TEN LOST YEARS

1 9 2 9 - 1 9 3 9

TEN LOST YEARS
1 9 2 9 - 1 9 3 9

Memories of Canadians Who Survived The Depression

Barry Broadfoot

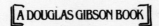

Copyright © 1973, 1997 by Barry Broadfoot
First published in hardcover by Doubleday in 1973
Published in paperback by Paperjacks in 1975
Published by McClelland & Stewart Inc. in trade paperback in 1997

Canadian Cataloguing in Publication Data

Broadfoot, Barry, 1926-
    Ten lost years, 1929-1939 : memories of Canadians who survived the depression

ISBN 0-7710-1652-2

1. Depressions – 1929 – Canada.   I. Title.

HB3717   1929   B7   1997   971.062'3   C97-930161-0

Typesetting by M&S, Toronto
Printed and bound in Canada

The publishers acknowledge the support of the Canada Council and the Ontario Arts
Council for their publishing program.

McClelland & Stewart Inc.
The Canadian Publishers
481 University Avenue
Toronto, Ontario
M5G 2E9

1 2 3 4 5 6   02 01 00 99 98 97

CONTENTS

PREFACE

I was a child of the Depression, born in Winnipeg in 1926. I was 13 when the Depression ended in 1939 with the start of the Second World War. Within three years, 400,000 men had enlisted in the armed forces and hundreds of thousands of men and women had been swept into vital war work. So the war became, in a very real sense, Canada's End-The-Depression Deal, because unemployment was basically what the Depression was all about.

The Depression has always interested me. Throughout my career as a newspaper reporter I have studied what I could find of it and talked to those who knew of it. By the time the 1970s rolled along I realized that probably 75 percent of Canada's 20,000,000-plus knew nothing, or very little, about those years – 1929-1939.

Canadians below the age of 50 are not to blame for their ignorance. For some reason a conspiracy of silence seems to have tried to hide the Depression from Canadians too young to remember it, to sweep under the rug those ten lost years that were the most traumatic in our nation's history, the most debilitating, the most devastating, the most horrendous. Those words are not used lightly. Text books used in Canadian schools tend to dismiss those ten years with half a page, three paragraphs, even one sentence. And if a student is interested enough to seek further information, there is precious little to be found in the library system.

Jamie is a very intelligent Grade 10 student in Calgary and has been taught much of the kings and queens of England, the obscure wars of Europe, early world explorations and discoveries, the history of the United States, and Canada's early days, from Jacques Cartier through Lord Durham's Report to the Riel Rebellion of 1885; so I asked him about the Depression:

"We have never been taught it, the Depression, the hard days. There's nothing in the school books, there might be something in the library but I have never seen it. They just don't teach it, at least not so far. No, I don't know why. Maybe they just don't want us to know about it. I know it was a time when no one had any money, not even the country. Yes, I know that. My Mom told me. She told me a few things about it, but that's all."

Why don't they teach it? It could be a full year's subject at a senior grade level, and every school has teachers who could use the "I was there" approach. Can 10 years just be chopped out of a nation's history? Should those 10 years be left blank in students' knowledge of their country?

The more I thought about it, the more I came to believe that everyone under 50 years of age should have a chance to learn about these hard times when a woman in a Quebec textile factory could work 54 or 60 hours a week for $5; when the people of Southern Ontario sent hundreds of freight car loads of fruit and vegetables and warm clothing to Saskatchewan, where millions of wheat-growing acres were burned out and blowing away as dust, and where families turned their backs on their hard-won farms and walked away; when a firm red spring salmon at Vancouver was giving the fisherman one cent a pound; and when, in New Brunswick, the net cash income of the average farm one year was just $20.

When the nation survived the war, and even emerged stronger from it, there seemed to be a general feeling that the Depression should not be talked about. A war had been won, great goals lay ahead, the Thirties were still a shameful smear on people's memories, so everyone should forget that it ever happened. And it has been kept out of sight – but not out of mind.

The Depression just didn't vanish without leaving a trace. On the contrary, even today, 1973, more than 30 years after it ended, the Depression still affects everyday life in Canada. It affects the 75-year-old pensioner who was scarred by the experience, and it has a traumatic effect on his 42-year-old son who grew up in an insecure home during and after the Depression, and it reaches out to affect his 17-year-old daughter. It does so in a dozen different and subtle ways, that I hope will emerge clearly in this book.

By now I hope it is clear *why* I decided to write this book. *How* to go about it was the next problem. I had been asking people for years about it – probably not really aware of why I was doing so – and I had been mentally filing these bits and pieces of information away. I also have vivid memories of some of those times, young as I might have been. But it was obvious that if I wanted to find out what survivors of the Depression in Canada felt about it, I would have to go out and find them. So, for nearly nine months I travelled Canada from Pacific to Atlantic, by car, train, plane, ferry, bus – and once I even had to hitchhike a few miles, and got a good story from the man who picked me up. I travelled at least 15,000 miles, through spring, summer and autumn.

I interviewed hundreds of people, so many I lost count. Some encounters were casual, the small talk of two strangers, but I would shift the talk around to the Depression and often they never knew why I did so. Other interviews were intensive, with the conversation firmly pointed on the subject for an hour or two. I interviewed people in their homes, in offices, in stores, in bars, in cafes, while travelling and while on the street. I even met people on radio hot-line shows, where the switchboard would invariably flash up red with people eager to tell their Depression stories.

Again and again an interview would begin with the man or woman laughing off the Depression, saying they could not remember anything – and then suddenly coming up with a hell of a story, something that happened to them or to a relative or friend or neighbour, something that happened long ago but is still burning vividly deep in their minds.

I was amazed at the detail they could remember. Understandably, some were fuzzy in parts, but they were the exception. Most could swiftly and surely remember dates, times, places, names, facial features, clothes worn and actual conversations – some paraphrased, to be sure, but accurate in subject and detail. To many it was as if the event or incident had happened yesterday; and others said, "I can't remember what I did last Tuesday but I can remember that day." And "that day" would be in July, 1932, or October, 1935.

I used a tape recorder whenever I could, but I also made notes or remembered the stories and words as closely as I could and wrote them down when the interview was over. I had to do some editing of most interviews because people just do not talk simply and economically. Listen to anyone tell a story and you will understand; they ramble. So I did compress the story where necessary, although I always tried to keep the individual flavour of the storyteller's style.

Stories often were shortened, but facts were never altered and facts vital to the story were never left out. Some of the stories were told to me on the understanding that I would not give away the name of the teller or allow others to be identified. This occurred quite often, and you will see why in many of the interviews.

In almost every case the identity of the storyteller is not given, their reminiscences appearing without any introduction. In some cases, I never did

know their name or their present occupation. But the decision not to intro-
duce individual speakers is deliberate; I believe that the stories, in the fullest
sense, speak for themselves. And if the anonymity worries you, leaves you
feeling that a certain story could have been told by your neighbour three
doors down the block, then you are getting the message of this book – that
dramatic and wonderful and terrible and foolish and funny and tragic things
happened in Canada's Depression to people you pass in the street every day,
people as ordinary as the woman three doors down.

The people I talked to are ordinary Canadians. If you want to know how
the Depression is recalled by the movers and shakers, the men who shaped
events in those dreadful days – premiers, cabinet ministers, judges, millionaires, financiers – then you must look elsewhere. And if you want to read an
academic account of the world economic conditions that produced the
Depression in North America, and an account of the high-level moves that
were made in Ottawa and by provinces and cities to counteract it, again you
must look elsewhere. This is a book about ordinary people. The survivors.
The soldiers, so to speak, not the Generals.

The title of the book, *Ten Lost Years*, is not my invention. It came in a
casual phrase by one of the Depression survivors I interviewed. But it
summed up perfectly my own ideas about the Depression, formed by the
people I met on my travels.

When I set out to find the survivors, I wanted to meet the old dust bowl
farmer and his son, and the clergyman's wife and the stock exchange clerk, the
school teacher who had been paid $8.50 a month, and the harassed grocer, and
the doctor, the trucker, the fisherman, the widow with small children, the
railway policeman, the youth with no hope of getting a job and his girlfriend
who therefore had no hope of marrying him, and the couple on the stump
farm in northern Ontario and the 19-year-old riding the rods back and forth
to nowhere and his sister working 10 hours a day for $4 a week as a waitress.
These are the people I knew could speak with the true voices of the Depression
and bring home to us today what it was like to live through those lean years.

As you read this book I hope you hear these voices echoing down from
the Thirties.

I hope that I reached out and touched these people. I know they touched
me. They told me their stories enthusiastically and honestly and as accurately
as their own years and those long years in between would allow. More important, when people heard I was doing a book on the hard times they would

often seek me out to tell their story. I cannot count the number of times I was told to go see such-and-such a person for a wonderful story, and could not go. For those who came to me, I thank you, and for those I could not see, I am sorry. Perhaps there will be another book.

To the people I met, the Great Depression is not to be swept under the carpet. To all of these people, their survival of those days is a badge of honour, to be worn with pride.

And as for myself, there was not a day during the researching and writing of this book that I did not wake up with a sense of eager anticipation.

Barry Broadfoot
Vancouver, January, 1973

Preface to the 1997 Edition

When I wrote that Preface almost twenty-five years ago I had no idea what would happen to this book. It proved to be a phenomenon, selling 100,000 copies in hardcover and many times that number in paperback. The book's success spawned a stage play, also entitled *Ten Lost Years*, which toured across Canada and at the Edinburgh Festival in the course of a major European tour. A number of productions are in progress in Canada as I write.

That was very pleasing, of course. What was even more pleasing was the reaction of ordinary Canadians, delighted that their own experiences in the course of their lives were being recognised as history. That led me to use my tape recorder to write a number of other books to achieve the same thing, showing that history was not just a matter of wars and treaties and speeches in Parliament.

Since 1973, however, some very displeasing things have happened, too. The words "recession" and even "depression" have reared their heads in Canada again. Many decent Canadians have gone through really rough times. Maybe we still have to learn the lessons about sticking together that those ten lost years in the Thirties should have taught us.

Barry Broadfoot
Nanaimo, January, 1997

During the late 1920s in Canada, the times were pretty good. Western farm crops were good, and mining, fishing and lumbering flourished. Manufacturing was at a high level. Employment was steady, and while wages and salaries were low compared with today, everything was in proportion because goods and services were low too. If the living wasn't easy, it certainly wasn't hard.

But there were danger signals. Wheat, Canada's blue chip export, was being over-produced around the world and the 1928 Canadian crop had still not been sold in 1929. The economies of many European countries were shaky, and had been since the First World War. Factories, especially in the United States, were over-producing, and since the market couldn't take the goods, their inventories and stockpiles were soon huge. The values of stocks on the New York Stock Exchange were grossly overvalued, but government and business appeared to ignore the signs. Things would get better and bigger, they predicted.

Canada was in a very vulnerable position. Despite the country's vast size, her thinly-spread population numbered only about 10,000,000. Her revenues came from export sales, and these sales were in vulnerable commodities – grain, pulp and paper, metals. The U.S. accounted for 40 percent of our export sales, and Canada counted on the Americans for vital money for expansion.

In October, 1929, all the black clouds met in one place, the New York Stock Exchange, and the thunderbolt struck. Stock prices fell disastrously, a sign that The American Economic System had been smashed. Things were never to be the same, in the U.S., in Canada, in the rest of the world.

Canada's markets began to collapse. The U.S., to protect its own, erected high tariff walls, shutting out Canadian goods. The prairie wheat economy tottered as the $1.60 a bushel price of 1929 skidded to 38 cents in 2½ years. By that time, even the weather had turned against us: the drought was destroying the West, and Canada like the rest of the world was deep into the worst Depression in history.

As the West and wheat went, so did the rest of Canada. Farmers stopped buying. Eastern factories closed, or laid off hundreds. Construction virtually stopped. Banks no longer lent money; instead, they called in loans. Less and less money was put into circulation and fewer and fewer goods were produced and more and more factories were shut down and the rolls of the poor grew longer and longer and the gloom and despair deepened.

Depression is a downward spiral and there was nothing to halt it. At times, the spiral was slowed, but it was never halted. When the upturn began around 1937 or 1938, it was a long, long struggle. The rains came to the prairies and that helped, and more and more men went back to work, but wages were still miserably low. Hundreds of thousands were still on direct public relief – a massive drain on the purse of a country that had precious little revenue anyway. Special projects and programs were reviving parts of the economy and the future did look brighter, but nobody could say that they really saw the end of it all.

But in Europe, Hitler's troops were marching into Austria and then into Czechoslovakia, and wise men knew that it was only a matter of time before Germany would smash into Poland. On September 1, 1939, Hitler gave the order and his tanks rolled. The Second World War had begun. On September 10, Canada declared war and a vast military effort got under way which was to require the services of every available man and woman for the next six years, in the armed forces, in defence plants, in factories and on farms across the nation. Everyone was at work.

The Great Depression was over. It had not been solved by the best brains in the country juggling with economic theories, but by the demands of total war, courtesy of Adolf Hitler.

CHAPTER ONE

What Was It Like?

Home, Wife, Land Gone . . . Let 'Em All Quit! . . . The Receipt . . . Entering The World . . . The Groves Of Academe . . . Living Like A King . . . Teaching From Eaton's Catalogues . . . Buying A Human Being . . . The Coal Selling Business . . . A Summer On The Farm . . . Just A Tank Of Water . . . In The Basement . . . A Regular Rip Van Winkle . . . A Prairie Preacher . . . Baby . . . Think About the Rest Of Us

———————————————— • ————————————————

I have arranged the interviews into chapters according to subject. At the head of each chapter all of the interviews that appear in it are listed by title.

As I explained in my Preface, the speakers remain anonymous; in many cases, too, the names of characters involved in the stories (as well as the actual settings of the stories) have been altered, to protect the guilty. But without exception, every break between stories marks the introduction of a new speaker. And in at least 9 cases out of 10, each speaker appears only once in the book, while nobody appears more than twice. Hundreds of Canadians talk to you in this book – not just a few whose stories have been artfully split up and spread around.

At the start of almost every chapter I have introduced the general subject with a paragraph or two of my own. In this first chapter – about how the Depression hit many people differently – I shall leave the introduction to an old man I met in a beer hall in Vancouver. Here's what he said: –

———————————————— • ————————————————

Home, Wife, Land Gone

"The Dirty Thirties! Just put in your book that you met Henry Jacobson and he's 78 years old. Might say I never took a backward step in my life until that Depression whipped me, took away my wife, my home, a section of good land back in Saskatchewan. Left me with nothing. Write that down."

Let 'Em All Quit

"The company was the Mohawk Handle Company in New Westminster and it was part of the Mohawk Lumber Company, quite a big outfit. It made a lot of wooden things including broom handles and I was in that part of the operation. My job was to paint those handles and we did it by dipping each handle into a pipe full of paint and by using several pipes and rigging up a gasket affair on the pipes and twirling the handle as we took it out, we could get the prettiest spiral effect in two colours.

We got 15 cents an hour painting those broom handles and the minimum wage in the province at that time was 35 cents an hour. Here we were, making 15 cents. There were about 300 men working for Mohawk at the time and they wanted to go on strike, they wanted the difference between what they were getting and what they should have got by law.

The directors called a meeting about this strike business and the superintendent told them, 'Let 'em all quit! I can replace 'em all by tomorrow morning if they do.' We all grumbled a lot, but what could we do? We stayed on the job and kept getting 15 cents an hour. That was the Depression for you."

———————————— • ————————————

The Receipt

"My mother was a widow and she shipped a steer, a big prime steer, from Saskatchewan to the Winnipeg stockyards because they told her she'd get a better price. But with the prices then and the weight loss and the trucker costs and the selling commission and what have you, she got a letter back from the agent saying *she owed them* $6. Without a word of a lie.

She was a proud woman and paid her debts and she really rustled for the $6 but she sent it off. And when the receipt came back in the mail she had it framed and it hung on the wall of our parlour until she died and we sold the house. Pretty good one, eh?"

———————————— • ————————————

Entering The World

"We had hopes. We had dreams. Certainly. We were the class of '35 in Newcastle and we graduated with the trimmings and then we were told, right turn, forward march and enter the world.

We did not know what the world was. No one had actually told us about the Depression. We knew not too many people had money. Doctors, yes.

Dentists, some. The merchants of the square. They seemed to do well. People who had good solid money kept it and made more. I do not think that there were many of what we called The Old Money who did that badly.

In late November I went out to work. Not work as we know it, so many dollars and cents an hour and each labourer being worthy of his hire, but piece work, axe and saw and cutting soft wood for the mill. In the woods. Piece work. There was deep snow that year, and prices for pulp was low and you had to be a damn-double-damn good man to make a dollar a day. Do you think I am kidding? You had to have shoulders like a bull and an eye like an eagle and the precision of a gang saw and the endurance of a pit pony and the hide of an elephant. It was also a good thing to have a wife and eight kids at home so that you knew that if you didn't produce for the company, then they would starve. You had to work, because you couldn't live off the relief. You could starve on relief.

The first month and living in Doaktown where I had a cousin and staying with him and walking six miles every morning with a lardpail full of bread-mush for lunch and working ten hours a day and walking out again on the road if I could not get a ride, I made about 50 cents. That's a day. Five cents an hour. Not so good, wouldn't you say? That was nothing! I lived with my cousin and walked, worked and walked 14 hours a day because I wouldn't live in the shanties.

You think shanties went out with the 1910 times, up to say 1920? The shantymen, the men, the Swedes, Finns, Slavs, the French living in those log shanties and eating that slop? No, they were still around. I was once told by a man who worked on the Trans-Siberian Railway that he had never, never in his working life, run into conditions like in the shanties. Some pretty big names in the Maritimes today, or the fathers, are connected with the shanties and the camps they ran. Sleep the sleep of the exhausted, eat breakfast such as it was, work, work, work, and at dark, back to the shanty and the stink and sweat and the toil, such useless toil of it all – and men came out of it after a winter with nothing.

They bought from the company store. At the shanty. Everything was on paper. You made so much, and so much was deducted and so much more was deducted if you broke a piece of equipment, and Lord God, if you bought a pair of boots that would cost you $4 in Newcastle, in the camp you paid $7 and the company was buying them wholesale and then this markup and if a company couldn't make 300 percent on boots or pants or even leather boot laces, then it had no right to be in business. It was theft, outright, and this was by companies run by the Scots and English of New Brunswick and Halifax and Montreal and Quebec City. Remember, not all the skunks were from Halifax or Saint John.

I'd venture to say that in a dicey season, the difference in some camps during the Thirties, and I'm speaking of profit or break-even, the black or the red side of the ledger, could have been those ship's stores the men had to buy from."

The Groves Of Academe

"I was an associate professor at Toronto in 1933, and I made $3,000. That was a good salary if you watched it, but remember, there were certain standards for a young professor, and I was 36 at the time. Certain methods of doing things, certain ways of conducting one's affairs, a certain way of life which is rigid. A university and even a liberal one is hardly a very liberal place.

So there I was, anticipation in 10 years or so of becoming a professor, History, and then, wonder of wonders, perhaps an appointment as a dean at some smaller university. Manitoba. Dalhousie. Somewhere.

That $3,000 worked out to $250 a month, minus income tax, club fees, et cetera. You know. I was married, two boys, two girls, no pets.

In April, the president announced cuts in academic pay and I was slashed, and that is the only word, I was slashed 15 percent for $650 per annum, and then my stipend worked out to less than $200 a month. Still all right for a man without a lot of additional financial obligations, but for an academic, let me tell you it was rough.

However, there are both ends of the scale. Those poor devils, the lowly lecturers making barely more than a $1,000 a year – and what greater love towards knowledge can a man have than that – he was knocked by five percent while the exalted, the chap on Mount Olympus at $8,000 plus, he was knocked 35 percent, and that is a hell of a crack. Just one hell of a crack. We survived."

Living Like A King

"I was paid $15 a month and I lived better than any millionaire in Canada. Hah!

In 1936 I was junior trader at the Hudson Bay post at Somerset Island. On the map that's several hundred miles from the magnetic pole. North. I made $15 a month but I was eating flour which cost the company $100 to get a 100-pound sack up there. Everything was the same. Everything we ate. Show me a millionaire in those days who was eating flour at a dollar a pound.

For a few crummy furs. A crazy world."

———————————— • ————————————

Teaching From Eaton's Catalogues

"I graduated from normal school and I was 18, not at all too young in those days for teaching, and it was 1935 and you know what that meant? Well, I'll tell you. It meant I would be lucky to get a job but I did, in a one room school in Saskatchewan, south of Wynyard.

The school secretary wrote me the district had been hit hard and he wrote and said they could not stick to the schedules, the graduated scale they paid teachers, but they would pay me $30 for a month. I knew the government grant was $300 a year for each room, so this district was just paying me the government grant. My mother told me to take it, it would be experience.

It wasn't a bad little school, eight grades, about 24 pupils and good kids. The district was Anglo-Saxon so there was none of the trouble some of the other girls had of trying to teach a bunch of Ukrainian kids who barely spoke English.

The first night I slept in the cloakroom with a horse blanket and my coat until the board could meet and figure out who would take me for that year. I got into a house of the farmer nearest, practically across the road, and I think, as I recall, the others paid their share of my board by working for him two or three days, ploughing or haying. No money changed hands. There was none. Hah!

I liked teaching, the children were a pleasure and the farm family I stayed with were nice people. Everybody tried to help each other, and I put on a Hallowe'en dance in the school and a Christmas concert, and the last day of school there was a picnic with races, old shoe races, egg and spoon races, things like that. They were hard times, but good times too, in a way.

I remember one thing. I had this terrific inspiration. The school books were practically useless, in tatters, and I thought, what will I do? Then I had this brain wave. I told every child to bring to school next day the Eaton's catalogue. The one at home, you see. Of course, some families had two and three children in school, but you know what I mean. I thought these would make wonderful texts for the older children. And they did too. But this is what happened. I'd be doing the grade sevens and eights together, and they had the catalogue and I'd let one child pick out to read what he wanted to. The girls would read aloud from the clothes section or the kitchen things, china sets, curtains, things like that, and the boys would read the harness section or guns or such and the younger ones would turn right to the toy section. I believe the Shirley Temple doll section was read two dozen times.

It was study, it was learning, it was fun. In other words it wasn't like school. But I began to notice that when one class, say the grade fives, and there might be four or so in that, when they were doing their reading from the catalogues, everybody else stopped their own lessons and listened. I began to watch and I found out that no work except the catalogue reading was being done in that little red schoolhouse on the Saskatchewan plains.

Everybody listened, everybody knew what everybody else wanted or liked, and no work was being done. I had to put a stop to that, send them home with their catalogues and go back to the old readers. It was too bad because it was such fun, for them and me too.

I often wonder why they can't make school books as enjoyable as the Eaton's catalogue. In those days it was opening a whole new world of colour and joy for the kids and that is what school books should be all about, don't you think?"

———————————— • ————————————

Buying A Human Being

"We moved to Montreal in 1933 and we found what we were looking for the first day, a perfectly lovely house in Westmount. There were houses for rent or for lease and you could buy them, everywhere. While we waited for our furniture to come out from the coast we all stayed at the Ritz. A grand hotel then, and it still is.

I phoned an employment agency and told them I wanted some staff and they asked a few questions and the next day a woman came over to the hotel. I told her I knew nothing about running a house and I wanted the best servants she could find. We drove over to the house and she worked it out this way. A chef and a woman who could be my maid and also serve the meals, and two domestics and a yardman, we had perfectly huge grounds, and a laundress who would come in Monday, Wednesday and Friday.

When our furniture moved in, this agency had people for us. The chef got $40 a month and his board and room. My maid got $30 and board and room. The first domestic maid got $25 and the second maid got $15. The gardener, and he was the chauffeur too if we wanted it, he got $25. The laundress got $2 a day, and she scrubbed by hand and ironed by hand and she lived at home. I paid her carfare too. Ten cents a day. Perfectly ridiculous, isn't it? Buying a human being, an excellent chef, for $10 a week, or a small maid for 50 cents a day. Nobody thought anything of it."

———————————— • ————————————

The Coal Selling Business

"I can't tell you too much about the good old days but I could talk for a month about the bad. Once I decided to go into the coal selling business. One winter. Gosh, it was cold. I had two wagons and eight horses, four I borrowed from Norman Scott's dad and four others I borrowed too. Eight horses. I used to haul coal from over here near Taber. That was 39 miles. In winter. Terribly cold winter that year. And I hauled coal from a mine west of Raymond. I had to buy the coal and sell it. It took a day of real good going to get there, managing two wagons over them roads, and then I had to load that coal. Shovel it. Back home, maybe two days sometimes, and that lignite never sold for much. For a week's work, going, loading, hauling and delivering, why I betcha I never made more than a few dollars a week. It was so cold I never had much of a chance to ride, I'd be walking beside the lead horses, leading them, stamping my feet, jumping up and down, trying every way to keep warm. You should talk to me about hard work in them hard times."

———————————— • ————————————

A Summer On The Farm

"When I was about 13, my uncle at Weyburn wrote and said a bachelor was looking for a boy to help him. The man's name was Coolihan, or Cowlan, something like that. A dollar a week and found. It sure as hell wasn't the money, a buck a week, but it meant one less mouth to feed at home and I was getting on in size.

Dad took me down to the freight yard and talked a brakeman into letting me ride in the caboose up that way. Free. You could do that sometimes those days. I got there and walked about six miles to this farm. Farm, huh! Two rooms in the house and I slept in the barn with about six of the sorriest looking scrub horses you have ever seen. Broom tails.

We ate pig mash mixed with hot, boiling water, mixed with molasses. One of my jobs was to walk over after dark to the garden of the family that looked after the nearest grain elevator, a mile away, and steal carrots, radish, anything what was growing. I never got caught because their dog was friendly. Never have a friendly dog in a Depression.

This Coolihan would go into town Saturday night and buy the cheapest meat. God, you could buy a barrelful for a dollar. Bacon that mostly was fat, but that was okay. He made his own bread, not fit for human consumption, and when we finished with the chores and ate, he'd put the plates and bowls down for his two dogs to clean and throw the rest of the loaf of bread back into the cupboard, like a pitcher throwing a fast ball, zip, and say, 'Well, Coolihan, if that was today, it wasn't much of a day.' Then we'd hit the sack.

I worked all summer, bloody awful hard work and you better believe it, and he didn't pay me. At most I guess I got a dollar over those seven or eight weeks in dribs and drabs. I didn't mind too much and when I got home and told my father he didn't mind either. Just laughed. But you know what? That was one of the best and healthiest summers I can remember."

———————•———————

Just A Tank Of Water

"I had this neighbour who was on a quarter section north of me and he was barely making her go. He had a coulee that held good water from the spring melt and he'd been able to keep a few head feeding pretty well on the grass in it and the water it held.

In 1937 he had eight good steers, but about early July the heat hit us and his water just evaporated and with it the grass went, and Aspinall tried digging wells or sumps but it was no use. There just wasn't any more water. He came over with a team and borrowed my tank wagon. I think it held 400 gallons, and if he could get water he could keep that stock alive until September when things surely would cool down. He drove that tank wagon about nine miles down to Maple Creek where there was a slough, lousy water but it was wet, and he filled it up by hand pump. That took three or four hours, and then he drove back to his place. He figured he could make out this way. His crop was lost anyway.

He got back about four o'clock and when he got to his yard he found that the tank, it was wooden, had a leak. I hadn't used it for so long it had opened at the seams, and about three quarters of his water was gone, dripped out along the road. I was there to help him pump out and he looked into the top of the tank and the smell of that water nearly drove him back, and he said, 'To hell with this, Mac, no more for me,' and next morning he drove those steers into town and sold them to the buyer as they stood, and those steers were in pretty good shape for the times and about 600 pounds as they stood – and he got about one cent a pound. He got $63 for them, and he'd been hoping for five or six cents a pound.

Within two weeks the Aspinalls were on their way to the Okanagan Valley and their place stood empty until after the war. Then some returned soldier bought it."

——————————— • ———————————

In The Basement

"The Depression passed me by. I'm only 43 now and my dad worked for the City of Toronto, an inspector in the maintenance department, so if I wanted an electric train or something for Christmas, then I got it.

No, nothing happened to me.

(He thinks a few moments and then says. . . .)

Wait. There was this fellow, Steve Metarski. He'd come over from Poland, the Ukraine, over there, as a kid of 14 or so and worked building railroad and became a sub-contractor, and when he married my cousin he was about 45. He was what you would call The Solid Citizen. A nice guy, and she was about 22 so she knew what she was doing. His first wife had died and he had this lovely house in a good part of Hamilton. I remember him laughing once and saying, 'I change my name to Marsh and I'm best damned Canadian you ever seen.' I think he was sounding us out. To me, Metarski was okay.

About 1930 – and I get this off Sally, his wife, because I was too young – construction just went crash and Steve lost his business in six months. Apparently it was just plain murder. Assets didn't cover debts at the bankruptcy auction so they – and who *they* are, I just don't know – but they took his house and he got his lawyer to work something out so he'd still have possession and ownership as long as he made the payments. Monthly. But man, he'd bought the house in, say the mid-Twenties, and he had a big chunk of a house left to pay, and it was a hell of a house, and interest was about 8 or 9 percent. We think nine percent high today? Think what it was then. I'm in the business and I would say it would be crushing.

Let's put this thing into a box, four sides, a bottom and lid. Here was Steve, no business, no job, no cash buried in the back yard and with some screwy deal between the bank and his creditors and where was his out? There was none.

Sally said he never made more than two payments, and had to sell furniture to do that. Then the house was swiped out from under him and sold at about a quarter of actual worth to some guy in Burlington. The guy moved in with his wife and kids and let Steve and Sally live in the basement, and Sally was the maid and Steve did work around the yard, stoked the furnace and was the guy's chauffeur. A chauffeur, for Christ sakes!

Look at it this way. Say, on July 1, 1930, Steve still had a business and a fine house and a nice wife. By January 1, 1931, six months later, he's zilch. Living in the basement in his own house and his wife is the maid upstairs, and the cook."

———————————— • ————————————

A Regular Rip Van Winkle

"I did not know there was a world or a Depression until I was 17, nearly 18. If you look at the map of New Brunswick, then look northeast of Fredericton, there is a huge area coloured green. Only a few roads, very few, and even the old trails must be gone now. Long gone now. That was 35 years ago.

We lived up an old logging road, miles from the end of the regular road, where it opened up into a clearing and this had been an old lumber camp probably about the beginning of the century. Say from 1900 anywhere up to 1915, I believe.

The family lived in there. We were comfortable. We had hay for the horses, a couple of cows, chickens – and I must say this, those chickens laid the smallest eggs in the world. About the size of your thumb nail. You see, they had no grain. Our house was warm and the bush was full of wood. We'd spend three weeks every spring cutting wood and by fall it would be dry, good for the stove. We could get a deer any time we wanted and there were creeks with fish.

My brother and I grew up this way, and I knew there was a place called Fredericton but I didn't know there was a city called Montreal or Toronto or London or Paris or New York. You could say without a word of a lie we were brought up in total isolation. Why, I don't know.

Every fall, my Dad would drive the two cows down the trail and be gone a week or so and he'd come back with the cows bred, so we usually had a calf or two, and he'd have two or three sacks of pig meat, hog, and a few sacks of corn meal. No flour. Sugar. Some coffee. Rubber boots for all of us. My feet are deformed from wearing tight rubber boots. He brought back :22 shells, shotgun, 30:30 Winchester, usually some new traps, rope, stove blacking, lamp oil. These sort of things.

We trapped and cut wood and fed the stock and that was our life and I can't ever remember thinking about another world. We just thought this was how people lived. Oh, I forget, we had no mother. She'd died of something years before. If she had been around I'm sure things would have been different. Nobody came up that trail in all the years I lived there and we never went down it. Don't ask me why. I had to learn curiosity, which is something a newborn babe has, putting fingers in his mouth, reaching for bright things. We had it, but only as it concerned our immediate life.

Then Dad sliced the side of his foot open with an axe. He must have had the sharpest axes in New Brunswick and by God, he did a good job. He lost some blood, not that much, but it was a big gash. He told us to go out and get a pail half full of mud from the creek and some handfuls of moss and we mixed it all together until it was real mush and then he put his foot in the pail and we packed the mixture all around, and in a way it was not unlike a plaster cast. It hardened, I mean. Not hard, but it became harder.

I remember my Dad saying, 'Okay, boys, I'll be up and around in a few days. This will do the trick.' In French, of course. We were French.

He sat up in that big rocker he'd made years ago with his foot in that pail and we brought food to him and he seemed to be getting slower in his speech and he'd break out in sweat and, well, in three days he was dead. The old nature trick, the way a fox or a wolf will put its broken leg or gashed leg in a mud mixture, that just didn't work on humans. Blood poisoning.

We buried him in a horse blanket with a torn up blanket wrapped around his face so the bugs wouldn't get at him. We didn't have a Bible, we didn't even know what a Bible was, and of course none of us could read.

I was the oldest and I figured I'd better hike down that road and tell somebody. I figured somebody should know about a thing like this.

They should have put me in the circus, right next to the Fat Lady and the Dog-faced Boy. I didn't know any English but there were plenty of my own people in the town. I didn't know what a car was, a truck, a policeman, a book, a picture show. I was a regular Rip Van Winkle, believe me. I could shoot the eye out of a squirrel at 100 feet but the first time somebody gave me an ice cream cone I didn't know what it was or how to eat it. I was 18. The records in the town hall showed that. That's where I'd been born before the old man went bush. Let's put it this way, I didn't know nothing. I was the only 18-year-old boy, unless he was in a cave on a mountain in Siberia, that didn't know what a girl, a woman was. You better believe it."

———————————— • ————————————

A Prairie Preacher
"Mr. Wade, my late husband, was a Baptist minister. But in the Thirties, everybody was welcome, just as it should be. There was this town, Bassano, and that was where the church was and as I recall, morning service would be at 9.30 which was a bit early for some people. At 10.30, Mr. Wade and I and our son Alex would get into our car, it was a Chandler more the worse for wear, but it had been a fine car in its day, and we'd drive southwest about 12 or so miles and there was a little schoolhouse on a hill by the road and we'd have service there at noon. Not the best time but it couldn't be helped and we'd get anywhere from 10 to 15 people. When there was a pretty school teacher boarding across the road there might be 20 people, and you can guess who those extras were. Young bachelors, right. After service we'd always have dinner with one family near.

Then, about 2 p.m. as I recall, we'd drive about 20 miles back west, past all those abandoned homes, and there was a little village and we'd hold another service in the hall. There might be 10 or 15 people there too. No, there would be more. That district had a lot of Baptists but it still couldn't support a ministry. Only the Mormon towns and those with a lot of RC's could do that. Then we'd drive to another school house and it would be about 4.30 by this time and you must remember, we did this Sunday after Sunday, no holidays for us, and in blizzard or summer's dust and that Chandler would just keep going. A service there and a light supper at one of the congregation's homes, just to lift up our spirits, and then we'd drive home and there would be evening service at 7.30. Mr. Wade was lucky because only a few, a very few, attended both morning and evening service so he could give the same sermon, and it was the one he gave on our circuit too, although he shortened it, of course.

We had this rack on the back of the Chandler and on it we could tie a portable organ, just a tiny thing, and we'd cover it with oil cloth and it went with us. Those sermons wouldn't have been much without a hymn or two. People wanted the music. Whenever we left the organ behind, they complained.

Mr. Wade was never what you would call a really inspirational speaker. He could reach people's hearts, but only in a quiet way and over a period of time. Sometimes a dollar would show up in the collection plate and then we'd know someone had felt his words. Mr. Parton, I believe his name was, at the first school, always gave a dollar. We could always count on that good man. A good farmer, a good father and a good Christian. A fine man. But all things said and done, except maybe just before Christmas and at Easter the collection wouldn't amount to more than $3 or $4 dollars at most. As I think of it now, $4 would have been good. I think we lived on about $25 a month and we had the house free, you understand. People would always be bringing in food, things like eggs and a chicken or a piece of meat, and these were appreciated.

We did our best. Sometimes it fell far short of what we hoped, and Mr. Wade would become discouraged but he would always rally. He was such a fine man. You must remember too that Mr. Aberhart was really our competition, if I may use that word. These were the years when Mr. Aberhart was up there on the radio and he would speak for hours on Sunday. I think he was on the air four or five hours there before he was elected in 1935 and there were other preachers, some our own, but even ones from across the line and wherever you turned on the dial, there was someone preaching. People wanted to hear Mr. Aberhart, he was a great favourite, and that is probably why our congregations were slim. People never, never lost their faith in God during those hard years but, as Mr. Wade used to remark, some people can carry the faith better than others."

––––––––––––––––––– • –––––––––––––––––––

Baby

"Oh, yes, yes, yes, we lived on the farm near Summerside, Prince Edward Island. Anne of Green Gables, that's all people knew about the island in those days. We were cut off in those days. You could see Nova Scotia across the Strait, Northumberland Strait, but it was as if somebody had just painted it on a giant canvas and hung it there. Nobody I knew went there.

We had this pony, Baby. Shetland ponies were wonderful for children, and Baby had been my brother's and then my two older sisters rode her and then she came to me.

Anyway, my father lost his job at a farm where the owner raised racing horses, the trotters and pacers they used to sell all through the States. Not many people wanted a good trotter in these days, and he had to try and make a living on our little place and you see, my father owned this small farm but he just didn't know farming. Potato farming or any other kind. All he knew was horses.

I'm coming to what I want to tell you. One winter we practically lived on potatoes. Don't laugh, but in the spring when they were sprouting, the sprouts became our vegetables, like bean sprouts. We ate potatoes. Mashed, boiled, mashed and boiled. I don't remember much meat and I guess we weren't on relief. An island Scot is a pretty proud bird.

The next summer my mother sent me for a week to an aunt, her sister in Charlottetown and I stayed a week, and when I went home on the old Toonerville trolley train they had in those days my father met me at the station and on the way home he told me that Baby had died. She'd got the bloat – they swell up horribly and you have to puncture their stomach to get the gas out – and they hadn't found her until too late. She'd been picked up by the truck from a fox farm down the road. I cried, naturally I would cry, but on a farm animals die, and I didn't feel that bad. I had lost a friend, oh yes, but that's the way it was. I was about 12 years old and understood these things.

Next summer I went to the beach because my father had got his job back at the track and mother had sold a lot of hooked rugs to tourists so they could send me to the beach with my cousins. One cousin one day, Marian, vicious little snit, she asked me how my horse had tasted.

Of course, she didn't come out with it, but her brother said their father, my uncle, had come over from Kings County to our farm while I was away visiting the other aunt and this uncle had butchered, had killed and then butchered my Baby. When he said that I knew it was true. It had to be, because we ate a lot of stews, cold cuts, and dishes you'd call beef Stroganoff now. We seemed to have quite a bit of meat. It was Baby, my old pony who we all had loved who we were eating. She hadn't gone to the fox farm. She hadn't gotten the bloat.

I never asked my father or my mother if it was true but I knew it was and if I did today, if they were alive, I know they would swear on our Bible it just wasn't. Oh yes, yes, very much so yes. But I knew. There are some ways you can't fool a child."

Think About The Rest Of Us

"I knew this assistant professor at the University of British Columbia. He had this big house down on the Blenheim Flats and at the back he had a chicken house, all disguised with ivy and flowers and trees, but it was still for chickens. He had about 200, and his kids looked after them and the neighbours bought fresh eggs for about 10 cents a dozen. He told me once that without those egg sales he just couldn't make ends meet, and he was a university professor. Think about the rest of us."

CHAPTER TWO

Three Overall Views

Ten Lost Years . . . A Conspiracy To Hide Those Years . . . A Crime To Be Poor.

As Alberta author James Gray said, "When the Depression came, our world stopped and we got off."

I interviewed hundreds of people right across Canada and no more than a handful claimed to understand the Depression, what had caused it, and why it hit so hard and lasted so long. Perhaps they belong to an exclusive club because even today there is still argument among the experts.

The average Canadian didn't know what was happening, but only that the economy was slowing down, slowing down. As the economic noose tightened, factories closed or cut staff by 25, 40, 60 percent. The vast and vital U.S. export market slowly and then more quickly was choked off. The drought hit the prairies, even as farm produce prices skidded alarmingly. Many mines closed. It was the old domino effect – one disaster causing another and so on. Municipalities went bankrupt, and even some cities. Relief was pitiful. Successive governments dithered. Nothing happened. Things just got worse, year after year. People still don't really know what caused it all, and they are still teaching different theories in university Economics classes. That is, when they teach it at all.

———————————— • ————————————

Ten Lost Years

"Some people just want to forget it ever happened, that God-fearing, third-generation Canadians starved to death in city alleyways and on their lousy farms out on the prairie. But it happened. The drought, of course, nobody could survive that, and that was just extra misery piled on top. At the time, the Canadian governments, the economists, the experts, did they know what was happening? No. They still don't.

President Roosevelt when he came in in 1933 took over an unholy mess in the U.S. and his New Deal started things going. He knew he had to spend money, even if he didn't have it. Why, print more. But get people working, so they could spend money, so other people could spend money so there would be money percolating through the economy. Roosevelt wasn't all that successful, but there was one thing so important that people have forgotten it. He had the appearance of success. I'll repeat that. He had the appearance of success. Other way of saying it, he gave people confidence. That fear was going away. Remember he said, 'We have nothing to fear but fear itself.' In a way, that was witch doctor stuff, but it worked. People wanted to be told, to be assured that things would go okay. And in about three or four years he started to get the country turned around and of course, Canada benefited too. Sure we did. There's no denying it.

But Bennett *(the Canadian prime minister)* did precious little for us and a lot of the things he did was bad, the relief camps for one thing, and William Lyon Mackenzie King? Hah! There was a winner. A tiny cautious man hyped on spiritualism who thought any problem could be solved by setting up royal commissions which would report back years later and by that time, by that time they hoped, the problem would have gone away. Or calling top level provincial conferences and all you got was the wealthy or the big provinces, Quebec, Ontario, British Columbia, their premiers ready and quite happy to sacrifice the weaker and poorer provinces so they could get a bigger share of federal funds. Oh, they were a bunch of dandies. Any man who was a Liberal or a Tory in those days cannot say he served his nation.

Of course, it all came out not too bad. The war, of course. People even talk about the Good Old Days now. Yes, and they still don't realize that Canada came out of the Thirties and Forties in good shape but not really through too much of our own doing. The Second World War, that gave us our leg-up, and then that crazy post-war prosperity when everyone had money to spend which they hadn't been able to spend during the war, and everyone wanted our goods.

But don't tell me we actually survived the Depression as such. No, it destroyed us for those ten years. Nineteen-twenty-nine to nineteen thirty-nine. The country stopped. Hardly a thing moved. Plans and all that, but not many were put into effect. Those that were put into effect, how many worked? Yes, ten lost years."

A Conspiracy To Hide Those Years

"One thing that has always astonished me is the way the Depression has been handled by school text books, histories, that kind of book. Even at the university level, the Depression is not handled in any depth. There are textbooks of Canadian history where the Depression gets three or four paragraphs, and I actually saw one book where it got *one* sentence, and went something like this: 'Between 1929 and 1939 the Canadian nation suffered a Great Depression, and the western wheat farmer was the most seriously hit.' Period. That was all. Then they went on to the war, as if the war, in a twist of meaning, healed all wounds.

It is almost a conspiracy to hide these ten years, although I hate to use the word 'conspiracy' because it often has a criminal connotation. Of course I don't think that. But . . . There seems to have been an attitude right up till now of 'Let's shove it under the carpet, let's not talk about it, let's not even admit that we walked around with holes in our soles and souls and let's never admit the fact we had to work for a dollar a day or we had to take relief and do things which our pride and our upbringing and our heritage would never allow us to do before.' I don't know why this attitude should prevail.

I can't come up with any true explanation, but it is a fact that in the U.S. and other countries this same attitude prevails. It is almost as if to say, if we don't talk about the Great Depression, then there will never be another one. Of course, it's true, too, that people were ashamed, collectively, that there was such a thing as a Depression, that the whole system just broke down and nothing could be done to make it work. But why have ten years of our contemporary history, ten years of the greatest trauma this continent has faced, and that includes all the wars, been virtually blotted out?

Remember, in some ways it was a tremendously exciting time. People found strengths they did not know they had. They learned they could endure, and endure and endure some more. It was almost a trial by battle. Yes, it was a battle in that sense and the Canadian nation came out of it stronger than before. Think about it. There was solid stuff there in the beginning, integrity, willingness to work and work very hard, faith, a defined goal and a good base of English, Scotch, Irish, French, German, Scandinavian, Polish, Russian, Ukrainian, Italian, all these providing a diverse but strong base to build upon.

But in the schools and universities today, what is known? A few paragraphs. At most, one or two pages. But more often, nothing! I meet people under 30 and I ask them what the Depression means to them. Or, to put it in more simple terms, what was the Depression? They will say, 'Oh, that was when times were hard,' or 'Dad said that was when he didn't have any money,' or 'That was when my parents couldn't go to the cottage at the lake each summer.' And of course, anybody in high school or university, likely as not, they will just giggle.

But there is a – for want of a better word I'll have to call it a conspiracy, and therefore it must be deliberate, to see no evil, hear no evil, speak no evil. And yet it was not a time of evil, as far as Canadians were involved. Canada was just caught in a worldwide squeeze."

———————————————— • ————————————————

A Crime To Be Poor

"I never so much as stole a dime, a loaf of bread, a gallon of gas, but in those days I was treated like a criminal. By the twist in some men's minds, men in high places, it became a criminal act just to be poor, and this percolated down through the whole structure until it reached the town cop or the railway bull and if you were without a job, on the roads, wandering, you automatically became a criminal. It was the temper of the times.

I was not a hobo. A hobo, by definition, is a regular bum, a professional bum, and there probably were hoboes in the time of the Crusades and there are hoboes now. There always have been that kind of people, whether they are on the highways or in the slums, in the Skid Roads or sitting beside a fire sipping Scotch whiskey in Rosedale *(a fashionable part of Toronto)* and living off their wife's inherited wealth. Hoboism is a state of mind.

I was, you could say, a wanderer. One of the unfortunates. A victim of the economic system? Perhaps. Certainly, most certainly a casualty in the battle between ignorant men who were running this country. There are two places in Ontario, in the fair city of Toronto and down at the even fairer city of London, where ancient records will show that I am a criminal. A criminal in that I violated the Criminal Code of Canada and thereby gained a criminal record for begging. Jail.

And I once got 30 days for riding a freight car long ago into a God-for-saken little Saskatchewan city which, thank God, the economic ebbs and flows of the past two decades, have served to reduce to a position of impotence. I refer, sir, to the metropolis of Moose Jaw. I am too old to check and not interested enough to care if the police court records have long since gone into the incinerator. But I do have a criminal record, and to me, as one who survived what we call The Great Canadian Depression, that is a badge of honour.

You will notice this train we are on? Perhaps it is indicative of how far our civilization has come, or gone, that I consider the passenger service between Toronto and Montreal of 40 years ago to be far superior to what it is today. If it were not for this drink in my hand, in this luxurious car, I would say there could not even be any comparison. Why, I ask you, can they not run the trains on time?

But enough, back to the criminal poor. I was born on a small farm across the Red River from a town called Morris, Manitoba, and when I was 14, in 1932, my father drowned in that river. The stupid son of a bitch tumbled into the river and that was the end of him. We didn't own the farm anyway. The bank did, and they were quick to assert the sovereignty of the Almighty Dollar. Four days after the funeral, we were out. Oh, no, not evicted, no possessions by the roadside. No, the foreclosure papers had been flashed through the courts. Judges seemed just as cooperative to those whom they deemed The Powers then as they do now. The judiciary and the bankers' association walked hand in hand, stopping occasionally to smile into each other's faces like lovers walking through a green park. We were not evicted. In fact, we were asked to stay. 'Mrs. Desjardins,' the man from the bank said, 'you and your family can stay here as long as you want.'

And why not? Why not, my friend? It made perfect sense. Who would rent 160 acres of grazing land, a house and its outbuildings in those years? No one, my friend. But if the widow Desjardins, who was a clean and industrious and honest woman, was induced to stay and if her six children stayed and continued to farm in the desultory manner of the past, a few cows and pigs and eggs sold in the nearby town, why, the house and buildings and fences and land would not deteriorate too much. It was a perfect arrangement, for the widow and her brood and for the bank. But it didn't work. My mother was a wise old hen and she clucked that man out of the house with some of the choicest language I have heard a woman utter. To this day I have no idea where she picked up those words. It was years until I considered myself fluent enough in them to use them in public.

So we left. (Snaps his fingers.) To Winnipeg. Our few possessions, a hundred dollars or so, and into the ghetto of North Winnipeg, by the Canadian Pacific tracks where the trains shook the house day and night and the little Jew boys got behind the counters of their father's stores on Selkirk

Avenue when they could barely see over the counter, and they learned the arts of commerce which have made that race paramount since long before Christianity inflicted itself upon us.

But I ramble. You obviously do not believe that the Depression should be kept out of sight, like the pregnant and unmarried daughter at the Christmas feast or the retarded son when the priest comes to call. Why have we run from those ten years, which, if I may set the record straight, could have continued on and on, yea, verily on and on until the last syllable of recorded time, if there had not been a war? A Hitler. For him, cousin, many thanks. Because Canadians, English-Canadians like you, French-Canadians like me, Ukrainian-Canadian, Chinese-Canadian, we were ashamed of it. Why? Because of what we call the Protestant Ethic, of course, which in essence says 'work your ass off all your life and do what the boss tells you and the big guy in the sky, when your time comes, he'll see you get your reward. The streets of Heaven are paved with gold, and hell is a fiery inferno.' We believe all this, you know. Even today, I believe it. You believe it. That gentleman and his wife over there, they believe it. I know.

So when I found out I could not survive in Winnipeg I left, I left that crummy house the relief had put us in, and before I left I hammered out pork and bean cans, hammered them flat, and then I nailed them over the holes where the rats came in and I told my mother not to tell the relief examiner that I was gone but to keep claiming my allowance, my share, and I said goodbye to her and Jean and Marie and all the rest and I took to the road with my two blankets wrapped around my Bible and my poor clothes and tied together with two leather thongs, and that is what they called a turkey. I roamed back and forth. I got in fights, and I was in one which concerned maybe 10 or 12 men and one man died later from his wounds, but by that time we had scattered to the far winds and he was just another casualty of that undeclared war. Potter's field for him. Tough, fellow, tough.

I worked in harvest fields for the cheapest farmers in Canada and I worked for some damn fine fellows too. I picked apples and I picked tobacco and I picked peaches in the Okanagan, and in those days, the Okanagan Valley was Paradise. I must go back to Paradise someday, and I wonder if a very fine family outside of Penticton named Williams . . . Williamson? . . . will remember me? I worked for them for several months and they treated me like a son. I was a skinny little 16-year-old. But, even so, when I would go into Penticton, because of the way I was dressed, because I had a French accent, maybe because of just the way I looked, the police would sometimes question me. I was a transient, but not a hobo.

If they wanted you to pick fruit in a hurry and get them out of a jam, you were an economic saviour, but the rest of the time you were shit.

If you were poor but had a house and sent your kids to Sunday school, if you had no money and nothing for food, then you were unfortunate and people looked after you. If you left home, like I did, so my brothers and sisters would have more food and more room to sleep, then you became a criminal. You did not have to commit a criminal act. Mr. *(R.B.)* Bennett saw to that. You just had to be you, without money. Throw the guy in jail. Get him out of town. Lay the stick to his backside. Hustle him along. There's no more soup and bread and there won't be tomorrow so you guys get the hell out of here, see! How many times have I heard these things.

I was not bitter then. No, I can honestly say that, but I didn't know any better. The Communists used to come into the jungles or ride the freights with us, but what they were saying just wasn't making sense to me, or anybody else. If they had talked about a little farm with good pastures and a nice stream with fish in it and big trees around the house, and some cows and pigs in it and maybe a car in the garage, then I would have understood. If they had talked about that, that I could have this and that, I would have understood.

But I didn't understand and I didn't care when they talked about Lenin and what was happening in Russia and that we should go into Vancouver and smash the telegraph station and break store windows and make the police so mad at us that they'd crack a few hundred heads. That kind of talk was just so much baloney. Bullshit.

I went to war like the rest and I saw a lot and I came back and I went to university and got in with this company, the one I'm with now. They've been good to me and I've worked hard and I make a lot of money. You could call me a success. My brothers and sisters did okay too. One's a doctor. One girl's a nun, but getting kind of restless, she writes me. It was only when I started thinking it all over, after it had digested for so many years, that I realized just how terrible things were in the Thirties and how it was criminal to be alone and poor and on the roads, when, for most of us, that was the only place we could be.

You've heard my story and I guess you're asking yourself, how could a guy that thinks the way this guy thinks be riding in this car and drinking Scotch and not doing anything about it. It is simple, and you should know it. The war smoothed out a lot of us, took away the memories of the Thirties, levelled off the bumps, like that, see. Most of us never had it so good, looking back on it. The great experience, eh? Then university. Money in the pocket, pretty girls. A big company. A good job. District sales manager. Fine, eh?

Now I'll tell you something, my friend; if there hadn't been a war, there would have been a revolution. Two, three more years, and then poof! Some leaders would have come along. But the war came along and it killed a lot of good guys but it did a lot for a lot of other guys too. Maybe I'm not saying exactly how I feel it, but it is all over and done with. Nobody thinks about it, because it is still a shameful thing to be poor in Canada. Things haven't changed that much. It was shameful to be poor then, and it is shameful now, except some people just don't seem to care about it all that much. That's my story, and for that, you owe me a drink. Ballantine's."

CHAPTER THREE

You'd Try Your Hand At Anything

Lemonade For Sale, Cheap . . . The Ma And Pa Resort . . . $25 A Month Trapping . . . Helping The Widow . . . Staying Alive On Gopher Tails . . . Gold Rush . . . Sunday Dinner For Tourists . . . Lots Of Supply, No Demand . . . Toronto Boarding House.

———————————————— • ————————————————

Inevitably, life went on. But it took a while for the lesson to sink in that the old ways, the ways of the Twenties, now called The Good Old Days, were gone. Times were going to be tough.

Some people developed the philosophy that whatever job could get them through the night was necessary, and therefore good. So people made 180 degree turns, as they realized that no job was secure any more. Women went out and worked for pennies an hour, or they opened tiny shops in their front parlours, or they took in boarders. Accountants went ditch-digging on make-work municipal jobs. Lawyers fought with teachers to become clerks in department stores. Store owners went bust and tried to sell vacuum cleaners door to door. Often the most important member of a family was the 15-year-old son who had a newspaper route.

Money was the name of the game. You turned your hand to any job, however hard, however menial, to make money – to survive.

———————————————— • ————————————————

Lemonade For Sale, Cheap

"I always was one to think things out, and there were some scorchers on the prairies in those years, summers when people were sleeping out down by the river at night hoping for a breeze. For three or four years this went on for weeks each summer. If it was that hot then anything you could provide which would make people cooler, that scheme had to succeed. After all, that's the whole principle of business, the law of supply and demand. You demand, I sell. If the price is right. First, of course, I have to make you demand, to want, but when it was 105 degrees in the shade at 2 p.m., then Mother Nature was on my side.

Lemonade. That was it. My wife and I figured that one out. Cold and as lemonadey as we could get it, and we had to get it to the people where they wanted it and that, obviously, was where people were concentrated. In the big office buildings on Jasper Avenue, and outside the department stores.

I didn't have much money but I went down to the wholesaler and bought several boxes of lemons. They were quite cheap. Sugar was cheap, about two or three cents a pound, and a 50 pound chunk of ice was two bits, and water was free. We cut the lemons in half and then each half into two and mashed them down with wooden mashers I made and put in a good helping of sugar and lots of chipped ice and filled the barrels – we used those small five gallon barrels – and drove down to Jasper and set up shop. We didn't know how much to charge but we were using glasses considerably larger than a Coca Cola and they were charging a nickel a bottle so we figured that would do for us.

Of course we needed a gimmick. We had the kids and they were the salesmen, the two boys and the girl, and it was they who went through the offices, with their red Super-Streak wagon. One would fill the glasses and one would take the money and the girl would wash and dry the glasses. She had to keep an eye out for the glasses as we only had about a dozen, but it worked. Here were these three kids making a good business, and selling a good product for a reasonable sum. Times were tough but I couldn't think of a person who wouldn't pay five cents for a glass of cold lemonade when the temperature was up in the nineties and more.

We had a friend who worked on the "Edmonton Journal" and he did a story with a picture over the article and that got the kids known too and by this time they had staked out their buildings where they worked and their mother and myself sold down the street. We did that for two years and the Lytle family, why we must have made $5 or $6 a day. The kids worked hard and we learned a few tricks and a thing or two about human nature, but every businessman does anyway. It certainly helped the kids and that venture led directly into the job I got which lifted the Lytle family right out and clear of the Depression. It was a case of one family helping themselves."

The Ma And Pa Resort

"It was a big Vancouver businessman who put me and my wife in business. We had a business but what a business! She'd got this little auto court from her Dad when he died, out on Fraser Highway, and as we were paying $18 a month rent in Vancouver and I was just doing odd jobs and she was clerking, we were going downhill anyway, so we moved out there.

It was run-down sort of an affair. Our house, which was okay because the old man had kept it up, and six little cabins scattered around four acres among old apple trees. There was a little stream, it was kind of pretty.

Business was so-so on weekends, picked up in July and August and was nothing in spring and winter, autumn too, and if we got the $72 for the taxes and could pay the light and water and our food and radio and truck payments, then we didn't ask for more. We would just wait out the hard times there.

One afternoon this big car comes in the drive. A big brown Advanced Six Nash, I still remember it. This fellow got out and wanted a cabin and he paid his $1 and drove around to it and about two hours later he drove back out. You see, he had this girl with him. He was maybe 50. He came into the office and you could tell he was a businessman. Right to the point. A nice little place we had, a nice spin out of the city, an hour's drive, but why didn't we put a rug on the floor and a hot plate and coffee pot and some sugar and coffee and a couple of cups and sort of clear a place out behind the cabin where he could park his car.

I knew what he was telling me. Increase your capital investment, increase your services, increase your price. My wife and I had kind of turned a blind eye to this sort of thing, big city businessmen bringing their girl friends or private secretaries out on Friday afternoon and stopping a couple of hours. Let's say we didn't encourage it, but by 5 p.m. you've got new sheets on the bed and rinsed out the glasses and you could rent it again.

This fellow said everything else was fine, the bathroom was nice and clean and that was important, but maybe we should stock up on ice. Chipped ice it was in those days, chipped off a 50 pound block with a chipper. He said he wouldn't mind paying $2.50 for an afternoon. He added that would be once a week. By the way, he owned a big store and later on would bring us out a smoked ham as a gift, a very friendly man. He also said he knew his friends, some of them, wouldn't mind paying $2.50 for a nice quiet cabin in the woods. On second thoughts, he said, charge them $3.

That's how it started. First, a few. Our Mr. X and then his friends, and then businessmen from Seattle with their girl friends, secretaries. You see, it was too far to Harrison Hot Springs for an afternoon, hell, even for a full day and night, and my place was clean and out of the way and we kept our mouths shut and if they wanted a tray, say around four in the afternoon, my wife would put some sandwiches and cookies and tea on it and put it by the door and knock three times and leave. That was another buck.

Then Mr. X phoned and asked if a man named Mr. So-and-So had phoned asking for a cabin and we said yes and he said not to give him one. Say we were full. I asked why and he said the fellow was trash. My wife didn't like that, and she asked what were we running, a whore house for the friends of this man, this Mr. X? I said no, nothing like that.

I told her our little Ma and Pa court, and that's what they were called in those days, was performing a social service, a vital necessity to the business community of Vancouver. She wasn't pleased, not pleased at my wit, and she said, 'We're selling out.' I said okay, she was the gunner. It had been her Dad's business and it was in her name and it had been very, very good to us in the past three years since Mr. X had come along and I said, okay, I'm not exactly in love with it, either.

I phoned him at his office downtown and he said how much, and I said we'd take $5,000, and that was a hell of a lot more than it was worth and he said, "I'll be out there this afternoon. Tell Annie to be ready to sign on the dotted line."

He knew a damn good business, a growth business, when he saw it. Sex."

———————————— • ————————————

$25 A Month Trapping

"Fur prices was good. An old Jew buyer with a truck used to come out from Lethbridge about once a month, he'd send a post card and we'd be ready. Some men were just foolish to go trapping but my Dad had trapped a lot in Minnesota – half the people in this district came up from the States about 1908 – and he taught me. I could set a badger trap as smart as anyone, and there were plenty of skunks and you'd get two or three coyotes. Weasel didn't pay nothing but other prices were pretty good.

For three years before the seven-year cycle ended there were plenty of rabbits. I've shot as many as 25 big fellows in one afternoon, just bang, bang, bang. A fellow who knew his business and didn't mind a lot of work, if he had a woman who'd help him skin them, they could do pretty good. One winter I made about $25 a month trapping and that was good.

The old Jew, Fewenberger, something like that, he said I was getting too good and I'd go on salary. I said okay, I'm game, put me on salary, but he was far too smart for that, I'll tell you. Trapping was okay if you had to do it, but nobody would want to do it all the time."

———————————— • ————————————

Helping The Widow

"The government was doing some rip-rapping along this river way up north of Ottawa. It was strengthening the bank and straightening the flow of water in this river for a power dam and the best rock workers were Italians. Maybe it goes back hundreds of years, but they could do rock work better. And besides, if it came right down to it, they would undercut anybody for the job, so it came right down to the contractor hiring dagoes.

There was a little town, a village, not too far away and a woman with two kids, her husband was killed in construction. There were about 400 workers at the time and they kicked in a dollar or two each for her, and because the village needed a cafe and she was a good cook, she opened a cafe. She opened it in another building right next to the hotel.

I don't want to be hard on the Italians because it just must have been long-time habit, but they wouldn't use the toilet in the hotel's beer parlour because it was easier to just step out the back door, and they pissed against the cafe wall. Not only was it a dirty thing to do, but it stunk like Billy-be-damned and this widow's customers were complaining. Wouldn't you? Damn right you would.

Billy Gilroy and I went down to the work yard and we got a long sheet of galvanized iron and I picked up a 12 volt battery out of a busted truck and we went back. It was dark, and we laid the sheet against the cafe and hooked up wires to it and the battery and went into the pub. Well, Jesus loving Christ! This guy gets up, steps out the back door and in about three seconds there is this scream. Like somebody was being murdered. The electric current had travelled up his stream of piss, the salt making it a good conductor, and just about blew him apart. He ran screaming down the road. I'd like to say we nailed about 10 other guys that night but it was no more than three more, and then everybody got wise. There was no more pissing against the widow's cafe any more. None at all. They learned their lesson well, and us being foremen, there wasn't boom-all they could do about it.

Try it on a tree in your yard sometime when the neighbourhood dogs are messing you up. Man, dog. Makes no difference. That's a mighty sensitive part of you. You might say that in the Depression we took our pleasures where we could find them."

———————————— • ————————————

Staying Alive On Gopher Tails

"There was this big family of Bohunks. Oh, sorry, we don't use that word any more. They were Ukrainians, and good hard-working people but somebody in a land office in Europe or Winnipeg had sold them the worst piece of land in the whole Shoal Lake country. Even in good times they could expect a fine crop of Russian thistle and mustard. I should say they could only seed about 50 acres of what they had. They sure got hooked by that land agent, but it was land, and when you come from the Ukraine, it don't matter what land it is, it's land.

In the bad times they were starving, but these people always had an inner strength to fall back on. Look at their sons and daughters today, doctors, lawyers, accountants, businessmen, nurses. Too bad so many felt they had to change their name. I can recognize them anyway, just the way their head is shaped and the way their faces are put together.

This family, Bodnarchuk, had 160 acres down the road from us, just first rate for gophers. The gophers lived on my wheat across the fence line, so I offered them a cent a tail bounty for each gopher. The government, or was it the municipality, gave another cent. Shells cost about half a cent each and if you got a gopher for every two shots you made a cent. Figure it out. So they had one kid with a :22 shooting gophers along the road allowances and he'd get maybe 20 or so a day, and that kid was a bloody good shot. The rest of the family – Momma in babushka, old man Bod as we called him, and about six kids – would fill up three barrels, those 45 gallon Imperial Oil drums, on a stone boat and go out to the gopher country.

They'd drive the horse to a colony of the critters and each kid and Momma would put her foot over a hole and they had a couple of scruffy dogs and they'd set them by two other holes. Gophers, you know, are always digging fresh holes so old Bod would go to the ones with the new dirt around them and start pouring in pails of water. It don't take much to fill up a gopher hole or a set of them, and the things panic too. You can hear them squeaking warnings to each other. One of the kids would yell in Uke and that meant she'd felt something push her foot. Up would come her foot and whap, the dog would have broken its back. Sometimes those Bodnarchuks would get four or five gophers in one deal, pappa gopher, momma gopher and all the little ones.

Those people would work all day at that. The sun could be blazing or the dust could be blowing, there they'd be, pouring water and whacking gophers. A doctor who visited my wife and me once from Winnipeg was fascinated, and he'd watch them far across the field for quite some time. He said it was like a scene out of some crazy, some nutty Russian novel.

I calculate I kept those people eating for about three summers, me and the government. I gotta give them credit too, they helped save about 10 or 15 acres of good crop for me too. That's how tough it was, because they couldn't have made more than 80 cents or a dollar a day. But then again, those people could live on next to nothing."

———————— • ————————

Gold Rush

"I took part in a gold rush once. The biggest farce I've ever participated in, but it was fun. I'd got my law degree back east but this town *(Vancouver)* was full of lawyers starving to death, and one of the big firms would be glad to give you a desk in a small office with three other young lawyers and work you six days a week, providing you wanted to work for nothing. Not even carfare. They had a great system in those days, and they were not about to change it.

Yes, the gold rush. Or that's what I call it. You'll recall if you had a gold mine in the Thirties then all was right with the world. The mining country of Ontario and Quebec was booming when the slump was everywhere, but Manitoba had a couple of mines as I recall and the country around Lillooet, up by Bralorne, Bridge River, in that way, up the P.G.E. was hot. It was hot, all right, but for the promoters and the whores and the merchants and the truckers and outfitters – there wasn't much for the little guy.

This was no Klondike, or California of the Forty-niners. There was gold in that country, a hell of a lot of it, but it wasn't for the placer operation except in the creeks and along the Fraser. In those days, to the gink who didn't know anything, gold meant a pan and picking nuggets out of it every three minutes.

You know, the burro and pick and pan bit, the old geezer on the back trails coming out every fall filthy rich to spend it all. But a lot of people who took part in that gold rush, it was in 1934, were your traditional losers, the ribbon clerks, the bank messengers, the taxi drivers, the guys who could work up a small stake, beg, borrow or steal, and head for the hills. I just can't recall just why everyone got hot on Bridge River and that country that year because I'm sure it had all been staked long ago. But away we went.

My Dad came up with 200 bucks, a lot of money then, and told me not to come back until fall.

We got to Squamish, and the Pacific Great Eastern was waiting for us. It seems to me they were starting a new run and this was the inaugural, maybe something like a Goldfields Special, and this was why there was so much excitement. But I just do not remember.

It took a couple of hours to get the ship unloaded and the train loaded and away we went, up through the Coast Range and into Lillooet and even though it was about three in the morning, the whole village turned out. More drinking, more bullshitting. A lot of talk about this being the land of opportunity, and watch our speed, and all that.

But it certainly wasn't a gold rush in the accepted sense, the classical sense, until I met The Old Man. The fact is, I met him through a Vancouver financier called Austin Taylor whom I had got to know on the train going up because he'd done business with my father. He suggested I go out with The Old Man, and to this day I never knew that guy by any other name. I wondered what he signed his claim papers with, or his free miner's license. Mr. Taylor was grubstaking this old geezer and he threw me in with the deal. I was 23, and Mr. Taylor said if the mining business suited me then I might go into his firm. Which one I don't know. He had a bunch of them.

After three days of mucking about in Lillooet The Old Boy and I headed out, back into the hills – *at six o'clock at night,* if you please – and this old guy kept muttering about getting out ahead of the rest of the mob and how they were always following him, and you'd think he was on to the bonanza of all time. We travelled about three hours and we and our horses were spilling and slathering all over the place and even a deaf and blind tracker could have followed us, and about nine o'clock, before it got dark, he went up a small canyon and this was where we were going to camp for the night. He got a tiny fire going, just a small Indian-type fire, and hauled out a fry pan and sliced open two cans of bully beef with a knife and then did the job on a can of beans and a can of stewed tomatoes and dumped them all into this fry pan and sizzled it up.

Know what he did then? He got out a big spoon and he began to eat. Nothing for me. Just this old bastard slurping away. Great slurps, and drooling. Then he passed the pan over to me and said, 'Hyar, Sonny Boy. Eat your fill and we'll have the leavings up for breakfast.'

Now there are several things I don't like, and one of them is being called 'Sonny' or 'Mac' or 'Buster.' Names like that. Secondly, I like food, not an insufferable mess of bully beef and beans and tomatoes. I could go on, but I won't, and furthermore, I had The Old Man figured for being crazy. So that was the end of my prospecting career. I didn't eat the mess that night and I didn't eat it next morning and I took my blankets and the bit of gear I had and started back down the trail towards the village. Before I left, the old bastard said, 'Knew you wouldn't last,' and I said I suspected that he didn't want me to last, to go with him. He just nodded, and then said, 'Yep. When I find it, it's all gonna be mine. Me and Mr. Taylor.'

He never did find boom-all, as you probably gathered. I hung around Lillooet, hiked or hitched into some of the camps, did odd jobs and pushed the summer around until it was September and I could go back to my father and say I'd tried. All in all, it was a good summer and I enjoyed it. Nobody I knew made any money but then again, nobody really lost. It still is very beautiful country in there and it will take more than that kind of strange gold rush to ruin it."

———————————— • ————————————

Sunday Dinner For Tourists

"My father was ferocious about debt. Simply ferocious. One of my brothers wanted a bicycle once and another boy wanted it and my brother had $5 coming to him for haying that summer from a farmer and was going to be paid in a week but father said no, he had to hand over the money when he took the bike. That's how the other boy got the bike.

We had this house, living room and dining room in one, a big kitchen, yes, a big kitchen, and three tiny bedrooms upstairs which weren't enough because my father and mother had one, my grandfather and his big dog had another and there were six kids so the three boys slept in a lean-to by the house, winter and summer. No matter how cold, that's where we slept. Kids grew up tough in Nova Scotia.

Dad came home from Pictou one morning and he looked upset and he told us kids to clear out, do your chores. I was hidden in the pantry off the kitchen and heard him say to my mother that the banker had said there was no loans left, especially for shore people, us, with no fish markets, and on and on and on. Dad was really ferocious about that banker, let me tell you, and he called him a 'damn Canadian.' He meant the man was from Ontario, an Upper Canadian, and that was not good. He wasn't from Nova Scotia. He didn't understand our ways.

I recall father saying, 'Lorna, there isn't a cent in the bank and there isn't a sou in my pocket.' I think it was the first time I'd seen him lose his self-confidence. He was low as a flounder. He just walked around the kitchen saying, 'Damn that man. Damn him.' That was bad, because father was Presbyterian. No cursing, ever. Scots. Old family. We were an old Nova Scotia family.

Mother asked what was the trouble, didn't we own the house and farm, about seven acres, and the bank couldn't take that away, and Dad said, 'Eat, woman, eat. How will we eat? Shoes. Dresses. Gas for the boat.'

Mother said, 'Dinna fash yerself,' and then she started to talk low and fast, and every time she said something Dad didn't like he'd take a swing at the sticky fly catcher hanging from the ceiling. They didn't see me, of course. When mother had finished, Dad said, 'You've done considerable pondering about this, haven't ye, Lorna?' and she said, 'Father and me.' That was grandfather, the permanent guest with the permanent guest-dog.

That's how we got into the restaurant business. Everybody pitched in. Except Dad, of course. I've heard this kind of story about the Thirties over and over, how the women took over. It must have made the men feel lowly, but the women took over.

The idea was sound. Dinners Sunday afternoon and evening. Nova Scotia dinners. Fish. All you could eat, and this was before we ever heard of the Smorgasbord. We just called it McGregor's Seafood Dinner. Underneath that was the word, Home-cooked. I scrounged a four by four foot Coca Cola sign and painted it white and my brother did the actual printing with green paint we used on the boat and mother had us move everything but the table and chairs and big buffet out of the dining room and we all decided – even Dad, because he was starting to come around – we decided what to serve and finally Dad said, 'We'll give them a feast from the sea and the land.'

Now how much was the price to be? In Pictou or over at Inverness or down at Halifax you could get a meal for 25 cents but funny, even today, those places don't serve much fish and the water's full of them. My oldest brother, Red, said we didn't want local people, they'd just criticize, and besides, they were too cheap and would eat at home. But what we wanted was those American tourists from Boston and New England and the rich people from Montreal and Ontario. There were no wealthy people in the Maritimes. Everyone was poor. If you wanted a good job you went to the States or Upper Canada, Ontario. We decided 50 cents. We'd go on that.

We gave them fish chowder soup. I'm just remembering that table now. They got fresh herring when they were running, and boiled salt herring. Fresh cod. Cod stewed for hours in milk, and our milk was like everybody's else's cream. They could have crabs and mussels in a garlic gravy. Mackerel. Smelts by the bucket if they wanted. Flatfish. There was always a big pot of steaming-hot potatoes, just as delicious as the fish, and there was a cold potato salad with boiled eggs sliced up and all spicy. Mother had a way with herbs. There was her own buns and thick bread and our own white butter, no colouring. We had three of the best little Jersey cows in the county, thanks to grandfather because he bought them. There was a rice and raisin pudding. That was all, for 50 cents, and I never saw a man, even the biggest, eat his fill.

Lobsters weren't considered much down our way then, and in fact, even today a lot of shore people don't consider them all that much even though they fetch about $2 a pound, landed. That is something fierce. But some people asked for lobsters. Why, they were out there pretty well for the taking so we added lobsters too, and they got to be so popular that mother had me write on the sign outside, 'Fresh Lobster.'

How did we do? We cleaned up. That table, which sat 16 with three extra leaves in it, was jammed from one in the afternoon until eight at night. Then *we* ate, if we hadn't grabbed something in the kitchen. Dad and the boys did the fishing Thursday and Friday and, I forgot to mention, we began serving on Saturday too. The boys brought in the vegetables too, potatoes, dandelions, swiss chard, turnips and carrots and Mom and us three girls, we worked hours at a time. I do mean hours at a time. Grandfather set himself up just outside the front door and took 50 cents from each person.

A thing like this spreads, you know. People would say they heard about the dinner in Boston and had made a detour and others would ask the tourist people, the ladies who ran guest houses, and they'd point down the highway towards our place. We had more than we could really handle and we just kept plugging away.

Fifty cents was just the right price and while a Scotsman is thrifty you don't see too many greedy ones. I guess 75 cents would have done but we felt 50 cents was fair and square. It was a dull Sunday when we didn't feed 100 people and nearly that, about 80 or so, on Saturday. We didn't make out too badly.

I remember a man from Providence, Rhode Island, who was in the hotel business. He had an inn. He said we could never make any money at 50 cents. He asked mother before he left how she did it, and she didn't know beans about the business so she said we just went ahead and did things. He asked what her inventory was and then he had to explain what that was and she pointed to the ocean and the garden and the cow pasture and he shook his head and then he asked what her overhead was, how much it cost to operate, and she looked at him with a funny kind of smile and said, 'Soap to wash the dishes and pans and salt and pepper for the table.' He just shook his head and told her she'd make a million easily.

When the war came, and especially when the Americans went into it, things dropped off. Rod and the next oldest joined the army and there wasn't enough gas and Dad went fishing under contract on a big boat and we just couldn't keep it going. Like the lady said, it was fun while it lasted."

———————————— • ————————————

Lots Of Supply, No Demand

"My dear husband died in 1928 when his team on the mower bolted and threw him. He didn't come in for dinner and my boy and I went out and found him. It was horrible.

We scraped along and in 1933 I was on relief getting $10 a month, for myself, the boy and my two girls, and with two cows milking and chickens and a garden, well, I'd say we got by. But then my brother came out from Vancouver to live and the relief people heard about it and they cut off the relief saying I had a man around the place now and he could do the farming. This wasn't so. We had no machinery or horses so how could we farm 80 acres? I ask you!

A man named Mr. Wood said I should make willow baskets and sell them, and that seemed a good idea. The kids went out along the Red Deer River and cut willows and I learned the ropes and I soon was making very good baskets.

Like Indian baskets, with designs. I tried to sell some in Red Deer but others had taken this Mr. Wood's advice and nobody wanted these fine baskets so Gerald (my brother) got a ride with a cattle buyer down to Calgary and he went up into Mount Royal to the wealthy people and tried to sell baskets, and I think he had a load of about 60. That was our whole winter's work. Good baskets. We were asking 50 cents each and in two days of door-to-door, he sold two. It was pretty obvious nobody wanted baskets so Gerald brought them home and I stored them away, the 58. I made another 35 or 40 the next winter just to keep busy and we put them on 50 percent consignment at the store next summer and hardly any sold.

Ten years later, this would be about 1945, I took them into the Bay in Calgary where we had moved, and they were beautiful and the man said he would give me $1 each and boy, did I jump at that. Nearly $100, which was still fine money, but we were in good shape then. But what $100 would have done in 1934, well, it just doesn't bear thinking about. What it would have done was keep that little family alive for nearly a year."

●

Toronto Boarding House

"Yes, oh yes. The Depression. What a lark it was. Mr. M. had died. Something to do with the ferry boat to Centre Island. Fell off or was pushed off or jumped off, the poor man, but I can tell you for certain some liquor was involved. He was a great man for the bottle.

I went down home and I didn't take to Halifax life any more, such a dull lot of people, and the fog, oh my God, the fog. The bloody fog. Is this all going down on your little radio? (My tape recorder.) Then for sure I must watch my language. So I came back, took the train I did and visited a cousin in Kingston and it was an awful place, all that rock and them narrow streets and the prison over there full of men ready to cut your throat in your sleep and the military. I've known military, Navy mostly, our grand and glorious two-for-a-penny navy, grand boys but such tiny ships, in Halifax and they mean nothing to me but did I ever see such a stuffed shirt bunch as them as was in Kingston?

So I came back to Toronto and what was I going to do? Char in some office or cafeteria? Washing floors in Eaton's or Simpsons? No, not on your life. I had a bit of money, Mr. M's tiny insurance after the undertaker had done his dirty work and my friend Mrs. Webb, she said one fine day, right out of the blue, 'Dulcie, you can cook and you can bake and you have a head for figures and the young people, they take to you. You know what your vocation is? You should buy a boarding house.' It sounded fine. I could cook, cook the feathers right off the angel's wings, and bake, I could do that, and if I had someone around to keep the furnace going, perhaps I could make out. I'd have a roof over my head. That's what a widow wants.

There was no trouble buying a house. Toronto was full of them, all these big red brick castles around here that they're tearing down so fast, all these Italians with their hammers and big machines just hit, hit, hitting everything, and next day they're around to knock down fine trees and before you turn around there's another building high as you can see.

The gist of it was, I bought a house. Off Yonge, a fine old one, not full of history but it did have its memories, of that I'm sure. By the time the inspector was through with me and I'd fixed up the kitchen and put in a fire escape and of course, my down payment, I had just enough to buy a sign for the window, 'Roomers Wanted' and a big accounts book.

They came, oh, they came. My boys and girls, from the university, from Ryerson, from normal school, from Osgoode. I could see I wasn't going to make much money off this lot, these students, but I did. A little. Honest as the day is long, except for maybe a quarter of them. One in four. I did well, and I still get a card or two, a letter, little things at Christmas and that was a long time ago. If I told you the things that went on in that house, well just multiply it by 10 and you'd have a good judgement. It was a madhouse.

I gave them breakfast and supper, 7.30 and 6, and be there sharp, not for my sake, but they was always so awful hungry the food would just go swoosh, like some big alligators just taking it all in in swooshes. I had about 18 to 20, any one time. Boys together, girls together, no mixing together. Ha! How little I knew. I knew of course, oh, I knew, but what could I do? Or care.

Boys paid $22.50 double, $20 single. Girls a dollar more, they used so much hot water. Washing their fancies every night. Some of those girls had but one pair of fancies.

We were all poor. Robert Kent, his parents lived near Orillia, he paid off half his bill in potatoes and turnips and apples. He stayed two years and each Thanksgiving he brought down this big old gobbler, the biggest turkey you ever did see. Some brought in all sorts of things. Butter. One's Dad owned a dairy at Peterborough. Milk. Cream. Eggs. Potatoes, country sausages, sauerkraut, blood puddings, this was free. It wasn't on their ticket. On late Sunday night this stuff would be stacked all in the lower hall by the door, the stuff they'd brought back from their weekend at home. If the truth were known, a lot of that food I really paid for, because I often made up the last 50 cents or so to some student to get home. You know what they say, if you've only got a quarter, 50 cents is an awful large sum. 'Tis true, you know. I've been poor too, you know.

There was Eunice. She was a student at the university and she was a prostitute too. She told me so one night, drinking tea at the kitchen table. I said tut tut, you know, and she said there is nothing wrong with being a prostitute. I said how do you know? She said her mother told her so. Now what can you answer to that, I ask you? You answer nothing, and she stayed. I liked her.

There was one lad, Frank Mutter, Frank Nutter, Nuther, something like that, and when he'd come home late, one, two in the morning, it sounded like an elephant going up the stairs. Thump! Thump! Thump! I put up with it for about four times, then I went out, I lived first floor, and turned on the lights and there was Frank staggering up the stairs with this girl piggyback. I said, 'Oh, good Lord,' and went back to bed. Next day I asked, 'Frank, what was you doing with that girl on your back? Was she sick?' He said no, the girl wasn't sick, she was his girl friend and they were going to bed, you see, and if he carried her then he thought I would think it was all right because I could only hear one set of footsteps on those stairs. Now there's a thinking lad for you. I hope he went into government. That's government thinking. Thump! Bang! Crash!

Once a boy came and he was something right out of Rip Van Winkle, tall and gangly and red faced and big hands, ugly but nice, and he had bad teeth and I said, 'Newfoundlander?' and he said he was and I said, 'Then come right in and get used to civilization.' It was a joke. The joke was on us. One of the nicest lads God ever made and he got some of the best marks at the university, such a sweet lad, such a future ahead of him, so good looking when we ironed the creases and spots out of him. He was killed in the war too. He wrote me once a week, on those little blue thin letter things, from England and Italy, and I cried my heart out when his mother wrote and said he had been killed.

They never left me, they'd stay in, come down for cocoa at nights after their studies were done, oh we had grand times. They talked and played bridge and chess and read each other their poems and stories they'd written and than they'd talk about them. They got better educations in my house than they did in the university, I can tell you that. I still have a roomful of books they left behind over those years. I suspect most of them were swiped. Oh well, books are for everybody.

Saturday morning was cleaning day, and everybody cleaned their rooms and the girls the upper halls and the den and dining room. The kitchen was my territory, so to speak. The boys did the furnace and the yard. Nobody had any money. Oh, we had grand times.

They came and they stayed and they left and I was Mrs. M. for six years, until 1940, and then it seemed so many joined up, the army, the air force, the navy, and they drifted away. I closed down in 1941.

I met one of them over on University Avenue not long ago and he said, 'Mrs. M., I wouldn't have survived without those meals of yours.' Dinner, my goodness, any night, piles and piles of potatoes and two huge bowls of stew, one at each end, and carrots and home-made bread and country butter they'd use to bring, and a basin, no, a tub of pudding, rice pudding with raisins or bread pudding and stewed rhubarb, not fancy food but good food, and every-one eating a mile a minute and laughing.

I can hardly think back on those days and not cry a little. They were my family."

CHAPTER FOUR

On The Farm – Those In The Bible
Never Had It Worse

Right Out From Under Our Feet . . . A Hot Sucking Wind . . . Laundry Was Never White . . . The Splash Of Hopper Juice . . . The Terror Of Nature . . . Dust From Your Hometown . . . Was It God's Punishment? . . . Like A Bank Robber . . . The Lovely Green Hillside . . . Farmers Did Funny Things . . . Weather All Upside Down . . . What Did The Experts Know?

———————————— • ————————————

The Western Canadian farmer is tough and as good a farmer as any in the world. He is not a quitter and can take adversity in his stride. But during the Dirty Thirties, when year after year he saw his land being eroded away, the fine and rich top soil blown away, his crop being frozen out in spring, hit by grasshoppers in June, burned away in July and blighted by disease in every growing month, even the toughest farmer had to consider quitting.

Worst hit of all were those in the famous Palliser Triangle, a great piece of land centred in Southern Saskatchewan but extending into Alberta and Manitoba, which contained about three million acres and on its farms, in its towns and cities, about two million people. It truly was a disaster area; some experts believe that in the bad years it was the hardest hit area in the world. Many experts now say that much of the Triangle should never have been used for farming, but kept only for grazing. That fact didn't help the farmer stuck there in the Thirties.

And if he did take off a crop – and six bushels to the acre was considered good – when he got to the elevator the price for wheat was rock bottom. Forty, fifty cents, not including charges and freight to the Lakehead. In those days, in those conditions, farming was a slow way of starving.

———————————— • ————————————

Right Out From Under Our Feet

"You see, the East didn't have a Depression as we had it on the prairies. They called it a Depression, and to them it was, but it wasn't a hell of a lot more than sitting around waiting for the jobs to come back, for the plants to get orders, for people to start buying new cars and stoves again, and they sat in their nice homes in Toronto and Hamilton and listened to soap operas and Foster Hewitt on the Toronto hockey games.

Now this is an exaggeration, and we both know that, but the East and British Columbia and the Maritimes, they didn't have a real Depression because they didn't have the drought. D-r-o-u-g-h-t. If you never experienced it, then it's hard to tell. Pictures tell part of it, but you had to see it, see the crops which were green and filling out in mid-June all across the prairies be down to nothing in two weeks, three weeks.

The dust storms. Nobody is ever going to write truly what a dust storm was like. We had them, I've seen them when you couldn't see the front of your car. Millions of acres just blowing away from all through the American midwest states and over towards the Dakotas and Minnesota, Wisconsin, up into Manitoba, Saskatchewan and Alberta. Things we'll never forget, and they could come again.

A while back I was telling my granddaughter about it and she asked, 'Grandad, what does drought mean?', and I was surprised, but then I told her because she's never known it. That's why I spelled the word out for you. Nobody knows it means five, six, seven years of dried-out crops, a great rich land without rain, and heat which would fry the edges off a muleskinner's boot, heat every day, too hot to fight and too hot to sleep in at night. Living in a dry sauna like in the motels, that's what it was like. I should have told that little girl 'drought' was desert, like in Arabia and then she'd have known, but there was no way she'd understood.

We had big crops for years, big ones in 1926, 1928 and 1929 and Mackenzie King *(the Prime Minister)* was selling wheat at $1.70 and up to $2, and wheat was king, and everybody just forgot that we were mining the land.

First, heat comes in cycles, years apart but years together when it comes, and who the hell is to know. We didn't have all that much ground water and what we had we were using up, the water table was dropping. The Palliser Triangle shouldn't have ever been broken to the plough. We know that now. Grazing, stock. The buffalo thrived like the green bay tree on it and so could cattle. We had this loose sub-soil that had no holding power and then we had the winds. Why them winds came, I'm not sure anyone knew, but I've seen them blow for two weeks at a time, blowing hard. Blowing the goddamned country right out from under our feet and nothing we could do about it.

We got around to contour ploughing later but for an awful lot of people, later was a lot too late. That dust, which was our earth and our livelihood, would blow for dozens of miles, scores of miles, and airplane pilots used to have to fly higher to get over them, they were thousands of feet high. You mistreat the land, take away its essential goodness and this will happen. It's been happening all down through history. So we had the drought, and everything else that went with it. That's why I could never get all that sorry for British Columbia and Ontario.

The West Coast didn't suffer like we did, and Ontario didn't either, and hasn't either, not as long as it's got the prairies to live on. Where we all made the mistake was the idea that Canada, the prairies, would sell high price wheat forever. When that fell to the bottom, when wheat was 50 cents, even less, everything went kerplunk. It turned out that what we were was a one-economy country and that was wheat. The prairies supply the world, Ontario manufactures machinery and goods for the farmers, B.C. chimes in with its fruit and lumber and fish and there you had it. Goodbye prairies, so long Canada."

———————————— • ————————————

A Hot Sucking Wind

"I'll tell you what that Depression was like. It was survival of the fittest and I read my Bible more now than I ever did and I never read of hard times like that, like we had in the middle of the Thirties. They was Dirty Thirties all right.

My boy and I were farming near Manyberries and it was dryland farming. No irrigation. You hoped for lots of snow and a slow runoff and good rains in June and July and sun at the right time. You hoped for everything and you got one or two, not everything, but you could make a crop and get by. It was grazing land, the Palliser Triangle, and it should never have been bust but there was a lot of land-taking in the early 1900s, Americans and immigrants, and my Dad was as much a grabber as the next. Just grab, grab, grab.

Here's how it was. Let me tell you. The wind blew all the time, from the four corners of the world. From the east one day, the west the next, and if you were working you didn't notice it too much but the women did. Ask my wife, but she's dead now, she said the wind used to make the house vibrate, and it was just a small wind, but there, always steady and always hot. A hot sucking wind. It sucked up the moisture. So this wind just blew and blew, and we had dust storms and times when we kept the lanterns lit all day.

Oh yes, here's how it was. I could walk, say in August when you couldn't have grown Russian thistle in a creek bed, I could go about 10 feet beyond the house fence and pick up a clod of dirt, as big as this fist. I'd lay it on my hand and you could see the wind picking at it. Pick, pick, pick. Something awful about it. The dry dust would just float away, like smoke. Like twisting smoke from that piece of land. If I tightened my grip, if I squeezed and crumbled her, then it would blow faster and right before your eyes in a few minutes that hunk of dry dirt would just blow away, even the bits of dust which collected into the wrinkles of your hand. I used to say the wind would polish your hand shiny if you left it out long enough. You've got to understand, this was no roaring wind. It just was a wind, blowing all the time, steady as a rock.

That dirt which blew off my hand, that wasn't dirt, mister. That was my land, and it was going south into Montana or north up towards Regina or east or west and it was never coming back. The land just blew away."

———————————— • ————————————

Laundry Was Never White

"I could never get my laundry white. I'd try and try. The children's things, the curtains and the sheets, why they all looked as grey as that sky out there. I'd work my fingers to the bone scrubbing, but it was no use. We were lucky to have a deep well and good water but even down that well, and it had casing in it, you understand, the water came up with dirt and dust in it. Even my husband, who was quite smart about these things, that was one thing he could never understand. Dust deep in a well. The wind blew that dust all the time. It never stopped."

———————————— • ————————————

The Splash Of Hopper Juice

"I was travelling C.P.R. towards Napinka, that's down southeast of here, and we ran into a plague of grasshoppers. Those in the Bible never had it worse. Millions of them, smashing and splashing against the coach. The train only had one coach, the rest was boxcars. They were small in those days. Soon you couldn't see out, with the grease and muck from those grasshoppers splattering the window, and then the train began to slow down and soon it was just making it ahead, less than a man's walking pace.

I was wearing glasses and I noticed they were fogging up, I couldn't see, and I took them off and there was oil on them. Now this is the funny part. I didn't catch on right off, but what that oil was, was mist from the juices of thousands of grasshoppers which the train's wheels was crushing and sending up as spray. I wouldn't have believed it. Grasshopper oil mist, penetrating right into the car, and it was over everything, ruining the ladies' dresses, well, everything. But soon the plague had flown on, they only lasted a few minutes anyway, and the train began inching forward. It had stopped, by the way, just no traction. It got going. Quite an experience."

———————————— • ————————————

The Terror Of Nature

"Remember Sputnik watching? People used to go out at night and look at the heavens and try and spot that first Russian satellite. We used to go grasshopper watching. Southwest of Regina, where we had a farm. My kids won't believe me when I say this but the clouds of grasshoppers used to go over and it was like a great storm. They were in their millions, tens of millions, and where they decided to stop all at once, then those farmers could just kiss that year's crop goodbye. If he had a crop.

We youngsters used to get pieces of glass, amber glass, like the colour of beer bottle glass, and we'd hold that glass up to our eyes and look into the sun and watch the grasshoppers go by, high, high up there. There were millions, as I said, but you could almost make out each individual hopper through this glass and, I tell you, I've never seen a more terrifying sight.

Nature on the loose, gone mad. In its own way it was beautiful too."

———————————— • ————————————

Dust From Your Hometown

"In 1933 I worked on a cattle boat for England, Liverpool, and the job of a bunch of us raunchy young buggers was to feed and water the cattle, keep them in good condition. In other words, get them there in market condition. It was long hours and there was no pay. You worked your passages but nobody thought a thing about that. Twelve days for a crossing, slow boat to China sort of thing. We loaded at Halifax, a load of good cattle from the Maritimes, Ontario, the prairies.

I was on the dock helping the dockers get them aboard and I got to talking with the foreman and I told him I was from the prairies. Where? Well, all over, I said, but Moose Jaw's my home town.

He said, 'Well, look ye up there,' and I did and the sun was sort of faded over by dirty clouds or something and he said, 'That may be from your home-town.' I didn't believe him but it was prairie dust, prairie dirt, or it was dirt from Kansas or Missouri or one of them states and the high, hot winds of that summer blew it east. This is no bull. That was prairie dust and if nothing makes you understand those days, that might."

—————————— • ——————————

Was It God's Punishment?

"Millions, billions, trillions. Yes, I remember grasshoppers. They would stop the trains. No traction. What a country! Dust would stop the trains and cars. The engineer couldn't see his bell and the car driver couldn't see the orna-ment on his water tank at the front of the hood.

But grasshoppers. Trillions. They would black out the sky and when they passed, nothing would be left. I've seen an ordinary kitchen broom leaning up against the side of a granary where we were crushing oats and when the hoppers were finished, all that was left of that broom was the handle and you couldn't tell it had been a handle because it was so chewed up except for the metal band which kept the bristles held together. Grasshoppers didn't eat machinery, but by God, I've seen them eat the leather off the seat of a John Deere tractor.

They had this juice. We used to call it tobacco. Actually it was some kind of brown and sticky liquid and I can't tell you what they used it for but Nature seemed to have a reason for everything, even the grasshopper, so it meant something. They'd come in the millions and fly into the sides of houses and barns and afterwards the side of a house would be stained a brown colour, and I've thrown a leather glove at the side of the house and it stuck. Splat! Stuck in this gucky juice. I tell you, God must have been punishing us for the sins of the world in them days."

—————————— • ——————————

Like A Bank Robber

"The heat. The 'hoppers. People at the door begging, for a sandwich, a meal, a cement patch for their tire, a glass of water, the school teacher who boarded with us crying because the board couldn't pay her any more and were closing down the school and she had to go away and she was in love with a local lad. Five cents for a dozen eggs. Oh, I remember lots of things.

The terrible winters. People getting caught on the roads and some freezing to death. Yes, that happened. Good friends leaving for the coast, and then writing back and asking how things were, were they getting any better, was there any point in coming back home again?

But most I remember the dust storms. When you were in them they were terrible, but from far away, when they were on the horizon moving north or south or west, they were beautiful, if it was towards evening. The sun would shine through, making them all rosy red and orange at the edges and a soft brown in the centre. Beautiful, just like in technicolour.

I remember my garden. Every year I tried a garden, radishes, lettuce, beets, peas, the few things a woman puts in. One year it blew, all the time, and when it was not blowing too strongly I'd go out and do some hoeing. No matter what, weeds always grew. I'd put a dish towel soaked in water around my mouth, like I was a bank robber, and then I'd rub vaseline into my nostrils. Yes, vaseline, good old drug store vaseline. This stopped the dust from blowing into your nose. It was supposed to stop dust pneumonia, stopping the dust from getting into your lungs. That killed people, you know. So there I was, with my Jesse James mask and my nostrils half plugged with vaseline, hoeing away, but it never was any use. Everything just grew a little and then died."

———————————————— • ————————————————

The Lovely Green Hillside

"I remember going to a town once, my husband was driving me, and we hadn't been over there for a few years but there was an auction sale advertised and I did love auctions, and we came down this slope into this valley and across the other side the hillside was a lovely green, it seemed for miles, just green as they say Ireland is.

My husband John said, 'I don't believe it, but somebody's got a crop. There's a man with a secret and that's a man we're going to see right now, if we can get in the line-up.' Well, we got to that place and it was just another abandoned farm and you know what that lovely green was? It wasn't new wheat. It was Russian thistle. Somehow it had caught on that whole hillside sloping down to the coulee. It was certainly a pretty sight, like just out of a magazine, but if good rains had come and everybody had replanted and come out of it, that farmer would have been in the most trouble. He had Russian thistle, and only the thistle seemed to beat the dust. I must say, though, he had a wonderful crop."

Farmers Did Funny Things

"Dust would cover up the fence poles and the farmers would come along with a wagon load of more poles and string another fence, on top of the first. I could never figure out why they did this because there were no cattle wandering at large, they had all been slaughtered long ago or taken to the community pastures. Farmers did funny things in those days. They still do, but everybody was just a little bit loco in that country then."

———————— • ————————

Weather All Upside Down

"My second son was born in January, 1931, and that was the year we got no snow and we lived in this old shack and our neighbour across the road summer fallowed, yes, in January, and we got half his field in our house. It blew, it blew steady, day after day, and the only time it stopped was after dark. I couldn't hang out the little fellow's diapers on the line, else they'd be black in five minutes. I'd hang them up on the line after dark and I'd get up before dawn and take them off and like as not, they'd still be grey. That was a crazy year. The whole weather was upside down. Nothing mattered.

When I had him, in mid-January, I was in the old Galt Hospital in Lethbridge and there was a tree outside my window that was budding out. It should have been twenty below outside. It was so unusual. We didn't get no snow until sometime in March and that wind just blew and blew and blew and it just took the topsoil away. Miles high, so it seemed, into the sky. They were really chinook winds. Southwest winds. Blew soil right into Ontario. We stuck it out because we're western farmers."

———————— • ————————

What Did The Experts Know?

"The worst thing was, we just didn't know what was going on, what was happening. We'd been going along fine in the Twenties, buying land, machinery, getting good, heavy crops and selling it all, and then crash.

Farmers and townspeople aren't university professors and those editorials in the Winnipeg "Free Press," those things were written for university professors.

One thing we did know. The Crash, the loss of millions and millions of dollars on the stock market, didn't touch us. We didn't have stocks. Our stocks and bonds were our land and our kids. What we had was the drought and everything that came with it. Oh sure, we couldn't sell our crop for anything nears a decent price but a farmer will keep growing wheat anyways because he doesn't know anything else. The stocks and bonds thing was for the city people. But what used to bind us was that nobody knew what was going on. We could look out on our fields and see them burning up in June, when in other years that was the time for good rains. Where were the rains? Where did all those billions of grasshoppers come from? And the rust.

It seemed every year you'd read that someone at some university had invented a wheat that would resist rust, but somebody was inventing a bigger and stronger rust. Musta been.

The thing is, none of the people who should have known these things, the scientists, the chemists, the economics men and the government, they just didn't know what to do for a while, a couple of years. Of course, what am I saying? No way they could have changed the weather and the price of wheat in England but, goddamit, they could have helped an awful lot of people feel a lot better. You see, all a farmer has is his land, and when he sees he might be losing it, then that is not a good thing."

CHAPTER FIVE

Moving With The Whistle . . . Off The Farm

The Call To Other Places . . . The Missus Said . . . I'm Pure Hell On Skeeters . . . Updating The Family Bible . . . A Place To Lay Their Weary Heads . . . Try Eating Puffed Wheat . . . $20 A Year Net Cash Income . . . We Just Loaded Up The Wagon . . . The Way God Meant Water To Be . . . I Knew All About Ranching . . . It Was Dog Eat Dog . . . And The Dust Moved In.

———————————— • ————————————

And so they quit. By the tens, hundreds, thousands, right across the west they left the farms, following the path of neighbours gone north to Peace River or the cool and green Fraser Valley of British Columbia.

What else could they do? There had been no crop for three, maybe five years, no money for fuel, clothes, even food. Their minds and their bodies were too beaten by searing July heat and terrible winters and the constant grind of poverty to really care much any more.

You could drive for miles down back roads and never see smoke from a chimney.

———————————— • ————————————

The Call To Other Places

"I loved the long whistle of a train, at night, moving down the valley six miles south of our farm, the long call to other places. Always at night, as I lay in my little bed in the attic. You know why I loved that sound? Because that train, a passenger train, I knew that train was going to Vancouver, or to Winnipeg and then on to Toronto. Escape. Get away. Leave the farm.

Maybe romance, if you really think so. But to get away. I was 20 and I had teacher's training and I'd have taught for free just to be given a chance but no, there was sweet, dear Margaret at home again with a family that was dying. Dying inside. The Depression was whipping us. Literally, I mean, because every time you went outside the wind, that constant wind whipped you.

I used to think that if the rest of the country was like us, lost and dying on 320 acres of Saskatchewan land, then Canada was finished. But there was always that train, that whistle. There was something in me, some kind of crazy clock, and I would wake moments before that whistle at night was to blow.

That train is going to Vancouver, through the Rockies and then the Selkirks and the Purcell mountains and then through the Monashee, oh, what a lovely name, and down to the sea and I would take off my shoes and walk along the sand and let every wave wash around me and I would write my sad thoughts with a stick in the sand and the waves would wash away the letters and those sad times would be gone for ever. Or to Toronto, and then Montreal, and we always thought it was busy and gay and romantic and Gallic and full of music and laughter, and then we'd get on one of those big Empress liners, all white, and sail for England. The Mall. The Strand. The Embankment and The Thames. Poets' Corner in the Abbey. Canterbury and Kent and quiet walks though flowery meadows in Devon in the spring.

You must be able to see what it was like, living on a farm, in a house that had not seen a splash of paint in 10 years, and my mother making do with nothing, like an old woman saving useless string and hoping someone would come along and buy string, and Dad up there, day after day, hot and hotter, on the iron seat of the cultivator trying to coax a little something out of the soil, and everything was dying and had been for years. A way of life was dying, and no one could weep. I've seen my father after dinner walk down the lane to where his first field began, beyond where the creek used to be full of good water and there was nothing. Once I saw him out there, and I don't think he was understanding quite what was happening to him. Sounds carry a long way in dry country and the call of a whistle came up then from the south and I saw him turn his head and look into the distance for a long time and then his head moved around slowly to the west as if following the train and I wondered if he was thinking that in British Columbia there was a country with fresh and cool and pure water right off the mountains, more than any people could want and here we were, dying for water.

I finally left. About two years later. Doesn't everybody? But I had stayed too long anyway. I went to Vancouver and it was just as I thought it would be. Even better. It was the whistle of the steam engine that kept me going in those bad years. Yes, I guess you could say that in those days the whistle meant romance and adventure and excitement and new places and new friends. We all needed that. Now, I'm 35 years older and when I think of the whistle or play my LP of train sounds you know what I think of? My mind goes right back to home, that farm in Saskatchewan. I can't help it."

———————————— • ————————————

The Missus Said . . .

"After the third bad year the missus said she wasn't going to take any more and somehow we got through that winter and lit out for the Okanagan Valley in the spring.

Sold what stock we could, gave the rest away, scrub stuff, there was nothing but scrub stuff by that time, and put two trunks on top of the car and left everything behind. Houseful of furniture, implements, crusher, harness, windmill, batteries, you couldn't give it away. The missus never looked back, just straight ahead down the road.

I had $210 in my pocket. I guess I was a rich man. Didn't even sign the papers back to the Bank of Montreal. Let them do the figgering. When we crossed into Alberta, the wife sang out: "One more border to go." When we got to the B.C. border down by, well we took the route south through Fernie, she sang out, "The promised land."

When we decided to go, and she was the one who gave the orders, she was a strong woman, she said, "Alan, I just want to walk into an orchard and reach up and pick a nice ripe peach off a branch, that's all I want." Well, that summer she did, and all she wanted, because nobody was selling those things. In a week she was sick of fruit.

I could see she was thinking about the old place back in Saskatchewan. I set her straight real quick. We're here, I said, and here we stay. You go back, you go alone. We stayed. It took her a couple of years to get used to the valley and we built up a fine place. Had a lot of help from the war, of course. Times were good after the war too. We did fine. I turned the place over to my son five years ago and the wife she up and died on me three years ago. You could say I miss her."

———————————— • ————————————

I'm Pure Hell On Skeeters

"We came to North Dakota, a shipload of us from Sweden, when I was a kid. This was about 1909, and about '22 a fellow came along and offered my old

man a fair price and he decided we'd head for Canada and we put the farm
into three boxcars and had a place near Deloraine for a couple of years and
then we moved up to Alberta, a place east of Edmonton and things were good
for a few years and then it got bad and then worse. Froze out, hailed out,
burned out, rusted out, and the grasshoppers ate the halters off the teams and
the catalogue in the privy and Dad was dead by this time and I had the family
and a farm. The government said there was good land up north and we could
see foreclosure coming on awful quick and we had a council of war one night
in the kitchen and we all said we should go. Even my old mother, and she had
got to like that district. So we head north.

Wagon travel. Just like on the western plains. Twelve, 15 miles a day. If you
wanted to be charitable, you could call them roads. You see, they froze in
winter, but in summer, muskeg.

We met people pulled off, and this was above the town of Peace River, back
there, who offered their outfit, horses and all, for a few dollars. It wasn't the
muskeg that got you but the critters that lived in it. I mean the mosquitoes. I
don't think I can describe them. We were down to two horses by this time, an
eight-year-old mare named Daisy and a gelding. He was called Spook. They
were thin, I wasn't giving them my grain – and I'd had to chuck off the cream
separator, a chest of drawers, a few sacks of coal, other things. We'd make do
without when we got to wherever we were going. All we had was an 'x' on a
map. But I could see we weren't going to make it. Those horses just didn't
have it in them.

The mosquitoes. God's punishment. My boy used to say there was all the
mosquitoes in the world just wherever we was but I'd say to go 200 yards away
and he'd find just as many. They drove them horses insane. Didya ever see a
horse rear up in harness, practically pulling the mate over on him, and lash
out and lash out and lash out, like a man boxing, and screaming. That was an
insane horse. Yet when a breeze came up and the skitters took to hiding, the
horse was quiet. We covered them with sacks and at night we built smudges
under them. Under their bellies and they sure loved all that smoke.

I've taken my hand and wiped it down a flank and my hand would come
away positively black and red. Black was the crushed bodies of the mosquitoes. Red, well, you know what the red was. A horse hide is pretty thick but
they could bore through.

I once saw four of them run down a moose, hamstring it and then kill
it. Ha!

I used to do that too with my face, brush it and have it come back black and red. Roll up your sleeve to the elbow and it would be covered with those devils in one minute flat. We must have had a smell that brought them, like sharks smell blood.

It got worse. There were no other wagons on the trail and it got so we didn't know if we were on the right road. One morning Daisy was so weak she couldn't roll over and get up. But the boys and me got her up and in harness, but she fell down about half a mile further. To you, half a mile means half of a 5,000 foot length. To me, them days, half a mile meant two, three days' work, using corduroy logs to build road, bull labour, not fit for a white man.

Next morning both were down and I just couldn't understand it. They wasn't diseased. They wasn't crazy, not that I could see. I mean, not full time crazy. I couldn't believe it was loss of blood and they weren't getting enough to eat for the work but enough to eat to keep going. I just figured both them horses had decided to die. Lost the will to live and it was the mosquitoes were doing it. Know why? Because the wife and I felt that way, too. Only the boys was too young and dumb to understand.

I said we'd camp for a couple of days. There was pea vine and vetch around for fodder and a creek was just boiling with hungry jackfish. We fed up the horses and added oats and slathered them with mud to protect them and kept smudge fires going.

The wife made some big feeds of booya. Booya? You know that soup they sell in fancy restaurants. B-o-u-, well, you take it from there. *(He meant bouillabaisse.)* Booya is what we call that in the north, from jackfish.

Third day, those horses weren't getting up even though the mud and smoke and wind hadn't made the bugs so bad. Fourth day, no. Fifth morning, I said I'm gonna boot your rumps from here to Great Slave Lake but you're gonna get moving and when I went over to Daisy with a hame strap, to belt hell out of her, you understand, she was dead. The gelding died that afternoon. It was like being stranded on a rock in the ocean, a bare rock, and watching the last ship in the world sail away.

I just looked at the wife and I said, 'Old girl, that ends it. We come into this world with nothing and at 44 years old, you're back to nothing.' We packed up what we wanted, clothes, pots and pans, some grub, a few trinkets, the rifle, little things, and we left the whole kit and kaboodle off to the side of the road. In three days of walking on our back trail we came to a farm and he

gave us a ride into Peace River. Seventeen days it took us to go in. The fault
was mine. Should have read the sun. We were way off the main road, miles
off, shooting off to a place nobody goes and a storekeeper in Peace River told
us, he was laughing, the fool, that if we had waited till winter some sleighs
and lumberjacks, loggers, would have come along. Appears we were on a
winter logging road and there was no farm land up that way at all. I lost two
good horses and all my patience finding out, and now I kill every mosquito
lands within half a mile of me. I'm pure hell on skeeters."

———————————— • ————————————

Updating The Family Bible

"There were places in the south country where people just picked up and left.
Some just turned their horses loose to live or die. You could drive down a side
road – if you could make it because there hadn't been maintenance for years
– and you could pass eight, ten farms on both sides of the road and no smoke
coming from any chimneys. All abandoned. They just packed up their
belongings, their few joys, put what they could into the truck or wagon and
headed west to British Columbia. Some went north, the government was
saying go north, the Peace River, up there, and they had a terrible time.

We farmed around Manyberries, that's south of Medicine Hat and it was
very bad times there and we wound up in Kamloops. My husband got a job
in a machine shop and we came through all right.

I remember, after the war he'd come back from overseas and I met him in
Winnipeg and he got leave there and we were going to have a Second
Honeymoon and his father lent him his car. Gas was rationed then, you know,
but there were ways of getting coupons and Bud's dad, he farmed near
Winnipeg, he knew all the ways, believe me. We got to The Hat and I said we
should go down and look at the old place. Bud didn't want to, but finally he
said okay and we got there and it looked the same after 10 years. The equipment shed had blown or caved down but the house could be made liveable.
There was even most of the furniture, what the rats and mice hadn't torn out
or eaten. I went into the parlour and even the pictures, of Christ and Our
Lord, were on the walls. It was scary. Bud came in and said he wondered if
the family Bible was still around, we'd forgot it, and I went to the china
cabinet and pulled out the bottom drawer and sure enough, there it was.

Old as old, been in my mother's family for four generations, but good as
it ever was. Nothing had changed. Right there and then I made two entries

for the kids I'd had in Kamloops and the death of my mother in '42 and we were right back where we started again. That Bible is in my home right now."

———————————— • ————————————

A Place To Lay Their Weary Heads

"I worked on the docks, washed dishes in a cafe on Granville, worked up to short order cook from 11 at night to 11 in the morning, did a lot of things, and in that job I fed a lot of guys free, buckwheat cakes and coffee, and that was because it was about '32 then.

That farmer out in the Fraser valley, named Patterson, walked in one day and saw me at the griddle and asked if I wanted my old job back and I said yes. He said things had changed, but he'd give me a dollar a day and no cows to milk and that was okay with me. He also said I'd have to keep a sharp eye out for the new people drifting in. Patterson meant the Saskatchewaners. Some from Alberta, those people who were being dried out. This was about '33 when they really started coming in.

They'd have a car and often they'd sawn the back off it and made it into a kind of pickup truck. Some truck. How they made it, I'll never know. They couldn't go through the States, over through Washington, so they just pushed her through from Fort Macleod, Cranbrook, up through the Okanagan, and down the canyon. Now in those days the Fraser Canyon was a bearcat. There actually were places where buses had to back and fill. You just wouldn't believe it.

But here they were, with their wives and kids and dogs and sometimes a few chickens and all that big mound of bedding and pots and pans and a tin stove all tied up behind. They wanted work, but mostly they wanted a place to just lay their weary heads. They weren't thieves, but if they had to, they could steal with the best of them. They were mostly good people, but on the run.

There was quite a bit of land in Surrey then, and a lot of it had gone back for taxes. They'd build shacks. Trees, they'd cut down trees and then they'd stroll by a lumberyard after dark and sometimes some good boards would stick to their hands. They wanted to work, but there really wasn't no work. Some on the roads, but not much. I think they were putting up or repairing some dykes on the rivers then but, you see, they were no better than foreigners, people from a distant land, and there wasn't even work for the valley people.

Not that there was much hatred, but you can see the situation. When times got better, starting as I remember about 1937 when prices began to work up a bit, then there was work, and then the war and the shipyards got going and other plants and they could buy up that little bit of land they had been squatting on, and by that time they were part of the valley.

But going back, they sure were a sight, those piled-up cars and trucks. They say some people actually came out in wagons, horses and wagons. They'd do all right once they got going though it must have been mighty slow, but them oatburners never broke down, and on the roads you were always seeing one car towing another. They were cheerful folks, though, lots of humour and I'm not sure I'd be that way in their situation. Everything left behind, land and kinfolk, friends and all they held dear."

Try Eating Puffed Wheat

"I had this farm 18 miles southeast of Regina and for four years I did not have a crop. The government boys gave me seed grain every spring and I put in 150 acres and by mid-July, sure as thunder, the Good Lord came along with the drought and grasshoppers and took it away.

I was really a cattleman. At heart, I loved a good herd and somehow I managed to keep the best together, feeding them marsh hay in winter and grazing them along the right-of-way and in the coulees, and we had a dugout I dug with a Fresno and that was tough work but it held enough water for about 10 cows and a bull until September when we could expect some rain.

Well, by 1935, I was finished. There was no rains in September, and I could get by on the water end of it by trucking it in but I needed feed and the government came along and they put me on the list for feed. Do you know what that feed was? Well, Billy be damned, it was barley and oat straw. Baled. Barley and oat straw, and they expected me to keep weight on 10 Shorthorns and a good bull with that. Here was the government with all its experts shipping in that kind of fodder.

You know what that kind of fare would do to you, to a human? Well, think what would happen to you if you ate puffed wheat as a steady diet, nothing else, for two months.

When I got hold of the government man in the next town and he told me that I'd have to bring those animals through the winter on that, I thanked him kindly, told him he was a horse's ass and then I loaded up that bunch and took them into Regina and sold them for what I could get.

I wasn't going to murder that herd, small as it was, day by day, just watching them slip away to nothing. Like hell I was. That ended the cattle side of the business for me. That ended it."

————————•————————

$20 A Year Net Cash Income

"There is just one way to put the plight of the small farmer in New Brunswick during that time in its proper perspective.

In 1933, the government in Ottawa came out with a commission report on farm incomes. Farmers were in rough shape across the country and the report was aimed, actually, at finding out the true position of the Saskatchewan farmer. But they did the whole nation, you see.

In 1932 when the survey was taken, the net cash income, the net cash income of the average New Brunswick farm – and admittedly some were marginal, poor land and poor farmers – but the average net cash income of each farm in that year was $20. That's right, I said $20. A nice and round and even $20.

There was produce too, vegetables and pork and blueberries that the people could eat, but the money they got from taking their produce into Moncton or Saint John or Fredericton and selling it on the open market was an average net cash income of $20 a year per farm.

I doubt if you want me to belabour a point but there were big farms, dairies and chickens and the like, which were money owners. So where were the chaps who were poor farmers on poor land, and remember a lot of their land was good only for conifers and when you have fir trees growing, you do not have land for growing cash crops. Where were they? They were nowhere. I hate to draw such a barren picture but there it was."

————————•————————

We Just Loaded Up The Wagon

"Everybody in that country was hard hit by the Depression. The school at Chilanko Forks had to close down, and we had four kids. They needed an education so we had to get closer to a school. The nearest one was many miles away, far too far for children to ride to. We tried to sell our ranch, and it was a good one, but nobody would buy it. Who would in those days when cows were selling for about $6 each? For a first class bull you wouldn't get more than $75. Finally the time came when those children just had to get to a school, so we just loaded up the wagon and drove away from it. We just left the ranch. Nobody wanted it, and we never went back."

———————————— • ————————————

The Way God Meant Water To Be

"When I was 18 there wasn't much use hanging around the place no more, the farm where my folks lived, because there just weren't no crops and if I left quietly no one was going to notice and so I got a ride with a cattle buyer and got to Calgary where it was 'Move along' and 'Keep moving, fellows' and all that, so you could see it wasn't the best place for a single man with no prospects.

One afternoon I walked out west of town and hopped a box car and settled down for the night and when I woke up the train was stopped and I looked out the door and by God, there were the mountains. All around me, pretty as you'd ever like to see, and just over there was a little stream, bouncing along and I got out and ran over and looked at it. I surely do think it was the first running stream I'd ever seen in August, surely not in southern Saskatchewan, which was my place of abode.

I looked at it, and then I jumped across it and then I jumped back over it and then I stepped into it, and by God, if I didn't sit down in it. Colder than hell but here was water you didn't have to strain and use over again and carry miles to use. This was the way God meant water to be, just running everywhere. Except for the army I never left British Columbia again. That was it. That water."

———————————— • ————————————

I Knew All About Ranching

"I got out of Saskatchewan in 1934, pretty well skinned alive. That part of Saskatchewan was a desert then and some camels and Arabs would have been right at home. I had $180, an old Ford truck and the gear I wanted, a six-foot hay mower, the rake broken down, four sets of harness, a saddle, blankets, a mattress, cooking stuff and some grub. I had no wife. She'd left me in '32, gone back to Brandon to her folks. I got as far as Kamloops and I thought I'd stop. Stay. It was ranching – I knew everything. Everything about ranching that country. I'll say I did, but not as much as any 10-year-old kid, I found out. I made a deal and took over 1,260 acres west of town, and pay when the cattle sales was held in the fall, pay that year's rent. The guy Crawford had about 100 head and he wanted two cents a pound, about $575 was the way I figured it and knowing everything about ranching, I just figured I'd cut him in half and I did and got 95 head, two-year-olds, culls, tail enders, junk for I think it was about $275. So there I was, a rancher, and I paid him $130 cash money and gave him a note for the rest and there I was with 1,200 acres and a small herd on green grass for $130, you could do it them days. He was a nice fellow and threw in a saddle pony free and I bought another, half down, for $25, and they was for the haying, and there I was, all set up, ready to go and nobody was ever more confident than the day Christ left Medicine Hat.

I get settled in and clean up the cabin and do some checking around and down at one end of the big meadow there is this piece fenced off and there is this piece of land with good shade on her and it's June and the grass is green and high, and I figure that is too good to miss. I cut the fence and drag away about five poles of it, so it's open and I know the cattle will drift down that way. That grass and a little pool, it looked like a picnic ground.

Next morning I'm riding around again and I see only a few of the herd and I think that's damned funny, where could they have gone to, and then I see one lying on its side there and another further over, all bloated, legs in the air, and damn it all to hell, I ride into that place, the place I'd opened up the day before, and there are dead animals all over the place. I counted 47 dead ones, and more looked like dead.

I ride back to the truck and into Kamloops for a vet but I don't find one and I'm trying to find the way to the government farm thinking they'll have one and I see this Crawford on the street so I slams on the brakes and tells him what happened. Where it happens.

He looks at me and then says, 'You goddam stubble jumper. Don't you know when a fence is where a fence is, that's where a fence should be. It's not there for fun.'

Then he tells me. Blue larkspur. The stuff may look beautiful and I did see it, but it is pure murder for cows. Poisons them. They fill up, drink, drink more and they blow up. The poison works and that's it, brother.

He said nothing could be done so I said what the hell, what do I do, and he said to forget it, pay him the rest what I owed when I got it and we'd tear up the rent agreement and I'd give him the truck and the gear in it. That was okay with me, I wasn't going to be no rancher anyway. Two days of it was just about enough for me and when I sent him $10 a year later on account the letter came back. The postmaster said he seemed to have left the country too. At least nobody had seen him. Maybe he ate some of his blue larkspur."

⸱

It Was Dog Eat Dog

"The farmers from the drought certainly didn't do me any favour. Wages was low enough as it was in the Twenties and then these sodbusters started coming in the Fraser Valley about '31 and if you had a job, you had better watch out. Say you was in the field, doing a repair, and one of them Saskatchewan fellows and his wife and kids would come in to the yard looking for a drink of water or a gallon of gas, sometimes before you knew it, that fellow had your job and his wife and kids was moving into your house.

Say you was making $30 a month with that little house, your vegs and spuds and milk free and the farmer let you run maybe two steers with his, so you had a bit coming to you when they sold. That looked pretty good, that house and garden and slops for a pig, maybe, to that Saskatchewan fellow. He'd get talking to the farmer and he'd say he'd work for $14 or something like that and his wife would work a couple of hours for his wife for $6, say, and, by bingo, you was out.

Maybe you worked for that farmer for five, six, 10 years. Loyalty didn't mean nothing. But $10 sure did. Ten dollars was an awful lot of money. Like a hundred now, more. This happened to me, by a dairy man up the valley and I said, 'Dan, how could you do this to me?' He just said, and he was ashamed, I can tell you, he said, 'I'm going under, and the slower I go under the better. Things might get better.'

He didn't ask me even if I would take a cut, which I would've, and I said, 'Dan, it grieves me to say this, but you ain't much of a man.'"

⸱

. . . And The Dust Moved In

"If you were to ask me to play the word game and you mentioned Depression, then I'd answer nasturtiums. When I think of the Hungry Thirties nothing comes quicker to my mind. I see a rutted road between two hills, leading to a cattle gate into a barnyard littered with rusting equipment. There is a house, unpainted the way they always were, and a barn whose boards have bleached in the sun. The house, one storey, six rooms, counting the fly-blown summer kitchen smelling of fresh milk in the churn. There are rows of beets and carrots, peas and corn, gulping for air among the weeds. But on the sheltered side of the house, there were the nasturtiums. Blazing in colour. The only sign of gaiety and bravery around.

That's the farm at Crestwynd in Saskatchewan which was home to my sister and her husband, three nephews and two nieces until my sister died of tuberculosis. From overwork. The dreaded T.B. of the Thirties. She died years ahead of her time. And when she went, the nasturtiums didn't get tended and watered again and the dust moved in and buried what was left and the family just moved out and left that whole section of land to the grasshoppers.

I've been back to Crestwynd once since then. The house is now used as a granary because the wind stopped blowing and the rains came back and the prices improved and everything got better, but the barn had keeled over from the wind and the equipment was all buried in weeds and mounds of soil of thirty years ago and the only living things were the gophers and coyotes, but they were always there and they always will be. That place represented defeat with a capital D for one man who worked his guts out and a woman who was drained by heat and wind and cold and hardship of all vitality. The nasturtiums are gone but they are still vivid in my mind because their brightness and colour represented, I suppose, the ultimate mockery.

In some ways the land never recovered from those years of the Thirties. The village of Crestwynd has a grain elevator and a couple of cottages and a railway station that was closed long ago. It used to have a general store and a lumber yard and other businesses and many more houses and a ball park. The roads in that part of the country are still mainly dirt, wandering up and down the hills, in and around the alkaline sloughs, seemingly going nowhere. The only sign of life for certain is the spindly-legged sand piper, a bird that apparently lives anywhere. Abandoned farm houses lean against low rises in the land and you can stand on one low hill or another, it doesn't matter, and see rusting railway tracks leading away into the distance, but the trains don't run any more."

CHAPTER SIX

Four Walls And A Roof

Like An Eskimo . . . Home For Two Young Ladies . . . We All Lived In Two Places . . . He Never Missed A Month . . . Both Free And Clear . . . Let's Put Up Monuments

———————————————— • ————————————————

People have great pride of place. They talk of "the home farm" or "the house in town" or "Grandma's place" and what they mean is that the place, wherever or whatever it is, is also theirs, a place they can go to, and be welcomed and be among friends or relatives. It is home.

In the Depression, uprooted people often endured great hardship to find new land, a new home, in the northern farming areas or further west. Those who stayed fought to keep what they had, even when all hope was gone. It was home.

———————————————— • ————————————————

Like An Eskimo

"It was about 1936 when the igloo part came in. Oh God, it was cold, day after day, and down around 45 degrees *(below zero)* but we couldn't know because a radio was an expensive thing in them days and getting in to town took enough out of a man without going around and asking about temperature. The house never was that much. Wood, no insulation then, fire burner in the kitchen and wood hard to get, and my wife said she was just waiting for the next big wind to blow us into the gully. The frost was an inch thick on the windows everywhere and the boys and me only left the house to get wood and feed the stock because we'd laid in a lot of Russian thistle and stinkweed and barley and wheat which never came to a head that summer before at all but was kind of a feed for the six cows I kept. People around said six cows was too many but I've always felt cows was something to fall back on. It's the countryman in me.

About the igloo. We'd got to know this lad in Regina who worked on the railroad and he drove down some time in January bringing some National

Geographics for the children and a can of pipe tobacco for me and a bottle. Gavin had been in the Arctic for years and he kept looking around the house not saying anything and then my wife said, 'I know, Gavin, God didn't, God never meant people to live like this in this cold,' and she started to cry. First time she'd ever cried front of the children.

Gavin started telling us that an Eskimo lived better in an igloo than we did, warmer, cosier, and then he turned to little Mary, she was just 10, and he asked if she would like to live in an igloo. She nodded yes and Gavin got up and told me to come out and me and the boys went with him and he walked over to the gully behind the house and he asked how deep the snow was and I cast an eye on it and I said it was at least nine feet deep. I remember him saying, 'Deep enough,' and then he said, 'Wind has packed her down like granite. She'll do.'

Well, my friend, we got shovels and we started to dig a tunnel, about yea high, I could just bend over in it, about five feet, and he went on to explain that the mouth faced away from the wind. You know about snow, I guess. She's a fine insulation. We took turns digging into the big drift and about 10 feet in, Gavin said he'd take over and he turned a corner and the snow, in chunks like concrete, came flying out and he said he'd now build the house. Mary came out with coffee and we knelt around in the tunnel and it was quite warm.

To make a long story short, we built, or we dug, a big room about 10 by 12 feet and five or so feet high. The boys went out to the barn and brought back horse blankets and grain sacks and straw and we laid them on the snow floor. Gavin got a broom and went up on top and said, 'If I break through, she's no good anyway,' but it held and he poked about six holes through with the broom and got empty tin cans and punched jagged big holes in them and set them over the holes and got them turned so the wind wouldn't blow down them.

By this time Jack and Harry were real excited and they went out to the barn and lugged in boards and we made some beds and they brought blankets from the house and so we had beds. Does all this sound loonie? Well, it all happened. Of course we brought out several lanterns and that made the place light and we had a little oil stove we set up on a board platform and they all provided plenty of heat and the stove was for cooking. We brought out all our food and magazines and everything we needed and we just walked away from that house.

Food? No, we never wanted for it. I had six dollars coming in every month, the relief, and Mary's aunt was sending her 10 every month by money order and two of our cows were still milking and there were a few hens. We did fine. Mind you, nothing fancy, but better than an awful lot of people who wasn't living in an igloo. I'd buy dried beans and dried apples and salt pork, sugar and coffee, corn meal, lard, flour, bread of course, and strawberry jam and we had our bacon. We killed quite a few chickens so we had chicken soup and stew and we were fine. We were warm, our igloo was the easiest thing to keep clean, and I guess it was between 35 and 45 below for a long time that winter and we never felt it at all. Cosy as cooties.

Going to the bathroom was a problem until I carved out a small biffy in the snow and we'd just cover it up. The thing I liked about an igloo was the maintenance, it was so simple. The boys just had to make sure that if there was new snow then that the tin cans over the air and smoke holes had to be cleaned and fixed again. A buffalo rug over the entrance and a horse blanket over the second entrance, into the big room, was all we needed. We were doing fine.

In about three weeks the kids decided to go back to school and pretty soon we were having visitors. They were bringing their chums home, and by golly, soon the old folks would be coming. Kept us going just making coffee for them. Sometimes one of them would come up with a bottle of his own home-brew and we'd sing and life wasn't too bad, except that we all was stony broke. I guess you could say we were celebrities. The police even came by one after-noon. They weren't looking for trouble, but they sure were curious. They wrote a report but nothing came of it. Oh yes, something did. The Regina newspaper heard of it and they sent a man down, quite a way you understand, but by that time it was getting into spring, sometime in March, and the snow house was drippy and we had moved back into the house. One thing about igloos, once they start to drip they're just no damn good. But we lived in her for about six or seven weeks and they were good times. Kids didn't have colds and they did their lessons at night without being asked and the wife and I got along better and we ate well and Gavin came down to see us once a few weeks after we'd moved in and he looked around and stayed the night and next morning he said we could show an Eskimo a thing or two.

That year our little farm got some rain at the right time and the wind stopped blowing so, and there was a bit of a crop. But we decided this was no life anyway and we went into Regina. But the kids, Harry was killed with the war, but Mary and Jackie, when they write, which is seldom, they always say did I remember what it was like, Dad, living in an igloo. I sure do, and they've never forgot it either."

—————————————— • ——————————————

Home For Two Young Ladies

"My family had this fine farm and my father and mother were of Scots descent, and you know how the Scots value education. I think education will always win out. My parents, since we were knee high to a grasshopper, had always told Mary, my sister, and me that we were going to college. To Varsity in Saskatoon, the University of Saskatchewan and we'd become teachers. A girl in those days could become one of three things, a secretary, a nurse or a teacher – and a teacher was the best.

We had no money, of course. We had a fine farm and cattle and there wasn't a real crop failure in our district but really, with prices so low, beef at a cent a pound and you lost money on every bushel of wheat, you were poor in a land of relative plenty. There was no sense in going into debt because if you borrowed from the bank, if you could, I mean, it usually meant that was the first giant step towards losing your land. I mean it. The banks were the ones giving farmers the push into bankruptcy. Farmers, at least the ones I have known, are not the best businessmen you will run into. Any businessman in Weyburn could skin the best farmer in the district without half trying. And so it is today, I think.

Dad was what you would call a canny Scotsman and he put an advertisement in the Saskatoon newspaper which read something like this: 'Two young ladies, Scottish descent, going to Varsity this fall, need room and board in quiet, friendly home. Will provide meat, poultry, eggs and potatoes in lieu of cash.' Et cetera. In words to that effect, anyway. I don't know how much of this went on but it certainly got results, the ad, I mean. Dad got, I think, about 40 or 45 replies. People wrote 10-page letters telling how homey their home was, how nice they would be, how quiet it was for studying, how everything. We even got two replies from people in Winnipeg, saying relatives in Saskatoon had sent them the clipping and they'd like to have us, and that the University of Manitoba was better than the University of Saskatchewan.

We were overwhelmed and spent about two weeks that summer at the big table in the kitchen going over the replies. We finally selected five and one day we drove into Saskatoon and drove by the five addresses and we could

eliminate two right away. Then we went downtown and phoned the one of
the three left that had a phone, and could we come out, and you could hear
the hurrying and scurrying around in the background and yes, of course, of
course, come out right away. Mother said that was a good sign, because it
meant their house was clean.

It was. It was just a lovely place, big and cool and nice inside, a lot like our
place at home. The Arnetts were lovely people and they had a daughter Mary's
age and, well, it was like being home. So Dad and Mr. Arnett got their heads
together and they made a deal and on the way home, mother asked what
arrangement they had come to so quickly. Father said, 'I told Mr. Arnett that
in exchange for them looking after our girls adequately, I would feed them
all adequately, just like the advertisement said. We shook hands and that is
the deal.'

It worked out beautifully. Mary and I lived in that fine old house and we
all ate like kings. When father said 'adequately,' it meant the way we ate at
home, and that was as good as the premier or the lieutenant governor. Sides
of beef and chicken and sometimes a turkey, eggs, cream, vegetables, and as I
said, we ate like kings. It lasted four years until Mary and I graduated, and
there was never a moment's friction. Their house was ours.

Mrs. Arnett told me years later, after her husband had died, that if it
hadn't been for that arrangement they probably wouldn't have survived
the Depression, and I mean keeping their home. As it was, they did pretty
well and so did we. I've often thought I should write a little book or story
on it but I always have been too busy. It's one of those things. But they were
good years."

———————————— • ————————————

We All Lived In Two Places

"We had been farming north of Shaunavon. We is my father and me. His
father had done it before him, coming in with two horses, a box wagon, three
kids perched up on top of the load to keep her down, a few cows and another
wagon following, driven by his brother. That was seed grain and other stuff.
They'd come across to Regina from Owen Sound, that's in Ontario, and
bought their outfit and they homesteaded.

By the time I'm talking about, in 1935, my grandfather and his brother
were dead and my father was getting on and I was 37, with five kids and
another on the way, and as far as I was concerned, we were right back where

we started from. We hadn't had a crop for three years but up north in Alberta they were getting 20 bushels of wheat an acre and that wasn't bad, except prices were down at the bottom. But where we were? Nothing.

The missus and I talked it over and decided to pull out, to go north, not around Edmonton but over in what they called the Peace River Block where they'd never had a crop failure and, as far as I know, to this day that holds true. Deep loam. Lots of sunshine. Rain just when you needed it. Course, the growing season was shorter, but with those three things going for you, that didn't matter. Remember the growing days were longer, and that helped. Someone said one night when we were discussing it that the Peace River Block compared with the plains of Hungary, which is supposed to be the best growing land in the world. I wouldn't know.

The government would help us. I hadn't taken no government help before, but by God, I would have taken the Parliament Buildings if they had offered it now. We didn't have no sale because my Dad and mother were staying on the place, my Dad to have another go-round with the Russian thistle and try and pay his binder twine and gas with his crop money and my mother, well, I guess she'd try and keep a garden going and see if she could figure out a new way to keep the dust from filling up the house, room by room. I gave my Dad $10 for his old truck and we piled in what we had and the neighbours donated a fair amount of stuff. Taking our stock and machinery was out of the question, but I'd figure a way out of that one when we got there. At least we weren't reduced to the level of a Bennett buggy. Too bad, we wouldn't have made it, and that would have been good.

At Edmonton, no, north of there, we stopped beside a little river for the night and soon another truck came along and soon two more and we got to talking. All heading for Peace River. All the same. Frozen out, burned out, dried out, rusted out, played out. There was a family named Miller and one from around Dundurn named Redway or Rodway and the McCormicks from Climax, around there. Well, sirree, it was the most natural thing to do. We'd form a wagon train and help each other along the way and in that way we'd all get there. You got to remember that the roads in those days were just terrible in the country and where we were heading, the Peace River, they were worse than that. You'd have to send your oldest boy walking ahead into a puddle to see if it had a bottom to it and if the gravel wasn't the dustiest I've ever run into, then the dirt was. But we got there, after a lot of breakdowns, but farmers always was good mechanics and the cars in those days weren't all that tricky and we could fix most of the trouble. To tell the truth, we had a lot of fun in those nine days and it all ended when we got to Dawson Creek, that's across the Alberta border into British Columbia.

Of course, the land is good. It still is. But Jesus H. Christ, I'll say this. What kind of a sappy government is it, or the land agents in it, who would tell people to go up into that country? They just said go, there's free land up there and it is so rich it will grow anything, even particles of country rock. Why stick around on these burnt out farms and starve? Mister, it was pretty powerful bait, I tell you. We went into the land office and the clerk just looked at us and asked, 'Saskatchewan?' We said yes, and he asked, 'Land?' Again, yes. Then I can remember his exact words and he said, 'It's not my job to tell you to turn around and go back home, please, because where your home is ain't no more, probably,' and he hauled out a big map and spread his hand over a considerable area and said, 'All taken up, long ago,' and then made a big circle with his hand and said, 'Open. Take your pick.'

Now I ask you, how the hell are you going to pick out a farm by pointing and saying 'there' but that's the way it seemed to be done. Then the clerk said, 'I'll give you a break, one of you. A fellow was in here yesterday and he's packing, leaving this country. You see those trucks heading back to the south? A lot of people are leaving, not from here,' and he showed the area where the land had been taken up a considerable time ago, but where he had offered it to us. 'One of you can have his place. He's got a house, a log house, and a barn and I expect you might find a few pieces of equipment around he didn't get rid of. One of you can have it. Means a bit of delay and red tape letting the homestead go back to the government and then you filing on it but it will give you a headstart. I'll pick out a number, one to 50, and the man who comes closest gets it,' and he wrote a number on a bit of paper. I guessed 35 and the number was 37 and so I won.

The clerk said, 'Okay, she's yours. Come back at one. I'm closing down now for lunch.' Miller asked why the man had left his homestead and the clerk said, 'Wasn't tough enough. Didn't have enough money. Didn't know how to farm this kind of country. Just lost heart. A few other reasons but that's enough.'

The upshot was the four of us went over to the beer parlour and got talking and when we walked out, this was the deal. It was early June and no way would the other three get in a crop, nothing more than potatoes and turnips. The place I'd got had 14 acres ready for seeding, so the four families would stay at my place, we'd all work like blazes, and during winter they'd use their time to start clearing and burning their land if they could get homesteads near mine, and it looked like they could. Everybody would also get a chance to see what the country was like in summer, fall and winter, and we had heard winters were a bastard. There were bound to be hassles, maybe the womenfolk fighting, or the men, but it was a workable plan.

So Miller and Rodway and McCormick filed and they got close by and we worked like dogs. Their families lived in tents, we all ate in our house and during the winter we all lived in two places, my house and a big log dormitory with a stove and a studying table for the 17 kids. Yep, 17. I'm going to make a long story short. We bought 10 weaners and four cows and that took most of our money. The rest went on four horses. We couldn't afford a seeder and couldn't borrow one, so we seeded by hand. Hell, you talk about Biblical times. This was 1935. We put in a big garden and I never saw vegetables grow like they did. Blackberries, chokecherries, saskatoons, wild plums. We got a good crop of barley and oats, but we had to spend five days building up the trail into our place, part over muskeg, so the thresher crew could get in, for half a day's work. We didn't sell the harvest because there was no price. Fed it to the livestock and bought chickens.

We damn near were eaten by mosquitoes, and that is without a word of a lie. Without a word of a lie. Plain torture.

Fall was lovely and there were plenty of deer and a moose any time we wanted to extend ourselves. We lived well, meat, porridge, milk, eggs, hootch that we made. We didn't do so bad. That was the plus side. There was no school, town was 17 miles away, but the worst was the winters. If you were ready for one, you still couldn't believe it could be so cold for so long. Half the time, Miller and Rodway and Mac just couldn't work on their places.

In the spring, both creeks flooded out the place. We just weren't tough enough, just the same as Gunderson, the guy who'd pulled out of my place, wasn't tough enough. It was a different kind of farming and if you can't sell your stuff, then is that really farming at all? I wonder. Just too many problems, and the government's offer of help didn't come through. Mac's little girl died of something, I don't know yet, and we couldn't get her to a doctor because there was a four-day blizzard blowing. I mean it, a four-day blizzard.

These are just the things I can remember, but there were so many more. One time we'd all moved about half a mile away to a little hill because of the flood and we were sitting around the fire, just the men and wives, and Rodway said, 'Hope the government is happy now. We're up here and out of their hair, not causing any trouble. Not that we ever did, but outa sight, outa mind.' He sure started off something, for within 10 minutes we'd all agreed to pull out and head back to the prairies, heat, rust, hoppers, shit, mud, blood, everything. And when I say 'all agreed' I mean it. It looks like each couple had been thinking the same thing for quite a while but each wouldn't say it, thinking the others would think they was letting them down, until Rodway came out with it. The upshot of it was that the kids lost a year of schooling, which didn't hurt them none, and the adults lost a year out of their lives – but what else was the Depression all about for folks like us, I ask you?"

———————————— • ————————————

He Never Missed A Month

"I'll tell you about my Dad. We had this little place, he called it a ranch, but it was just a little outfit near Lethbridge and there was a creek through it and we had a few cows and Mom kept chickens and what with that small cream cheque every week and such, we made out. Call it about 50 acres and you'd be pretty close.

I was – just a kid, about 12 when the Depression ended, so I really know nothing, just that we didn't have anything and we didn't expect anything and the Eaton's catalogue was for people in some other world. You know what I mean.

About three years ago, 1968, Dad died, quickly, of cancer. I don't want to talk about it, but they just opened him up and shut him up and told him there was nothing they could do. He was gone in three weeks.

Being the only child I had to clean up, help the lawyer, sign papers, arrange for the auction, and do what had to be done. There was this box of papers, the size of an apple box, his birth certificate from some town in Pennsylvania, army papers, all that, the deed to the ranch, but there were these slips. You'd call them receipt notices but they were on all kinds of papers, and a lot were from the Depression days.

You know what that old man had done? He had been paying off that land at $2 a month, $5, sometimes 10, sometimes the receipt would read that instead of money, Connor, the owner, had taken a steer as payment. The things made me just break down and cry. Every month, he never missed a month, Dad made some sort of payment. Just the interest sometimes; and a big deal for him was a bottle of whiskey at Christmas and sometimes a package of Picobac for his pipe.

He scraped and scraped and scraped and scraped some more and he kept us, mother, me, my cousin from Calgary who was an orphan, he kept us on that farm. In those days a man would hang onto his land as if it was life itself. I guess it was. Those old and faded receipts. Two dollars, four. His life's blood."

———————————— • ————————————

Both Free And Clear

"I worked on the railroad, braking, and being far down the ladder when the bad times came I was laid off. Not fired, just told I'd be called when things brightened up. Well, sir, they never. My wife and I had worked like coolies during the Twenties and bought one house which we rented and one which we lived in. Both free and clear. All ours. The little house rented for $18 a month. Actually we had to cut the rent down from $30 and then $25 and then $20 because otherwise it would have just sat empty. The taxes didn't go down, though. So here we were getting $18 times 12, total $216 in rent, and the taxes were about $195 and we had insurance to pay and in those days like today you still had to do maintenance, a new water pipe or something, and I sat down one night and figured out our taxes and expenses were about $230 a year. It was costing me good money to keep that house and the difference was coming out of my savings, which were just about gone. It was a damn good house, brick, sound as a dollar, and it had a garage – and I had a tough time getting $1,000 for it.

That's how things were in Edmonton those days. A sound $5,000 house going for a thousand, otherwise the city would take it back for nonpayment of taxes. If it happened once, it happened a thousand times in those years."

———————————— • ————————————

Let's Put Up Monuments

"I don't really remember much about the Depression. I was born in 1930 and by the time it was over I was still a youngster but I know something about it because I've heard my mother talk about it. I remember mostly my father.

We lived in Regina then and I can't even tell you what street because we left for here in 1940 or so, but apparently before 1929 a lot of people were buying new houses. The city still wasn't very big. My father was something in farm machinery, selling, and all that went for a shit when the farmers had no money and he took a real thick cut in salary, just to hang in there. The way mother tells it, they had bought our bungalow for $8,000, which was a pretty high price. I remember the house. Nice, and you couldn't get it for less than 25 or so now, and because times were good, and this was about 1927, the interest rate was high, but it looked like there was going to be good days forever. Anyway, they bought. And then boom! You know all about it. Boom! Boom, right to the bottom. My Dad had put his savings, and I think it was about $3,000, into this house and the mortgage was for $50 a month, I think mother said, and at seven and a half percent. Dad was only making about $100 a month, yes, $100, but even a hundred was considered okay in 1933 or so, especially when relief was about 40 or 50. At the very most. Well, anyway. At 50 a month, you're sure as hell not cutting into that principal, are you? And only 50 left. Fifty. My father was Scots, a guy who knew money and what it was all about. He pleaded with the landlord, the guy who held the mortgage, to cut the interest. It seems other interest rates were being cut, but this bastard, another Scotsman by the way, said no way, because, you see, he wanted that house, he wanted all the houses he could get by foreclosure, and I understand he got quite a few.

My mother tells it this way, that on pay night, the end of the month, my father would have worked himself into a frenzy. Pure hate for this man who held the mortgage and wouldn't give him a break. She said he'd be almost crazy and couldn't eat his dinner, wouldn't eat his dinner, yelled at my brother and me, and I can remember that. Then he'd put on his coat and walk the half mile to this man's house and pay him his stinking dollars and he knew he was paying most of it in interest and he still had to pay the taxes on top of that, and it used to kill him. One night when he was especially bad my mother phoned her brother Fred and he drove around and parked across the street and when, well as soon as the landlord opened the door, the old man started yelling at him, cursing him. Like he was crazy, and I guess he was. The landlord would take the money, shut the door in my father's face, and then come back and give him a receipt.

Those nights I can remember him taking off his coat and going into a room he'd built downstairs where he made jigsaw puzzles and made a few bucks a month selling the silly things and he'd have a bottle of booze, we'd call it a mickey now but I don't know what it was called then, and he'd drink it in an hour.

Well, that will bomb anybody. He'd sit down there and curse the banks and the landlords and everybody and, you see, he was a reasonable man and this was very upsetting to us kids because he was a good father. He was a very good father. And you can see the effect it had on my mother. Well, let me see, about nine o'clock or so, Dad would stumble up the stairs and go into their bedroom and I could hear, because our bedroom was next door, I could hear my mother going in and saying, 'Now, dear, there, there, everything will be all right. You'll see,' and she'd sit and hold his hand until he went out like a light. You know, some of the tough ones of those years, I guess, were the women. Next morning Dad would be okay, shaky but okay, and everything would be okay for another month.

(He breaks down and cries for a few seconds)

You've got to think of it in his terms. One hundred bucks a month or whatever it was. A wife, two kids, a house. That mortgage. Fifty off the top. Taxes. No vacation. Nothing for the kids. How they did it I'll never know. Let's put up monuments all over this country to our folks. Why, the wife and I blow $200 in a weekend in Montreal, without even trying, and we don't even enjoy ourselves. Just to keep our marriage from falling apart."

CHAPTER SEVEN

On Relief

One Family In Five ... Soggy Firewood ... I Sat By The Stove ... On Relief In A Shack ... In The City Relief Office ... Talk To The Old Timers ... Two Years Of Shame ... A Vocational School ... Cod Liver Oil Or Food ... Jamie's Got Relief Boots ... Your Liquor Permit, Please ... Our Only Claim To Fame ... No Shoes At All.

———————————— • ————————————

There came a time for hundreds of thousands when the mortgage had been sur-rendered, the insurance abandoned, savings gone, heirlooms sold for pennies, and they had no job, no money, very little food, only worn out clothing, and no hope.

Then they turned to relief, "the dole," "the pogey." This was a new concept in government help to the poor, an admission at last by the politicians that the poor were not to blame for the desperate plight they were in, and that they needed assistance.

Despite its faults, and skimpy as the payments were – in some provinces a couple with two children were expected to live on less than $10 food money a month – the system worked. Many still went hungry, but on relief you did not actually starve. Even its worst critics – often those fortunate enough not to have to go on relief – had to admit it helped hold everything together.

Necessary legislation it was, but the shame and bitterness can never be legis-lated out of the recipient's mind. If he had been a proud and hard-working wage earner only a year or two before, the most shameful moment of his life was walking into the relief office for the first time. I know that to this day men still remember that moment.

———————————— • ————————————

One Family In Five

"Sure, we got relief. It was a federal thing. But mind you, it takes a little explaining. Not like welfare today. Not on your life.

When Bennett brought it in, yes, '31, I was in the city hall in Lethbridge. Now it was a nice little city in those days. A farmers' town. Ranching. People came in and bought their supplies. Some coal miners around, but a quiet place.

I was helping with the paperwork. Not like today, you didn't get so much for the man and wife, and for each kid and so on until a family could get $500 a month. It was like this. If you qualified you as likely as not got $10 for food a month, or $10 in vouchers, and coupons or chits for necessary clothes, say in the fall, and oil, and the city or municipality would pick up your rent. Rent? Hah! Five bucks, ten a month got you a nice little house. If your wife's old lady and her brother jammed in with you, no matter. Right across the board, ten bucks.

Lethbridge in '32, and I'm sure, quite sure of that date, had about 20 percent unemployed. That doesn't mean what it does today. It meant 20 percent of the *men who had worked* were on the dole. Men on the bricks. It *didn't* mean wives who might have wanted to work, or had once worked because, you see, not many women worked. Waitressing, five and ten, a few banks, secretaries. That would do it. And it didn't mean young people who had come out of high school or school and couldn't get a job. There were no jobs for them, and they were not listed as employables. I can't remember what the hell they were. I guess they did not exist.

So here's my point. The do-gooders and fellows in Parliament look at the unemployment figures today and they say six percent and say, 'Fire the government.' Baloney. What would they have said 35 years ago at 20 percent in a small city with absolutely no prospect of things picking up.

Here's what I mean. That six percent today is six percent of people who are out of work, want to work, or have registered to work even if they don't want to work. Get it?

Put that back into 1933 and it means nothing. But then remember that the 20 percent of 1933 was only the men, the heads of families. It meant one father of a family in five had no work and so his wife and their five kids were on the relief too. Total all that up and it makes a terrible high total.

Another way. One family in five was out of work. Two families were not on relief but so deep in debt and so far into poverty that they would have taken relief if they could have. The fourth family was just getting by, and the fifth family, the merchants, the lawyers, all the professional men, the grain people and the retired people living in town, they were doing very well. Very well indeed.

Sometimes all these figures confuse me, but you know what I mean. Being on relief then wasn't like being on relief now."

---•---

Soggy Firewood

"I come from New Brunswick, Bathurst. There was no work, no mill, no nothing. Just people on the dole.

We had this house, and I think we rented it for $15 a month, and you should remember, times were not good even in the mid-Twenties and then about 1930, well, New Brunswick just wasn't a place to be. As I recall, we moved into another house and we paid $7 a month for that, in rent, and the money came from the county. We were on the pogey. Relief, you understand. It had huge rooms, oh, ceilings 18 feet tall, and we used only part of it. The kids in town called it The Big House. It had been owned by a lumber baron once, centuries ago.

Summer was fine and in autumn we got along even though the nights were chilly, but in winter when the county delivered the wood it was heavy, about 15 inches through and wet. Soggy. Dripping, you might say. Where they got it, God only knows. There was our family, a family of mother and father and five children living in the kitchen and one downstairs bedroom with county wood so wet that there was no way it was ever going to dry out. You understand, there was no way out of all this, because we had our winter's supply of wood strewn all over the back yard but there was no way to dry it out and so there we were, freezing, literally freezing to death beside a mountain of wood. Wouldn't you think it would drive a man mad? I think it drove my father mad."

---•---

I Sat By The Stove

"They may have built 10 new homes in Winnipeg in 1937. I don't know, but I bid on a contract to dig the basement of a house for a doctor in Riverview. A big house. There must have been 20 or 25 other fellows with teams bidding, but I got it.

In those days we used a Fresno scoop, you hitched it to a team and manhandled it from the rear and it was the most brutal work a man can do. There's a knack to it, just like there's an easy way to do everything, but a man still was so bushed he didn't know his left foot from his right at the end of a day. I hired a good man, a shovel man, and he did the wall scraping and the corners and I paid a kid $2 a week to sleep with the team, two damn good horses, feed them, curry them, and have them harnessed when we got there. The contractor was at me all the time. Anyway, after I'd paid the man $2 a day and the boy and the team's feed, on that contract I figured I made 13 cents an hour for myself. Of course, we ran into hard clay and that made the job longer, but it also just about finished me and finished the team, two big fellows who could pull with any in the country. I never bid on another job. Just sold the team and equipment for $40 and went on the relief. Just sat by the kitchen stove all day with my feet up, for years."

———————————— • ————————————

On Relief In A Shack

"We lived in a shack in the bush, dirt floor and a lot of the stucco had fallen off. We must have been the sorriest lot in the district and yet my grandfather, James Macdonald, was one of the first settlers around and owned plenty of land. But his son, my father, was just a no-good bum. He knew it and so did everyone else. My mother wasn't that much better, but she had just lost hope.

Grandfather was still living down the road and he wouldn't do anything. Not even for his grandchildren. Us, and my brothers. It wasn't all the Depression that made some people the way they were. Some were just no good from the start, and my father was one.

Jesus Christ, what an upbringing. The old man would get his relief, and don't ask me how much it was. Twelve, fifteen dollars. He'd come back from town with a sack of flour, some potatoes, a few pounds of baloney and that was it. He'd buy a couple of big bottles of orange Kik for us kids and a pound of peanut brittle. That was what he considered providing for his family. Then he'd roar off in that old car of his, riding around the country, drinking bootleg whiskey with every dumb Polack and Hunyak for miles around until his money was gone.

It may have broken his Dad's heart but he was a stubborn old Scot and there is nothing more stubborn. He would do nothing."

In The City Relief Office

"My own personal opinion, you must remember, but I'd say that Canadians today aren't a patch on Canadians of those Depression years. I worked in the city relief office in Edmonton for a time and I must say that was unusual because those jobs were taken by men, and how often when I was at the desk I would overhear remarks like, 'If that woman was back in the kitchen then maybe there'd be more jobs for us,' but I wasn't back in the kitchen, I was doing a good job on the relief. Today, it is welfare-this and social assistance-that and where will it all end? It's nothing but gimme, gimme, grab, grab, my share, my share and part of his too. Look around you and think about it.

In the Thirties Canadians had their pride. My God, how they had their pride! Relief was a disgrace. Men would say that never in the history of their family – and they'd usually mention something about the British Empire Loyalists, or coming West with the first C.P.R. trains – never had they had to go on relief. These were men whose families back at the house were without food. I'm not sure many people actually starved to death but there was a great deal of hunger, just not enough food, not enough vitamins and proteins and calories, and you had malnutrition. You can see it in that generation of Depression babies today, the effects are there in some.

These men, a few told me they had to walk around the block eight or a dozen times before they had the nerve to come in and apply for relief, 'the dole' as the people from the Old Country called it. I've seen tears in men's eyes, as though they were signing away their manhood, their right to be a husband and sit at the head of the table and carve the roast. It was a very emotional time, that first time when a man came in and went up to the counter.

You know, I never really could figure out how they arrived at the relief figures they did. You see I was just at the counter and got them to fill out the forms with all the information and then one of the men at the back, the regular workers, I was just part-time, would decide how much. Of course, there usually was a further investigation, a visit to the house, talk with the man again, the wife, maybe the children's teacher, but not too often. Just a visit to the house. But why would an able-bodied single young man of say, oh, 25, get $10 a month relief for himself, and a 40-year-old man with a wife and four children get only $10 or $12.50? That always puzzled me. It seemed so unfair, the young man could somehow get by on $10 but the family of the older man would be in for a very rough time. I suppose it might be the same today.

Another thing, people had too many babies in those days. It would be nothing for a scrawny little man to come in who had been nothing but a carpenter's helper or a labourer or a sweep-up man in a bakery and he'd put down nine or eleven or seven children and when the investigator went to check, sure enough, they'd find a horrible little shack at that address and a worn-out woman and seven or nine children. People didn't have too much sense in these matters in those days.

But I was talking about pride. The system worked against people with pride because some of the hand-outs, and there I go using that word "hand-out," which I hate, but coal, wood, some food, some things like that, boots, shoes, clothing, they were in the form of vouchers. You went to a coal yard or a grocery store or a clothing store and the clerk would know you were on relief, and the owner would find out, and soon it would be all over the neighbourhood. This kind of thing, I'm sure, stopped some people from coming in. Pride, just stupid pride, pride all the way to the grave.

I knew lots of people who were on relief, a couple of my uncles, and I do not know one, not one, not one single one who was on relief, or should I say out of a job, because of their own laziness, stupidity or whatever. This was the way it was all over Canada. Of course, the strong survived. I mean, if there were four workers in a warehouse and two had to go because there was no business it would be likely that the two oldest and weakest, the least productive, would be let out. Temporarily, of course. That's what they always said, 'We'll hire you back when times get better.' Now you know and I know that this system is cruel, but the law of business is the law of the jungle and it always had been, until the unions came along. But I never knew one who was fired because of something other than economic conditions. This was happening all over Canada.

So you see, a man had worked for a firm for 20 years and then he was let go and where was his pride? Oh, I know, the present generation won't understand what I'm talking about, but the old timers will. There he was facing the wife of those 20 years, and telling the children that Daddy would be home for a while, and knocking on dozens of doors and no work, and standing in line-ups for one day's work as labourer, you know, the whole thing, and then the going to the counter in that awful yellow and green welfare office, well, the whole thing.

It left its mark on many a good man today, let me tell you. Ask anyone who went through it. The wounds of war leave scars, but the wounds of humiliation and lost pride leave their scars here, up here in the mind. Oh, I could have wept for some of those people, those Canadians with all that pride in them. And the worst part of it all was this, the worst part of it all was that *they didn't know what was happening to them.* They just did not understand it at all. Some still don't. I'm not sure I do."

———————————— • ————————————

Talk To The Old Timers

"The real story of the Depression, and I mean the saddest of it all, that story's dead. The people are in the graveyard. The old age pensioners. The old timers who got the pension. There is a terrible time and it sure ain't in no history books, you bet. I know why.

My parents. Why, there were thousands like them. The old man came over from Scotland, it was always called the Old Country. That man worked his ass off until he could work no more and then the mine owners had no use for him. They had the deputy tell him to clear out. That was in the coal mines of Nova Scotia.

There was this government old age pension and the government made a lot of fine music about it but really it only kept a person alive a little longer. In the long run you still starved. At 70. Seventy years of age and when you went underground at 13, I can tell you there is damn little left of a man by 70. Maybe sharp blue eyes, but the body has gone.

There was the Means Test. A diabolical thing. They took a list of what you had and if you had an old car they could make you sell it. Never mind if it was 15 miles to town, old people didn't need transportation. If you had a piano they could tell you to sell it or sell it for you, because why should an old couple like my Mom and Dad have a piano to sing a few hymns before going to bed at night? That's what they did. Godly people. If you had two pairs of Stanfield underwear, well, maybe they could even make you sell one set. The worst set. Hah!

When you applied for the old age you delivered yourself into slavery. On paper you became destitute. The government, I guess, could take away even your chamber pot. Yet they took it. Who was worse, the prime minister or the mine boss? My parents were simple people and they thought the owners, the government always did best for people. I say bullshit. Here are people who have worn themselves out, squeezed dry for Canada and what do they get? A handful of sand in their eyes. Die, old people, you are no use to us any more.

I was in British Columbia when my Dad in Nova Scotia applied to go on the pension. He'd worked in the mines and above ground all his life and the mines were shutting down and there was no pension. Dad had paid in, of course, but all those profits of better years had gone into dividends! Nothing set aside. Oh yes, times were never all that good in Cape Breton and most people lived in poverty even before the Depression, and that is something a lot of people don't know. But the big companies made profits and bugger all went towards the workers because it went into dividends. Damn little for mine safety. They'd just laugh at the government. Nothing for ventilation or decent change rooms or, let us not forget this, decent wages. The company report proudly announced every year that the dividend had been maintained. Damn the dividends. My father was the dividend that should have been maintained. Anyhow they applied, my father and my mother, and my father was given the pension, the old age pension and it was $14.40 a month. This was about 1936. My mother, I think, got a little less – say $11. So about $25 for two old people for a month. Work that out just on food in those days and two old people could get by, just get by. They'd die slowly. But they had taxes, and by God you paid your taxes or you were out. Too many friends of government were just waiting to pounce on those wee homes and buy them up for 70 bucks or so. They paid light, and they had to buy firewood, and the old man liked a smoke after dinner. Not a cigar, a cigarette. Just a cigarette. If the relief people had caught him smoking they could have cut his pension. Yes, yes, they could have, because they've done it to others. And yet that $14 wasn't too bad when you consider Prince Edward Island paid only $10. Ten lousy, stinking dollars.

Finally a neighbour wrote me in B.C. where I was working and I was doing not too bad. I had an old car, and I drove back to Cape Breton and I told them I was going to sell the house and move them out to Powell River where I was. And by this time they were so beaten that they didn't say much, just 'Okay son, do what you think the best,' and I got practically nothing for the place but it was enough to get the three of us back out to the coast, and they never spoke much about the people they'd left behind, their life-long friends, because they realized they were spent, finished, all washed up, and only their son gave a damn what happened to them.

My Dad liked the mountains and my mother had been born beside the sea in Scotland so she liked the place too, and I think they were fairly happy until they died. Within a week of each other. Dad first and then Mom. I was glad to see them go. They'll be a hell of a lot better treated where they went than where they came from.

If you think of $25 or so for a month, why I can spend twice that on booze for a few friends in for a party, some poker and some talk and food and think nothing of it.

You ought to find somebody who was a old age pensioner in them days. Course you can't. They're all dead."

———————————— • ————————————

Two Years Of Shame

"My father had been killed cutting pulp wood. He sliced his leg open with an axe and bled to death. There was my mother, and my sister Eva who was 16, and my brother Dick who was about 13, and I was 11 when this happened that I'm going to tell you about.

The relief people had found us a big room in a house on Higgins *(in Winnipeg)* and we all lived in there. We had a good stove and the toilet was just down the hall and I used to spend a lot of time in the big library just down the street and the place was kept warm. Mom was like Ma Joad in *The Grapes of Wrath*, things would get better. She was pretty and had a good figure and laughed a lot.

When you got relief they were supposed to come around and check you. I've heard some were real mean people, like they'd look for a man's hat in the closet or sniff for the smell of pipe tobacco. You weren't supposed to have any other support. We were in what was called a relief house, everybody was destitute, and the examiner or inspector, whatever he was called, usually came about every six months.

Not with Mom. This man came every month, and sometimes every three weeks or so. He was short and had a belly and, Oh God, he was enough to put a woman off men for life. He smelled. His feet. It got so he was there a lot, when we'd come home from school, or when Eva came back from looking for a job.

One day, I was in alone and Mom said, 'Joan, you take your books back to the library. It's children's day, and stay for about half an hour.' I did, and this happened more and more – go to the store and get some bread, go out and find Dick, do this, do that.

In spring and summer we lived on the streets, us kids, and I knew what was going on, and so did Dick and Eva but this man was giving my mother bits of money, and when I needed a winter coat and goloshes he signed the chit without a word, and we got other things too. A special allowance for milk, I think, and more clothes, and this man arranged so Dick could go to a Fresh Air camp at the lake.

Once in bed – I slept with Eva – she whispered that she wondered why the man didn't try for her because she was a woman now and would like to give Mom a rest. She said she'd hate it, but she'd do it to help out Mom. We thought of writing a letter to the relief people telling them what this man was doing, which was illegal in the first instance, and immoral in the second, but we figured that if what he was doing was illegal, then what we were doing, taking his stuff, was illegal too. Mom finally did it, though; she asked the relief people to move her because she said the neighbourhood was too tough and men in the street were pestering her daughter, Eva, not me. So they moved us out of this creep's territory. He came around once, after we'd moved down on McMillan Avenue, but he never even got his foot in the door.

I look back on those two years with shame, but maybe he was the only one like that. A mean little man in that kind of a job in the Depression had a lot of power."

———————————— • ————————————

A Vocational School

"When the times got bad it wasn't just a case of the working men sitting back and folding their hands and waiting for something.

It was in 1934, I remember, and things were as bad in Nova Scotia as anywhere in the world, maybe, and we had a lot of good lads around, lads who had left school and had never found a job and I think they were not even listed as unemployed. They were just there, around the street corners.

Some of us, we set up a work bench in one of the big rooms in the labour hall in Amherst and we brought down some of our tools and material, wood and pipes and things we could find, and it was our intention to teach these lads to be useful. To learn a trade, to be able to go up to Upper Canada and maybe find an honest day's work.

It just didn't work out. The lads came, oh yes, come they did, but learning carpentering and such, there wasn't much point in it, was there, when Nova Scotia lads who was carpenters in Toronto was coming back home and us, who set up the school, was teaching and lecturing these lads because we had no work either.

In a few weeks anyone could see the silliness of it all, and the union didn't seem interested or the government, and the lads just stopped coming, and that made us despairing, and so the thing just quit.

The same thing is called a vocational school now, with million dollar buildings and better equipment than most tradesmen ever see, and all that money coming in from the government to train lads as carpenters who would rather ride around on motorcycles and get girls in trouble."

Cod Liver Oil Or Food

"The city paid the rent, which was $12 a month, and delivered a ton of that Souris coal, which was nothing more than solidified mud, and gave me $10 a month and that was for myself and two children, Reggie, nine and Marion who was seven. I had no husband because he'd been buried to death in a gravel pit.

One winter I didn't have the shoes or clothes for the children to go to school, even though it was just a couple of streets over and the school, or maybe it was the city, sent a nurse around. Why weren't the children going to school when they were registered? I told her and she made a note in her book. She looked at Reggie and then Marion and she said, 'Mrs. Thompson, these children are undernourished, they're suffering from malnutrition. Look at their complexions.' Then she said we'd need better food and a big dose of cod liver oil once a day. I said the $10 relief only lasted about half the month so how could we afford the big bottle of cod liver oil, which was expensive? Would the city provide it? The nurse said no, there were no funds available, blah, blah, blah, blah, and so I asked what was best, to buy a bottle of cod liver oil which might last a month but would use up about three or four days of our food, or what? The nurse said the children had to have the cod liver oil but they certainly should never be deprived of any food. I was a beaten woman by this time, four years of this kind of nonsense, but I pushed the woman out the front door, yelling. 'Get out of my house, you tiresome bitch.'

The woman probably filed a report against us, but the clothes and shoes did come, so it showed someone was thinking in the right direction."

•

Jamie's Got Relief Boots

"I don't remember the Depression much. I'm 45 now, and all I can remember was the growing up time. You see, I wasn't like my Dad, who could compare the Depression with any other time, a better time.

But yes, I do remember one thing. We were on relief and I wanted a pair of boots because I was still wearing those canvas and rubber things and it was well into October. My father one day took me out of school and we went down to the relief yard, and I believe it was somewhere up where the Royal Alexander Hotel was, and there was no arguing or anything because the clerk looked at my feet. Running shoes, that's what they called them. He looked and then wrote out a chit. I forget the amount but my father looked at it and said we'd have to go down to Notre Dame. For your information, that was where the cheapest clothing and shoe stores and second hand stores were. We went into a shop and the old Jew was kind enough, I remember that, but the only boots he could offer were what I'd call clodhoppers. The kind L'il Abner wears.

They were red. Ever seen red boots before? I never did before and I never did since. And the stitching was white and showed up. I hated them but I had no choice. Nine years old, what choice does a nine-year-old have? We got home and I put on the boots and God, I remember they were stiff. The kids were playing road hockey out in front and my mother said, 'Jamie, go out now and play. You've got to go out and face them sometime.'

I went out and began to bat around with them and one kid spotted those L'il Abners and yelled, 'Relief boots. Jamie's got relief boots,' and everybody laughed. A couple of others made smart remarks, and the first time we were scrimmaging with the ball I gave the first guy a swift kick in the shins. The two other guys got it shortly after, and there were three guys sitting on the curb holding their ankles and shins and crying. No one laughed at my boots again."

Your Liquor Permit, Please

"In those days the government in Saskatchewan, like it does now, sold all the liquor. They had the stores and there was the permit system. I wasn't a drinker but I always had a bottle around the house for guests. Let's see, a 40-ounce bottle of government rye was about $2.40. Something like that. Hard to believe now.

In '36 I finally went belly-up. I had 16 horses and in the fall of '35 I turned them in to a community pasture and maybe rustlers had been at it, although who the hell would have wanted them skeletons, but comes spring and I've got to get to work, I can only find three. The rest could have been blown into Manitoba. No horses, no chance to prepare the land, the neighbours couldn't help and so I couldn't get the free government seed. By this time I was so off farming that I was ready to give the place away for a train ticket for my family to the Fraser Valley.

I went into our little town, and I said to myself, 'Fred Davis, you've tried, and you've lost, and now it's up to the government.' I figured some of that tax money I'd paid all those good years should start working towards my old age. I got through the relief office okay and I think for me and the wife and the two kids still at home I got $19 a month, close to that, and we could live on that. It would be tight, but the wife was pretty canny.

Then the relief clerk, hell, a guy I curled with every winter, he said, 'Fred, I'll have to ask you for your liquor permit.' I asked what for. 'Nobody on relief can have a permit. I don't make the rules, Fred, that's just one that is there.' So I hauled it out, not mad but kind of disgusted because I wasn't a kindergarten kid and in no way was I a drinking man. It was just the idea of the thing. But that wasn't the worst.

This guy said, 'There's another thing. I'm not sure this is a regulation but the district office says we got to tell you. You or anybody. Beer. If you're seen in the beer parlour and somebody squawks, then your relief can be cut off, just like that,' and he snapped the desk with his pencil. I felt sick. Applying for the dole was bad enough but being treated almost like a criminal was bad, very bad.

The clerk, he said, 'I know, Fred, lousy, and when I walk into that beer parlour I am as blind as a bat. But some ain't. There are people in this town who would just like to squeal on you or the next guy. Just a meanful nature, hoping they might make it hard on you. Three families already have been cut off, and one guy was drinking hell and gone over towards Regina when he was spotted.'

You see, that was nearly 40 years ago and I can remember every word that clerk said, and there was not a damn thing I could do about it. They, the government, had you where they wanted you. I can remember it so well, I can remember the colour of his pencil. Yellow. There was a calendar on the wall, a lumber yard, and the picture showed a guy fishing in a stream in the mountains, and I remember every word that man said. Not his fault, but I remember."

———————————•———————————

Our Only Claim To Fame

"We lived down near Medicine Hat. My mother told me this. I was too little to remember. My grandparents still had three kids at home, on the farm, and Dad got $10 a month relief. What with what they had and food parcels from his brother on the coast and by hooking and scrounging here and there, $10 cash money got them by. Just by, and no more. Rolled oats and potatoes.

So they figured that if their oldest boy, who was my Dad, moved back home, he was getting $10 a month relief too, then they'd have $20 a month and if they were going to starve, they would all starve together. By their figuring, with the few cows they had left and two extra hands, my Dad and Mom, they might make something out of that place. Fine, except that the relief people heard about us moving in. Mom said there were a lot of snitchers those days. People would inform on their neighbours, hoping there would be something in it for them. What, I don't know. So they said to my Dad, they said; "You're moving in with your father and he has relief money and a few horses and a few cows, so there is no reason for you to have all that money." All that money! Ten dollars.

They cut him down to $2.50 a month, and that was for Dad and Mom and me, and so the whole damned family was worse off than ever before, and all because they were trying to improve their situation. It must have been a crazy way of life then. A relief official later told my Dad he had never heard of a family getting so little money, no matter what the circumstances were. I guess that was our only claim to fame in the whole thing."

No Shoes At All

"I grew up on a stump farm about 12 miles from Carrot River. In Saskatchewan. I remember not going to school my fifth grade, about 12 years old, because I didn't have shoes. My sister Helen went, though, because she could use the ones I grew out of. My mother was a widow and she asked the relief people for $2 for shoes for me but they said no, there were folks who needed things worse than me. I got around, doing chores and that, by making sort of moccasins out of deer skin, rubber from an inner tube and binder twine and staples but my mother wouldn't let me go to school that way. Foolish pride. I missed that year and I never went back. I missed a lot by her pride. I would have gone in them moccasins."

CHAPTER EIGHT

Starvation? Depends On What You Had Before

She Said They Were Starving . . . We Starved . . . There We Were – Stony Broke
. . . Bundles Of Rags . . . Good Old Ketchup Soup . . . The Best-Looking Livestock
. . . Gopher Pie? Sure . . . Alfalfa Makes For Healthy Kids . . . What Is Starvation?
. . . Ever Eaten Wolf? . . . 10,000 Calories . . . Bags of Bread Crusts . . . What Makes
A Man Like That? . . . Just The Usual Thing . . . They Ate Their Seed Grain . . . A
Violation Of God's Will . . . Potatoes For Christmas . . . Cod Liver Oil . . . A
Round Orange . . . They Were My Sister's Kids.

———————————— • ————————————

*People have told me that they starved during the Depression, but starvation is a
relative word. Unless you were rich there is no doubt that you ate less, and were
a little hungrier. But you did not starve, although you called it that. At worst,
you suffered from slight malnutrition.*

*I have been told that men died in the hobo jungles on the prairies and
beneath the bridges of Vancouver, victims of starvation. My informants were
obviously sincere, but I would guess that death was probably due to rotgut wine,
exposure causing pneumonia, and a lack of food – a deadly combination. Judge
for yourself. Certainly there was terrible hunger in Canada during the
Depression, as these stories make clear.*

———————————— • ————————————

She Said They Were Starving

"I had this small truck farm way up out Yonge Street, a few good acres and
I sold from a cart with a horse. I was working in my gardens one morning,
it was spring and things were starting up again, and Mrs. Schreiber came
over, with her three little kids, and she said, "Mr. Wozny, my children and I
haven't had a thing to eat for two days. We are starving. Can we have something to eat?"

This was about 1934, around there, and this was Canada and my neighbour, a widow lady and three children, she said they were starving.

I got them into my house and I fed them, just taking cans and jars and things out of boxes and making a meal, a big meal, and they sat and ate an awful lot of it. We didn't talk but I was thinking that she was a nice lady, a widow, and her kids were behaved and I was alone, didn't have no woman, and maybe she should marry me. Maybe I should ask her. I was doing okay.

Then she got up and said thank you, and the kids all said thank you and they went home and I thought, I'll wait until tonight and take a bunch of stuff over, eggs and bacon and peaches, and I'll sort of work my way around to find out at least what she might think of her marrying me. So I took all this stuff over and there was nobody home. The door was open so I put the stuff in the kitchen. When I was walking home I met my other neighbour and I asked if he had seen Mrs. Schreiber and he said he'd seen her and her three kids about noon walking down Yonge Street towards Toronto, and he said the widow and the oldest kid, about eight, each had a suitcase.

I never saw them or heard of them again. They just vanished into the city."

———————————— • ————————————

We Starved

"We starved. Yes, I would call it starving. We lived in Dundurn and that was starvation country and we were told there was good land north of the Carrot River. There were half breeds back in there but it wasn't for a white man. Not a city man, anyway. We went up there. We called it The North. It really was.

We had potatoes and saskatoon berries and chokecherries and if Dad got a moose, then we were okay. I remember two years in a row he didn't shoot a moose. Then we starved. Some days in winter mother wouldn't let us get out of bed, the three of us. She said it was too cold and we'd lose our strength. Everybody forgot us, it seemed, and when the government came and took us out after a big flood it was like being rescued from a prison. We were in a prison, starving in a prison those years.

This was how the government thought they were helping the burned-out farmers."

———————————— • ————————————

There We Were – Stony Broke

"My father was a designer of jewellery and in Toronto in the Twenties we did fine. Our own house, we ate well, we belonged to a skating club. By 1932 we weren't doing so well at all; there were still plenty of his clients around and prosperous but they were thinking of other things. A lot were buying houses, land, dirt cheap and not thinking of bracelets and such.

Dad lost the business, of course. That came about early in '31. Then the house went because we couldn't hit that mortgage payment every month. Then his savings. Broke. He wouldn't take relief. There we were, the four of us in two rooms on Danforth. Stony broke.

He couldn't get a job anywhere. The truth is, he couldn't do anything. He once said he thought he had a job sewn up. When he reported for work in this freight shed, the foreman shook his hand, then the foreman looked at his soft white hand and said no, no job. He said Dad had never done any hard work and he could get 50 men who had. Fifty men with calloused hands.

So Dad got a "Liberty Magazine" route. You've got to picture it. A man of 50, tall and slim, white-haired. From an old and proud Austrian family and peddling door-to-door that trash called "Liberty Magazine." Five cents and he got a cent commission. Then he got "Saturday Evening Post" and "Silver Screen" or "Photoplay," some of those movie magazines, and soon he was selling about 400 a week. He must have been a super-salesman or his looks must have wowed those housewives. The $4 or $5 he brought in every week kept us from starving. You see, we had been starving before. Yes, starving.

We paid for the rent by looking after this ratty apartment block, sweeping halls, washing windows, all that, and I made $2 a week on Saturday as helper on a "Toronto Star" delivery truck. My sister baby-sat. Ten cents an hour. Thirty-five cents until midnight.

With $5 a week coming in and rent free and baby-sister making 50 cents a week, we were on Easy Street. It doesn't sound like much, but my mother made it go and we weren't starving any more.

Starving? Yes, before that we were starving. We actually went two or three days together with nothing but a slice of bread and molasses or lard and we drank water. Lots of water. And if that is not starving, then let me know what is, because I'd like to hear."

———————————— • ————————————

Bundles Of Rags

"Anybody who says people wasn't going hungry, why he was a little wacky. I was a plumber, and that's not the same as being a plumber today. Oh boy, no. You got two hours one day and none the next and one the next, week after week, month after month, and it was best if you had 11 brothers and sisters all married in town and living in houses with bad pipes. Otherwise it was dog eat dog.

I said to hell with it and went up north. There was no hunger there, not in Dawson City. You got $2 a day in Vancouver and paid your own transportation and up in the Yukon it was about the same, but all the difference. People was happy, they helped each other out. There was no starving there, but if I come down to Vancouver for December and January I saw lots of starving. I seen bodies in doorways down on the waterfront, Cordova, Skid Row, east of Main. At the hospital they'd have a fancy name for it, you know, malnutrition, but a dead body was still a dead body. In doorways early in the morning, especially if it was a cold night. Bundles of rags. Yes, I seen that."

———————————— • ————————————

Good Old Ketchup Soup

"One of the guys got to know the night cashier at this cafeteria over by Yonge Street. She was the boss because the company were too cheap to put on a night manager and as I remember she handled things pretty well. The guy who knew her was one of our gang and he was laying her. Anyway, she let us get away with a lot. There was no work around, this was about 1934, and believe me you couldn't even get a job shovelling snow. People were starving and we couldn't get relief.

'Go to Montreal, there is work there,' the guy at the job office would say. Bullshit. Those Frenchies were starving worse than anybody. 'Go to St. Catharines,' we were told. We did, walking most of the way, and got run out of town. 'Go to Vancouver.' When we heard that, we laughed in their faces. Vancouver was the last place to go. To hear it told, everybody was starving there, or fighting.

Anyway, this night cashier wouldn't let us steal nothing. No pie, nothing, because she had to account for everything. She was a tough little gal, from Cape Breton and they know what a paying job is down there, and she had the staff in line, nobody would rat on her, but she wasn't doing us any favours which could get her nailed down.

Ever heard of ketchup soup? Or catsup stew? Okay, we'd go into the place and Lily would say, 'Hi, fellows.' We'd buy a glass of milk. Five cents. Scoop up a big handful of those oyster biscuits, like little pillows, of cracker material, and they were best in oyster stew. They floated around. Then we'd go to the boiling water urn and take a soup bowl and fill it up. Still with me? There was a sort of cabinet where they kept all the sauces and stuff, and I'd grab up a bottle of ketchup and go to a booth. Then I'd dump about half a bottle of ketchup, or as much as I figured I could get away with, and the other guy would do the same. You got to remember that Lily had to account for those condiments too, and if those lousy owners, probably Jews, saw too much ketchup disappearing, they'd begin to wonder and it would be Lily's ass that would be in a sling. Now you stir up the ketchup into a soup and then you unload your oyster crackers and you crumple them up, like so, in your hand and you pour it all into the ketchup and water and stir it around and put salt and pepper into it and you've got, mister, right there you've got something that tasted pretty damn good in those days. Top it off with a glass of milk and you were good for the evening.

That was pretty much our diet some days and I never saw anybody die from it. Of course, you couldn't go out and shovel snow on it, either."

————————————— • —————————————

The Best-Looking Livestock
"I heard of farm families eating gophers, but I don't believe it. But if you were to eat a barn rat in a stew, unwittingly, now that could be another matter altogether. Those rats were plump and grain-fed around the barn and were just about the best-looking livestock I had around the place in those days."

————————————— • —————————————

Gopher Pie? Sure.
"Now what was wrong with eating gophers? Cows we eat. They eat grass, grain, Russian thistle. What's the difference between a gopher and a red squirrel? I ask you. Sure, gopher pie. You'd send the kids out and they'd come home with 20/30 or so and you'd skin and clean them just like squirrels. Squirrels are a delicacy, ain't they? Paris sort of delicacy. You got a casserole dish and you lined it and then you laid down about eight strips of gopher because you got two strips of sides and bellymeat off of one of them. Then you laid a thin layer of sliced potatoes and some onions and then gopher and then a layer of potatoes and so on, and when you were ready you folded the dough over the

top and put it in the oven. Some people put in sliced dried apples, although I did not always.

It was quite good, that gopher pie, but I always thought it best if you told any visitors you were eating squirrel pie. You could make stews too, out of gophers.

There was nothing wrong with the meat, it was just the thought of it. But what is wrong with a gopher? Just the thought, that's it. Crab meat? Well, crabs live off other dead life under the water and a man once told me that when they brought up a body in Vancouver harbour once it had about 15 big crabs on it, them just gobbling and greedy-gut away on it. I'll take gopher, thank you kindly."

———————————— • ————————————

Alfalfa Makes For Healthy Kids

"I'd done some post-grad work in grains at the University of Iowa. Ames, Iowa. I knew the nutritional value of grains. Wheat, mainly. I won't go into it but this natural food faddism is nothing new. Not at all.

In '36 I came back to Saskatchewan and things were still pretty bad, but I went on a sort of campaign trail, a prophet for grains. Any mother I'd meet I'd tell her to get some good grain, seed wheat if she could, and wash it for dust and feed it to the kids. Make porridge. Grind and put in soup. Gruel. Feed it to them until it was coming out their ears.

Kids chewed grain in those days, chewed it until it was kind of a gum. That was their gum in those days. I haven't seen a youngster chewing wheat for years.

I also told people to cut grass like alfalfa early in the morning, put it in the hot sun and let it dry slightly, and then cut it up fine and use it in soups, stew. Load up the stew with it. I'd tell them there is no finer food. Just loaded with goodies. I had to talk in that language. Loaded with nutrition. Vitamins were coming in, they were the big thing in those days but as usual, the advertising and the huge food companies generally had it all haywire. Alfalfa. About 27 percent protein, you know. Makes for healthy kids.

Anyway, in our neighbourhood I was the wheat man. Considered somewhat of a nut. A nut 25 years before his time."

What Is Starvation?

"If starvation is what they do in India, then I never starved. If being hungry is not having a scrap of food for more than two days, then I was hungry lots of times."

———————————— • ————————————

Ever Eaten Wolf?

"Along about 1935 I was hauling wild hay from a big marsh that was about seven miles south of us. The hay wasn't really good stuff at all but it was something. I worked on it and got it in stacks in summer and I hauled it back with a rick in February or so. I was trying to keep some cows alive, and my work horses.

One day about two miles from home, coming back, I saw this wolf just loping along, and it was the first wolf I'd seen in that country in years. About a week later coming back, there he was again. That got me thinking. That fellow must be running on some sort of a schedule, as though he had this territory staked out. It was something to ponder and the next week, the same day the next week as the two other weeks, I took along the rifle on the seat with me and I'll be goddamned if just about three o'clock, not 200 yards from where I'd seen him last, there he was coming along the fence line.

I stopped the team and let one go and it went under his belly. I could see the snow kick up, and the next one hit him square and he flipped over and when I got to him, by God, he was a big son of a bitch. I skinned him out there and threw the carcass and skin up on the load and never said nothing about it. Next Saturday I went into town and sold the skin to the livery store man, Old Man Charles, for $5, and when the wife and kids was at church next day I started a stew of that fellow. Kind of surprised my wife, but I said I'd shot a few rabbits, they was thick that year, and with lots of vegs and flour and such, it came out that way pretty good. Nobody knew, not until this day, that the Rainford family once ate wolf.

You know, I didn't have to shoot that fellow. You just did. Nowhere in the Bible does it say you can't eat the flesh of the field, and that means wolf. Course, that fellow wasn't doing anybody any harm, but the prairies was a tough place to live in those days."

10,000 Calories

"My father called me in from outside, kick the can or one of those games we used to play, and there was a man with him and he said, 'Sam, this is your cousin Bert. He's taking you with him back to his farm at Salmon Arm and you'll live with him. I don't have to tell you why, do I?' I said no, I knew there was hard times getting worse and the old man had been laid off, he worked for the city, and Vancouver was getting rough for people without work.

So I packed up and left with this cousin Bert and he had this old truck, but we got there. Some farm. Mostly stumps, but he had a few Jerseys and hens, but his wife and him were almost as broke as we were. Maybe more, but they had the cows and didn't pay no rent, you see.

There was food, but I wasn't getting it. They was selling all the eggs and cream and feeding the skim to the pigs.It didn't matter that they didn't feed me. I fed myself. Scrounged, I did. I'd suck about five or six eggs a day, and they got their cream by putting out the milk in these big flat pans in a little shed and I'd sneak in there and I'd put my lips down to the cream and just suck up that rich cream, slick as a whistle. I always left enough so they never got suspicious, but I could sure suck up cream in a hurry. I ate a lot of hazel nuts and raw potatoes and sweet corn, juicy, right off the stalk.

When I was 14 I had shot up to about six feet and weighed all of 200 pounds and that was a very big lad in those days. Hell, it still is. If I had known what girls was all about I'd have had a Roman holiday.

No, those people were sure stingy but I outfoxed them. A smart city kid. Eggs and cream and hazel nuts and ham and spuds and everything else I could filch. Once I ate two pounds of granulated honey just because I had it. I guess any doctor would say maybe 10,000 calories a day is a pretty bad diet, but I seemed to thrive on it."

———————————————— • ————————————————

Bags Of Bread Crusts

"I went to work when I was 14, but I looked 16, 18. Big bust, big hips. A cafe in the 700-block Robson *(in Vancouver)*. I made $4 a week and worked a 12-hour day. Tips? I never saw a tip. Tips, you've got to be kidding. This was 1934.

We never served a customer a sandwich with crusts in those days. We cut off the crusts. The sandwiches cost five cents, 10 cents, and you were very well fed on a 20-cent sandwich. Open-faced. Roast beef with lots of good gravy.

So we had all these crusts from the bread, and the word got around that

Alice, that's me, was putting them in brown bags and giving them out at the door on the lane. I am not telling you any lie when I say I have seen as many as 100 men lined up there about seven o'clock, closing time, waiting for crusts. These were starving men, and I am telling the truth when I say I've seen men pass out, yes, just fall over. I did what I could, but it was first come, first served. There would be men there three hours ahead, like at four, you know. There was never any trouble.

My boss, he didn't like this, but I told him this was business he was never going to get anyway, so why throw good bread crusts away. He was a Greek, and I've never been fond of Greeks, but he was okay.

Four dollars a week, and I was glad to get that job. If I had quit there would have been girls ready to grab it at three-fifty. You just can't imagine what it was like. Nobody can. They should teach a special course in the schools."

———————————————— • ————————————————

What Makes A Man Like That?

"Some guys were rats. I remember one when I was walking over the old Skyline Trail, from Princeton to Hope. Not where the highway is now but up on the skyline. Eighty miles across and 120 up and down mountains. There was no work in the Okanagan and I thought there might be work in the Fraser Valley. In those days we thought nothing of a five day hike over an old miners' trail to look for work. Just hitched up the old turkey (*the hobo's bedroll and possessions*) and took off.

About noon of the third day I came to this survey gang. The boss was one of those university engineers and I asked for work. No, no work, all hiring done in Victoria. I asked for a meal, because the cook tent was right there. He asked where my papers were. I said I had none. Okay, he said, no meal. Now imagine it, a guy starving 40 miles from nowhere and the bastard wouldn't give a starving man a piece of bread. He's lucky I didn't kill him. The cook caught my eye and when the engineer went back to his paperwork he told me to go down the trail and wait by the creek there.

Well, I waited two hours, and then the cook came. He had a big packsack stamped 'government' and he must have cleaned out the camp. There was bacon and beans and honey and flour and jam, Christ, enough to feed an army, and that cook, he was a real nice fellow, he said to keep moving a few miles before I ate. Just in case. Jesus, that pack must have weighed 80 pounds. I go along a few miles and cook myself up a big feed and lie back beside a creek and snooze and then four other guys come along, and these fellows are heading for the Okanagan. No work, I tell them, not even fruit picking, but I said for them to sit down and have a meal and they cooked up a monster of a feed and I joined them again when the guys clanged the gut hammer. There's still about 40 or 50 pounds of stuff so I take about five pounds of bacon and beans and some lard and coffee and I tell them to take the rest, but for Christ sakes, when they get near that government camp they should make a hell of a wide detour into the timber because that pack sack had that government stamp on it and if that engineer saw it, then there was one cook who was going to be out of a job.

That engineer. Now, what would make a man be like that? Refusing a hungry man a meal. Something's gone very wrong since the days when you could walk into any house and help yourself and if you went by that cabin a year later and you had some spare grub, then you'd leave it. Not refusing a man a meal. Is it only me that thinks this way?"

---•---

Just The Usual Thing

"I was walking down past the post office, where the steep hill is down to the pier on the waterfront, and there was this tall laddie just ahead of me and he seemed to be walking in a funny way and then he went down hard. I thought he had had a heart attack or something because I was on my first visit from Ontario where nothing like this happened, and I didn't know the score the way it was in Vancouver.

I called the police from an office next door and they came along and I was standing there and I asked what was the matter. 'Oh, it's just the usual thing. This poor bugger hasn't had a thing to eat for a few days,' said the policeman. Well, what were they going to do? The policeman said, 'Oh, we'll just put him in the car and take him down to the Salvation Army.' I saw that laddie collapse right in front of me, and that was starvation."

---•---

They Ate Their Seed Grain

"I was a telephone lineman down in the South Country, around Shaunavon and Eastend and LaFleche in Saskatchewan and I saw farmers as poor as any native in a backward nation anywhere on earth. The government gave them seed grain, registered grain to plant, and this was to be their next year's crop and if things went right, the right rain, the right sunshine, no hoppers, no rust, then things would be better.

Those poor bastards couldn't wait until spring to plant, not when they saw their children starving before their eyes and they boiled the seed wheat, they made porridge and gruel and bannock out of it, and this is the way some of those farmers got their families through the winter. That was starvation in one of the greatest and richest nations of earth."

———————————— • ————————————

A Violation Of God's Will

"My mother would have no truck with relief. None at all. She said it was sinful, a violation of God's will. Things like that. My father had been killed by a broken neck when a horse threw him and my mother was still a widow. She said marrying again was a violation of God's will. She was like that. Not a fanatic, but, you know.

There was my sister and the three of us lived up near Orillia. North of there. Let me say this, it was not a land of milk and honey. We had nothing. A tiny farm, rocky, poor drainage, everything was wrong with it. We had two but sometimes, often, we had one meal a day. Milk, potatoes, bread, rice, beans. No variety. We had a garden, but there was never a day I wasn't hungry. Always.

One day mother said, 'James, remember this day. It is the blackest day of my life.' She said there was nothing in the house, nothing. It was in April as I reckon, the cow was dry, there was nothing. The larder was bare. Her little money was gone. Mother worked for women in the town when she could. I'd pick up the doctor's wife's laundry and bring it home and mother would wash and iron it and I'd deliver it. Things like that. But nobody had any money that winter and that had just dwindled off. That night we ate a paste of water and the last of the flour. Baking it, she said, would lose the nourishment. The next day we had nothing. I said she didn't believe in relief so now you couldn't see her asking the neighbours for help, could you? No.

So there we were, starving quietly. Now I had 70 cents. It took me half a year to save it, running errands and such, and it was hidden in a little box that chalk came in at school. The teacher gave them out as rewards for good marks. This box was hidden in my room. On the third day I went and got it and gave the money to mother and the tears were streaming down her face and she said, 'It is God's will,' and she kissed me and my sister yelled, 'It is not

God's will, it is Jamie's money he was going to buy a camera with,' and my mother asked me if that was so, and when I said yes, she boxed my ears so hard I can still feel them ringing and she said, 'That's for putting a thing like the Devil's instrument ahead of the good of your family.'

Things got better because about two days later, right out of the blue, my mother got a job as one of the cooks at the hospital.

Today, I guess you'd call her a religious nut."

———————————•———————————

Potatoes For Christmas

"My father had drifted away somewhere and an uncle who lived in the Peace River Country in Alberta sent mother train fare for her and my brother and me to live with him. He had a homestead but nothing else. He had a team but he took the horses with him and went into the bush for the winter to cut wood for some company. Maybe the railroad.

Mother and Donnie and me, we had nothing up there, not a cow, not even a chicken, but there was lots of firewood my uncle had cut and a huge stack of potatoes in the root cellar. He'd only been up there a year and potatoes were his first crop.

We ate potatoes all that winter. Nothing else. At supper we'd each get a big potato on the plate and mother would cut off one end and say, 'Now, this is your soup, and isn't that good?' We'd eat that. Then she'd slice off another piece and say, 'Here's your meat,' and another slice and, 'My, isn't that a fine piece of carrot and look at all those nice peas,' and then she'd pick up the last piece left and she'd say, 'And here's your chocolate pudding, and isn't that nice?' It got so we'd almost believe her. Yes, children have a tremendous capacity for make-believe.

Along about January my uncle sent $20 and things were better after that, but here's one little girl of those days who remembers a Christmas dinner with all the trimmings – made up entirely of potato."

———————————•———————————

Cod Liver Oil

"You talk about poverty? Let me go into my night club act about how poor the MacRaes were. There was this long street, downhill to the wharf, and if kids up the hill were acting up, their mothers would say, 'Laddie, you'll be sent down the MacRaes' for supper.' That meant they'd get bugger all. Late potatoes, potatoes we'd picked off the fields after the farmers had taken what they wanted. They were usually frozen and going bad. Fish heads, guts, boiled, in a big stew, and the goddamn ocean was full of fish. Tea. Not store tea, Indian tea, spruce buds my mother had collected out of the woods. Maple sugar, what my mother and the kids scraped out of the sugar boiling vats in the spring. That was it. And every morning, two slices of bread with sugar, the crust out of the vats, and that goddamned cod liver oil my old man, when he wasn't drunk, would brew out of fish guts the captains would give him. The left-overs.

If we were acting up, raising hell, my mother would threaten us with another tablespoon of cod liver oil. Like mothers in cities might say, 'Be good or the policeman will get you.' If we kept it up, we'd get another dose. It was a weapon.

We had no shoes, not even in winter. We used woollen socks and rubbers and that was better. We had nothing. I've seen us without coal oil for the lamp so the whole bunch of us, Mom, Dad if he was home and not drunk, grandmother, me and four other kids, two of them cousins, we'd be in bed just after supper. Say, six o'clock.

Shit, what a life.

One thing, though, we were the healthiest kids within 20 miles of Truro. Even the school doctor said that. Rosy cheeks, bright blue eyes, tough as nails, and stinking of cod liver oil."

———————————————— • ————————————————

A Round Orange

"During the Depression, for three years of it, we lived near the Cypress Hills. You might say that was as hard-hit a part of Canada as there was. We didn't live on a farm as such, but we lived in a house which was on a farm owned by a man in Medicine Hat. My father, my mother, my older sister and myself. We were poor as church mice, although I can't say we starved. We just didn't have enough to eat.

One Christmas I was hoping for an electric train, an improbable thing because we didn't have electricity, but those Lincoln trains looked so wonderful in the mail order catalogue. That Christmas I got an orange. A round and orange orange. That was all, and that's what my sister got, too. Nothing else, you understand. Just an orange. It was beside our plate when we sat down for our breakfast mush. You know, I can't look at an orange today without thinking of those two oranges."

————————————— • —————————————

They Were My Sister's Kids

"R. B. Bennett said nobody in Canada was dying of starvation and if he meant like Biafra, kids with big bloated bellies, no, not that kind of starvation. But I know one family which lost three children from hunger. Lack of food, malnutrition, then diarrhea which they couldn't fight because they were so weak – and that to me is dying of starvation. They were my sister's kids, and every day if Bennett is in hell I curse him a thousand times, even today, and if he is in heaven, I curse him a thousand times and wish he was in hell. I will do it until I die."

CHAPTER NINE

Government Relief Camps –
They Treated Us Like Dirt

They Wanted Us Out of Sight . . . Some Depression Reasoning . . . A Nice Little Medical Racket . . . A Relief Camp Loophole . . . They Weren't All That Bad.

———————————— • ————————————

In time the government began to worry that the thousands of unemployed single men clogging the cities were ripe for revolution. To avoid this the relief camp scheme was invented; feed them, clothe them, pay them 20 cents a day and keep them in the hills, in the mountains, far from civilization, far from the haranguing of Communists and other dangerous agitators.

They would do good works – clearing parkland, building bridges, brushing out hiking trails. A healthy life, all the fresh air they could breathe, learning sound work habits and, most important of all, keeping out of trouble. The economic crisis would soon be over and they could come back, rarin' to go.

The young men saw it differently: sometimes they were actually grabbed off the streets to be sent to these isolated slave camps. There, their overseers were the sergeant majors of the last war, the life was dull, the camps dirty and drab, the work was mindless and meaningless, and the 20 cents a day was an insult.

It was a hopeless system from the beginning, according to most of the single men. But the politicians and civil servants claimed that on paper it was a very good plan – but they scrapped it after a couple of years, before rioting broke out in the camps.

———————————— • ————————————

They Wanted Us Out Of Sight

"You've got to realize this, in the relief camps of the Thirties we weren't treated as humans. We weren't treated as animals, either, and I've always thought we were just statistics written into some big ledger in Ottawa. I was 18 and had come out west from Brantford because there was no work for a young fellow in that part of Ontario and in Calgary about October, early October, I got to know a city policeman and one day we met in front of the

103

Palliser Hotel and he asked me what I was going to do. Well, I was 18 and what did I know about what I was going to do? I remember him saying, 'You better get out of this country, Bob, before the snow flies or you'll be in real trouble.' He said it as a friend, not as a policeman so I headed for Vancouver where at least I wouldn't freeze to death, but we were harassed there and kicked around and so I joined up for a relief camp.

It was one of several up the old Hope-Princeton Trail, made up of board and canvas tents, and buildings they called cabooses where we slept. There was about 150 of us in this one, guys as young as 16 and up to 35 or 45, I should guess, and the thing was, we were all single and no jobs, stony broke and no future and the politicians considered us as dangerous. Their thinking was that if we were isolated then we wouldn't be hanging around vacant lots and jungles listening to Communist troublemakers.

The truth was, nobody really paid much attention to these agitators. They were more a laugh than anything. Who the hell cared about saving the world out there when we had no world to save right there for ourselves. When we arrived we got some underwear, a brown shirt and pants, socks and good heavy boots and the agitators said the reason we got such good boots was because some politician in Ottawa had a brother-in-law who had a boot factory and was charging the government sky-high for them.

If that sounds like a uniform and if a uniform sounds like the army, then you'd be partly right. They were run like the army, except when I joined in '39 and everything was disorganized as hell it was still a hell of a lot more organized than those relief camps. They'd march us out in the morning and we would be widening a trail or putting in a culvert or cutting and stacking wood for winter and every day there was a quota but after about an hour the guys would just sit down and wait for lunch and then sit around all afternoon snoozing or bullshitting or playing cards or, if there was a stream close, we'd go swimming. That was in good weather. In bad weather we'd sometimes not even leave camp.

They'd turned the running of these camps over to the Department of National Defence and while the guys in charge weren't army, they had been in the last war and let me tell you, a guy who has been a captain or a sergeant major has a hell of a time forgetting he was a captain or sergeant major. We were under K.R. and R. (*King's Rules and Regulations*) so we were under army law, so to speak, and they could pretty well do what they wanted. They couldn't keep you in camp if you didn't want to stay, but if they wanted to kick you out, then they could do that and in winter, 100 miles from nowhere and a supply truck coming in once or twice a week, that could be a real hardship. Believe you me. You thought twice about walking out anytime, and you minded your P's and Q's too.

We were paid 20 cents a day. Twenty cents a day. I've told this to people today and they always say, 'You mean 20 cents an hour, don't you?' and I'd say no, 20 goddamned cents a goddamned *day*. There was one guy in charge at that Hope camp who used to call us slaves. 'Okay, slaves, off your asses, we're going to cut trail today,' he'd say, and that was really what we were.

You've got to consider it this way. Across the country, but mostly in the west, there were 10 or 15 thousand men in these camps. I read once that they figured about 200,000 men were in them, all told, in five years. That's 200,000 young men who were really pissed off at society, the government, the politicians, the army way of doing things, and that 20 cents meant slavery.

Suppose you worked in a camp, or suffered through one, for two months. Okay, that's about 40 days' work. That's eight dollars. What can you do with $8 in town. Live a week? We were like loggers, come in to town with a big stake. We'd blow that in a night, some beer, a big meal, some whiskey, maybe a woman, a flop for the night and she's gone. I heard there was a tobacco ration too of one and a half cents a day but I know damn well nobody in our camp got it, but I'll bet it went into the books and the quartermaster split it with the commandant. There was a lot of room for graft. I've seen the truck come in with 10 sides of beef, good beef, and I've seen that truck go back out with two of those sides under canvas and you can bet your bottom dollar that the trucker had passed some money over and bought those two sides. Same with the other things. Axes, tools, dynamite, things like that, and canned goods.

No, we never starved. The food was good. I mean good when it arrived but it was pretty awful when it hit our plates. There is something about mass cooking by cooks who just don't give a damn which takes the spunk out of everything they touch. They could even foul up chocolate pudding and porridge. I knew guys from good homes, Dad gone broke, maybe, who would live on bread and butter and peanut butter and strawberry jam and prunes and canned milk and raw potatoes and oranges because they just couldn't stand the sight of them big pots of greasy soup and watery stew.

There was nothing to do either. In our camp I saw two Finns, cousins, get into a Joe Louis-Jack Dempsey type of fight over who was next to throw horseshoes. We only had one set of horseshoes. The government provided sweet bugger all. Absolutely sweet bugger all. Cards, dice, checkers, the guys provided them. Nothing to read, unless if you were acting up one of the commandants would shove King's Rules under your nose and tell you to read section such and such. I've seen a guy spend all Sunday, week after week, throwing an axe from 40 feet into a tree and every time he hit it dead centre he'd yell, 'Got ya, ya bastard.' He was pretty good, could hit that tree dead centre about once out of two throws. The bosses tried to stop him and the first time he just looked at them and said, 'Go ahead and try.' They never did. I hope he got a job in a circus or something.

It wasn't too good a situation because they didn't screen anybody, and every camp had a few perverts and us young guys, well what did we know about that. Some older guys gets friendly, helps you out, gives you advice, loans you tobacco, the old con, of course, and there were a few young guys who became bum boys. Too bad, but if the other guys found out, they'd usually run Herbert the Pervert out. Sometimes the kid too, because these young guys would get pretty cheeky. In some ways we policed our own camp in the way an army platoon will police themselves. The old silence treatment sometimes worked, but bumps, shoves, accidental trippings, sometimes a good kidney punch got the message across.

But it was the monotony, the jail of it all. It was jail, you know. What else would you call it? All the fresh air and sunshine you could stand, but no women, no music, no streets and people, no place to buy anything, no beer although some guys used to make homebrew, and no sound of streetcars and kids playing. Just the wind through the fir trees, it blew all the time, and guys lying around bullshitting. After a while you forgot what you looked like. If you thought the army was bad, then you don't know about one of those camps.

Nothing has ever been written about them because I think the government was too ashamed when it was all over. Down the line the CCC *(the U.S. Civilian Conservation Corps)* did good work, so I've read, because they paid their guys and had decent leaders and discipline that made sense but you know what, I think down there a guy, well he didn't mind working in a camp. They had pride, they gave their guys pride. Parks built, dams built, roads a fellow could drive over years later and say to his wife, 'I helped build this road,' just like a guy could take his wife to Europe and drive through a little French town and say, 'I helped liberate this town.'

But in Canada, not on your blinking life. It was 'get these dogs off the street before they offend the people.' You know, it was mostly the guys from the relief camps north and east of Vancouver who were on that Ottawa March which wound up in the Regina Riot. That wasn't no riot in the sense of what those guys could really have done if it had taken place in Vancouver when they all came out of the camps in the spring of '35. Why, shit, if they had had three good leaders, not the reds, but three guys who made a lot of sense and would have been up front with them, they would have taken Vancouver apart. That's why McGeer *(Mayor Gerry McGeer of Vancouver)* raised $6,000 in an awful hurry and gave it to the boys to get them out of town. He knew about the camps and he could see what was coming.

Everything about those camps was wrong, but the thing most wrong was they treated us like dirt. And we weren't. We were up against it, broke, tired, hungry, but we were farm boys who knew how to work and so we were shit. Dirt. Slaves. I said it before to you. We were slaves. What else would you call a man who is given 20 cents a day and is expected to believe their bullshit that he is an important part of the country. They just wanted us out of sight, as far out of sight as they could manage."

———————————— • ————————————

Some Depression Reasoning

"If people were to get relief, then a lot of people in official places – mayors, councillors, administrators – felt they should work. Now there is nothing new about this idea. It probably goes way back in history. The Romans, the Greeks, maybe?

You did work for your few dollars and it came out in funny ways. There were several theories, and one was that you got a bunch of men and they cleared foot paths for hiking, or parks, and these were things that were pretty far from the nub of things, really. It has to be a pretty wonderful hiking trail through the back country before you can get a bunch of men to work as though they even half meant it.

Another way was to let the machinery stand idle. Let the men do it, for their 90 cents a day, so you had the crazy situation of a $3,000 bulldozer and a steam roller sitting by the side of the road while 50 men went at the dirt and rock with shovels and picks. Now, under any conditions, those men weren't going to make the dirt fly all that much, and it took many times, say 10 times as long, for 20 men to dig away a clay bank on a municipal road than for the bulldozer man to drop his blade and clear the whole thing out, once and for all. So good machinery stood idle, costing the taxpayer money as you'll understand, but by the Great Balls of Fire, those 20 or 30 guys who were accepting relief would be doing some work.

Maybe it made the council feel better, but if a taxpayer thought it over he'd see the stupidity of it all, and some of these men were suffering from malnutrition, some were really too weak to be on the end of a shovel or pick or eight pound sledge. But the municipality was getting its pound of flesh so everything was just fine.

So many stupid things like that went on, all the time, all over Canada, and they were all the work of men with the best of intentions. That was the pity of it all, good but stupid men."

———————— • ————————

A Nice Little Medical Racket

"There was a doctor in our town, and he still lives there, but he was just one of the guys who had a nice racket going for himself in those days. They had these relief camps, and I was in one, up past the town of Hope on the old Hope-Princeton Trail. You got a roof over your head, meals, and 20 cents a day. Big deal, big benevolent R. B. Bennett. These camps were strung right across the country, as I recall, and their main reason was to get the young men, the single men, off the roads and out of the cities because they thought we'd have a revolution. There could never have been a revolution because we never had a single leader worth a hoot.

Anyway, this doctor. These federal camps were voluntary, you didn't have to go, but if you didn't like starving and being hammered about by every cop from Kingston, Ontario, to Vancouver Island, you went. A lot did. They were way back in the bush, these camps, and a lot of guys didn't want to go to them. Especially city guys. The city or municipality was handing out relief in those days and they were always denying the $6 or $10 you got a month as a single guy, saying go into one of the relief camps. They actually forced a lot of single guys into them, and these camps were hell holes, most of them. But to get into a camp you had to have a clean bill of health and you could get that from a doctor who examined you, and now here's the kicker.

If you couldn't get into the camp because you had a hernia or something, then the city had to put you on relief and brother, you were home free. Now the whole picture opens up, doesn't it? It's like these Chinese brokers in Hong Kong with connections in Canada who can get a Chinese man into this country on payment of $500 or $1,000, or whatever it is.

This doctor set himself up the same way, letting the word go round that he'd give a fellow a rejection, hernia, bad knee, heart murmur, something, for $100. The doctor got $80 and the tip-off guy, the guy who brought the work to the doctor, took his $20. It was a sweet racket and nobody ever caught on, not in Victoria or Vancouver.

Everybody knew this doctor. He was like a doctor who does abortions in a city, everybody knows him. He just kept on and on, making out these phoney reports and laying his reputation on the line every time he signed his John Henry. *(His signature.)* He played it right, he never got all that greedy, just charged $50 or $100, enough to live like a bloody king in them days. If there was money around, there are always fellows who know where it is. But $100 or $50, that was a pile of do-re-mi in those days, but again, a lot of guys would do anything to get on relief. That was easy street."

———————————— • ————————————

A Relief Camp Loophole

"I never saw it fail. The government would come up with some scheme and in about two days some guy would come up with a loophole. There were more frustrated lawyers in those government relief camps than I ever saw in the army.

They paid us 20 cents a day and all they wanted was to get the young guys off the city streets. Some jackasses in Ottawa thought we were going to start a revolution. Yep, that's right. We weren't. I made the relief camp work for me, and here's how I done it. Simple. You could sign up under any name because I don't remember an identification card then. Joe, Mike, Pete, be what you wanted.

You got a pair of 1914-1918 army boots, two pair of socks, a pair of overalls, a shirt, pants, heavy underwear, a pair of mitts and you could go into one camp today and get your clothes and leave it tomorrow. Nobody gave a damn. These camps were scattered all over the west.

So I used to make for the track gangs, the Canadian Pacific. These gangs were mostly Italians, dumb wops, they were getting two bits an hour. Good native-born Canadians could only get 20 cents a day in the relief camps but the garlic-eaters got two bits an hour on the railroad gangs. Pretty good, eh? So we'd head for the crew and you could get $5 for this whole outfit of clothes, so we'd sell the clothes and go back to another camp and get some more. It took you five weeks to make $5 in a relief camp and I could make $5 a day. Of course, this couldn't go on forever, but I must have done that 30 times."

————————————— • —————————————

They Weren't All That Bad

"The relief camps were fine. Just a question of adjusting. I've seen lads who came off a New Brunswick farm and hardly knew how to cash a dollar into change in a corner grocery, I've seen them bitch and rattle on about conditions when I knew damn well they slept four to a bed and ate potatoes three times a day back in Good Old N.B. and they were complaining because the camp wasn't the Chateau Frontenac or the Palliser Hotel.

You had to adjust. Say to yourself, 'Well, I'm getting clothes and food and a roof over my head and it's 15 below outside,' and then you knew you were all right.

Better than being in the Clink. They were throwing lads into jails all over the prairies, in the winter. For their own protection. Railway Act violations. Trespassing. Loitering by night. Vagrancy. Public nuisance. The charge didn't matter. Give them 60 days and turn 'em loose when the crocuses were blooming and the first crows came back. Spring.

I was in camps in B.C. Some were good, some not so good. Dirty, clean, chaos, anarchy, order, pleasant, a lot depended on the supervisors. A good supervisor, a good camp, and that was about the size of it.

The food was good, but it was like putting good beef through a grinder. Sometimes it came out as baloney. Good food, poor cooks. No motivation. If nobody cared up above, it was a poor camp.

The agitators used to come in. Clever fellows but too clever. They'd say, 'You're worse than galley slaves. You're scum, and Bennett wants you off the streets. You're buried here and buried things rot.' I'd always talk back and the arguments I had, when they added up to the common sense of food and shelter, the boys usually went for them. I never saw an agitator thrown out bodily but when guys a month before had ridden in boxcars in 10 below zero through the Kicking Horse Pass and come just that far from freezing, a relief camp made a lot of sense. There was never much argument from the agitators on that score. I used to ask them, 'When did you last hit a boxcar at midnight in the Moose Jaw yards?' Something like that. The commies, if that's what they were, never did that. Too smart.

Yes, I agree. Yes, the 20 cents a day was an insult. It was the worst part of it. But you forget that quickly. I only think of it four or five times a day now. *(He laughs.)*

Yes, I'm sure there was a better solution than the camps, but I'll wait around an hour or so until you think of one. I can't. Not under the circumstances of the times. You must remember the country was down for the 10 count. Knocked out."

CHAPTER TEN

The Bush Was Still There

A Winter On The Frontier . . . We Got Along, Pals Together . . . Living Off The Country . . . A Detour From Alaska . . . My Little Indian . . . Venison, Caviar And Wine.

———————————— • ————————————

The cities and towns were dead-ends. Destitute people were not wanted, and transients were considered troublemakers and often run out of town. Many said to hell with it – "I can't do any worse up in the bush than I am in this lousy town."

Their way was always north beyond civilization, or west to the coast. Their belief was that where they were going – although few of them had a specific destination – a man could be free, far from interference and the hassle of rules and regulations. And, with a lot of hard work, they knew that they had a chance of producing enough food to live on. So they headed out to take their chances in the bush.

———————————— • ————————————

A Winter On The Frontier

"People were saying, 'Mac, you crazy? You'll never come out of that country alive.' I got tired of hearing it. I was telling people I was tired of these hard days and how the white man was screwing up the whole Cariboo country and I was going way west to the mountains, way out west of Williams Lake and Redstone and Lee's Store and out north up into the mountains. Towards the Ichkas.

This was '33 and the whole country was belly-up. But furs were fetching good, 'cause another of them goofy fashion swings had come along and I wanted to catch it.

I knew what I'd do. A good big horse and two pack animals. Indians over at Springbank or just here on the Sugarcane Reserve were selling them for nothing and I'd get out slowly towards Riske Creek and then on and when I got where I was going which I'd know when I damn well got there, well then I'd cut north. An Indian told me moose were coming back into that country and there were plenty of deer and I figured that ten years working on the Vancouver docks hadn't knocked all the bush out of me. An axe was an axe, and if you were taught good to handle it, then you could always. I'd make me a lean-to for the horses and try and put up a little fall hay for the horses and get together a 10 by 12 cabin for myself and hell, I'd be in business. I figured I'd need a hundred or so traps and they was almost for the asking in that country that year. Folks had just lost the gumption to go out. Spirit gone. Mink, marten, beaver, and some bigger numbers for coyote and wolf and maybe a bear. I had to have a .22 pistol and a 30:30 would do me. A good bush rifle. You could buy a handful of shells for two bits, and I wouldn't need too many. I'd knock down a moose and jerky it, and the rest I'd put up for pemmican for my traps, around the trap line, you see, one spreading out north from my cabin and one south.

The game officer of the government at Quesnel issued me a permit. He said, 'where?' and I pointed to an area on his map which was empty and it was north of Takla Lake and south of the Westroad River and I dropped a 50 cent piece on the map and took my pencil and went around it and I said, 'There,' and he laughed and said, 'There isn't no there,' but he made out the thing anyway. A good guy. Most of them were.

I wasn't too fussy about people knowing where I was, anyway.

It was early August by then and I got my outfit and left and didn't say bye-bye to anyone. I'd meet the odd rancher and sometimes a few Indian families. Poor creatures, every one of them. At that time they wasn't getting no relief and sure, they were living off the land as they always done, but the government grant to them, the federal, was $5 a month for any size family, and I don't know of any Indian knew enough English to apply. The priests sure were no help. Vanilla extract was their only fun, and some gambling games and screwing. Funny though, when tribes live like that, some sort of birth control takes over, because you don't often see Indian families up in the Chilcotin with huge families. Sure, a lot of babies die too. Law of nature. Anyway. These Indians would want tobacco, and I'd ask them about out to the northwest, and they'd say big country. I gathered there were lots of mountains and they meant running streams and that meant beaver, and beaver meant coyotes and deer and muskrats and ducks and, well, you see, beaver is kind of the key to it all in the wilderness. Where there's water, animals come.

One old Indian said he'd been into a village and it sounded like 'Ulchake' and I kept that in mind and I took out a map and asked him to point where, and he was a bit confused by then but he put down a mark after looking at the map for a while. Then he pointed to me and the gun and my traps bag on my pack horse and he drew a line east and north of this Indian village. He was telling me it was good there, and I knew that must be up around Swannell Mountain, as she is called.

They had a girl with them, oh, 15 or 16 or thereabouts, and I pointed to her and to me but the old man said no, that was out. He talked to the rest of his gang and they all laughed like hell, and I guess he was suggesting they offer me the oldest bag in the bunch, but then he pointed to the map and to me and laughed and what he was saying was I could get a woman for the winter up there. I didn't want a man partner because too much can go wrong, but a woman who can cook and skin and keep your loins from burning up, then that's better. An Indian woman, though. Nothing else. Anyway, no matter. I didn't get one.

There wasn't too much trouble because there was old Indian trails north of the trade post at Anaheim. Now you've got to see this country in your mind's eye. Even today it is still wilderness. I've heard it said that some Indians there haven't seen a white man in their lives, and others say it isn't so, but back in the Thirties I knew there were kids of 16 and 18, and for them seeing me must have been like seeing Christopher Columbus. No shit. I stayed clear of the tribe although I saw their sign often. They'd find me soon enough anyway. You know Indians. Suddenly one day I'd be cutting wood or something outside the cabin and a dozen would ride out of the bush, and eat you out of house and home and smoke half your tobacco and just watch you for an hour and then ride out. That's the way it usually happened.

I found a place I was looking for, and it had a salt lick near, which I wanted. That was like putting out grain for deer. There was good timber shelter, lots of logs, good water, and beaver sign.

The first day I was cutting logs for my cache and I looked up and there was a bull moose about 60 feet away. You know how they look when they get mad. Their ears flatten down. Well, this big bugger's were flattened down. My rifle was right there and when he charged he got two in the neck, almost on top of each other and he coughed, went down on his knees and over and I didn't even have to bleed him. There was my 800 pounds of winter meat.

What I'm trying to say is this, yeah, the Depression was tough but if a guy had the savvy he could make it. He could make it. The Cariboo and Chilcotin was my country, so I was lucky. That was some winter. I really needed a woman but nobody had one to spare and I'd spend half my time cutting and skinning and making frames and if I'd have had a woman, or even a partner, I'd have cleaned up. As it was, by thaw-up I had 28 beaver and they said there wasn't any beaver in the Chilcotin. Nothing on the eastern side but on the west, plenty. I found out later I was poaching those beaver. Illegal as hell. Thirty coyotes, and I got 22 of them with poison bait. I hate doing that, but it's the only way. I got nine wolves, big timber wolves, and six of them in an ambush, them coming up a river running a couple of deer and I had six shells in the rifle and every one went home. They just didn't know which way to run. The wolf is usually smarter than that, but the echoes I guess were bouncing every which way in that canyon and I just picked them off. About 30 foxes and 18 mink, and three were the biggest I ever did see, like as big as martens, and I got $40 each for them. We had a terrible freeze in February for about two weeks and I reckon it went down as far as it ever does in that country and it gave me time to do a lot of skinning and framing and pondering.

I decided that without a woman this life wasn't for me, so next time it was going to be with a woman. Then a chinook *(a warm wind)* came and it was 30 or 40 above and this was February and two of the horses came in and they was in pretty bad shape and the third, he was down and the foxes had been at him so I had two horses. For that reason I didn't take any muskrat although there was thousands, and 300 or so would have been $300 more but I wanted to get out of that country, and in another month I got out.

I hit an Indian trail into those big hay meadows south of the mountains and met an old man and his squaw and they were going to Nazko. Poor devils, I guess I saved their lives. Funny thing about Indians. People think an Indian is born to the bush, like he is able to provide soon as he can walk. Not so, he learns, like anybody else. There's no instinct involved. These two were like babies, they had lost all their instinct, and all they could survive was cold and hunger. I fed them pemmican and beans and tea and we got out to Nazko.

Now we're into 1934 and I give the horses to the old people and hire a truck to take me to Quesnel. The trader is mad because I won't deal with him, and the bastard's on fifty-fifty. Know what that is? Fifty percent cash, 50 percent trade goods. I don't want no shells or flour or beads or calico or rubber boots. At Quesnel I ship my pelts by the railroad and every mile of the way I'm sitting on top of them in the baggage car, reading western magazines, all that cowboys and Indians bullshit, and drinking beer with liverwurst sausage on buns. I take the boat into Vancouver and haul my winter's work up to the raw fur sales room and they pour me a drink and I get a good price, more than $1,500 for everything, and that's enough.

I don't go back to the bush."

———————————————— • ————————————————

We Got Along, Pals Together

"Now, we were different. I had been to university two years, Jack Dawson was a minister's son – and they are supposed to be generally bad – and James, Jamie Dawson was his cousin, and then there was Anton. I won't try and spell his last name, all c's and z's, but he was a good guy and we met on the farm of an old geezer who was hiring a few pickers up on the Naramata Road. That's by Penticton.

Pay was 50 cents a day for apples, maybe 60 cents. They had no lead picker, some slob you had to keep up with. 'Just work at your own time, fellows,' said the fruit farmer. 'I can't sell the damn things anyway.' He had a great sense of humour, and his wife was always laughing and bringing out apple pie and soft cider. Not hard cider. Hard cider, we'd have fallen off our ladders, the stuff was so powerful. He fed us. Milk, you bought a four quart can for five cents. That was raw, of course, or skim, and all you could handle. Hamburger was five cents a pound at most and there was a big garden so no matter how much we ate, it was only the trouble his wife took to cook more for us that cost them. That cost time more than anything.

Apples are the last crop and then we got a bit of haying in, and Jack and I got a job digging up around telephone poles and scraping away the rot and painting them, and we threw everything in the pot. Now, anybody can figure out a man can't live on 50 cents a day, but consider this. Four men could live well on $2 a day.

The farmer said we could have a cabin in the hills up above his house. Just one thing. Rent. Rent was to build a fence to keep range cattle from drifting down into his watershed and screwing up his creek supply and that was easy. 'Take your time, boys, them cattle have been up there for years,' he said. He was the greatest take-your-time-boys fellow I ever knew.

The cabin was pretty, and first thing I did was carve on a big board, and stain it, a saying from Thoreau: 'At a certain season of our life, we are accustomed to consider every spot as the possible site of a house.' I was a student of Thoreau, and this life suited me fine.

We'd saved money all summer and most of fall and we went into town and begged winter clothes from the Sally Ann *(Salvation Army)* or whoever it was. We would go to the butcher and ask for the pork butts, that end part of the big ham that hangs from the hook. After a while it gets this big hole worked through it and pretty tough. Nobody wants it, so we'd get it free. Tomatoes? You could buy them for $15 or so a ton. Nobody wanted them. Apples. Peaches. Cherries. Bread, all you wanted at three, four cents a loaf. I've bought hamburger at 20 pounds for a dollar. Good beefsteak was 20 cents a pound, and even that we thought was too high. There was deer along the creek. Firewood, no problem. We had to buy flour and grease and you could get a big pail for next to nothing and kerosene and salt and pepper and sugar.

We stayed for another summer and fall and then Anton went to California, I went back to Toronto and the Dawson boys went down to the coast. Nobody wanted any part of the prairies and funny, that's where we had all come from. Alberta and Saskatchewan.

We lived together for nearly two years and there was not one incident, without a word of a lie, between us. We were happy, of course, in our own stupid way.

Everybody around us in the Okanagan Valley was bitching, and yet, even though prices were poor, they had their land, their cars, their nice houses. Some used to ride. Polo. To the hounds. There was a cricket league. Fishing was good and so was hunting. As I remember, they had some pretty fancy balls, dances, too. But they bitched. They still bitch, but they do it now while they're vacationing in California."

———————————— • ————————————

Living Off The Country

"Oh, we didn't live too badly off. But there is one thing you've got to remember. We didn't have any money. No, barely a sou, but again, who did? Those big shots on the Winnipeg Grain Exchange, I guess. But we lived fine.

How did we? Well, I had this place near Lac Du Bonnet. East of Winnipeg. In the bush, we called it a stump farm, and I had about 20 acres in crop and another 10 in pasture. The rest was bush. I doubt, yes, I'd say the whole thing, barn and house and sheds, in those days was worth maybe a thousand. Maybe less. Farms all over Manitoba were lying empty. Just walk in and start living if you wanted to. We had four cows and two was always milking and we raised the calves for food. I may be forgetful but I think you could get a three-day-old calf for a dollar, or maybe for free. We had milk, and Mrs. Renault would make butter and cheese and ice cream, blueberry ice cream. On a hot summer day, nothing better than Mrs. Renault's ice cream. I had some wheat and barley and we ground that up in the old fashioned way, and that was nourishing. Things like meat was cheap and how some of our neighbours made a living selling beef cattle, well I'll never know.

We had a bunch of deer around and I'd start feeding them a bit of hay about September and take one every time we needed some more meat. The country was full of deer. They was a nuisance. God, you could get one or two every time you went to town just driving along the roads. And people in the city they say was starving, and good meat only 60 miles away! I'd always get my moose. Part of my land had a small marsh on it, marsh hay and that kind of growth. First day of the season, bang. That's 600 pounds of meat, and as good as any steer.

We took wild rice, over by the Winnipeg River. The Indians squawked like hell the first time and I told the old chief, I said, 'Look, chief. We're all in this together. Your boys will never harvest all that rice and I can use it, I've got five kids and a wife, so any time I can watch out for you, I will. Fair enough?' He was a pretty wise old fellow and he said okay. The very next week I heard in town that the police were looking for two of his lads, and it was serious, assault, a fight. So I passed the word along that very day and the two fellows got out of the country. Well, they got picked up in Winnipeg weeks later but that was their own fault. I did my job. After that, why, I tell you I could have taken five tons of that rice. Not rice really, it's a sort of grain. You have a venison stew with wild vegetables and that rice and you've got a meal and a half.

The wife had chickens and so we were fine in that line. I got all the ducks and geese I wanted in the fall, dozens of them. We ate those. Mrs. Renault had a special jelly for ducks. Saskatoons, blueberries, wild plums, chokecherries. Hell, we had all we could eat, and we made a pretty good wine. The kids looked after a garden, yea big, maybe an acre, and we would give vegetables away. Potatoes, why we had spuds coming out our ears. Corn, that sweet corn. Peas, carrots, well, we sure had those vitamins coming in. This was about 1933, and a few years after.

Did I mention the trap line? No. Well, we had three, one legal and two not.

You never saw the way prices went up and down, why fashion was as bad then as it appears now. I never sold to the buyer. Right straight to the auction. The boys really worked on them, making those skins soft. Let's see, weasel, lots of muskrat. Do you know, I was catching a few beaver each year when even the game warden didn't know there were any in the country. A wolf or two or three. Several bear. Foxes. That surprised a lot of people. Foxes, they didn't know they was in that country, but if you've got lots of rabbits, then you've got foxes. I remember one year I could go to a place where there was lots of willows and stand quiet and then start firing those little .22 whiz bangs and pop off maybe 15 rabbits by not moving but just turning in a circle. They was that frequent. Next year no rabbits, no foxes.

There was more money about 1937 coming into the country and by that, I mean more Americans coming up from Minneapolis and Grand Forks and Duluth and Chicago to fish and hunt. I'd do a bit of guiding and Mrs. Renault would feed them if they wanted to stay at the house. We could always squeeze in a couple or three fellows. They'd rave about the food and we'd have a few skins lying around, oh, a wolf, a bear, some weasel made into a sort of woman's scarf. The girls, I had three, they were specially good at that. These guys they'd say how pretty they were. Talk back and forth, you know. Finally, one would say his wife would like this scarf, or that would look good in his den. I'd puff my pipe and let them talk themselves into buying. We got damn good prices. You know why? Because we didn't want to sell. Like hell we didn't. But who was they to know? Soon, out would come $30 or $40 and I'd say, no that's too much, that skin is only worth 25, something like that. They'd think I was the most honest guy in the world, that Renault was really one fine fellow, and they'd come back next year and they'd send their friends too. That developed into a good business. And that's how we got money for things.

We bought through the catalogue and the wife and girls would make their own clothes. Breeks and pants and shirts for me and the boys. Sugar, we could buy, and salt and pepper, and we didn't need no flour because we had our own, but things like tea and cocoa and shells and gas and nails and things like that. We had all the wood we could use. We had a whole country full of wood. We'd sell wood in town, vegetables, fish in winter, nets through a hole in the ice.

We lived good, there was always plenty of food and some to give away and the kids were always warmly dressed, and they went to school and made something of themselves. I can't even write, but times have changed. I mean

I couldn't write then. Now I can, because I learned myself and it was some-thing to do. We never got a newspaper and I'm not sure just what the radio system was like in those days but sometimes it was a long time before we heard of things. People didn't complain. We knew it was hard times, but I don't remember anybody using that word 'Depression.' We just knew every-body was in a pickle, but for me and my wife nothing ever did come easy.

One of our boys was killed in the war, in Italy, and the other is a business-man. The girls married nice fellows and have lots of kids, French Canadian kids. Mrs. Renault is dead. A good woman, and I miss her. The thing about the Depression for the Renault family was we was independent. We lived out there in the bush and buckled down and worked for what we got. In those years before the war opened up a lot of jobs I can't remember us – Mrs. Renault did the book work, so to speak – I can't remember us ever having any money over at the end of the year, but we sure didn't do without. We lived good, by our standards, and there was no grousing and complaining to the government. Perhaps just lucky or maybe we were just dumb-headed French Canadians who didn't know no better. Oh, well."

———————————— • ————————————

A Detour From Alaska

"There was no sense trying to make sense of life in Vancouver at that time because I had no trade and there just wasn't any work anyway. For a couple of years we just moved from house to house, living with friends until we wore out our welcome. Six kids we had, and that's not too hard to wear out a welcome: say five days a kid, about a month. Finally the wife wouldn't put up with it any more and her Dad sent her $50 from Toronto and she took the three youngest, the three girls.

The three boys and me were living in a tent on False Creek, on the south side, down among a lot of willows where there were a lot of fellows, and one night we hear this groaning and we go down to the water and there is this skiff bumping against the shore and there is a man on the shore. We carried him in a blanket, one at each corner, over to the Granville Street bridge and a police car just happened along and they called for an ambulance and took the man away. Next day these two boys in blue come down where I'd told them I lived and they said the man was dead and what did I know? There wasn't much to it, I said. We heard this noise and this guy came staggering along the shore and we took him up to where they'd seen us. I didn't say nothing about no boat and they didn't know about a boat. They seen the boat but they must have thought it was mine. So that's how it came mine.

That's how I got into the fishing business. Of course I don't mean I made a living fishing. You could if you had a big boat and good equipment and a good crew and knew where to fish. All I had was this 16-foot skiff, but she was well made, and an anchor, some lines, a box of grub, the usual stuff a drifting type of Swede would have. This boat was his last will and testimony. He'd been beat up, but the cops wouldn't ever find who did it. There was always guys around the creek who would kill a man for $2 and change.

I asked the boys what they wanted to do, it was May and they weren't going to school anyway. The school just wouldn't have them. Donnie, he was the eldest, he said, 'Let's go to Alaska,' and that suited the other kids. I knew we wasn't going to Alaska in that thing, but going north was better than hanging around the creek. I knew a fellow who slung beer down at the Anchor Hotel and I walked over to see him, that place was always full of fishermen and tugboatmen, and he introduced me to a guy who had a packer and he said yes, he'd take us north as far as he was going, which was Campbell River. We got ready for the trip, bought a few things, lard, beans, flour, a ham. He was over at Campbell Street and he had to catch the right tide through First Narrows and the boys and I rowed out and picked him up off Siwash Rock. We slung onto him and had a nice ride and he was a nice fellow and took us through the bad part of Johnstone Narrows, Ripple Rock, on the slack tide and then he went skidding and sliding back to Campbell River.

We poked around there for a while, a few days, grub getting low, and then we hitched another ride on a big seiner going south and we worked our way over into Desolation Sound. Now that's a big body of water, islands everywhere and damn few people, and them that was there minded their own bloody business. They didn't want no police boat in there. We found an old Indian village and were ready to settle down there, but there were rats and where there's rats, there's disease. Everybody knows that. It was a spooky place too, graves in trees, that sort of thing. But further along we found just the cutest little log cabin on an island and there was sweet water on it and we got along.

There was a big logging camp across the sound and I'd borrow the caretaker's rifle and in those days you could buy one cartridge, not a box, and I'd get me a deer with every shot. The camp had a dynamite magazine and I took a box of the stuff when the caretaker had his back turned and kept it dry and used about one third of a stick for C.I.L. lures, that's when you dynamite fish. You'd be amazed the number of fish one small blast would bring up. I'm still amazed. You could fish in that spot all day and nothing. Toss over a C.I.L. lure, and you'd have stunned fish all over the place.

There were berries and roots and we had a potato garden and we'd go over to Campbell River and prowl through the garbage dump or the dump at the logging camps along the way, and the Indians on Quadra Island got to know us and like us and we'd go over to their place. All in all, in those three years, what with selling a bit of fur, and I sold six claims for $300, the boys and me did pretty good. We were never hungry."

—————————— • ——————————

My Little Indian

"Hee haw, hee haw. That's a horse laugh. I didn't suffer during the Thirties and I had a damn good time and there wasn't much I couldn't do and I always had me a good horse and a woman and booze and I lived by my wits, just a poor but smart sailor boy from Iowa. I seen a lot of the world and in, oh, 1932, I got into a fight in a bar in San Francisco and pounded a guy half to death and a couple more punches and it would have been the marble orchard for him. I could hit. With my crime sheet and then this, well there was no way I wasn't going to be behind bars for a long time and believe me, in them days, a navy brig was worse than any Siberia. I headed for Canada and stole a truck at Everett and slipped across the border on a back road at night and I puttered along into New Westminister and went into a used car lot and picked out the oldest wreck I could see and undid the license plates. You see what I'm getting at. The U.S. Navy teaches you a thing or two. Or three. Then I put those plates on my pickup and threw the Washington State ones in the river. So I had a Canadian truck with Canadian papers, from the old wreck, understand, and they were good enough that I sold the truck for $260 in Mission. It was a good truck. I also sold a box of tools that were in the cab of the truck so I had a stake of about $275, plus what was left of my navy pay after buying clothes after I took off from that bar.

I caught a bus up to the Cariboo, Jesus Christ, what a ride, and I bought a horse at Clinton and a saddle and a bit of an outfit and rode around the hills a week learning to ride that horse. It was a brown gelding and it had it in for me every morning, every day for five years. Many a stick I broke on him. My first job was with a good guy named Marriott in that country and he knew I was no hand but he gave me a job that summer and I spent it nursemaiding calves and figuring how I could beat the system. That fall after work was done this guy, Marriott, asked me to stay on, no money, but room and board, and I said no.

He didn't know it but his count was three short because I'd driven three of his steers up into the hills and so there was no brand and I had three pretty good animals going for me. I rode out of his place in October, first snow was flying, with $27 for three months work, and I circled back and loaded up my horse with a couple of axes, two saws, a file, gunny sacks, candles, a lantern, plane, chisels, sledge, a lot of stuff I'd swiped, worth no more, I'd say, than 20 bucks. Added to the wages and the three young ones, it made a decent summer's wages in the style to which I had become accustomed. U.S. Navy.

I bought a pack horse for five bucks and loaded her up and headed across to the country over against the Fraser River and I got a woman, too. Just rode into an Indian camp and made a deal with her old man. Louise, a pretty fine woman, a girl then. For $10 and one steer, and she brought her own pony, an Indian pony that would go forever. The old man had a Winchester 44-40 and I bought that for ten, I think he skinned me on it, but he threw in a box of shells. I told Louise to bring along anything she owned but did you ever see an Indian girl with a hope chest? Ha! Ha! She had some blankets, some clothes, a skinning knife, a honey pail full of pretty rocks she'd gathered for years in the creek, and some of those small pamphlets which the missionaries, the priests, gave out with the covers showing God and Jesus floating up there in the sky. The first night we used one to light the fire and my little squaw laughed like hell. Laughed and laughed. So much for religion in the Woods' household.

We went back in the hills and found a trapper's cabin in good shape and I patched up the stove and put some shakes on the roof and we both worked like hell, me on the north end of the axe and she dragging the poles with the gelding to the cabin, and we got in our wood and then we had to decide what to do with the steers. You see, we had no hay, and horses can winter in that country, but cows just can't. They can't scrape through the snow crust to the grass below. Louise knew what to do. You know what she did? She just walked over with the knife and she put her hand just above the tail and ran it along the backbone and when she got to the steer's neck, snick, in went the knife and the beast never knew it was dead. Then I knew I had me a real woman.

There was none of this steak for breakfast, lunch and dinner. No sir. She butchered them down to the last ounce and every bit of fat, and she made jerky and she made pemmican. You grind up the jerky and put in berries, anything to give it flavour, like raisins, and you mix it up with tallow and store it in airtight bags of leather, and you take a pound of that pemmican into the bush on a 30 below day and it will keep you going forever.

She was quite a gal, and remember she was only 15, and she loved her white man with the tattoo on his arm. She used to study it for minutes at a time and talk to herself in the Indian tongue and I never knew what she meant.

There was the odd moose to the north of us and she could find them, she knew where their yarding-up places would be although she'd never been there. Some Indians know these things. They say an Indian has to be taught to live in the bush just like a white man, but this is just not so.

She helped me a lot, that little girl. I began thinking like an Indian and she like a white man and we got along fine. We lived together for four years and in the summer I went cowboying and she would work in The Lake *(Williams Lake)* or somewhere, and we were both stealing them all blind. Our cabin back of Big Creek was getting to be a fine place, a garden in the spring which didn't seem to grow weeds and we had corn and spuds and pumpkins in the fall and I guess we lived on about $200 a year cash money. Two hundred a year, and that included giving pretty good Christmas presents to her folks. The old Winchester always got us a moose. God! It threw a slug that would stop a freight train. We had fool hen and plenty of fish and some vegetables and we bought sugar and flour and salt and beans and kerosene and grease, cloth, latigo, some oats for the horses and a crock of hootch for Christmas and we made an awful lot of stuff and I taught her to read and write and she taught me the bush.

No, no kids. They just never seemed to come along.

Once the B.C. police came up, and they seemed awful curious and Louise fed them a big moose steak, out of season, of course, and I always bought a steer from a rancher each fall and got a bill of sale so we ate beef and deer and moose all year on that one bill of sale and usually it was a beef that Louise had given the old treatment to. The friendly voice, the hand on the backbone and the creature would just wait for the knife.

She made me vests and chaps out of leather and she kept the place clean and she put up magazine pictures on the walls and even kept flowers in winter. Red geraniums. I'll never see a geranium but what I'll remember my little Indian. I'd say we lived four years on less than $800, from haying, a bit of cowboying and Louise sold a few vests and jackets of deerskin and coyotes in winter prime, beginning in November, got a good price of about $8 or $10 with the trader, so we did okay.

Of course, it wasn't all peaches and cream, not that we ever saw cream. Or peaches either. Louise gave me some trouble but not because she was Indian. Because she was a woman. Those pictures on the walls. The lady magazine things. Out there, goddammit, was another world. Shiny cars and long dresses and champagne. Why couldn't we go out to Vancouver? Let's go to Vancouver, Woodsy? When we going to see Vancouver and the moving shows? I told her that outside there, the whole world was going belly up.

It was the Dirty Thirties, of course, but here was a girl 19, as pretty as a mountain lily, tall and slim and smart, and she had never seen a moving show or heard a radio or worn a right dress and, well, for Christ's sakes, it was only a matter of time before I caved in. So one morning I said, 'Okay, get your gear together. We'll ride over to Clinton and catch the PGE *(The Pacific Great Eastern Railway)* and we'll go down to town. Vancouver.' She was like a kid with a new red wagon. I had a mind to steal a car, pull the old used car lot plate switch, rustle up some money any way I could, and I had a few ideas. Not a very nice fellow, am I? Well, no, I'm not. Anyway, we were going to live and love it up and no bullshit about it.

Three days later we closed her up and I went and saddled the horses and if you don't believe me, then to hell with you, but when I brought them around there she was standing by the door in an outfit I couldn't believe. It was high society you'd call it, just like the smart city outfits in the magazines and she'd somehow bought the material, the fall before, I guess, and studied the pictures and made these clothes, hat, jacket, skirt, blouse, the works. Her feet were still in moccasins.

Well, I oohed and aahed and she giggled and we started down the trail and she was sidesaddle, the skirt you see. Sidesaddle on a western saddle, if you want to believe it. Ladylike as hell. We came to the first creek and her pinto, one of those Indian scrub, he must have caught an eye just then, a flash of her red skirt. Red, hell, it was scarlet. He gave a sideways jump, more of a skitter, but Louise was sidesaddle and that was enough and off she went, sort of tumbling, not sliding, and I heard this crack. A distinct crack. Her head had hit a rock in the stream. Somehow, something told me she was dead before I got to her. She was. Not even a smile for me at the end. Just dead. I tied her in the saddle and went on leading her pony and her Dad's place, you'll remember, was about 20 miles down the road and we got there before dark and next morning we buried her in her pink and scarlet city clothes by some pretty poplars, out of sight.

We didn't need no priest. We didn't even think of one. It was me and Louise and the rest of the world, all your goddamned records and social security cards and car insurance cards and names in a big census book in Ottawa didn't exist. It was just me and her people buried her in a board casket and I stood at the head of the grave as her brothers and cousins dumped in the soil and I said, 'Goodbye, Louise. I loved you, and I'm glad you didn't see the city.' I told her people I wouldn't be back and the cabin and everything in it was for them, and the brother Manuel said he was going to put a white cross on the grave and he'd send me a painting of it if he knew where I was going to be and I said I didn't know where I was going to be and I got on my gelding, the same one I'd rode into that country on and seen Louise, and I got on the horse and I rode out of that goddamned country and I never went back."

(He breaks down and cries.)

———————————— • ————————————

Venison, Caviar And Wine

"Remember the old pier at English Bay? They were selling off their boats, 17-foot, clinker-built, double-ended Peterboroughs, good boats, and I bought one very cheap and loaded it up with a small tent, axes, a cross-cut saw, rifle and grub and so on, and I rowed out of Vancouver harbour and headed upcoast, not knowing where I was going, but I figured it better than hanging around. There was no relief then, but you could get meal tickets. There were a lot of us who didn't want to take anything.

I rowed up to Pender Harbor and then to Powell River and old Doctor Henderson said that Mike Schuster up at Melanie Cove had died last year and left his place to the hospital and if I wanted to pay the taxes on the place, which was approximately $2 a year, then I could take it over.

So I went up and I found the hole in the wall entrance and found Mike's place and I settled down. Mike's cabin was in good shape because he'd just died the year before. He was one of the last of the old hand loggers. Quite a hunter. I had to clean the cabin out when I got there because he had deer and cougar hides spiked to the floor, six inches thick. When I got them up there was a copy of the Vancouver Province newspaper of 1892 underneath them.

I fished, handlining, no rods, a line tied below each knee, and I rowed. He had left an orchard there he had built by hand, with terraces, planting an apple or a cherry tree when he created a bit more space by bringing in earth in a bucket. Four acres of that. He had a fence and a rigging of fish net about 10 feet high to keep the deer out. And then a blackberry vine over a trellis over 50 feet long. The domestic kind, not the wild kind. And he had a cider press and he was known up and down the coast for his hard cider. A little creek came down about 150 yards from the cabin and once or twice a week anyway, you'd be able to pick up a deer there if you wanted.

That was the year the price of salmon went so low that the price of white spring went down to half a cent a pound and the fishermen wouldn't sell it, in protest. I salted down in barrels all the springs I could catch and I filled the rest full of blackberry wine and hard cider. Mike's apples were cider apples. You could take a mouthful and you'd have a mouthful of juice and a little cotton wool left in your mouth.

The result was that by curing up some of the salmon roe, I could live on venison and caviar and wine, like a gourmet, but I'd row 10 miles to Refuge Cove on Sunday with my fish, and if I could trade them for a pound of sausage and a couple of bottles of beer, then that was a real feast. It was a good life, but a lonely one.

There was no hope of getting anywhere, of course, but you were keeping yourself alive and staying off the relief roll. I stayed there for more than a year, exploring the coast at times, and it was nothing to row 45 miles or more up north just to see what the country looked like. It was a good life, but after a while I had to have the city life, people around me. So I left. If anybody took over that place, they'd have found several barrels of salted white spring salmon there. It may still be there."

CHAPTER ELEVEN

Employers Could Pick And Choose

You Could Pick And Choose ... Four Weeks In Four Years ... Out! Out! Out! Out! ... An Objectionable Little Creep ... On The Rockpile ... Hard Times Killed My Man ... All The Loopholes ... What Is A Day's Work? ... Just A Good Bunch Of Lads.

———————————— • ————————————

During the research of this book a thread began to appear, running through the stories of many of the people I interviewed; many still remembered with bitterness the treatment they received at the hands of unscrupulous employers during the Depression. They would remember the employer's name, his business, the work they had to do, the pitiful amounts of money they received, and the indignities they suffered at his hands.

Perhaps the law of the jungle always applies; but in Depression times the claws of the predators become longer and sharper. Thus a woman making $2 a day in a garment factory could lose her job in a moment to someone who walked in off the street and offered to work for $1.50. Or the wholesaler could dictate to the manufacturer the price he would pay for a garment, and the workers' wages would be cut accordingly.

It would be fair to say that there were thousands of good employers in the Thirties, distressed when people had to be laid off, and trying to be honest and Christian men. And then there were the others; the survivors remember them, the venal employers, out to gouge their workers, to extract every possible ounce of labour for the least possible amount in wages.

———————————— • ————————————

You Could Pick And Choose

"I think the true test of many a man, employers, came in the Dirty Thirties. Look at it this way. Help was a commodity that was in fantastic over-supply. You could pick and choose, and when you did you could then pay exactly what you wished. If the worker complained then you just told him to move along and you took the next application off the pile, which was ten feet high.

It was a form of slavery, except I understand slaves in the American South were treated better.

Women working in textile factories, doing piece work, often fine sewing which ruined the eyes in a few years, they often made only $3 or $4 a week, and there were line-ups for their jobs, at that!

You talk about exploitation! The banks have always been among the worst employers of all, poor salaries, and a man of 25 with several years service, working 10 hours a day, Monday to Friday, and half day Saturdays and some night work every month, a man of 25 could be paid $7 or $8 a week.

Farm hands got $5 a month, and grub. Maids got $5 or $6 a month. I've seen newspapers where the only jobs offered were for domestics. Pure labourers got 10 bucks or so, winter and summer, and lucky to have a job. Don't tell me about store clerks. Paid practically nothing and expected to dress neat, look neat, always smile and go to church every Sunday. Mail men and people who worked for the government didn't do too bad, and their jobs were fairly secure.

The banks were the worst, I think, and they kept their people in a form of slavery. Respectable poverty. You even had to get permission to marry, and I know one young fellow who was fired because he played golf every Sunday. With his father. His bank manager saw him on the course and didn't think it was right that a young fellow should be wasting away his time on a Sunday. Hard to believe, isn't it? The insurance companies weren't far behind, paying wages you couldn't keep a reasonably-sized dog now in Gaines Dogburger. I mean it.

If a man's true colours showed, in those days, it was when some employee would say, 'Mr. X is a good fellow, he treats us fine.' Too often it was the other way, dog eat dog, exploit, grind away until you had the lowest possible wage a man would work for. Why some of these owners didn't wind up in the river, throat cut, I'll never know.

The indignity of it all. I knew one man, a wholesaler in fruit and vegetables, and he did very well, one of those fellows who would do well in a roaring blizzard in the Arctic, he just had that knack. He threw big parties. How much did it cost, really, when booze was dirt cheap and food, you could serve 50 people for $10? This fellow made his office staff girls come to these parties and act as maids in black dresses and frilly white aprons and the men, yes, men with families, they had to come and serve as bartenders and waiters. Free. Not a drink for them, only what they could steal, sneak off. If that party went on until 2 a.m., then they still had to be at work at eight the next morning, ready to go, and as I recall the last streetcar stopped running at 1.45 so they had to walk.

Do you wonder why some people are bitter, or just want to forget the whole thing, the whole ten years of it and say it never happened?

There are two generations of Canadians who think that. The Depression brought out the worst in a lot of people, and some of those big fortunes you see around today, I can tell you from personal experience that many of those were made by ruthless and totally unlikeable men in those years, and what they piled up in those years they doubled or quadrupled in the war years. From '29 to '45, if you knew how to make money it was there to be made."

———————•———————

Four Weeks In Four Years

"There was no work for anybody and certainly no work for girls, women. For four years after I graduated from school I had four jobs, a week at a time each year in the Christmas week.

Oh yes, we were well paid. It was in the small department store in the town. We got $5 a week and we worked from nine in the morning until 11 at night for that Christmas week."

———————•———————

Out! Out! Out! Out!

"My mother operated a sewing machine in a factory in the East End of Montreal. They made pants, other things, and her salary for five days a week and nine hours a day was $3 a week and there was a bonus system that if you could go over your quota you made so much more.

There were 120 or so women in that factory and my mother said no woman ever made a bonus. Never ever.

If you went to the bathroom more than twice in a shift you were docked and there were just two toilets for those hundred women and they ate lunch at their machines because there was no washroom or lunchroom. No fire escapes. No sprinklers. No ladders. Windows sealed tight.

There was no union. If you even thought union, it was out. Out! Out! Ask for a raise? Out! Take two days off sick. Out! Think. Out!

The supervisor and the foremen were paid to keep the workers down. They were on some sort of bonus they got to run that place as a sweat shop.

Three bucks a week, and she walked four miles to work, there and back and that money kept her and Dad, he'd lost a leg in the bush, and me alive. I won't say how, but here I am to prove it. Alive and kicking.

The war came along and all the Rosie the Rivetters were making 20, 25 bucks a week in the shipyards and building trucks, and here were all these women on the machines still making about six or seven bucks. Coolie wages. They didn't speak English, they didn't understand what was going on, just those heavy machines going hours on end. Not even looking up, making sailor suits for the navy and uniforms for the army and other things for war.

It was slave, slave, slave, taking dirt and eating dirt, and if anybody had given them a kind word those women would have fallen over dead from the shock. I know that. Bodies lying all over the factory floor.

Somewhere along during the war the man who owned this factory and his son were given a commendation from the Canadian government because of their valuable contribution to the nation's war effort."

———————————— • ————————————

I Was A Bunkhouse Man

"My name is Per Thornsteinson. A Swede, Dane, Norvaygan, whatever you want. On the books I was Steinson, because a railroad contractor's clerk cut off the Thorn. Didn't have space on the form, I guess. I'm between 80 and 85 and that's the best I can tell you because in those days a birth certificate didn't cut much ice at all. You became what you wanted to be. If I didn't have this Swede accent my name could be Joe Bachinski or Antonio Berelli, two of my friends long ago.

I was a bunkhouse man. Never heard of it, did you? A bunkhouse man. Navvies. Railroad work. Construction. Never hear that term any more, navvies. It meant a construction worker, work your ass right off but we, the Joe Bachinskis and the Antonio Berellis and myself, we built a lot of the railroads. North of Lake Superior. Hudson's Bay. Alberta Northern. If I told you how much a day we made you wouldn't believe it.

Things got tougher in the late Twenties, and it was just us, the old timers who could go 12 hours a day with only Sunday off, who were getting the work, but by 1931 or so, and I was a foreman then, the pay was dropping. A dollar a day was pretty good, and three bucks was clover. Rain in the desert. Not too many got that, and you had to be doing real complicated work, in a mine, or running a machine, maybe on the trestles, which is tricky stuff. There were not too many men who could handle this hard work because it wasn't like farming, farm labour, because you had to keep up. The goddamned contractors would even hire pacers, guys with no more brains than a keg of nails, but they could work and you had to stay with them. Same thing in the vegetable and tobacco fields, they'd bring in a pacer, a knothead, and you stayed with him or you died. There was a lot of dying in those fields, guys who just didn't have the strength.

Everybody was taken advantage of. Everybody. The meanest men were the contractors. The commissary, the war chest. You're 30 miles from the nearest store so the contractor is the store. Mitts you need, three bucks. A dollar and a half in town. Boots. Six dollars. Four dollars in town. Even tobacco had a boost-up. The only thing they didn't screw you on was mail, and that was government and if the contractor, or usually the sub-contractor, if he fell down on that he might find he had no working force after the next weekend.

Food was poor. The usual, of course, beans, salt pork, salt cod. Jesus, salt cod! Ugh! Even a Scandihoovian couldn't take that. Bread, strawberry jam. Lots of tea. Some contractors thought they could keep us going on bread, jam and tea.

We had one thing in common, I guess. No kin. Family all lost and gone. Homeless men. Some of us would work from spring break-up to Thanksgiving and then head south, $100 in our pocket if we were damn lucky. Oh, it would be closer to $40 or $50. Down into the American South, or maybe as far as Mexico, or just Vancouver. We would just live off the bread lines. Hoboes, they called them. I usually worked through winter with two weeks off at Christmas and New Year's. The money was much better and, in fact, that was where you could get your $3 a day and much better food, and the contractor had to keep the bunkhouses warm to hold the men. As a matter of statement, the winter men were a much better class of worker and man, more reliable, willing to work together.

The Swedes – and all Scandihoovians kind of had the nickname 'Swedes' – I would say they were the best, the kind who got up to foreman and sometimes superintendent and sometimes even sub-contracting. The whole system sort of broke down during the Second World War. It couldn't last, not under those conditions and at those wages. No, it couldn't last."

———————————— • ————————————

An Objectionable Little Creep

"Yes, I'll tell you a story. After I got out of Commercial College there just weren't any jobs for a girl with no experience. Absolutely none. There wasn't such a job in all of Edmonton, I would say. A friend of my mother, my father had died, said he knew a girl who was leaving her job as a cook in a small restaurant, a four o'clock to 11 p.m. job, and the owner didn't know she was leaving yet, and he gave me the name.

I bustled down there next morning, no, that's wrong, I went that very night and saw the girl who had the job. It wasn't a restaurant, the way we think of one now. It was a hole in the wall on a street that runs north and south across Jasper. Oh well, never mind. I told this girl who had sent me and she said yes, she was leaving and was giving her notice the next day when she went in. She asked if I wanted to know what it was like, the routine, the boss, that sort of stuff, but something in her voice told me I didn't want to know. I said no thanks, if I got the job I'd find out for myself, and that gives you an idea how much I needed the job.

Next afternoon I saw the owner and my timing was perfect because he was boiling mad and had just fired the other girl, just like that, get out, and there I was, a better cook than most 19-year-olds, fairly pleasant looking and a very, very good Scots name which made me respectable. McIntyre. He hired me on the spot, a dollar a day, and my supper, and showed me how to work the till and waved up where the menu was printed on the wall. The stuff was all there, hamburger, wieners, bacon, eggs, sauerkraut, cheese, bread, beans, tomatoes, you know. Just a one-armed joint. He said he always checked the till at four o'clock and at 11.30 and I was never to leave, never to close up until he'd checked out the receipts. He'd take the money and leave a float of about $4 for the opening-up man.

This owner, and I should say he could have been Greek or Syrian, something like that, smooth, olive and oily skin, a most objectionable little creep, he lived with his wife and kids in an apartment up above. I wouldn't have been surprised if he had owned the building too. Hamburgers were a nickel, milk whips were a nickel, coffee was a nickel. The highest thing we had, I guess, was spaghetti or beans on toast with coffee, 15 cents. But he still made money because he had about 15 stools and four booths and, my God, he paid his help nothing and you were running at the dead gallop half the time. He did well in that flea joint, I'd say.

The first night he stayed with me on and off, showing me the ropes. The second night he came down at 11.30, checked me out and even counted the meat patties in the fridge so the day man wouldn't be pulling a fast one. Then he called me into the little storeroom in the back and pushed me against the wall and lifted my dress and pulled down my panties and there it was, there, just as calmly as I'm telling you now, he shoved it into me. It wasn't my first time, I'll admit, but I've never been more surprised in all my life. In fact, since that day I can't really say anything has ever surprised me all that much. There it was, rape, whichever way you like it, and I stood there and took it. He was out in a few seconds, over with. He said to get myself decent and walked out and I followed, and he said, well, that was part of the job. That's what he said, getting screwed was part of the job.

Then he opened his wallet and handed me a dollar and that was my pay for my shift, but I didn't know whether he was paying me a dollar for screwing me and I was working for him seven hours for nothing, and of course, as I've laughed a lot about it since, that made me a whore. Or was he paying me for my seven hours, this dollar, and I was opening up for him because I thought he was kind and generous and trustworthy? Something to think about.

I never said anything, that's how badly my family needed the money. It kept us alive. My poor mother, she would have died.

There's more, of course. Isn't there always? About a week later Janet, that was the first waitress, the one who got fired, she came in and asked, 'Is he?' and I just shrugged my shoulders and nodded. She said okay, now here's what you do, and told me how to beat him. You buy your own hamburger, your own buns, about 15 cents would buy enough for ten hamburgers, and you sneak them in when you start work and during the evening you use what you've brought in and that never gets into the till. That gets into your pocket. There was no way Numbnuts was ever going to find out, only if he stood over the till for seven hours and he never showed his face until 11.30 for his bang-bang. I worked Monday through Friday and he closed the place down at four Saturday and all day Sunday, so you might say I had total control. First I was taking an extra $1.30 or so home each night and then I got that up to about two bucks because I was a happy-go-lucky little tyke and if a guy ate one burger, I could usually smile and kid him into another. That kind of stuff.

Oh, I could have made a real nice living but I quit after six months and went off to a better job in a better restaurant because no matter how often he took me into the back storeroom, to me he was just a vile and repulsive and slimy man. A really awful person."

———————————————— • ————————————————

On The Rockpile

"My wife and I were married in Halifax in 1927 and life there even then was intolerable. I had no job and she worked as a waitress 12 hours a day for $2 and then she lost even that because of kidney trouble and when the big Canadian depression moved in on the usual Maritime hard times, well, that pretty well finished off a lot of people.

Civil servants were okay and there was always some shipyard repair work but it was a case of who you knew, not what you knew, and I was closed out of the shipyard, and the fishing jobs all went to friends and friends of friends, and we were pretty bad off. We both had been raised on farms and I can't ever remember anybody starving on the land so we walked out of Halifax one spring day. I would put it about 1931.

A fellow in a truck picked us up and he offered us a job. This was the set-up and remember, we jumped at it. We'd get a house, and not a bad house. I could cut wood from his wood lot, do the chores, help with the haying. In other words I was a hired man. Eleanor, she's been dead since 1954, was the cook, the housekeeper. We got milk and meat and we could keep a pig or two and there was a vegetable garden he wasn't using. He was a bachelor. From May to end September I would get $40 a month which was real good wages. The rest of the year, nothing. I worked for the roof over our heads and Eleanor got nothing. She got nothing the year round. We came as a package so to speak, but it still wasn't too bad. Part of the deal was no farm work except milking on Sunday, feeding the stock, and one day off a week to go to town. That was okay, but if you ask me that two people worked year round, and hard work sometimes, for $20 a month I'd have to say yes. Our first boy came along in '32.

My real trade was meat cutter and I'd use that day off to work at it because there was always somebody around, or in town, who was slaughtering, and the word got around that I was a good meat cutter. A lot of people, even in towns, raised their own meat and in this way in about four years I was able to save about $400. That was a fair amount of money in those days, to be able to put your hand in your pocket and pull out that red bank book and show a balance over $400, but remember that money meant walking many a long mile with my meat cutting tools and I always suspected my employer had figured I had done too shrewd a trade when I got that extra day out of him. I always felt he resented it, but he knew he still had a good thing in Eleanor and me and so he let it stand. It wasn't too bad an arrangement, as it stood.

Until. Yes, until. We'd got the feel of the land again and every man wants land to work, his own acres to walk over at dusk, and I did and there was a tax sale of 98 acres not too far away. I figured I could work it after work, after chores were done at the place and on Wednesdays and Sundays, so I went to the government agent and I asked what he thought it would go for. It was a sealed bid. He hemmed and hawed and said it was not much and did I know it had gone back to turf and weeds and that the buildings were in bad shape. My God, man, I had been over there so much I could have told him how many nails were needed to put the house back into any sort of shape and he took out a piece of paper and wrote a figure on it and folded it and handed it to me. When I got out I looked at the paper and it said '$300.' That was $3 an acre for what really was raw land. Not bush land, more like prairie land. I was game and in went my sealed bid for $300 and, and this is the way fate plays her little games on you – I was the only bidder. It could have been mine for $200 or $150. I think $150 was the reserve price, but so badly did I want that chunk of land that I felt everybody else would be slavering after it, like damn land-grabbers.

So we had 98 acres and I needed some of it ploughed and I went to the man I worked for and asked to borrow a four horse team and plough and he said no. I couldn't have been more shocked. Thirty acres I wanted done and he said he'd do it but it would cost $4 an acre. Four dollars an acre, remember, when the land cost only three. That was a shocker but the wife and two boys, we'd had another son, they were all set to move down the road, rough as it was going to be. I said no thanks and hunted around but there was nobody who would do it. If I could have found someone with a big tractor I'd have jumped at him but it didn't work out that way and it was late May so I had to swallow my pride and go back to the boss and he did the job. It was just light covering, almost a heavy, heavy mulch but it had to be ploughed and no two ways about it. Well, I signed a paper, a note, saying I'd pay it back, the $120. I didn't read the paper. I admit that.

When he finished, he said, 'Well, farmer, you can start work tomorrow. I want that field cleared off as soon as I can.' I asked what field, and he said the one over by the deer salt lick and swamp and I asked him what the hell he was talking about because I sure didn't know. He said hadn't I read my copy of the deal to plough my 30 acres? He said it said payment would be in cash, a lump sum upon completion of the job or, failing that, the debt could be worked off by labour. Now I knew the field he meant. We called it the rockpile and it was just that. Rocks in it like mushrooms after a spring rain, rocks everywhere. Some fields are like that. One will have thousands of rocks coming to the surface all the time and half a mile away the ground is clean.

He asked if I could pay. Of course I couldn't pay and I couldn't give part payment because it said payment in full and I just had $100, less than that, and I needed it to buy seed and rent a seeder and a team and get tools and other things. So we were stuck. At his terms. We'd pick rocks, the wife and I, a thing I had refused to do when I worked for him because that isn't white man's labour.

Do you know what that bastard said? Forty years later I can still hear him and I can still hate him. He said I would get 60 cents a day and if my wife wanted she could earn 30 cents a day. Well, there went that year. It was pick rocks or lose our little place. He didn't want the farm, no sir, but he wanted to make me suffer and he did. That whole year. I planted my 30 acres. A kind neighbour loaned me a team and some rye seed and potato starters and we worked on Sundays and after six at night and kept things going somehow. Eleanor's niece came down from Sydney to baby-sit and we worked 10 hours a day in his fields. If you figure it out, that's 6 cents an hour for me and three for Eleanor. If a man was ever tormented that summer it was me.

One night I went up there to kill him. Yes, to kill him, and I wound up sticking my knife through the jugular vein of his pedigreed bull. The poor beast. It knew me and let me walk right up to it and it died throwing up big gobs of blood, coughing them up. That was an awful thing to do.

I should have gone to court over that contract, the agreement I made, but in those days people had a much wider respect for the contract, the word or handshake was everything and the written thing was everything again. We also felt that lawyers and judges and bankers and wealthy people were working together against us, and there are a lot of people who think that today, but it was much stronger then. I was a populist by politics, and I felt I didn't have a chance. Of course, today that agreement would have been thrown hell and gone out. In jig time.

It took us well into September to clear off that debt, well into September as I recall and it was only a man in the village who told me that if I didn't get a quit claim, I still owed the debt. I went over to the big house and saw this farmer and asked for the settlement paper and he wasn't going to give it to me. He said my lawyer should see his lawyer. He knew I didn't have no lawyer, he well knew that. I did what they do in books, I counted to ten and then I took this big jack knife out of my pocket and I sort of bounced it up and down in my palm. I didn't open it, but I said, oh, I said it so quietly in case his cook was listening, 'Too bad about your prize bull, wasn't it, getting its throat cut and all.' He just looked at me for a few seconds and then at the knife and then he went over to the desk and he wrote out the settlement thing and gave it to me and said, 'God damn you, get out' and then he said, 'I'll get you if it's the last thing I ever do,' and I said, 'No, you won't, Mr. McDonald, because you're in more trouble than any three men should have. You've got me for an enemy.'"

———————————— • ————————————

Hard Times Killed My Man

"The coal killed my man. Just as sure as if he'd been on the field of battle, through shot and shell. He worked for a coal company, first in Winnipeg and then we came to Toronto where my relatives were. This was 1935. Hard times, I assure you. Nobody wants them again. Why my husband couldn't do anything else but haul coal I will never know.

You had this truck. In Winnipeg it was painted yellow and it had a box and you loaded it with these sacks with bulky coal, it would stick out everywhere and push into his back, and then you drove to the house which wanted the coal and you carried each sack to the chute. My man used to say each sack weighed 125 pounds, 16 to the ton, and you parked in the lane and it was a 60 foot walk to the chute and you had to make your own path and the snow always was two feet deep. When you're hauling coal, what else have you to think about. He could count to 16, all right.

Home after dark, maybe seven or eight loads on an ordinary day, and he got $2.50 a day. His pay packet on Saturday night was $15. About 60 a month for the hardest work one man ever ordered another man to do. He'd come home and I'd say, 'You look like a coal man,' because his face would be black with dust and he'd say, if he had the strength, 'No, I look like a whipped nigger.'

He would be strong at the start of winter because in summer they just hauled ice and that was simple, easy, and the pay was the same. Ice door to door was a vacation. But you could just see him running down in winter. How many's the time, oh hundreds, that he has just lain down on the kitchen floor and I'd be taking off his wool jacket and pants and one of the kids would be working away on his boots. The dinner would be steaming on the table and the dear man would say, 'Eat, it'll get cold.' Sometimes he'd have a bowl of vegetable soup and some bread and then go to bed and sleep right through, not a movement, not a whisper until next morning. Ten, eleven hours of the sleep of the dead.

How could there be a man-wife relationship that way? The man never saw his children. He slept all day Sunday, or just stared out the window. He never cursed. By God, I did though. I used to go to church and I'd curse Mr. Bennett, the prime minister, and then when he was out, I'd curse King, the new one.

In 1939 my man fell and with this load of coal on his back something snapped. The doctor said he couldn't do hard work again, so the company hemmed and hawed and finally put him in as a checker. He weighed the trucks and filled out cards, but it was no use. He just kept going down and down and although he was only 33, the army wouldn't have him. He wanted to go, for his country. His own country didn't want him. Bad back. They had a name that long *(she holds her arms out wide)* for what he had, and that was it. He died next year. That's how the hard times destroyed my man. And me."

———————————— • ————————————

All The Loopholes

"There were a lot of small garment plants in or near the edge of downtown Toronto, 10, 20 or 40 workers and many doing special piece work for the big companies. Just little joints and the owners were usually a family with poppa as president and momma as accountant and the sons and daughters as managers or foremen, the ones who made these sweat shops go.

Women. They employed women. Those who might have come in off the farms, towns, northern Quebec and Ontario. The province had set a minimum wage law for women at $12.50 a week. Now remember, that's a week. What's a week? How long is a piece of string? That week could be

48 hours to 70 hours, whatever these people figured they could get away with. They knew all the loopholes.

I forgot what they were, but they could pay a woman $8 or $9 a week, which was way under the minimum wage. There were ways of going around it. There were lawyers for these owners who just worked looking for these holes.

So a woman complains, the owner says you want your job? Your husband is out of work, and aren't the kids hungry? Okay, you go to the minimum wage board and tell them you are only working so many hours and that's all there is, you see what I'm saying, and the board will make up the difference between say $8 and the $12.50. They'd do it, too.

Well, then what do we have? We have the government subsidizing the garment shop owner and he is still selling his product at the same price and you, the customer, are still buying it at that price and you, the customer, you're also paying taxes so you are subsidizing that factory owner. A racket, eh? Sure, there were dozens of them. Everywhere. If you weren't trying to screw the government, the employee and the customer, then you were a schmuck. You know what a schmuck is? That's a guy who ain't smart. Like us."

—————————— • ——————————

What Is A Day's Work?

"Wages never was much good in B.C. I don't care what others say. I can't remember no things getting good. Nobody else I know too. It was just hard work and most of us on the river worked at day labour. That's all there was. There was a mill down on the river across from New Westminster and you got $1 a day for stacking heavy shingle blocks. A day could mean five hours or 15 hours. The day meant as long as the company needed you. It could mean 24 hours straight, and sometimes it was. If there was shingles to handle, you stayed because you got paid at the end of each day and if you left, then you was blackballed. It was just about the only mill working on the Fraser around there, so what could you do?

One day an organizer joined the crew and he told us we was working worse than anyone in Canada. We said we knew that. The foreman heard us talking and he said if we walked off, he would have another gang on the job by that afternoon, or next morning. We didn't quit, or strike or wildcat or do nothing. Just kept piling those blocks. You didn't have time to do a thing. If you got off, paid off about seven o'clock, then you went home and fell into bed, and the wife used to take off my shoes and socks because I had fallen asleep. Out. Then about midnight I'd usually wake and she'd be sitting up, mending or sewing or something, and she'd feed me a little supper and I'd fall asleep again until six in the morning. Day after day. That wasn't living. That wasn't even existing."

———————— • ————————

Just A Good Bunch Of Lads

"I had a dandy job with the Canadian National at Moncton. It was the head-quarters for the Eastern Region between Montreal and Halifax then. Not now, but then. I was considered one of their bright lads, going places and I did later, but mind you, I worked hard. This is being taped, isn't it? Okay, no swearing.

There was sort of an informal group, a bunch of us, management at a lower level than plant superintendent or what have you and we used to meet and drink a bit and play poker or go fishing up on the Miramichi or sometimes deer hunting and it was a good bunch to belong to and I enjoyed it. Just a good bunch of lads. All reaching for the next rung of the ladder, you understand?

But what I saw in the first couple of years of the Thirties would curl your hair. Here were men I had fished with and gambled with, and we'd be sitting around and one would say something like, 'Well, Bert, I'm going to trim off some more fat this week.' This might have been a foundry or a sawmill. Bert would ask how many, and the other fellow would say five, three, six, what-ever, and Bert would say, 'Okay, Harry, if you can, I'll wait a week and match you,' or he'd say, 'That's the way you see it, eh? Okay, let me know if there's a ruckus, and if not, I'll do the same.' This type of thing went on, week after week, and I saw maybe 15 or 20 of my good friends dealing in men's lives, their wives' lives, the very futures of the children, maybe two dozen chil-dren, and doing it just like they were raising each other at stud poker. This was all, to me, disgusting but I could not say anything, and I was not included in this sort of thing because I was with the railroad – the running trades and roundhouse and the telegraphers, they were all union – but I was there and I listened.

I guess you could say I saw many hundreds of men's lives destroyed, and if I had said once, 'You rotten sons of bitches,' then I would have been out. There was no club, no constitution, no blackballing, but I would have been out nevertheless and I don't think I was a coward not to speak out. There was just nothing I could do.

Some guy in lumbering would say, 'I'm asking my sawyers to take an eight percent cut.' He meant he was *telling* them they would be cut eight percent. No ifs, ands or buts. No union, so bugger you. If it worked out – and there was no such thing as work-to-rule and that in those days, not really – then the next guy would do it and in a month, the whole industry in southern New Brunswick would have sawyers making less a shift, and in another month, that rate would be standard throughout the Maritimes. See how easy it worked?

This club, and it really wasn't a club and few, I suspect, ever knew of its existence, it was an owners' club, but the owners never attended. It was done by their bright young men, men of 35 and 40 like me, and if you wanted confirmation of this, then you'd be looking today for old men of 75 or so. Like me. And there are darn few around.

It was a system, or call it a management device, which worked perfectly. The workers had no union. They were a pretty beaten-down lot, you see. Anyway, things just kept going down, a bit by bit thing, you understand, but these jolly lads I knew greased the skids. And you know, to this day, I sometimes wonder if they knew *they* were being used, manipulated, up and down like jumping jacks by their own bosses. They were so eager to get ahead, move one more step up, that they probably didn't think so, and I know they weren't thinking of the mass misery they caused. You know, looking back, it was quite incredible. I wonder if people will believe this?"

When the Depression hit Canada, the first people to suffer were the poor. Husbands were laid off, money became scarce, and families began to fall behind with their rent payments. Then evictions, like this one in a slum district of Montreal, followed promptly.

[National Archives of Canada]

When the people in this Toronto house were threatened with eviction, the neighbours turned out in force to prevent it.

[*Toronto Sun*]

These unemployed Toronto men soon found that they had to become transients to have any hope of finding work.

[National Archives of Canada]

At the other end of the country, in Vancouver, a large number of men found themselves without jobs. They started to drift eastward.

[Vancouver Public Library/1299]

The only way for a penniless man to get across the country was to jump on a freight train.

[Glenbow Archives/NC-6-12955(b)]

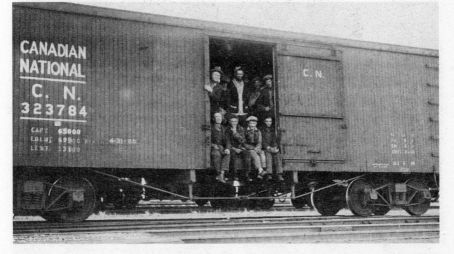

If you could avoid the railroad "bulls" and could find an empty car to travel inside—not on top, or clinging to the rods underneath—you were really in luck.

[Glenbow Archives/NC-6-12955(e)]

Soon hoboes of all ages became a common sight in Canada as they drifted to and fro across the country in a hopeless search for work.

[Glenbow Archives/NC-6-12955(j) (left), NC-6-12955(c) (bottom)]

These unemployed drifters formed a sort of floating community. They gathered just outside the main towns on the railroad in informal camps known as "jungles."

A hoboes' jungle on the outskirts of Toronto.

[*Toronto Sun*]

Housekeeping in the jungle.

[*Toronto Sun*]

Occasionally the drifting paid off. These men are bound for temporary work in the tobacco fields of Southern Ontario.

[*Toronto Star*]

But even seasonal jobs were scarce, and more often the hoboes drifted on from jungle to soup kitchen and back again. Here hundreds of men line up for a meal at the famous Port Arthur soup kitchen.

[*Toronto Star*]

The interior of the Edmonton soup kitchen in 1933.

[Glenbow Archives/ND-3-6523(b)]

On a vacant lot in Vancouver unemployed men of all ages line up at a soup kitchen. The man on the left is about to receive a potato. In the background ladies are arriving to supervise the good works.

[Vancouver Public Library/12748]

CHAPTER TWELVE

Hoboes – Coming From Nowhere, Going Nowhere

Brother Meets Brother . . . The Lowdown On Jungles . . . The Science of Riding The Rods . . . The Wonderful Omelette . . . Mrs. Collins' Kitchen . . . The Doctor Named Lindsay . . . Just Moving On . . . The Killing of A Hobo . . . Honolulu City . . . There Were Tricks . . . Meet Mother Melville . . . The Soup Kitchen Line-up . . . Going Absolutely Nowhere . . . The Mouth Organ Symphony.

———————————————— • ————————————————

Riding The Rods is a hobo term, but it is now synonymous with The Depression, especially in Western Canada. In those days thousands of men rode on top of freight cars, inside them and sometimes even went through the bone-jarring and mind-searing ride on the long rods underneath the cars. Usually they were coming from nowhere and going nowhere.

Why did they do it? Some left home because their belly was just another one to feed in a home without enough food for the little ones. Some fathers just quit because they could no longer take the shame of hanging around the house any more. Some, usually the younger ones, sought adventure, to see the Rockies or the Pacific Ocean or Montreal. Others just found their natural bent in wandering. And some were thieves running from the law and finding anonymity in the large masses of men moving about.

Of course, the rationale for most was that they wanted to find jobs, but they quickly learned that there were no jobs. So they just kept travelling around, hoping for something.

———————————————— • ————————————————

Brother Meets Brother

"She's a sunny morning and we've got our shirts off, sitting on top of a boxcar in a hole just east of Calgary and this other freight from Vancouver comes along to go by us and she stops and there is my kid brother Billy sitting large as life and twice as ugly not six feet from me.

I say, 'Hi Billy, how's the folks?' and he says, 'I don't know, haven't seen 'em for some time,' and he says, 'Where you headed?' and I told him I was going into the Okanagan Valley for the summer and he gets up and says, 'I just came from the Coast but it's pretty country through there so I'll go along back with you. Somebody's got to look after you,' and he jumps across, with hardly a thought, turning right around the way he'd come.

That's the way we were them days, in the Thirties. Coming from nowhere, going nowhere. Like gypsies."

———————————— • ————————————

The Lowdown On Jungles

"What was a jungle like? Well, you could say it was home to the hobo. Some writers screwy enough to even think of us called us 'The Knights of the Road.' That's right, 'Knights.' We were just about the farthest thing a knight ever was, I can tell you that. We didn't dress any better than I am now. *(He was filthy, a real Skid Roader.)*

Well, the jungle was where the hoboes gathered, and it was a place where the cops didn't bother you. It was a place like the Skid Road here where they know you'll be if they ever want you, if you're still alive and in town. Why do you think towns had Red Light Districts? Because it was a place where the cops could keep an eye on the madams and the girls and the pimps, the gamblers and the bad eggs. Same with us.

Now there used to be a lot of jungles, one, two, three right on False Creek and down on the flats and out by New Westminster and another at Port Moody where we sometimes used to hop off. That's when the bulls were laying for us. Chilliwack had one, and Kamloops, quite a big one. One at Golden, the people were pretty good there, always a handout of some kind if you wanted to split a bit of wood or fill up the reservoir in the lady's stove or dig a bit of garden. Calgary had one outside the Ogden Yards. A couple by the river. Moose Jaw, Regina, a few around Winnipeg, like at Transcona and there was a place near the grain elevators and the rats were thick and that's where I saw a fellow roasting rats on a stick once.

I told him I didn't think that was quite right and he said rats were clean, look at the food they ate, good grain, and they were delicious meat. He offered me some, but there just wasn't any way I could make myself try it. If he hadn't mentioned it, well, then it would have been different because, as I recall, I was hungry.

Yes, that's right. I have an university education. It never did me any good because when I stepped out of those hallowed halls, I put my foot into about two feet of nice and sticky Depression mud and I never pulled loose. University of Alberta, class of '30. Some prominent men in that class.

Well now, about the jungle. You'd find them easily at night, spring, fall, summer because of the fires. Cooking fires mainly. On the road, riding the rods those days, everybody was a great talker. We sure as hell knew what was wrong with the country. If Bennett had stepped down and said, 'Ok, boys, it's your round,' why, there would have been ten thousand takers, and each one would have done just as badly as R.B. did.

I've seen a train passing through Headingly going west and it would be black with men, hundreds of them, all heading west looking for work, just heading west looking for a dollar a day, and that train would pass another, going east, you understand, and it would be black with men, heading into Winnipeg and on out the other side, and guess what they were doing. Heading east, looking for work. A dollar a day.

It was the craziest of times. From R. B. Bennett down to the lowest of the low, some bohunk smelling of garlic and not knowing a word of English, why we were all in one huge lunatic asylum. We'd meet in the jungles, and the guys, well, say it was Kamloops, the guys who had just come in from the Coast they'd say there wasn't a job of any kind to be had. Ab-so-lute-ly zero. And the ones who had just come in from Calgary, they'd be waiting for a night freight to the Coast and they'd say things like, 'Is that so,' or 'Yeah, things are tough' or some such foolery and when the freight came along, there they would be, ready to hop her and on to Vancouver. You'd say why, why go there when there is nothing doing and they would say something like they had a buddy they'd promised to meet at such and such a place. Aimless. Just wandering. Going nowhere.

Those jungles. There was always a stew pot going, one of those gallon tomato tins. Somebody'd throw in some meat. Carrot tops. Spuds. Spinach. Handful of flour. Salt. We always carried our own salt, a big spoon, a knife, and a shingle or can would do for a plate. But salt and a spoon, everyone had that. It wasn't the Royal Saskatchewan but there were times when it was so good I can still taste it. All over the jungle, there'd be fires, oh, maybe six or eight, and a few guys around each, dipping in to the mulligan and telling each other how they'd run the country.

Look, I've got to go and meet a fellow."

The Science Of Riding The Rods

"You didn't just jump on a boxcar and away you went. No sirree. There was science in it, you had to calculate. In those years I saw too many bodies, guys with bodies cut in two, legs off, head off, to think anybody could hop a freight. I must have seen eight or 10 dead guys in those days.

First, the train was moving if you were leaving a city because the yard bulls patrolled pretty hard and unless it was black dark you couldn't get in. After they began to bear down on the Canada Railway Act that is, in '35. So the train was rolling.

Usually you didn't have a packsack because you needed your speed and timing and a turkey, a bed roll, got in your way. Carry stuff in your pocket, and your extra clothes you wore. Like two suits and over them, a sweater and overalls. Good shoes slung around your neck. That way.

If you could get inside a boxcar then you were on Easy Street, but mostly you rode on top. Not many rode the rods, that was hanging like a bat to the rods which slung under the car and it was hell, sheer hell every mile of the way. Mostly the cars were full, or empty but locked, so you rode on top. On a sunny spring day it was joyful but in fall, raining, snow, it was bad and of course, something awful had to be happening to you if you rode on top in winter. There was a quick way to die.

Some of the guys could judge speed, right to the button, like 20, 15, 30 or so. You had to be able to run a quarter of the speed of the train, so running on slippery grade, sloping gravel, you'd never try to swing on a train going faster than 30. That's where a lot of the guys never made it, catching on, bumping along, letting go and then sausage meat. You ran along as fast as you could and when you were going your best lick and the train was whizzing by you figured how fast it was going and when one car went by then you got ready for the next, and as it went by you jumped for the ladder and your own speed would help you swing up. Then you'd lickety split up to the top and lie flat for a few miles and then nobody would bother you. All the bothering was done in the yards, anyway.

The best thing was to travel the branch lines. The trains were going the same place eventually but they weren't going as fast and if you dropped off at a little town, chances were they didn't see many drifters in that town and the food and hand-outs were much better, and besides there weren't railroad cops. Less likely, anyway.

Most of the riding was done in the prairies and the boys used to gang up on Vancouver in the winter, the climate, and there was some riding down to Toronto but not much beyond that. Montreal, well they just seemed tougher there and in the Maritimes, everybody was leaving there anyway. One-way traffic.

You can see the need for travelling light, that swinging up and jumping off. It was a young man's business and I don't remember many old guys. The old guys starting about their forties would lie around a jungle somewhere and bum food and smokes and tell tall tales and they had nicknames, every one of them, like 'Oklahoma Slim' and 'Big Red' and 'The Winnipeg Cyclone' and 'Nanaimo Joe' and I figured they were names they gave to themselves. They were mostly a lot of real phonies."

———————————— • ————————————

The Wonderful Omelette

"I'll tell you about the famous Calgary omelette. I made it myself. There was a cutbank on the Bow, on a curve, and there was a kind of jungle there because the boys used to like to jungle up where there was willows and shelter and this was one place where you had to know it to find it. Sort of like the Glencoe Country Club of jungles. It was about five miles into Calgary and that was one place, Winnipeg and Sioux Lookout and Vancouver were others, where my dear old mother would send me mail, general delivery. So I went in and sure enough, there was a letter and I'll be damned if two one dollar bills dropped out.

I had four beers in that tiny downstairs parlour at the Palliser and then I started hiking back, and on the way I passed a little farm, oh, a few acres. There were a few out that way, in the city but still farms, and a sign said Eggs For Sale. Well, I thought half a dozen eggs would be a very pleasant way to settle the beer which had made me a little tipsy so the farmer came out and I said to give me 15 cents worth of eggs. He said, 'Fifteen cents?' and I said yes, and I'll be darned if he didn't come out with a big brown bag and he said, 'Handle it carefully. Keep one hand under it.' Well, my friend, there were four dozen eggs. Forty-eight eggs. The farmer said he only got three cents from the buyer so he sold them for four.

I asked if he had any bread. How many loaves? Five, I said, and a pound of butter. His wife came out with the loaves, five cents each and a jar of butter that she said was two pounds and I said fine, and she said she'd give me some garden stuff and took a knife and this Swiss chard stuff, I got a bunch of the leaves and half a dozen onions and while they were figuring it all out I offered 50 cents for the works, and boy, they sure grabbed it. So I guess I was over. But I took the whole kaboodle back and dug out one of those purple-enamelled washpans one of the boys had found somewhere and I made up an omelette. Try imagining it. Forty-eight eggs, about two pounds of butter, half a dozen good sized onions, sliced up chard leaves and chunks of bread. When it was over the guys just lay around gasping, and my friend, that was the most famous omelette ever made in Alberta and they are still talking about it. Barbecue dinners for the Yankee oil barons had nothing, absolutely goddamned nothing on Rupert Gill's Great Omelette of 1936. Absolutely nothing."

Mrs. Collins' Kitchen

"My mother was an angel. A woman sent from heaven above, in the bad days she ran her own soup kitchen. It wasn't much but she was doing something, and you couldn't say that for everyone.

We had this house, an old sad thing of a house, by the Canadian Pacific Railway tracks just outside the city limits of Winnipeg. And on that lot there was a garage, and in that garage she set up, I helped her, we set up a wood cook stove, a Majestic, big and black as I remember, which cost us nothing because the man next door gave it to us, and I scrounged up boards and planks and we made a table and benches. Her purpose was to feed the hungry lads as they dropped off the eastbound trains, the freights, just over our back fence and on that north end of the garage I painted 'Free Food.'

It wasn't the greatest food, just porridge and bread when we could get day old stuff and grease to spread on it and tea with lots of sugar. No milk. Mother would get up about six and it was too far to the church for mass so she'd do her bit of praying by the kitchen table while the tea kettle was boiling, and she'd have her tea and a piece of toast and then yell for me. The fellows on the freights, they always passed information back and forth about where to go and so on, and one told me once that when they saw smoke coming out of Mrs. Collins' garage chimney they knew there would be something waiting for them. All it was was porridge, but it was porridge and a half. The night before, she'd soak about three pounds of dried peas and beans in water, let them stand overnight. Then she had this huge open kettle, black iron, and she'd fill it with oatmeal and dump in the peas and beans and several handfuls of raisins and salt and in would go the boiling water and she'd stir and stir and do whatever you had to do with porridge and soon it was a big heaving mass, like you see those pictures of volcanoes with bubbles coming to the top. We needed a lot, because some days there would be as many as 60 for mother's breakfast.

Towards noon, if there was any porridge left, Mother would take it – and it was as tacky as putty then – and she'd slap it into cakes, about hamburger size, and fry them in grease and the fellows that came along after would drink the tea and eat the porridge cakes.

I often thought she could expect more of the men – and there were quite a few boys too and even the occasional girl – they might have helped split wood, or washed up. Oh, some of them did, but most of them would mumble thanks of a sort and leave. But if you consider that these were beaten people, that they were down so far they had no hope of ever looking up, then this behaviour might be okay. There were a few who helped, but not all that many."

———————————— • ————————————

The Doctor Named Lindsay

"I remember one time there was this freight pulling into Moose Jaw and this fellow must have seen the fires of the hobo jungle so he swung off and bang, smash into one of those signal lights, screaming and he was badly banged up.

Some men came running up from the jungle and one guy took charge and started ordering us around. I had been a Red Cross man in the war and I could see that this guy knew what he was doing and he could see I knew what I was doing so we worked together and we kept the guy going until the ambulance came. We got him loaded and I said he knew what he was doing and he said, 'I should, I guess. I'm a doctor.' I had to believe him because I had worked around them enough to know, and so I asked what happened.

He'd finished his internship and could not get a job so he went to this town in Saskatchewan where most of the township was on relief, about 95 percent he said, and he told the town clerk he'd be their doctor if they'd give him a house and coal and light and relief. It was a fair deal, no more than what a lot of other people were getting. They wouldn't, because he said they wouldn't believe a doctor couldn't get a good job in Saskatoon or somewhere, and if he couldn't get a job then he must have something wrong with him.

So he said to hell with it and he travelled the freights and stayed in a crummy hotel in Vancouver during the winter, and if a guy was hurt or sick, he helped him. I never saw him again. He said his name was Lindsay."

———————————————— • ————————————————

Just Moving On

"The guys who were real hoboes, and there were a few girls and women too, were hoboes long before the real Depression hit us, and they were hoboes long after it was finished. Sometimes, waiting at a crossing or seeing a freight go by along the Lougheed Highway you will occasionally see a chap riding the rails and you wonder, 'Now, did I ever know him?'

There were the professionals, who were the hoboes, and the amateurs, us, the guys from every part of Canada, and from the States too, who just didn't have jobs. I don't think you can say we were actually looking for jobs, for that commodity was in very short supply. A bit of seasonal work, harvesting on the prairies, some fruit picking, but it is fair to say there just was no work. We were just moving on, more of an adventuring life, seeing the country.

There was no use staying at home, eating food that younger brothers or sisters needed. There was no sense getting married if you hadn't a job. So you put some clothes and personal things in a bag one day and said goodbye and sometimes you didn't even say goodbye but sent a postcard from a divisional point in the next province and that was it.

You could always tell the professionals if they can be dignified by that word. First, they were dirty. Lice. Crabs. Fleas. But just plain dirty. They would wear three or so coats and three pairs of pants in summer, just so nobody would steal them before winter. If they could have worn two pairs of boots, why they would have. They always needed a shave, always a three-day beard. Never a one-day beard. That used to puzzle me.

They were rather contemptuous of anybody else. They knew all the tricks and doing 30 days was a holiday. Sometimes they used to get caught deliberately, and sometimes the civic or town authorities would truck them five miles out beyond the city limits and lay a billy club on their backsides and tell them to keep moving.

Each had their own nicknames and their own set of stories and they used to tell them around the fires in the jungles and you knew damn well they had made them up or stole them from somebody else. I've seen me in a jungle, say under the Georgia Viaduct in Vancouver, and there would be a lot of guys around the fire and somebody across the flames would be telling a story and I'd think that I heard that same story in Brandon or Winnipeg or Toronto and I'd get up, and sure enough, there would be the same hobo telling his same little pack of stories. Then somebody else would come in, picking up smoothly where the other had left off, and they could all have been written by O. Henry, the short story writer, they all had that little surprise twist at the end. In every story the teller was the hero or big shot. The joke or the trick was never on him. Never.

But all in all, they weren't bad guys. A few were homosexuals, and that was when that word was pure dynamite. No women on the road, that would be the main reason, or they would have been ostracized by their own community. They'd pick up youngsters as, well . . . as their playthings. These kids were called punks. I've seen them as young as 12 and tough as nails. Smart little thieves too. One wonders where they went to. But all in all, from what I've seen of the world, the professional hobo was not a hell of a lot different from some of the guys you can see in a labour union or in a warehouse or in an office. They knew how to survive and they could do it without any work. That's not my way but they were masters at it and they never minded passing on their knowledge. How to swing onto a freight, what cars to choose, that sort of thing.

They also had a grapevine, which was valuable because there was considerable harassment by the railroad police, the bulls as we called them, and some were very vicious men. Anyone who survived a year or so on the road, riding the freights, never had much respect or even use for policemen. That bit of authority they had, which was actually quite considerable, brought out the worst in many men. After those days it was pretty hard to have much respect for the railroads themselves. They took all and gave practically nothing.

There always seemed to be enough food if you really wanted it. Oh, I've gone for a day or so without grub but there was a certain amount of share-and-share-alike, and there were the kitchens, the soup stations, the sandwich line-ups. Winnipeg had a couple, Edmonton, Calgary. Vancouver as I recall had three. It was enough to keep you alive and besides we were all young bucks in those days. Among the amateurs, us, you didn't see all that many older men. Quite frankly, they just couldn't stand the gaff. The cold, the poor food, the tension. There was always tension, the threat of police. You might be killed dropping off the next time, and as in a war there was the tension.

Speaking of the war, when it did come along an awful lot of the guys joined up and one sergeant told me it took them weeks but he was exaggerating, but it took considerable time getting the coal dust out of some of those fellows. You see, it was steam then, coal burners, and in those tunnels in the Rockies you literally had coal dust shot into your very skins. The Connaught Tunnel and that other one, the Seven Mile, wasn't it, out of Field, B.C., and Jesus Christ, a man could suffocate in those if he was not in a car where you could shut the door. Lying on top or between cars was murder. They were always finding remains of guys who had passed out or fallen off in those tunnels."

The Killing Of A Hobo

"I saw one man kill another man one night in a jungle at Kamloops in British Columbia. It wasn't about food or money either, let me tell you.

One fellow said Roosevelt was president of the United States and another said no, it was Mr. Coolidge. One thing led to another, they always do. The Roosevelt man grabbed the other fellow and threw him and he fell and his head hit the iron arrangement we had to keep our pots over the fire. It appeared to me the iron point end went into his ear. Well anyway, it killed him. Or we thought so. Certainly 'peared dead to me.

The Roosevelt man took him up to the tracks and soon a freight came along and squished his head to nothing, so where was your evidence? I reckon 50 men saw that killing, if one saw it. To this day, that was a drunk asleep laying his head on the rail. It happened all the time and I never heard of anyone getting hanged for that. I'll freely grant you that, mister."

Honolulu City

"Honolulu City was at Kelowna, a big hobo jungle with rules and regulations and why it was called that, I don't know. Maybe Honolulu in Hawaii was supposed to be a nice place. This Honolulu had a kind of street lay-out and a sort of elected mayor and this was where the action was.

It was a good place. Quiet. Orderly. It was all pretty much sensible business, otherwise they'd have mobilized those Rocky Mountain Rangers or some other militia bunch and run them out. Why run them out though? City council at Kelowna once asked why not. The guys said, 'Okay, run us out and we'll run all over you. You won't know where we are. We'll be sleeping in your cellars, cleaning out your barns, selling your harness. You better watch out.' It was like the Red Light District. The police like the Red Light District because then they know where everybody is. Where the tough nuts were.

We could never find out what was going on. Nobody knew. Go to Toronto. The steel company at Hamilton is opening up again. You can take train loads of cattle through to Halifax if you can get to Winnipeg. You know, the same thing you must hear in these places where the kids today jungle up. There wasn't much hope. Nobody had any hope, except they hoped next year would be better. More jobs. Better food. More wages. Less obstruction by the railroad police. The town police.

Things were on a simple level. Job. Food. Money. Peace and quiet."

There Were Tricks

"Suppose you looked like a bum. I mean a real bum. Dirty, ragged, smelling, and I think you know what I mean. A lot of houses had big dogs, and often those housewives didn't have to send the dog after that kind of person. The dog had enough sense to do it himself.

There were tricks. You never went up and down a main street, or a residential street within four or five blocks of the rail yards. Never within four or five blocks of a main highway. No. Just common sense. Those people had been asked, had their doors knocked on for years, even before the Depression, when the hoboes worked the area. You went off a distance, seven or eight blocks, where they weren't sick to death of people."

Meet Mother Melville

"There was this old lady in Calgary, they called her Mother Melville, and she used to go down to the jungle on the Bow River and she'd have a purse full of envelopes. Envelopes with stamps on them and a sheet of paper inside each one and she'd go among the guys, all these guys riding the rods and she'd hand out these envelopes and say, 'Write your mother, son, please write her just a line or two. She's worried, I know.' After Mother Melville had gone through, you'd see 15 or 20 guys sitting around, passing a pencil around, writing notes home."

———————————————— • ————————————————

The Soup Kitchen Line-up

"They didn't serve at different times in these soup kitchens. Six o'clock, the Sally Ann or the nuns or the city, all at the same time and I guess I'd have done the same. That meant there was no line-up at noon and another at three, say, and a third at six. You got one line-up meal a day. Let's see. Of course it was the cheapest food going around, baloney, head cheese, cheese, sausage meat. Sometimes a small bottle of milk and on special days or if they had been given a good donation, there would be tobacco, a bag and a package of papers. At Christmas you could usually find a place which was serving a Christmas dinner and you got a cigar, a White Owl, or the makings. The city usually sprung for that, and I remember once getting a package of razor blades and a pair of socks. Fancy ones too, the kind they called MacIntosh socks, all coloured squares and that.

At the mission you would get a sermon, say 15 minutes of religion from a sky pilot but they weren't such bad fellows and then it was grub time. The Sally Ann was good in some cities and bad in others and those rosy-cheeked girls and fat young fellows in their uniforms, well, I always wondered how much actually gave a damn for God and religion and how much they cared about good clothes, the best of food, and a place to live. Joining the Sally Ann must have been like joining the police force. Security, and not a bit danger-ous except you had to stand out on the street corners and bang that drum.

Six o'clock meant you had to be there by four or four thirty and you got to know the guys. Everybody was in that line. Just look at the old pictures. They're all there. Young Canada and old Canada. I just wonder where they are now. Of course, the war swallowed up a hell of a lot of them and you know, they were a pretty bright lot. Some fellows I used to stand with, and it was almost like having reserved seats at a football game today because every-one had their place. A lot used to practically live at the public library. They did a lot of reading and had read a lot too. There were engineers, and one doctor who had a booze problem, and jewellers, and accountants, and a couple of guys who used to play hockey professionally. There were winos but not too many, and of course, there were the kids. Sixteen, seventeen, eighteen, from Cape Breton to Vancouver Island. Just roaming about.

Someone would say that there was work in Edmonton and if you didn't click, well, the kitchen there was good. There was an old lady in Calgary, some Holy Roller type, and she fed the boys. Those line-ups were clearing houses for information right across the country. Somebody got killed falling off a train at Swift Current and a few guys might recognize him. Where the worst railway bulls were and believe me, some of those guys were bastards. That's spelled r-a-t-s. Some guys went into the mines, because they knew somebody who said there were jobs. We all lived on 90 percent hope and 10 percent I-don't-know-what.

If a guy had a shot at a job we'd go over to the public toilet at Main and Hastings, about five of us, and one guy would give up his shoes because they were good, and another his suit if it fitted. Shirt. Tie. Fifteen cents for a hair cut. So this guy could look presentable, yeah, presentable so he could stand in line for four hours and get a job at $6 a week. Oh, well, better than nothing.

Single guys who couldn't establish residency in Vancouver, well they got nothing. Just back-of-the-hand charity or Matthew-Mark-Luke-and-John sandwiches. That's what we called the lunch at one mission. They even sermonized at us while we stood around eating their sandwich and drinking their coffee. Ever heard of saltpetre? They put it in the coffee so we wouldn't rush out into the streets and rape all the women."

———————————— • ————————————

Going Absolutely Nowhere

"Our farm was just east of Chilliwack, land that is now homes, part of the city. When I was 19 I rented a fair chunk of acreage down the road and began farming myself. Every morning I'd cycle down to my land and I had two dogs with me and I'd send them into the barn first thing to rout out any hoboes. The track ran nearly alongside the farm. The dogs would flush out the men, often a dozen or more of them.

They were good fellows, just looking for a warm place to sleep in the hay and there wasn't much damage. A broken padlock or something. Only a few, and very few at that, caused any trouble. I remember one fellow was going to come at me with a pitchfork once, but he soon dropped the idea. I couldn't offer them anything but they were welcome to sleep in my barn if they wanted.

What never ceased to amaze me were these men, going nowhere, up and down the country, riding back and forth, and fairly cheerful about it all. There would be nobody around when I'd leave in the evening for home and in the morning they'd have found the place in the dark and there were often 12 or 15 or more. How they found it I don't know. The freight trains were covered with men, men just riding back and forth going absolutely nowhere."

———————————— • ————————————

The Mouth Organ Symphony

"You ever heard a symphony made up of mouth organs? No, and you never will now. I think the mouth organ is gone for good, but in the hard times, on the road, it was one of our best friends. I remember once near Hamilton about 100 of us were in the basement for a factory or something which had stopped being built because of the hard times. The country was full of basements like that.

We'd been picking fruit. I remember it was in the fall and there were about five fires going and everybody had a bit of money and was cooking stew or warming up cans of stuff and there was a good-time feeling. It got dark and soon everybody was around one big fire in the middle, about a 100 guys, I'd reckon, and everybody full of food and passing the rollings around and one guy brought out his harmonica and that's the fancy name for a mouth organ. He started to play, and Christ, that man was good, and everybody soon stopped talking.

We always used to talk about what the government was doing, and how we were being screwed and where jobs were and where we had this terrific meal, things like that. Food was always important to us. Funny, but women weren't. I guess we just didn't have the energy. Besides, there were no women.

Anyway, there was this guy with the mouth organ and soon another guy brought one out and another until there were about ten. Now, remember, I guess not two of these guys had ever played together before. But it was as if they had played together for years, and remember you can buy a harmonica for a lot of money or a cheap one for a buck or two, but when they were all together quality or price didn't mean a hoot. I guess you could say they were inspired, and that's why I asked if you had ever heard a symphony of mouth organs.

They played for about two hours, and I guess every guy there was thinking of home, of mother, sweethearts, brothers and sisters, sitting around the tree opening Christmas presents, sleigh rides, the way the creek made a loop and the water was warm and soft for swimming, the smell of bacon and eggs and stewed tomatoes for Sunday breakfast and walking over crisp snow with a .22 looking for rabbits with your dog running ahead, bouncing around. These were the things I was thinking about, so that's why I mention them. We were all thinking of home. The good days. The other times.

They played songs like 'Mother Macree' and 'There's A Long, Long Trail A-winding' and 'I'll Take You Home Again, Kathleen' and 'Flow Gently, Sweet Afton' and 'Girl Of My Dreams' and an awful lot of others. Some we sang, some we just kept quiet. Nobody said we'd sing one and not another. It just happened, you see. Songs, of course, you never hear today. The old songs. Good ones, I'll tell you.

That was the night when the fruit picking was over, except for some cleaning up, and so everybody went his own way next morning and I've often wondered after that night how many decided to chuck the life on the road, this moving from town to town, and go back home. If they could find it. I know I did, but I didn't go home. I just kept going and going because there was absolutely nothing at home for me. I would just have been another mouth to feed, and I would have been taking food out of the mouths of the little ones. So I just kept on going. I was 17 at the time."

CHAPTER THIRTEEN

Pride – A Commodity In Generous Supply

Sneaking Down Alleys . . . Steel In The Lad's Spine . . . Lucille, That's My Dress . . . Those Jones People . . . White Gift Sunday . . . Nobody Ever Thanked Me . . . Impetigo! My God! . . . For The Dog . . . Two Or Three Lousy Dollars . . . A Loaf Of Bread . . . The Shame Of Suicide . . . One Grey Blanket . . . Days In The Library . . . Gerry And The Benjamins . . . The White Wedding Dress . . . Just Tired Of Waiting.

———————————— • ————————————

They never took a dime in relief or a tin plate of stew from a soup kitchen, nor a single apple from an Ontario charity train – and they'd had to sell precious seed wheat to pay their taxes.

It's called pride, Depression pride.

To paraphrase a dozen conversations I heard: "Why should we take stuff to get by? My people came from Antigonish (or Sarnia or Ayrshire or Minneapolis) and they had tough times, but they never asked for nothing. They stood on their own two feet, and my wife and I did the same thing."

This was true pride speaking, but as this chapter will show, there also was stubborn pride, which translated into plain old pigheadedness. There seemed to be plenty of both kinds around in those years, and it seemed to help most people to dig in and hold on, revealing surprising inner strength.

One woman was greatly surprised when I asked her about the Depression because "that's all old stuff." But when she got talking, her words tumbled out far behind her thoughts and, like an old soldier contemptuous of a non-combatant, she pointed to a house down the road and said, "They never paint that house. Pigs and chickens loose in the yard. The boy's in prison and Lord knows where the two girls ended up. What can you expect? They were on relief during The Thirties. They were never up to much."

I said many people were on relief through no fault of their own but she rebuffed me, saying, "It shows now. They were never up to much."

Sneaking Down Alleys

"The winter I was 14, that was my year, the time when it was my turn to get the supplies.

We were on relief, the dole, you see, and they gave out tickets, the vouchers, and you took them to the grocery store, the one they told you to go to and you gave them the vouchers and they gave you what you were supposed to get. And so once a week I would get up about six in the morning and get the empty kerosene can and the can for the molasses and it was my job to go to the store in the village.

You must remember, for proud people – and my mother was proud but my father was the proudest man I know, I will *ever* know – the relief was the most terrible thing. It was truly the end of everything. It was, truly. This was instilled in me.

I would take the cans, both of them, and the vouchers and I would go out, and this would be in the winter at that time and it was pitch black, but I would still take the back alleys and pray to God that nobody would see me because if they saw me taking the two cans to the store people would know. It was so shameful. Yes, the store opened about 6.30 in those days and stayed open late. Those poor clerks. They worked 14 hours or so for nothing.

Once I made it safely to the store I was all right because they knew we were on relief so it didn't matter, and they delivered to the houses so nobody would know. It was such a shameful thing.

On the morning I was to go to the store I could hardly sleep the night before and my stomach would be churning, sickness, nausea, and even when I think of it now there is that feeling. That is what it was to have a Scots Presbyterian upbringing in Nova Scotia. Yes, I can feel it now. I still find it hard to talk about. Believe me."

———————————— • ————————————

Steel In The Lad's Spine

"One morning I was in the kitchen and I heard a yell and this lad was bouncing along the road on his back and an auto was high tailing it out of there. It had struck the lad, just glanced him, but he and the road had a bit of a scuffle. I took him in the house and his clothes were torn and his arms scraped but otherwise, he was okay.

He was an English lad, a fine lad, and Mrs. Bruce and I were impressed with him. Peter, he said his name was. She fed him a hearty breakfast and he had a bath and his clothes were in tatters, his shirt and pants, so she said he could swap for one of my shirts and a pair of my pants, they'd fit, and she'd throw away his torn ones. Would that be all right? Oh, it was fine, he said. In that way he'd be more presentable if a chance at a job came along. So it was done.

He left us that afternoon, no thanks, he wouldn't stay the night and he was going to walk towards Saskatoon. That was maybe 200 miles away. Maybe there was a job along the way.

The next morning close to noon the door knocked and it was this English lad, this Peter. Could he see his old shirt, please? Of course, but why? He felt in the breast pocket and undid a safety pin and now, if there wasn't three one dollar bills pinned there. He told us he'd walked about 10 hours before he stopped for some milk and sardines and there, at some little store, he had no money. So he had to walk back, another 30 miles. Sixty miles altogether and he was tuckered out. Played out. The money, he said, was all he had in the world and, in fact, he said it was the most he'd ever had at one time.

We gave him a meal and another bath and he slept almost until next morning. It was four in the morning and we heard him moving around and he said he must be off. He might be missing out on a job. I gave him an old pair of boots and two pair of socks because he was worn out of his and he got his breakfast and a lunch to carry. That and his only baggage, a razor, some soap, his towel and an old jacket.

You wonder to this day about these boys. How they made out. Pretty well, I should say. Lads like Peter had a strip of steel down their backbone, and in the few hours we knew him he always had this smile on his face."

———————————— • ————————————

Lucille, That's My Dress

"Dad had some sort of executive job with a farm implement company and you know what happened to that industry. No crops in the west, no work in the East. The plant was tied, literally, to Saskatchewan by a long cord and when that snapped, well, good bye Mr. Carter. Mom kept us going, though, and for a year I was kept on tap dancing and elocution. My God, does anybody under 35 even know what the word 'elocution' means? To me it means Shirley Temple. Mother figured I could be the next Shirley Temple. So did 150,000 other mothers across the country and 1,500,000 in the States. Shirley Temple I wasn't. A kind of gangling, shy and mousy-haired little girl I was.

Things were hard for us, but we got by. Ever have ox tail soup and carrots day after day with stale bread? Nourishing, maybe, but not gourmet fare.

Yes, clothes. There was this woman down near the city hall *(in Toronto)* and she had set up some kind of depot. Her name was Mrs. Phillipson, something like that, and I can always remember her as being tall and lean and sitting in this little shop with clothes piled every which way. Tons of clothes, it seemed like. You'd walk in and she'd wave. She always had a cigarette hanging from her lips, like a tart in an old French film. She rented this little place and she apparently had been high society once in Toronto and her rich friends brought all their children's and their own clothes to her, what they'd give to the Good Will truck anyway, and she'd sell it cheap. In a way she was doing a very real service.

When you brought up something to her, say a fine coat with fur at the collar and hardly a mark on it, she'd barely look at it and say it was a dollar. Or 50 cents. I sometimes thought these were the only prices she knew, a dollar, and 50 cents. Mother took me there often and so I was as well dressed as any kid in school. We still lived in the same house in this good district and I went to the school and you know why I hated school? Why I dreaded hearing that school bell and walking into the hall and into the class – and this went on every day from the time I was eight or nine until I was 13 or 14? I lived in dread that one of my friends – or not one of my friends – whose fathers still had good jobs and went to the cottage every summer, I dreaded that one of those girls would come up to me and say, 'Lucille, that's my dress you're wearing,' or 'Lucille, that coat you've got is the one my mother gave to the lady at the second hand store.'

I would have died, and as it was, I died a bit every day, every day I was at that school. As it turned out, we finally did move and I went to another school, but that fear never left me and I'm almost ashamed to say it, but it is still with me and I guess it will always be."

———————————— • ————————————

Those Jones People

"Too many people tried to keep face, and it's natural I guess, but it was too bad they felt that way. We lived in a nice district in London and our city wasn't hit all that hard. In fact, it was quite a good time for us because everything was so low in price, food, things for the house, and help, yes, you could get a good maid for $5 a month, some girl from Saskatchewan or the Maritimes where they were hit hard.

Once we went up to visit my sister in Toronto, and on the Saturday after we arrived we went to this party at a neighbour's. It was a fine party, I must say, and the food was good and there was liquor if you wanted it. There seemed to be quite a bit of liquor, and a small band for dancing. These people had quite a large house. When we got home my sister said the man had lost his job in an insurance company a year ago, and they had sold their bonds and their car, and their children often went hungry, just some tea and a piece of toast for breakfast. She had often, oh many times, she had fed them their lunch and they really needed it, the little beggars, but this couple had to put on a face. Two or three big parties a year, music and everything, just to keep up with the Joneses.

This was the sad thing, really, everybody knew that man and his wife were in desperate trouble financially because after all, hadn't they fed their kids lunch and even dinner at times? They were like those little Arab youngsters you see begging on the streets in the National Geographic magazines. I asked, if this was the case, why didn't someone tell them so and tell them to stop throwing these parties like they did in the old days, and my sister said, 'Oh, we wouldn't want to hurt their feelings.' Their feelings, my eye!"

────────────── • ──────────────

White Gift Sunday

"I remember one thing quite vividly. I was an elder of the church, the youngest one and pretty proud of it. Our congregation was, well, you could call them middle class and upper middle class. A good district in Calgary. Do you remember White Gift Sunday? I think most churches had it. The idea was there would be a children's service along with the adults before the 11 a.m. service, about four Sundays before Christmas, I'm sure you remember this, and each child was to bring a gift, wrapped in white tissue paper. I can't recall whether this custom was started before the Depression for the needy, because there always are needy, or did it start during the Thirties. I just can't recall.

Each parcel was supposed to contain, oh a couple, three or four cans of beans or corn or peas or some edible. You could bring a 20 pound bag of apples or some clothing, but the whole idea was that the gift had to be useful.

That was the whole idea. Or toys. Yes, toys, certainly. The children would pile the gifts up on the altar, around the altar, and it was a pretty sight, all those white gifts.

As I said, I was an elder and after service the elders and their wives would get to work and unwrap those gifts. You see, they went to a central depot where they were repacked into cartons and sent out. Well, I'll tell you this in all frankness, it was about 1934, I guess, when we noticed that a few of those nicely wrapped boxes and packages were empty. Or they had a piece of wood in them to give them weight. We talked about it, but didn't really think of it too much. I think our explanation was that some families had been caught up, had forgot about it and had just done this before leaving for church that morning. You can guess that we were a pretty complacent bunch.

Next year, next Christmas there were exactly 23 gifts with nothing in them. There was only about 110 gifts, as I recall. Now you can figure out the percentage. Somewhere around 18 or 20 percent. It dawned on us that about one fifth of our own congregation must have been in such tough shape that they couldn't even afford 50 cents worth of food for the poor. We didn't need to feed the poor in Bassano or Drumheller. They were among us. And I recall it shook us.

There really was nothing we could do, it wasn't the sort of thing anyone in that neighbourhood was going to admit, you know, but I remember looking at those 12 or 13 men and women in that room and asking myself: 'Does one of those empty gifts belong to you?' There was no answer to that one, now was there?"

———————————— • ————————————

Nobody Ever Thanked Me

"My name then was Margaret O'Sullivan and older people around Melita might remember me from those days. I cut quite a figure at the Saturday night dances, a different escort every week. It must be the Irish in me, both sides, as far back as Ireland's oldest stones as my mother used to say.

I had a one-room school west of the town with a small teacherage off to one side and the school board paid me something like $35 a month, which was pretty good in the middle Thirties, and my stove fuel and a farmer down the road threw in a horse and saddle for loan and that saved him from feeding it over the cold months and it got me around.

It wasn't long before I found the children, many of them, were coming to school without lunches. Of course, you can say that these were the children from farms with problems, and by problems I mean large families and low income. Poor farmers on poor land, in other words. I knew I had to do something about this because a hungry student is a poor one. I know, I could mark every one of them 'Approved' or 'Passed' in June, but that hardly seemed the solution when they couldn't do their lessons. I spoke to Mr. Garth about it, the head of the board, and I told him that porridge was good and he laughed and said, 'Do you know what oats are selling for? I'll give you all I've got and then we'll clean out the pool elevator.'

We had a big black stove at the back of the room that the boys kept clean and lit every morning and I got one of those big blue enamel pans, more like the kind you'd put a big Christmas turkey in, and every morning about 10:30 I'd start porridge. Crushed oats, raisins, prunes which you could buy for practically nothing, grated cheese which was cheap and onions I could get by just asking for them. Everything would go into the pot with the water and one big tin of condensed milk and there would be this tiny, black-haired teacher standing back at the stove about 11.30 every morning instead of being at the front of the room and stirring with a spoon I'd whittled from a poplar stick and calling out the lessons. 'All right, Grade Fives, turn to page 26 and do two pages because I've got some questions to ask you.' That sort of thing. It worked.

The kids had their own bowls and spoons and they'd clean up the pan and I even got those who had brought lunches to share with the others, a communal sort of thing, and everything went well.

Some of the parents weren't too happy about this because they darn well knew that I was paying at least $2 a week from my own pocket for the milk and prunes and things. They could figure that I was also buying rock candy for the children as a treat and $2 would buy a considerable amount, a lot of food in those days. They might not have liked it, and perhaps they might have taken it as an insult that they couldn't provide lunch for their children, but nobody ever came and said I should stop.

In fact, nobody ever came and offered to help, except Mr. Garth and the Oldham family that sent along a few pounds of onions and potatoes each week. In fact, and this is the last 'in fact,' nobody ever thanked me, either. People were funny in those days. There was this great feeling of working together, we're all in the same boat sort of thing, but I guess a city girl coming and feeding their kids at lunch was just a bit too much. Perhaps you can't blame them."

————————————— • —————————————

Impetigo! My God!

"Those were the worst days my man and me put in, just the worst days. He could get a day's work for the city *(Halifax)* about once a week but there was nothing for us, there was no clothes, or a movie, and a bottle of rum was years back when he worked on a dragger, but our babies got enough milk. There was the boy, five, and the girls three and two when I'm talking about the worst time.

The baby got these scabs on her face and between her fingers and then the little girl and the boy got these sores, these awful sores on their faces and my man said to go down to the clinic and I did.

Yes, I did and the doctor told me it was impetigo. Impetigo, I bet you never heard of it? Awful sores, and here my kids had it and I thought it was just the worst I had ever heard. We thought it was just for poor people, those people living in slums that pick up this ringworm bug from garbage. Impetigo was such a nasty word. I broke down, I cried and the nurse told me not to be a fool, that some medicine would cure the babies up quick, but she didn't understand that we'd always thought impetigo was a dirty thing, like a bad disease, and only people in slums got it and my little ones had it and we lived in a nice small house, and it was clean and we had food on the table most meals, not expensive but nourishing, and here we were no better than people over in the slums. There never was such a shock to me before."

————————————— • —————————————

For The Dog

"Momma would say, 'Now, kitten, you go to the Butcher Man and say you want two pounds of hamburger and something for the dog.' I remember hamburger was about five cents a pound if it was that and not full of all that fat you get today. You call that meat? I'd go down to the shop near the Strathcona Hotel and I'd ask for the hamburger and I'd get it and pay the man. I think his name was Mr. Field. He was quite English. Then I'd ask for something for the dog, bones or something like that. Of course we had no dog. He'd give me free some ox tails and some bits of liver and kidneys and other stuff, all stuffed into a big bag I'd bring along. Canadian people didn't eat things like that, kidneys and what they called guts. We did, though. We were Old Country and over there, Momma said, you ate everything. It was good.

So Mr. Field would fill up the bag and then he'd reach over and stuff in a couple of bones and say they were the dog's dessert. Sometimes he'd throw in a couple of onions and he'd say they were for the dog because the oil or something in them would make his coat shiny. Then he'd wink. He knew we didn't have a dog.

When my brother came back and got a job on the railroad we had some money in the house and we bought everything we could off Mr. Field. There were a lot of good men around in those days, like him, ones who would help a poor family. Of course, there were a lot of rats too."

———————————————— • ————————————————

Two Or Three Lousy Dollars

"Ever hear of front yard auctions? I don't think they are legal now.

When a family was evicted, the landlord had the right to sell their possessions to get his back rent and boy, some of those landlords didn't have any scruples. The sheriff's officers would pile the possessions out in the front yard and the auctioneer would start, and things like a bed and mattress would go for a dollar or a chest of drawers for 75 cents. All the family's dishes might go for a half a dollar, and the kid's bike for 25 cents. It was murder. Often I've seen me go to an auction of a family in the district and buy $2 or $3 of stuff, stuff I considered essential, bed, stove, dishes, the stuff I've mentioned, and give it back to them. Hell, what was two or three lousy dollars when a family was standing up on the porch watching their stuff go and, I guess, dying inside with humiliation and shame.

Sometimes when I'd give them the tickets to get back some of their stuff they'd just look at me. I've seen a man cry when I did that. Hell, I wasn't trying to be a Good Samaritan, I was just doing what I thought was right."

———————————————— • ————————————————

A Loaf Of Bread

"There was the story of the loaf of bread, and I can't remember much else about those days. Dad was out of work, and we lived all in one room in a rooming house, living room, kitchen and bedroom all rolled into one. My mother's aunt paid the rent, oh, about $10 a month, and maybe not that.

She also sent me to the academy, a boarding school, but the nuns took in day students too. I went when I was six and I was skinny, a skinny little beggar. A nun one day stopped me in the hall, and remember I was only six but I remember it well, and she said, 'Rickie, have you had breakfast this morning?' I said yes, because you didn't lie to a sister and even though it was only a piece of bread or something like that, I said yes. She took me by the ear and led me back into the kitchen and told one of the women there to feed me, this boy. I ate pancakes and ham and eggs and milk and had a rare and wild old time and then the nun came back and told me to go home and I could come back tomorrow again. Why she sent me home I can't remember, and she gave me a loaf of bread to take home.

I got home and was all excited and yelled to Mom that they had given me a loaf of bread and breakfast too. My mother snatched up the bread and put it in a paper bag and handed it to my Dad and told him to get right down to the academy and tell that nun we didn't need their charity, didn't need their relief, something like that. My father left and my mother started to cry and I couldn't figure out what was wrong and then she rushed over to the window and opened it and yelled out to my father down below, and she told him to come back, right away. When he came back up the stairs she took the loaf from him and put it in the cupboard and then she looked at me and said I could go back to the nuns the next day. Just before that, when she had given the bread to my father, she had said I was never to go back to that place.

I guess she felt, what was the use? She was the strong one in that family, but there are times you can't be strong enough. Poor woman."

———————————— • ————————————

The Shame Of Suicide

"Some people made the mistake of living beyond their means, but I guess they had to because that was the way they were made. There was a man in our town named Douglas Jones. Everybody knew him as Doug Jones and he was a good man. He had this business, sand and gravel and cement, and in the Twenties he did well. The companies were building elevators around the country and the farmers were building extra bins and new houses. Good times, I can tell you that.

Then along came the Depression and you know what? No business. Doug Jones wasn't sending his jumpers (*thoroughbred horses*) for his kids to ride them at the Brandon Winter Fair and there weren't any of those expensive trips to the Royal Winter Fair in Toronto where they'd rent a boxcar for the horses. They still kept their horses, though. He let one man go and then another, and finally he just had one man left to handle the few orders that came in, and no girl bookkeeper in the office. They still kept up that big house over by the creek and kept the gardens as lovely as ever but about 1935 the two girls didn't go into Winnipeg to private school, and that winter Doug drove out in the country and put a hose from the exhaust pipe through the window to the front seat and just sat back.

Kids on their way into school next morning found him. The police said they had found half a bottle of whiskey on the seat beside him and they said he was frozen stiff. Mrs. Jones closed down the supply yard within two months and moved to Toronto with the children. She didn't know a pinch or a sniff about business anyway. She just wanted to get as far away from it as possible. There was a terrible shame about suicide in those days."

— • —

One Grey Blanket

"No, no, we never went on relief. We could get by and we didn't need to. Oh yeah, a lot of people did go on relief, a lot of people go on relief now too, welfare, when they don't have to. You know, parasites. We managed.

I had to sew, making over every bit of clothing for the three kids, for us. I had a big garden, very big garden. My husband did some trapping in the winter. He picked up odd jobs around the district. I cooked for road gangs three or four times. Twenty cents a man a meal and I made money. We did a lot of things we'd never done before.

Was it pride that didn't let us go on relief, you ask? No, no, it just never occurred to us. You know. We were getting by, it was hard scratching. A neighbour gave my husband $10 a month to do their chores and haul their water. Relief for a lot of people was the easy way, you know. Even if they didn't get real relief they got free seed wheat and hay. We never did.

The only thing we ever took was one blanket. We were in town and a lot of blankets had come in, those old grey army blankets, and the man who was passing them out stopped us on the street for a chat and he said he had a few left, ones he hadn't found relief people to give to, and he said did we want one.

So I said, well, if he was giving them away free and other people didn't need them, we'd take one. One grey blanket. That's all we ever took."

———————————— • ————————————

Days In The Library

"My Dad's brother, my uncle, and his wife visited us in Calgary one summer for two weeks, driving out from Kitchener. Dad was out of work and accountants were a dime a dozen. When my uncle and his wife were at our house my Dad would get up every morning, have breakfast, leave the house and come home at 5.30 at night. He'd spend the day in the public library or walk in the park or do something, but there was no way he was going to let that brother of his know he was out of work. I don't blame him one little bit."

———————————— • ————————————

Gerry And The Benjamins

"I guess you could call this a funny story. A tragic one, too, and it wasn't too uncommon.

We lived in the better sections of Hamilton in those days and our church was about a mile away. Every Sunday about 1:30, Sunday school was at two, I'd take my little brother by the hand and we'd start out. I remember this very well. About half way there one day little Gerry had to go to the bathroom. It came on him all of a sudden but he wouldn't go forward and he wouldn't go backward, to church or back home. I can see him yet, the little fellow. He was four or five, and he just wrapped his arms around a tree in a front yard and started to scream, sob, the poor kid was so frightened, and I couldn't do anything with him and I ran all the way home.

My father was in the front yard raking the leaves and I told him and we got into the car and were up there in a minute or so but Gerry wasn't around. Dad said he knew the people where Gerry had sort of set up his fort, he said their name was Benjamin and he had met him somewhere at a convention, business. They had a lovely house.

Dad and I went up the front steps and the door was half open and we could hear Gerry's voice so he tapped and we went in and there was Gerry in the front room eating a Graham wafer and happy as any five-year-old. Dad thanked Mr. and Mrs. Benjamin and made a bit of conversation and then we left and we didn't go to Sunday School that day. It just didn't seem like a good idea.

Later I heard Dad talking to mother and he said that there wasn't a stick of furniture, only an old table and a couple of chairs in the dining room, a couch, one of those steel Winnipeg couch things in the living rooms and nothing in the den or hall. A few days later I heard him say that he had checked into Mr. Benjamin and he apparently had lost his job months ago, he worked for some building company, and I remember Dad saying, "They must be selling their furniture bit by bit. Maybe taking it out by the lane at night, just to keep up that big house. They looked like they were down to nothing," and mother said, 'Oh, those poor people,' and my father said, 'I guess you could call that Keeping Up With the Joneses, Depression Style.'"

———————————— • ————————————

The White Wedding Dress

"I was getting married at 19, and my father said I'd be married in white. It meant a lot to him, a great deal, and I can remember one Saturday that man packing up his Encyclopedia Britannica, the whole set, which cost him a lot of money several years before, he was very proud of that set, and he said he was going to take it down to a second hand store on Notre Dame. Then at the last minute he went back in the house and he came out with his golf bag and clubs over his shoulder, and he looked at my mother and said, 'Just in case.'

For the set of books and the golf clubs – and he loved to play golf before hard times hit – he got $4. Just $4, and maybe that was good. I don't know. It was just enough to get the material for my dress, and my mother and I made it, and it was lovely, but there was a lot of heartbreak in that dress.

He never did get the books back because there never was enough money to redeem the books. Or the golf clubs either."

———————————— • ————————————

Just Tired Of Waiting

"We had this big house on the island (P.E.I.) and Mother rented rooms to tourists. No such thing as a tourist industry then, let me tell you. But the people who used to come up from Maine and Boston and as far away as Philadelphia in the summer became friends, and they sent their friends to Mother. Notice I say Mother, and not our place. Mother kept the world turning, every day of her life. Dad just cut the lawn and met the people at the ferry dock and brought them home and tended our big garden, such a huge garden, acres of it, and kept the furnace going at winter time, and sometimes he'd do a week's work on the boats – if he could get it – and be paid off in fish. We had our church, and there was school, and we had good friends – and they are friendships we still keep to this day – and we had our Highland Dancing, of course, and every summer we'd go to the Gaelic Mod over on Cape Breton Island, and that was just about our life. We were poor as church mice, of course, and a nickel was to be kept for weeks before you decided how to spend it.

Then father went to jail. The shame! In those days the law was the law, and judges showed no mercy. I don't think it was actually the judges, it was the times. If you did something wrong you had to be punished. I guess Dad was tired of waiting for the ferry, looking for a car with Pennsylvania license plates and telling them how to get to the house, tired of telling these tourists he had to take in summer people to live. To survive, I mean. He joined up with a bootlegger and when they were chased by a police car, Dad was driving, and somehow the police were forced off the road. A story ran in the paper, and then somebody must have told, and they came and took my father away and he stood up in court next day and said he'd done it. Eighteen months, and people said he was lucky. Father had never stolen a nickel in his life and to this day I don't know if he actually was working for that boot-legger or if he somehow had just gone along for the ride. Anyway, water under the bridge. He said he had done it.

When he came out, he came home and it didn't work out. We'd always sort of got along without him and for 15 months or whatever it was we'd never even mentioned his name. Mother wouldn't allow it. Poor Dad, he stayed around a week and then said he was going to the mainland to work in one of the collieries. I remember Mother saying, 'Work in a wet coal seam for all I care.' I think that took my father out. I know he loved Mother and he knew the shame he had caused her. The shame on all of us. 'Your father's in jail.' Could you go to school and face that every day? My sisters and brothers and I did, every day, and in a town where everybody knew everybody's great great grandmother's first cousin.

So Dad went away – and what is more hypocritical than a God-fearing Scot – none of us, all of us who loved his ways, not one of us went down to the ferry to say goodbye. He just went away.

(Her face crumples, and she cries a bit, shakes her head and says, 'Sorry, I'm a fool.')

Three days later they found his body. A fishing crew found his body in their nets, and we didn't even know he was missing. He'd jumped overboard. I know we all expected him to come home because anybody with half a brain knew there was no work in the mines, in New Glasgow or Springhill or anywhere, and not for an island man either, for what does he know about the collieries?

Oh, to make a long story short, my father came home, and I can tell you this, it wasn't much of a funeral. Not what you'd expect for such a good man."

CHAPTER FOURTEEN

Prejudice – It Takes A Long Time For Old Habits To Die

Hunkies In Town . . . And If You Were Jewish . . . French Versus English . . . Long Before Pearl Harbor . . . He Didn't Even Charge Interest . . . Two Shinplasters A Year . . . Born A Bohunk.

———————————— • ————————————

As you must have noticed already, there was plenty of prejudice in Canada in those years. When times get tough and people close in together, back to back, to protect themselves from the intruder, then prejudice becomes sharper and meaner and stronger. In some cases, it also became well organized.

If you were Polish, Ukrainian, Japanese, French, English, Irish, German, American, Spanish, Chinese, Russian, Italian, you found prejudice against you – and you also handed out the hatred as best you could. If you were Greek Orthodox, Jewish, Roman Catholic, Presbyterian, Mennonite, Anglican, Baptist, Hutterite, Methodist or United Church of Canada, you dished it out and took it too. If you were Negro or Indian, Chinese, Japanese or Syrian, you took more prejudice than others.

There always had been prejudice in Canada – lots of it. But when it was a case of too many men struggling for too few jobs, then the prejudice became deeper and more vicious. And when your life was so poverty-stricken that it gave you little to be proud of, then you started to take great pride in the fact that you were Norwegian, or Scots, or Loyalist, or whatever.

Then new dimensions were added – blue collar worker against white collar worker, farmer against city man, young against old, neighbour against friend, men against women and women against women and my side against your side.

And what threw it all into stark black and white was money. Or the lack of it.

———————————— • ————————————

Hunkies In Town

"My father was a doctor. We were Polish. He was and mother too, but the kids were born in Canada. What's that make us?

We'd lived in this town in Saskatchewan but it wasn't big enough to support two doctors. It was dying, you see. Dad was the youngest of the two doctors so he pulled up stakes and we moved to a nice town in Ontario. My brothers and family still live there, not too far from London.

It was wall to wall Anglo Saxon. Scotch, English, United Empire Loyalist. Presbyterian and Anglican. We didn't even have a church to go to.

The people were very kind. A new doctor, a young doctor in town and they needed one badly so we got the real treatment. People can be very kind, you know, and Dad was soon in practice and Mom had some new friends and we were in school and when Dad asked for a loan to buy a house, the down payment, the bank came through just like that. Easy.

Dad had a brother in Alberta who wasn't doing well and so he wrote him and told him there was plenty of work for him. He could be his partner. Uncle Andrew came and his family and then his wife's cousin was leaving Dundurn, burned out, and he was going to the coast but my Dad and uncle persuaded him to come east and he set up on a farm right on the edge of town. See the pattern? Here was a good place, and now there were three Polish families, and a year and a half before there were none.

The cousin bought a little feed and grain store on Main Street and one day Dad and Uncle Andrew and this cousin Nick are standing outside in the sun talking and I'm walking by the bank and this banker who lent Dad the money, he is with a friend and he points down where my Dad is talking with his brother and he says, 'Looks like the miserable hunkies are taking over this whole town.'

That's the way it was. I remember that about the Depression. I was upset and I told Dad and he was upset and he said to me: 'I guess that proves we'll just have to be twice as good citizens as anybody else.'"

———————————————•———————————————

And If You Were Jewish. . . .

"There was this certain area in Winnipeg about five streets across by six blocks long and in it there existed The Caveat. Now, to you a caveat might mean a warning or a document forbidding some action and that's what this meant. It was not a document but an understanding among all the good people living in that area that they would not sell or rent their homes to Jews.

I don't think there was anything actually on paper and I don't think it could have stood up in court but in the years I lived there, from 1930 to 1938, not one Jewish family ever moved in, and it was a very desirable middle class area. Big homes, lovely trees, quiet, good school nearby. Not much unemployment. Practically none.

Now mark you this, this was in the Thirties, not in the Dark Ages, and I suppose there were other areas in Winnipeg like it, and Toronto and Montreal must have been riddled with such exclusive areas.

This didn't apply just to homes. Men's clubs. The Junior League, I believe. Golf clubs. Country clubs. Certain summer resorts, including one run by the Canadian National Railway. Christ, think of that! There were quotas on Jews in the medical schools and in the law schools. Just ask any Jew over 50 about it all and you'll get an earful. Just like the movie, 'Gentlemen's Agreement,' but who was the gentleman?

Back to Winnipeg. So one chap did buy a house and he was a Scotsman. Hell, he even had a Scottie dog, which was the favoured breed in those days. He also had a Jewish wife. A lovely woman, and beautiful. Well, the buzz-buzz-buzzing that went around that neighbourhood of upright Anglo-Saxon hypocrites, you wouldn't believe it. You just wouldn't.

Meetings in living rooms. There must have been a dozen of them. What to do?

I went to one finally, and because I taught English in the school and my wife and I went to Mexico every year we were put down as odd-balls, and I listened to this bullshit until I could take no more and then, and mind you I was not taking on any role as the Great Defender, but I told them I doubted if there was one of them who did not have a hideous skeleton in the closet somewhere. I also said that because of the breeding that has been going on in the world for several thousand years I doubted if half those present did not have some Jewish blood. I told them to think it over. It did no good, of course. I was just a nut.

You know what they finally came up with. They decided that this Scottie had married his wife *and not known she was Jewish*. Therefore he couldn't be blamed, so okay, then it was fine for him to stay and his wife too. Hah hah! After all, mistakes are made and this looked like an honest one. What the hell that proved I don't know to this day. The kids today would call it a cop-out. No, I told them, you have to get out your Caveat, your paper, and appoint a delegation and go see this fellow and his wife and tell them they have to move. That ended it right there. There wasn't an ounce of guts in a carload of them.

Next month I had a corn roast in my backyard and I invited this couple and I made a damned determined point of introducing them to every single couple there, using first names and the whole business and by the looks on some of their faces they were astonished that she wasn't eating gentile babies instead of an innocent corn on the cob. She was a delightful woman.

I think that finished off the Caveat business right there, but it didn't end discrimination against Jews. That's still with us."

———————————— • ————————————

French Versus English

"In a city or town where there were a lot of French and a lot of English it was usually bad for the French. Take Moncton. It is now the centre of French culture in the Maritimes and the French-English split, you could say it is about even. Fifty-fifty.

But in the Thirties, in what we call the Depression, Moncton was pretty much of an Anglo, well, an English-speaking city. At that time all the commerce was done in English and consequently all the work went to the English-speaking people. The split might have been 35 percent French and the rest English, but all the jobs, the good ones in the city, were for the English, and this was not good. This was bad.

A chap who is now a senator, his name was Calixte Savoie, he formed a group suggesting to the French people that when they went into a store or a house of commerce where English was used that they speak French in order to try and create a demand for French clerks in the stores, to create jobs, to help out the French who needed it badly.

So, you had the English-speaking league on one side, which confronted this situation and you had the French on the other side and so you had a Tong sort of thing, a war in a sense between the French and the English. There was such a backlash from the English-speaking people about this, about this small situation that they over-reacted and then there was an over-reaction from the French people and it got worse.

It was not the start of Separatism, what we have today, not on any scale but it was the start of something, that the French had to get together if they were to survive. It died out about the start of the war, but it was a start."

———————————— • ————————————

Long Before Pearl Harbor

"I was born in Vancouver in 1902 so I have the advantage of looking at the problem from three sides – from my parents' side because they were born in

Japan, and from my side as a Canadian, and third, also from dealing with Japanese and Canadian people all those years.

People really know nothing of our problem. They only think of the evacuation of the people, the 27,000 people, in 1942. A terrible thing, people say. Too bad. Yes. Yes, but a good thing too. It broke up the ghetto concentration of the Japanese people around Vancouver, they moved to the Interior, to the prairies, to Toronto and they began new lives. They began new careers. They became successful.

The non-Japanese think that the attack on Pearl Harbor, the declaration of war, the British and American and Canadian involvement in the Pacific war was the reason for the evacuation of March, 1942, and the internment camps. No, that was not the whole reason. That was the excuse. The decision to move the people out had been made before that. The decision had actually been made in 1940 and the studies to arrive at this conclusion had begun years earlier. In the 1930s, the Japanese government's war on China had been the excuse then and the politicians were just waiting for the right time. The Pearl Harbor attack was the perfect excuse.

If you look underneath it all, back of it all, it was economic. You see, we were Japanese. Canadians, but still Japanese. Look at our size. Small, aren't we? Our skin. Dark. Not white. We weren't white men. Only about half spoke English, and while there were thousands of German and Italian and Chinese and even French in British Columbia who couldn't read a newspaper in English, we were in the wrong because we were Japanese.

It goes back into the 1880s when we first came. We didn't segregate ourselves. The whites, what you would call the red necks, the politicians, they segregated us. We set up our own schools because how else could our children learn? Our own churches, Christian, but also our own religion, yes. Newspaper. Meeting halls. Restaurants, hotels. Stores. Where else could we get our food, the things our old people wanted, the food that was favourable to our diet? Yes, we became a ghetto.

A Japanese is a good fisherman. There is something about fishing which makes him good or better than anyone. The whites, through laws and pressure, tried to force us out of the fishing through the Twenties and Thirties. Our women could work in the cannery because they were so fast and efficient, not because they were wanted as Canadians. Even the Chinese were against us. Naturally so, I guess. Old hatreds stretch back through the centuries.

We moved into the woods to work, and laws and brutality forced us out. Farms. The Japanese are excellent farmers. Vegetables. Each little plant is treated with care, with tenderness, fertilized and watered. If we had the land, we could not be forced out. A farm which might support two families would have six, and everybody worked from dawn to dark and there, that was the way vegetable prices were kept so low. The same with stores. Wholesaling, tailoring, laundries. Undercut the white competition. You had to to survive. Live in the back of the stores, three or four families in two or three rooms.

It was the whites who forced the Japanese into this position where the white businessman could no longer compete. The Japanese was forced into the worst kind of labour.

Do you know that the 1930s, the period you are asking about, most of the Japanese in British Columbia were Canadian citizens. Born in Canada. Canadian citizens. But we couldn't do this and we couldn't do that. First, we couldn't vote. Yes, we couldn't vote. A Japanese man with a doctor's degree couldn't serve in the provincial legislature, and neither could the market gardener. No Japanese could. Or be an alderman, or a school trustee. You couldn't be a hand logger or a lawyer. Not a druggist. You couldn't work for the government either, even with a shovel on the roads. You couldn't serve on a jury. You don't think this is possible? It is.

I don't say there was all that hatred by all the people but this was the Depression, and things hadn't really been too good in the province for years anyway, and people saw the Japanese Canadians as a threat. An economic threat. Somebody who just might, just might take a dollar a week out of your pocket by being a sharper businessman, a harder farm worker, a faster stuffer in a cannery. And I don't need to tell you, it doesn't have to go much further than that to translate this economic fear into action. What kind of action? Political action. Kick them out.

A report called the Special Committee on Orientals in British Columbia was published in autumn of 1940, *a year before* Pearl Harbor. This report said there was a great hatred of the Japanese by the whites in British Columbia. The report could not back up its findings with any specific instances, just that there was a great hatred. They said the Japanese were underselling, undercutting their white Canadian competitors. What is competition all about? What we have in the supermarkets now? Do you call that competition? That is monopoly. The report also talked about great smuggling of Japanese nationals in to Canada through B.C., and they talked about spies mapping the coast.

This was proved over and over again to be rubbish, so what they came up with was that the Japanese had to be protected from the whites. So they must all be kept in a position of surveillance, watched by the authorities, registered. No military training, because they were not to be trusted. You see what this did, don't you? When the war with the Japanese did come along, the Japanese were all lined up, so to speak, located, numbered, marked, ready to go.

One thing to be said for the committee, its members were not unanimous, but the anti-Japanese obviously were in the majority.

You will have a hard time convincing any Japanese of my generation that all this was not economic, that those whose ox was being gored were not screaming the loudest. A shameful, disgraceful period, and the true story still has to be told. But, shameful as it was, the Japanese accepted it with courage and honour and for that, more credit to them all. For many, as I've said before, it did open up a whole new world, but that was a fortunate end result.

It was never my intention to mean that all the white people were bad, or against us. That definitely was not the case. But that type were there in sufficient number and they made enough noise and the time was ready for them, and there were enough politicians who saw in it a means of getting votes. And this, mind you, at a time when from the docks of New Westminster and Vancouver ship loads of scrap iron were being sent to Japan, and the politicians knew that metal would be used in munitions and that Japan had lined up with Italy and Germany as an ally. That's a politician for you. There are still a few of these men around. I wonder if they have changed. If the faction of West Coast Canadians who were against us in those days had had their way, our children and grandchildren would still be working in coal mines. As slaves."

———————————— • ————————————

He Didn't Even Charge Interest

"You'd better let me describe my father. He was Jewish and he was a good man. I'm not too sure of his background but he did come from Russia and I know he worked hard because when he met my mother he was selling off the tailgate of a wagon in southeastern Manitoba, in cotton goods, sewing materials, wool, ribbons, soap, safety pins, string. He was what we would call a mobile notions store. The fact is, he was a Jewish peddler. Then he sold the horse and wagon and bought this store and married my mother. I guess that was her father's command – 'Buy a store, so you can look after my daughter.' It was a wooden place, on a corner, surrounded by a sea of Anglo-saxons, from shore to shore, as far as the eye could gaze. My Dad versus the enemy.

Looking back on it, I don't think my Dad was such a good businessman. Are all Jews supposed to be good businessmen? Apparently. I said earlier it was my Dad versus the enemy. That's the way I felt after four years in Canada's democratic armed services, the air force. I don't think he felt that. After all, there were quite a few Italians and Ukrainians around the neighbourhood and you couldn't feel at the bottom of the social ladder when you saw the way those people lived. Especially the Hunkies. There I go. The Hunkies. It takes a long time, doesn't it, for old habits to die?

This is getting away from my old man. Well, he died. Horribly. Cancer of the gut. I was overseas and Reva wrote and said Dad had died and she'd try and carry on the store and she did but it went downhill and so she and Mom sold. My brother, by this time, had been killed in the war. Bomber command. When I got back my share was waiting and it was nothing really, so I went to Reva and she got all huffy as if the war was my fault and we went to the lawyer up on Notre Dame and he spread everything out on a desk and opened ledgers and flipped through those order forms, the kind with carbons in them, and he said, 'Do you know anything about accounting? Ledgers?' I said no, of course not, I was just a dumb flying officer on discharge furlough. He picked up a ledger and held it towards me and said, 'This represents $21,000 in unpaid accounts, money that your father did not collect between 1931 and 1942. Money that is owing him, money that you will never see a red cent of, money that you can kiss goodbye.'

I told him to go on, keep talking. He said Dad had never charged interest on overdue accounts. Maybe no small grocer did in those days, too much bookkeeping. There are 20 kinds of credit you can get now, all equally incomprehensible to the average Joe and all equally gouging, but then, it appeared there was none. Of course, of course the wholesaler charged interest, about one percent per month on overdue accounts, and my old man had some dillies. Out of sight. So he owed the wholesalers thousands and there was $21,000 he couldn't collect, but he was probably paying interest on that to the wholesalers too, and people had robbed him blind. Imagine having the cash register at the back of the store, and people just lifted anything they wanted on their way out the front door. Thank God there was no sales tax, or he'd have owed millions on that score.

When Reva sold, she was selling a run-down old building that didn't even have heat. No basement, and heat came from a coal stove in the centre of the room and in winter, remember some of those Depression winters, the old man would stoke up a real big fire in another stove in the backroom to keep it warm so his potatoes and bottled goods wouldn't freeze. Dad used to go down there and sleep and he had an alarm clock which would wake him every two hours and he'd build up the fire again.

Oh yeah, those beady-eyed Jewish grocers, hating the goyim, the gentiles, screwing the public with high prices and buying apartment blocks and rooming houses downtown and living in big homes in River Heights. B.S. I'd say my dear and dead father, rotten Abie as some of the kids used to yell at him, was a pretty typical Jewish grocer in those days, pretty typical. Sure, he stood behind the counter with his blue five o'clock shadow by noon, the dirty white cloth tied around his middle, the cigar half burned in his mouth. No, he wasn't a pretty sight, I admit. Straight out of some cartoon.

But look what he did. He didn't ask no favours. He gave poor people credit, and they never paid him, and when they had money they'd go a mile up to Safeway because the peanut butter there was two cents cheaper a jar and a dozen eggs one cent less. But he helped a lot of people along and he knew he was eventually cutting his own throat because the wholesalers were eventually going to close him out, and they did, to my sister.

She was dumb, because she just kept on doing business my old man's way. From that store he should have made $20,000 a year which was a fortune in those days because he had no competition. The nearest was half a mile away, maybe. He should have been making a fortune, but our family ate baloney and potatoes and cabbage like everybody else. I guess I'm trying to defend the old man because people like him are natural targets for abuse, because they always appear to be as they are on the outside, and that is the negative view. The hard-eyed Jew. The Shylock. I know most of those families intended to pay off Old Abie when things got better, and that each family thought they probably were the only ones he was helping. It was tomorrow country. Tomorrow, things will be better and he'll get his. They didn't know he was probably carrying, well, hell, he was carrying 20, 30, 25 families the last four or five days of every month, and writing it off. Writing it down in the account books, but writing it off in his mind.

After everybody got theirs, the wholesalers, the suppliers, the government, the lawyer, you know how much was left because that little grocer had too big a heart? Exactly three thousand, five hundred and eighty dollars and 12 cents.

I wish that little old neighbourhood Santa Claus had got his proper respects. Reva said just two customers went to the synagogue and none to the graveside. Hell, can you blame them? She said it was a rotten day."

———————————— • ————————————

Two Shinplasters A Year

"Now I was born in Riviere du Loup, in the province of Quebec. That is across the river. In a white house on St. Marc Street, and in my mother's bed. In those days you speak of, a woman did not go the hospital to have a child. Right in her bed. The midwife came, the doctor came, the sisters and aunts came, and then the baby came. No kids died.

We were French, you see, and there is this big-shot uncle, my mother's older brother and he sells jewellery in Toronto. He goes on the road, you see, and he would make a lot of money. This jewellery was not so hot but in those days the French in our province did not have much money either. Some from fishing in the river and the guys used to go in the woods, up around Edmunston, and make a few bucks in the winter. Nothing much, just a few bucks.

This uncle, he doesn't want people to know he's from Quebec, you know, that he is French, and when I hear him speak English somewhere later he is perfect. That guy could have been in the House of Commons and nobody would know, not even those French guys. He's good.

But when he comes to our house then my mother is sort of half and half. We don't have a penny, not one, and how we lived, well, my friend, to this day I just don't know. My father has a net so we eat fish, fresh fish and there is stuff to be picked up. I guess my father and my bunch of brothers are the best scroungers along the river. Remember, 15 in that family. By one woman. So when she knows this brother André, the jewellery man is coming, mother doesn't want him to know we are poor but she isn't going to let him get away with being a smart Anglais. Speak French, speak your tongue, she'll tell us. How the hell else? We don't understand English. Only the guy in the filling station and the restaurant girls know. Nobody speaks English on that street, in our school.

Twice a year this uncle comes. On his route, you know. His rounds, like. He stays at the Windsor Hotel but he has dinner with this poor bunch of people but my mother she puts on what we call the dog. Borrow this from

Mrs. Savard. Borrow that from Mrs. Beaulieu. Borrow from the lady across the street. Why not? Everyone does it. Silver, plates, gravy boats, lots of fun.

So the great day! La la! He comes, in a nice grey suit and I'm telling you this, he's got a monocle. The thing in the eye. Up here. I've never seen a thing in the eye like that except in English officers in the army. We think he's a god damn phoney. A French guy who wants to be English.

So there is this meal. Like in the Ritz or the Bonaventure. That old lady sure could cook. Like a dream. We talk French. He talks French. We finish and the great moment arrives. Remember shinplasters? They are bills, like dollar bills, and they are worth 25 cents. Two bits. You understand? Sure. Well, out comes the shinplasters and each kid at the table gets one. We go up and shake Uncle André's hand and he's handing out these little bits of paper and my old man, he's thinking that phoney French brother-in-law is selling this cheap Toronto jewellery stuff, these rings that are supposed to be gold and the red stone is supposed to be ruby, and for about 400 percent mark-up, you know, and here is this guy giving out two-bitses to half a dozen kids.

That was not my way of thinking then, but maybe it is now. I was 10, 12, 14, 16, those years when I remember my uncle coming to our house and I know this, those shinplasters were the only money I ever saw those years. Not a bit more. That is what it is to be poor. That's hard times for a French guy. I didn't think that uncle was a phoney. To this French kid his name was Santa Claus and he came twice a year. There!"

———————————— • ————————————

Born A Bohunk

"My name was Alex, for Alexandra and that was aristocratic, and there the high-faluting thing breaks down, for my last name was Gurofsky. Sounds Jewish, but I don't think so. We were Ukrainians who somehow wound up with a foiny name.

My parents had migrated to Minnesota about 1908 with their parents, as kids, but the Swedes and Norwegians had made it so rough for them that, well they just headed up to Manitoba about 1926 or so. They'd got married about 1920 and along came me and by 1926 I was four years old.

I think it was 1926 and Dad got a good deal on a piece of land east of a town. A little place. A couple of grain elevators. I haven't seen it for 25 years but if it is still alive today it probably has a sign on one side which says 'Welcome' and another which says, 'Thank You, Come Again.'

We lived in the marsh. The land was no good. It was boggy and wouldn't drain. We dug canals. You know, ditches. We did everything. We starved, and nobody in the village knew us. Everybody else got credit, because they were all old-time Scots and Irish settlers from Christ knows where and they were all inter-married, or in the process, of which I will say no more. Other than to say, if a girl got knocked up by a neighbour boy, both families cheered. But if she went to Transcona or Winnipeg, she was worse than any slut.

We built a house on the land we moved onto. It already had a barn. We built a house, poplar logs stuck in the ground, chinked with gumbo mud, mixed with chicken shit and lime. No kidding, real chicken droppings. It did something. This was splattered with a trowel over a wire mesh and it made a good wall. The floor was dirt.

I'll say this. It was cleaner dirt than a lot of oak floors I saw in homes I saw later when I was teaching. I taught far away from home and my name was definitely not Gurofsky. Believe me.

My sister Carlotta – and you can see my mother did have high-falutin' ways, a daughter as a Russian queen and another as an Austrian princess. Oh, well. Carl and I went to school, down that dirt road to the little school at Oak Bank. You think the Swedes gave my parents a hard time? I don't know how hard, but those Scots and Irish and some high-flown Polish, they made life miserable for Carl and me. Really miserable.

Like how? Like ignoring us. Like choosing us last in any choose-up game. Like throwing our coats to the floor in the cloak room at least once a day. Like putting a dead barn rat in our lunch bags some time before noon. Like writing mean, dirty things on the board so the teacher would think it was us, but that never fooled one of them. I can say the teachers were okay.

Want me to go on? Like talking a gibberish they thought was Ukrainian, a gobbledygook, you know, when they talked to us. Putting pony shit in our rubber boots. Some rode ponies to school. Talking gibberish, you know, that's what got me, and then the one who was doing it would turn to the others and somebody else would start up the same gibberish and then like on some kind of signal, they'd all laugh.

You're right, yes, we were Ukrainians. Proud of it. What a culture that little country has, and what a struggle!

We had four miles to walk, I think it was, and once there was this blizzard. In November. Nobody should have been out, but there was Carlotta and this nutty one fighting our way down the road and along comes this car, no school buses then. It stopped, and the driver looked out, and then rolled up his window and drove on. It was a man named McKenzie. He was taking his kids to school.

Carl was in the fifth grade, I remember, and that would just about put me in the eighth. We were bright kids. What else did we have to do? Our Dad put the kerosene lamp out at 10 and then everybody into bed and there was no reading in that house except a Bible in the old language so we fought, stole, bribed and hung on in there to get reading material. Red River Cereal. The picture of a Red River Ox Cart. Remember? Want me to recite the recipe? I can. We learned everything we could. No radios. No newspapers. I have actually run half a mile on a windy fall day to catch up with a newspaper page blowing down the road, just for something to read.

We found an old house when Dad had taken us out rabbit shooting. We ate rabbit. Lots of them. There is only one way to make rabbit and that is in stew, simmered for 24 hours – and it still tastes like rabbit. We came to this old farmhouse, an abandoned one, somewhere near a place which was called Cook's Creek and in a shed we found newspapers piled up. 'The Prairie Farmer,' Winnipeg. We carried as much as we could, and Dad got two good shots on the way home so that was quite a day. This is the way we learned.

Of course we spoke English. We were born in Minnesota. But what I'm saying, each of those issues was a small part of an encyclopedia. Just jammed. And what were we doing? We were just putting ourselves head and shoulders above those other kids in school. We didn't understand it; they didn't either. We were just those smart Bohunk kids. Understand?

I never had a childhood, in the sense that after eight or nine or ten, a child enters a new phase of his life and progresses through what you would call puberty and the high school scene, dating and the dances and the nice dresses and the boy coming around to the house at seven and sitting on the sofa and making conversation with my old man until I swept down the stairs looking like some Scarlett O'Hara. Not for me. No hay rides. No toboggan parties. No going to the Winnipeg Art Gallery for the two-bit afternoon tour. God! I saw that a few years later and thank God for that, anyway!

We felt it deeply. We knew we were poor, very poor. You didn't need to be a genius to see that my Dad was wearing himself out on that lousy 160 acres that nobody wanted, land that had been picked out so some Bohunk could be sold a bill of goods in Minneapolis and passed on to some shyster in Winnipeg, and 'Please sign here, Mr. Gurofsky, and then the farm will be yours.' I watched my mother go down, and you tell me how a woman can go 16 hours a day working in the fields, in the barn, in the house, and still look like something Frank Sinatra would take out, and if you do, I'll line you up with a publisher and you'll make a million.

I haven't put this well, right? I know it, but if you were a Bohunk kid growing up in an all-Scots plus Irish and English community, a farm community, you had a fight on your hands. It made you tougher, and now we're on top.

You see, we were poor. I can remember seeing pennies, and dimes, you know, silver. I can't remember ever seeing bills. We always ate well. You wouldn't eat it today, but you could. You'd eat the leather buttons off that Harris Tweed jacket you're wearing if you had to. Sure you would. But we were never hungry.

It was what you, god damn your lousy breed, it was what they did to Carlotta and her sister. Sorry, that's me! It was what they did, those nice little Anglo-Saxon absolutely rotten bastards. Sorry, I'm getting angry.

When I was 16 I was built. That's the term. I was lush. What would you think if the guy you had adored, for about three years in high school and he asks you out and he's got his old man's car and we go to a movie. Christ, but I wanted that guy to ask me. I sweated it out every day, every night. The things I used to do to make him notice me. He wasn't your football-hero crap. Just a guy I wanted, but I soon found out a lot of others wanted him. One of those kind of guys. Got him. Yah! *(and Mrs. X reached out and, ferociously, grabbed a handful of air.)*

After the performance . . . Oh yes, we went to a performance of Gilbert and Sullivan, and I think it was 'Pinafore,' and after a meal, we started home, and he wheeled into an empty parking lot and grabbed me and said, and these are his words, 'Okay, Hunkie, pants down!' I could handle him now with one finger but then I didn't know up from down. Oh, well, the upshot was, I gave him a raking on the face, he punched me in the face, I got out of the car, he made a sort of half-assed run at me with the car, and I walked two or three or four miles in my fancy high heeled some-actress shoes and a guy, from a town near us picked me up in his milk truck and drove me home.

Sort of a long way from a Depression story. Sorry. . . ."

CHAPTER FIFTEEN

Dishonesty? Just A Word For Survival

It Really Wasn't Stealing ... The Bathtub Saloon ... Sausages And Maggots ... The Old Kentucky Trick ... Golf Balls For Dinner ... Sonny The Swoop ... China Booze To L.A. ... Gold Is Where You Steal It ... Skipping ... Driving 'A Commodity' ... The Bloody Gun Was Shaking.

———————————————— • ————————————————

A woman in Richmond in British Columbia admitted to me: "Stan was a good thief. There wasn't a building he couldn't get into," and she was proud of him. He never got caught, and he only stole to keep his family in food, and when he got a job, then he quit being a thief. That was 30 years ago.

Dishonesty in the Depression meant many things. It meant the kid who swiped an apple from a market barrel; he could be sent to Juvenile Court and put on probation for six months. It meant the father who stole bread and two cans of beans for his hungry family; he could go to provincial prison for three months, and no public outcry would be raised. It meant the rich man who used his good old horse sense to ship thousands of cases of legal whisky out of Vancouver, knowing that it would wind up as illegal whisky in Los Angeles during prohibition; he was admired and envied. After all, if the Americans couldn't enforce their own laws, well, too bad for them.

———————————————— • ————————————————

It Really Wasn't Stealing

"No, I never once considered I was doing a truly dishonest thing by stealing. I stole a lot – often. We all did.

I could walk slowly through a drug store on Jasper Avenue and buy a package of razor blades and then I'd just saunter over a couple of streets and into a beer parlour and I'd go into the men's john and sit down on a toilet and the things would come out of my pockets. More razor blades, maybe a couple of razors, maybe a fountain pen or two, maybe a cigarette lighter, the bullet kind, and aspirins and candy bars and a magazine or two and a Kodak film, all the stuff that is on the shelves of a drug store. Bars of scented soap. A shaving brush. Shoe polish. Little things, of course, because you couldn't have any bulges they could identify.

I'd sort things in different pockets and then go out and there would be a table of men, guys, oh, one or two I might know, and I'd pull up a chair and make some remark about having what they wanted, but not any girls and they would catch on quick, or they would say, 'Well, what today?' Something like that.

These were working guys, stopping off for a few brews before going home. These were good fellows, hard workers the lot of them, I'd say, and they usually had a little money. I'd run off what I had, patting my pockets as I'd say 'Two safety razors' or 'Three packages of envelopes' or 'Some Baby Ruth Candy Bars.' Then I'd say, 'Oh, hell,' and I'd take out the candy bars or the salted peanuts and hand them around and I was a good guy. I'd sell all the rest, holus bolus, every pocket, for a buck or two.

Some guy would go home with that loot and be a hero to his family, and I must say it was pretty nice for me too. Sometimes I'd sell things separately, a dime, 15 cents and it would work out to more than a buck or two but I was in a hurry and didn't want to bargain or trade. I always dressed well, a suit, shirt, tie, fedora, and I looked like I was on top of the world with enough money to cover any man's $10 bet, but I was out of work and I lived by my wits.

Now you look at it this way. If I had walked into that drug store, or the department stores, a hardware store, say, and looked like a bum, a tramp, just off the freights, out of work, why the manager would have trailed me all over that store, step for step. But I was respectable, a businessman looking for something and with jack to buy it. So while he was trailing some poor down-and-outer, there I was picking things up just like they were apples off a tree. I never got caught, and I stole every day for two years.

Funny. I'd be told never to go back to a place you'd stolen from. That's wrong. I stole from only a dozen or so places, day after day. I was Mr. Brandon who owned an import-export agency down the street, or I was Mr. Carter who worked at Eaton's and I established myself in the owner's mind and with his clerks and every time I went in, I'd buy something and pay for it and make some conversation about the news or tell a little joke. I've even taken cheques to the bank for a store owner when he was too busy to make a deposit.

Trust. That's the key word, trust. The little old lady cashier in the small bank in the States gets away with a quarter of a million. How? Trust. They trusted her. They trusted me. I was the solid citizen.

Why didn't I get caught? You know, I've often wondered that. Maybe the good Lord looked down on me. Anyway, I didn't consider myself a thief in the common thief sense of the word. I was just making a living in desperate times. A friend who was a real thief – and he was always behind bars, it seemed – once said to me, because he knew how I was operating, this friend said, 'Harvey, I'll bet you could go up to the Hudson's Bay and pick up a 16-foot Peterborough canoe and get it out through the revolving doors in the main entrance and nobody would catch you.' Now, that's what I call a compliment."

———————————— • ————————————

The Bathtub Saloon

"I was up at Sayward cruising timber with Watt Urquhart and I got $90 a month and that was mighty good money in them days. Jesus Christ, I was single then and 90 once a month, you could do an awful lot with that. Then a wire came, and the whole deal was through, we were fired. We got our cheques and bingo, that was it.

I went over to Port Alberni and I got a job cooking. I could do anything. I was cooking in this hotel for a while, and it was busy all the time and the kitchen was hot, and the poor old lady who ran this hotel, Mrs. Stewart was her name, she said, 'Look, if you want any beer, just ask for it.'

The kitchen was just an ordinary one, a stove and a table and a pantry and shelves, and right across the kitchen was a big bathtub full of spuds. She said all I had to do was rap on the wall, which was the beer parlour, and this window thing would open and the bartender would give me beer. Well, a few days later I thought I'd like a beer so I rapped on the wall and it opened and a great big bloody pitcher of beer was shoved at me. Well, Christ, I couldn't drink a big pitcher of beer, not even if I was thirsty. So I drank it anyway.

There was a man who used to hang around the kitchen sometimes, he'd come in and talk, we'd talk about authors and such, and he was a chemist, a very well educated man but he was an absolute alcoholic. His name was Dixon. One day I told him my troubles, I told him my troubles were that I had too much beer and how I'd knock and the little door would open and there would be a pitcher of beer. I wanted a glass, I got a pitcher. All the beer in the world, just by rapping. Dixon said, 'Jesus Christ, this thing closes at 11 o'clock at night and these guys all want more beer.' Then he looked around and here was this tub and he said, 'Can't you find any other place to put those spuds?' I said I guess we could put them in sacks, so we did that and then he washed the tub out and whittled a cork, he made one out of cedar, you know, and it fitted tight as a bung. Popped it in the hole. Then he said, 'You start rapping on that goddam thing and every time you get a pitcher of beer, pour it in the tub. And at 11.15 tonight, you be here and I'll knock on the door and I'll have half the guys in that beer parlour with me and we'll sell this at 10 cents a glass. Hell, we'll sell this beer for two bits a glass.'

I thought this was a hell of a good deal, I get it for nothing and sell it for two bits a glass. So from then on, I'd pound, a pitcher of beer, into the bathtub, I'd wait about 10 minutes, pound again and I guess that bartender thought I had a gut like nobody else. Pound, beer, into the tub.

At 11.15 that night, I'm supposed to be in bed but I'm in the kitchen and Dixon is there and all these guys lined up behind him in the alley and then he started to sell it to them at, what was it, yeah, 15 cents a glass. Why, we was making 15 cents a glass. It was buckshee, and goddam, both of us were getting stakey as hell.

This went on for quite a while, and then one day I realized that I'd just about reached the end of my string. Half the town was tight every morning, everybody was getting tight on my beer. What made up my mind was that one afternoon, when the United Church Ladies or some such group were having a meeting in one of the hotel's public rooms, the police came swarming down and they were going to raid the joint for bootlegging. I was listening close by when the sergeant was explaining what it was all about to poor old Mrs. Stewart and, Jesus, I just went upstairs and packed my duds and blankets and I tore out of that place and headed for the docks and there was a boat just casting off called the *Elway* and the skipper and his brother were on this boat and I yelled, 'Where ya going?' and they were going hell and gone up to Ketchikan and I said I wanted to hire on and the skipper yelled back did I know anything about diesels.

'Christ,' I yelled, 'I was born with a diesel in my mouth.' So I got a job and I didn't know a goddamn thing about a diesel and there I was a few minutes later down in the engine room with this big Cummings diesel and I didn't know the front end from the rear end. We went to Alaska, then to Bellingham, packing for Farwest Cannery. This was all pretty much of a show because what we were doing was rum running.

I presume the police at Port Alberni were looking for me, and here I'd taken a running jump off the dock onto a boat and wound up in the rum-running trade. Bootlegging both ways you look at it."

———————————— • ————————————

Sausages And Maggots

"I'll tell you a little story about my mother going out, to this woman who was having a baby, and my mother was the kind of wonderful person, she was always there when someone was needed. She was always in the neighbour-hood, helping. She just seemed to know when someone was needed to help. Most women in New Brunswick then had their babies at home.

I remember her coming home after helping. She didn't get riled too easy. In fact, in our house if one of us said 'damn' we got our ears boxed. I had never heard her swear in her life. And she came home that day and she was saying, 'Damn! damn! damn!' and I thought the world was going to fall right in on our heads. I was young and I worried so much about my mother saying these things.

What had happened? The man in the relief department for the county was the one who said you will have such and such, this food and that, and you will get it at this store or that store, and so he was very powerful. This woman's doctor had told her she should have soup, good heavy soup, certain foods. She had been sick while the baby was coming and the doctor said she had to have better foods and her husband went to that man, this man who handed out the dole, and asked if his wife could have different foods, like exchanging ones they were supposed to get for nourishing ones, the soup and milk she needed, and he said no. He said no. And this son of a bitch who was the man who handed out the dole and said what was what, *he also owned the store!* Now do I need to say anything more? No. But!

After the baby had been delivered and the house was settled down again, my mother went to get the other children some breakfast, and there were some sausages and she said you could see the maggots in them, and great big fat strips of fat pork, no meat at all, and this was what this dole man's store was giving to the people with the vouchers, and he made a fortune. That's just part of what went on in those days.

Now can you see my mother, who probably had never swore out loud in her life before, coming home from that poor man's house and saying 'Damn' over and over again?"

———————————— • ————————————

The Old Kentucky Trick

"No, I didn't suffer none in the Thirties because I was buying cull potatoes around here at three or so a ton and making booze and selling it, and everybody for 20 miles up and down this valley knew it because they was drinking it, and the provincials *(the B.C. Provincial Police)* knew it but they couldn't catch me.

You had to have a good recommendation before I'd sell you my stuff, you being a stranger. I had a way. I'd ask 'you want a tiny matchbox?' That was a quart. 'Or a big matchbox?' And that was a gallon. If they wanted two quarts or two gallons they'd say, 'Gimme two.' So I'd sell them a big matchbox, a gallon, for about $7, and that was quite a bit in the Thirties, but my stuff was good. It would take the hide off your horse but it wouldn't kill him. In that matchbox was a piece of paper and on it was drawn a map, with an 'X' and that was where the jug was. Usually simple, like the third fencepost west of the Serpentine Bridge, and all they had to do was scratch around and they'd find the hole with a piece of sod or grass over it. That way, I never actually passed liquor to anyone and all they got for their money was a matchbox with a paper in it, the map. This was the way they did it in Kentucky, some of those places.

In those days the police weren't too popular and besides, there weren't that many of them so I could cook up a run and get my boy to hide it around and we did real well.

We kept friends with our neighbours too. If, say, the Malloys who used to live on that ridge, they were having a party I'd sell them a gallon and they'd mix it with orange Kik or something, maybe cranberry juice, and they'd say I should come over. Well, sir, I'd wait until that party was going full blast and maybe a few people were worrying about how long that jug was going to hold out, and I'd walk in and without saying a word I'd lay two quarts of the government rye on the table. You should have seen them dive for that. I may, after that, have made only a couple of dollars on that party but if anybody was thinking unkindly about me before, they sure figured I was king of the castle then.

To me it was a business. I bought a product, potatoes, that the farmers couldn't sell and I made a champagne out of it. Champagne, hah! And I sold it. People in those days always had money for booze, or as I like to put it, money for a party. I've seen fishermen from the river, Sunbury, Annieville Slough, out towards Guichon, and I knew they weren't making more than a couple of cents a fish and yet they'd get the money and regular. Farmers. Five cents for a quart of the best cream you ever saw. Prime beef, the two best quarters for five cents a pound and they almost kissed you for paying you that much. There was a guy who lived in a scow house near the bridge and he made a dollar a day painting company boats but he'd be along every Saturday afternoon.

I had lots of good customers, lawyers, doctors who would send somebody but I knew who it was for. Aldermen, you know, councillors. Businessmen. Don't use my name but if you did, those men would stand up in the grave and swear I never sold a bad batch. I made thousands of dollars in those days because I had guts and if I had wanted to go big and sold in Vancouver and Westminster I could have been a millionaire. But I was contented. Never caught once. Others, but not me. I never did feel I was breaking the law."

———————————————— • ————————————————

Golf Balls For Dinner

"I lived on $3 and three dozen stolen golf balls for one month. One whole month. Thirty days. My father had lost his business, importing. Who was buying? Then he died. My mother let the house go and took an apartment, not much of a one but for a few dollars you could do quite well. So I had this place to stay and we'd play ball up at Fletcher's Field, move down into the waterfront places and bum beer, over to McGill to watch the girls, down to the YMCA, quite a pleasant way to pass the time but generally useless.

Then mother died. Suddenly. She was there and then she wasn't. I found out the apartment was paid up for a few months. Anyway, it was a roof over my head. The lawyer was a family friend and after the funeral he reached in his pocket and gave me a five dollar bill. That was what the estate would be, he said, so you might as well have it now. I went out and drank $2 of that in beer that night and that was one incredible lot of beer in those days. So I had $3 and my clothes, they were still in good shape.

I met a friend, Jimmy, over near Pine Crescent and he told me what he was doing. He was stealing from the big stores and bartering it off for meals.

Well, I wasn't about to do that, and then I thought, why not? After I left him I went into a restaurant over there in behind Ontario Street somewhere and I heard the owner complaining to another fellow that he liked to play golf, but the cost of balls was too much. Golf in those days was a bit of a crackpot's game. Not all that many played it, not like today, and there weren't many courses. I said, I told him I could get him golf balls cheap. Dirt cheap. It came to me as a spur of the moment thing.

He asked me how cheap, and I said the best for 10 cents each. Hell, I didn't know what the best was, and I certainly didn't know if 10 cents was a cheap price. I just guessed, and this Greek said okay, bring them and I could take it out in food. A dollar is always a dollar to those fellows. With his mark-up he'd probably be getting each ball for seven and a half cents, but I couldn't care. I had a hungry mouth to feed, my own.

So, to make it short and sweet, I walked down to Morgan's and into the sporting goods section. I found the golf balls and the ones that were displayed the best and that looked the best were Spaldings, and I just picked out three boxes and put them under my coat. I didn't even think about it. Just put them under my overcoat, held my arm down hard on them and walked out. I don't think even one clerk looked at me.

So I got home. Now I was a thief. That's how I became a thief. Thirty-six golf balls. Next morning I took one down to the Greek. He looked it over, bounced it, did everything but test it with his teeth. Then he said okay, and he gave me three pancakes and coffee. That gave me one meal a day. Not much of a meal, but enough. You'd die on it if you went long enough, but that was beside the point. I got to know him, this Greek, and he'd mix up the menu on me. One day it would be stew, and the next pot roast, and then back to pancakes and coffee. Sometimes milk.

Then, you'll remember, I had that other $3 from the lawyer's five dollar bill. That was breakfast. Around 10 I'd go to a little cafe where I got to know the waitress and I'd have an egg and a piece of toast and tea. Ten cents. If no one, her employer, was looking she'd slip me another slice of toast.

A free slice of toast and a glob of strawberry jam, free, not paying for it, why that would set you up and feeling good for the rest of the day. Funny how you remember the little things like that."

Sonny The Swoop

"There was a guy we knew called Sonny the Swoop. His way of making a living was to sit on the porch of an empty house down in the West End or over in Kitsilano. The house would be vacant but the woman wouldn't know nobody lived there, I guess, and a man sitting on a front steps on an evening would look innocent and like he was taking the air before going to bed. So they wouldn't be afraid, and Sonny the Swoop would get down off that porch and rush up behind them and snatch the purse, swoop down and grab it. He used to do this several times a week.

Half the time, more I guess, the women wouldn't report it. Why? Well, Sonny used to say that mostly they wouldn't have anything in their purses, no money, just a few women's things. No money at all. He'd even take the pennies but there would be none.

He used to say, 'Where the Christ has all the do-re-mi gone?' Maybe that's why the women never reported it. Didn't have a phone at home and not a nickel for a public payphone."

China Booze To L.A.

"You couldn't find a man on the waterfront to admit it, but it was good money for a lot of us before Mr. Roosevelt got Prohibition repealed in 1935.

Rum running wasn't legal anywhere, but in Vancouver nobody asked any questions. You could buy bonded liquor, as much as you wanted, from the government warehouses and have the bill made out for a China destination, but an awful lot more of that booze wound up in Los Angeles than it ever did in China.

I'd say more illegal booze went out of Vancouver and some from Victoria to California than ever was landed from Ensenada, and that was the big Mexican port.

These people were big, and some of the big fortunes in this part of the world got their start in the Prohibition days. The names might not be familiar because they all had front men. They used converted sub-chasers and even bigger boats and it was nothing for a boat to load up 20,000 cases and head out on the Canadian side of Strait of Juan de Fuca and then cruise south about 40 miles out and meet the American boats off Catalina. Then it was their problem getting the stuff ashore. Not ours.

There was quite a bit of violence, gunfire, you see, because who was going to mourn a rum runner who had been hi-jacked? It happened, and men went out that never came back. There was one case where two hi-jackers were hanged at Nanaimo. That never taught anybody a lesson.

Down below the arena on Denman Street by Stanley Park, that was no-man's land. Beyond the law. The police never bothered anybody down there. Carbolic Joe and a few of his cronies ran it. It was all fishboats and house-boats and you never saw a uniform down there.

It is hard to imagine a fish boat going down into American waters, Puget Sound, without a few bottles, a few sacks of bottles aboard. We'd go down the waterfront and ask around and there was always somebody open for takers. Usually at night. We'd unload at a spot just south of Blaine *(an American town on the border south of Vancouver)* and there never was anyone around. Nobody watched that place. Of course, a few palms were being greased.

There never was much danger for the small guy. He was too tiny a minnow, especially when there were sub-chasers to watch.

There was another dodge the big boys played. You could buy a boat load of Scotch in England for a few cents a bottle. The stuff is dirt cheap to make, millions of gallons at a batch. You bought it and had it on a through bill to Vancouver bound for China, and you got around the government taxes then. The other way, you paid excise. This way, it could be through Vancouver, held in storage and then to China, Hong Kong, anywhere. All you had was the warehouse costs and you got rid of it as you found buyers. Twenty thousand or thirty thousand cases was not a real big order, either. The buyer would be fictitious, and the companies involved, here and at port of destination, would be phoney too. Everything was phoney but everything was legal, if you know what I mean.

Millions were made. Millions and millions. Everybody who had a finger in the pot got rich. It was sweet while it lasted. About 15 years. Prohibition harmed everyone. What was respect for law and order when that was going on, the millions being made? The only people who came out on top were the fellows behind it all, and they wound up laughing their heads off. The big guys wouldn't know a real live rum-runner if he knocked on their front door."

Gold Is Where You Steal It

"If they had ever jugged me for all the gold I stole I'd be in jail yet. I was in the mines. I was only a school kid when I went into the mines. Underground. I was 16 and I told them I was 18. They gave me a job mucking in a drift which was the toughest job in a mine in those days. I weighed 145 pounds and they laughed at me when I applied. Men of 200 pounds they wanted, but I got the job. How, I still don't know. They paid me $4.80 a day, that was absolute, and then you were on bonus. You were on contract. Some guys could make up to 12 a day. You worked like a dog, but a good man – and there were plenty of them there – could make about $10 or $12 a day – besides what gold you stole.

Yes, I highgraded. That wasn't a sin in those days either, you know. They just fired you if you got caught. If you could get that pure gold out of the mine you were home free. I've gone down to Toronto, down to Detroit and across the line and sold it, as much as $3,000 at a time. That was an awful lot of money in those days and there wasn't much chance of you getting caught if you watched yourself. Later, of course, they made highgrading a crime but the guys still did it.

No, I won't tell you my name or the mines I worked in. Just say the north shore of Lake Superior, over that way. Anyone who was there can figure it out."

——————————— ● ———————————

Skipping

"I have no idea what you would call it now, but in the Thirties it was called skipping and today you could probably go to jail for it but then, why, it was done everywhere. My family must have moved 30 times in five or six years. Just like gypsies. It was tough being a landlord in those years. Yes, very tough.

For a few thousand dollars used in the right places, mortgage sales, distress sales, estate sales, a man could buy several good houses. A good house, of wood and brick, but good condition, oh, say, for between $750 and $1,200. Then it was his job to keep tenants in it, people who would keep it from being vandalized, wrecked, slept in by bums because a house that is not lived in goes to ruin pretty bloody fast. Rents were $15 a month and up. Two families often rented a big house for $18 or $20. Like everybody else the landlord was waiting for an upturn in the economy. Happy Days Are Here Again, that kind of crap. So he wanted people in his house and as long as they weren't Zulus or something, okay.

If you pushed a bit then you could get a break. An incentive. He'd often give the first month free, no rent. Then you'd plead that you lost your job, or were just on the point of getting one, or your relief payments were going to be boosted, so you could usually keep stalling the landlord on the second month's rent. As I said, it was unlikely he'd throw you into the street. That cost in legal fees and time and it was pure and simply a pain in the ass too, on both sides. So you'd have two months free, and about the 20th of the second month you'd line up another house.

My old man usually tried for a house in the same district because all of us were still going to school, and that was easy because there were houses for rent all over the damned town. Dozens of them. That was no problem.

We'd move about the 28th of the month. A transfer truck cost maybe $3 and with all us kids flying around and a couple of neighbours helping, that truck could be away from there and on its way to the next place in half an hour. We really had nothing – a few beds, chesterfield, kitchen stuff, a few chairs, and that didn't take much space. Of course, this was done at night and in Montreal in those days there must have been more moving at night than in the day. One day a family would be there and the next morning they wouldn't.

As I said, the landlord could have traced us easily enough through the post office or the school but I can't recall one ever doing it.

The fact is, we just didn't have the money. You did what you could, and I can remember my old man saying he hoped his evil ways wouldn't brush off on his kids. He was laughing when he said it, with a big tumbler of dandelion wine in his hand."

———————————————— • ————————————————

Driving "A Commodity"

"There was this uncle, Dad's brother in Winnipeg so I thought I'd hop over there. I didn't know where it was, how far, no nothing but I'll tell you one thing: I soon found out. Half way around the bloody world, but I got there riding in freight cars. He owned this garage on River Avenue and it's a funny set-up. He's got big cars, but there's only a driver's side. Get what I mean? No passenger seat up front. None in the back. Just open space and he said, 'Frank, think you could handle one of these?'

I looked one over, a Graham Paige, engine bloody big enough to drive the Queen Elizabeth and he said three cars would go together and load up at a warehouse, and he said it was 'a commodity,' and then we headed for the border about 60 miles away and if somebody stopped us, we just banged on through and if anyone chased us we just went as fast as we could, just outran them and if we did get caught then our tough luck. Farewell, so to speak. The commodity, of course, was Scotch and it was Prohibition in the United States and a big and fast car like that could carry a lot of booze. When he said the pay was $50 a week I said he was on.

He also said that there wasn't much chance of being caught because it wasn't the Mounties' business and the Americans were paid off but he said, 'Sometimes . . .' I asked him what he meant. He said, 'Well, sometimes, some cop wants to be a hero. Then it takes a month or so to get him transferred.' That sounded fine to me. Just fine.

I worked for a year and one month, until they knocked down Prohibition. Until booze became legal again. I got paid $50 a week and later $60. I smashed up two cars. I got shot in the leg once. A friend double-crossed me and stole a load and I often wonder what happened to him. I had a girl friend I kept in an apartment in St. Boniface, and I had another girl in Grand Forks in North Dakota. I made three runs a week. I risked my life every trip and I never saved a cent. I had fun."

———————————— • ————————————

The Bloody Gun Was Shaking

"Crime wasn't too bad, as I remember. Oh, I was held up once. I was coming back from a late meeting and when I put the car in the garage a fellow came down the lane. He had a gun. He told me his wife and kids hadn't had anything to eat for three or four days. I think I had $7 on me and that I gave to him, but what frightened me was the way the bloody gun was shaking in his hand. The goddamned thing might have gone off."

CHAPTER SIXTEEN

You Go A Little Crazy

A Serious Federal Offence . . . Do You Laugh Or Cry? . . . Stamps By The
Millions! . . . The Funeral Wreath . . . The New Grain Truck . . . My Son The
Vegetable . . . We Were Hung Up On Food . . . The Great Gideon Mystery . . . My
Tobacco, Your Tea . . . Let's Get That Guy Off The Street . . . Gold Fever . . . The
Church Was My Wife's Life . . . He Never Let Me Forget It.

———————————————— • ————————————————

*Under the strain of the Depression, many people went a little bit crazy. Their
lives dictated by poverty or lack of a job or just not having enough money to live
as decently as they thought people should, they often said, 'To hell with it,' something snapped, and they did crazy things. Perhaps for the first time in their lives,
and perhaps for the only time – but it was not always so.*

*Sometimes the strain showed in almost comical ways; more often it was
tragic.*

———————————————— • ————————————————

A Serious Federal Offence

"It was about a week before Christmas in 1934 in Edmonton and I had no
money, no place to stay. I guess you could say I was as low as a human being
could be. I was walking back towards the High Level Bridge after trying to
find some sort of work over by the university and I saw a woman get out of a
big car and stuff a lot of letters in a mail box.

I walked up to it, propped open the slot with a chunk of ice, lit my hankie
with a wooden match and when it was going good I stuffed it into the mail
box and walked away. I don't think anybody saw me or knew what I was doing.
It had all the effect of dropping a pebble into a canyon. Nothing happened,
and I didn't feel any better and I was just as cold and hungry as ever, but I
dropped a blazing hankie in among His Majesty's mail and that is a serious
federal offence and I could have gone to the penitentiary for a long time.

Why did I do it? I really don't know to this day."

Do You Laugh Or Cry?

"We lived on Lind Street in Toronto and I think everybody but my Dad was out of work on our block. In the summer they'd just sit on their porches, arms folded, and wait for something to happen but nothing ever did.

There was this little man living a few doors down the street from us. Yes, you'd have to say he was a nothing, the type that never said anything much. You know. It was six miles downtown to where the unemployment offices were and you had to get there about six in the morning to have any chance of a job, so this guy would get up about 4.30, winter or summer, and down he'd trudge, day after day, but it seemed he never could get a job. Then he'd walk home.

One day he came home about 7.30 at night, walking as usual, but somehow he'd got a job. He'd made $5 that day and he let everybody know it. I guess you could say he was the proudest man in Toronto that day, and he sent his girl, about 10 or so, down to the nearest store to buy two quarts of ice cream and some other small stuff. There was going to be a celebration.

But somehow, on the way back between the store and the house she lost the change. Don't ask me how it could happen. She just lost the change. You could see it in pantomime, her father gesturing on the front walk and the girl going through the little pocket of her dress and looking into the bag, but the money was gone.

Now here's a man who apparently never got mad, but he lost his cool. He started to thrash that kid right on the front yard. Hit her, push her, hit her again, screaming all the time, and the girl just stood there and took it.

Oh sure, all the men in the neighbourhood saw this, but they could figure out what had happened. Usually if they saw a man beating a child, two or three of them would go over and plough him. Not this time. They just sat there.

Finally the guy threw himself full length on the steps and started to cry. Sobbing. Hard. The first time he'd made any money by his own labour in maybe three or four years and it was gone. He cried, big sobs. And you know who went to comfort him? The little girl. She went over and sat beside him and spoke to him and put her hand on his shoulder.

Christ, you don't know whether to laugh or cry."

———————— • ————————

Stamps By The Millions!

"You see, my Dad had had his own surveying company but he couldn't keep it going when everybody was leaving the land and the soil was blowing over to Manitoba or up north or into the States, across the line. The government offered him the job because his knowledge was very valuable, so he started way up the ladder. That wasn't enough. He had this terrible feeling of guilt, that he had let his employees, his family, everybody, down. He started doing odd things, but the oddest was the stamp business. He read in one of those magazines that a company in the States was looking for used stamps. All they could buy.

It was quite easy to understand, you see. Stamp collecting was a mania then, and these stamp companies needed stamps, any old kind and by the car load. So the upshot of it was, my father would go around to the departments and big stores and tell them to save all the letters that came in. Hundreds, maybe thousands a week, and he'd lug them home and we, mother and us kids, would sit down at the dining room table and tear out the stamps from the envelopes. Then, well if I ever see a Canadian King George the Fifth one, two or three cent stamp again I think I'll cry. We saw thousands, millions. They had to be soaked off the envelope, and Dad had a friend make a bunch of big flat trays, just like cookie trays although three times as big, and in would go the stamps. Each night, the kitchen table and floor was covered with these trays of stamps.

It was crazy, but there was no way to tell Dad that. He had a family to support, and although we were living well, very good for those days, he just had to earn more money. He was thinking of pre-Depression, in the Twenties, when he had thoroughbred horses and all those trappings. They didn't matter any more. I'd hear him about midnight, putting those trays down. They made a little flat slap. And then the dear man would be off to bed, and next morning about six, he'd be up and he'd have big pieces of blotting paper about a yard square and the stamps would come out of the water and onto the blotting paper to dry. Then they had to be packaged, in ones and twos and so on, and that was a family job too. On weekends. I've even had my boyfriend recruited on Saturday night. Finally, the last step in this hideous process, the stamps would be packaged and sent off to this stamp place in New Jersey, and Dad, of course, paid the postage too. Thousands of stamps, God, maybe millions.

We didn't know it at the time but Dad actually was around the bend. Poor man. I never knew what his returns were for certain but mother used to shake her head. She saw a cheque once and it was for $3. That was for one big package, because they paid by weight. Dozens of hours' work, all that sleep lost he should have been getting, that worry, the house cluttered up with pans and blotters. It was a perfectly awful time, and we put up with it. He was actually bending a little more each time, his mind, and this went on for a long time. Those pitiful little $2 and $3 cheques, just such a tiny part of his salary. He thought he was helping the family so much. The dear, dear man. The best father anyone ever had, and he died every day. Finally his mind snapped and I won't tell you about that, I just can't bear to. He died in the mental hospital at Weyburn just after the war.

You can say Dad was a victim of the Depression just as surely as the farmer whose land blew away."

The Funeral Wreath

"People did some pretty strange things. Almost as if some sort of madness had a hold of them.

There was this family named Thompson across the street and the father died. They hung a black wreath on the front door and, well, that sure impressed the kids in the neighbourhood.

The day of the funeral, in fact when nobody was at home because they were all at the funeral, some of us kids saw a man go up the walk of the Thompson house and stand there. He was pretending to ring the door bell, I guess, and then we saw him slip that wreath under his coat and walk away. We followed him on our bikes, just kind of goofing along, and he went around the corner and over a couple of blocks and into a house and then he came out and hung the wreath on his own door. I told my Dad and he checked and found out the man's wife had died the night before."

The New Grain Truck

"Some men would just not admit defeat or admit that there even was a Depression. I mind one August, probably 1938, I was working for a man west of Brandon and a new grain truck came bouncing across the field and that was strange because this farmer was old fashioned and tight as the bark on a tree and do you think he'd phone for a truck? No sir, he kept his sons busy all winter hauling wagon loads to the elevator six miles away. Saved a few dollars that way.

The driver of this GMC was insistent that he be given work. In fact, he was downright insistent. Demanded work until finally the son grabbed a pitch fork and practically drove that man back into his truck. In fact, he did drive him back, and there was some pretty strong language.

We heard about him in town on Saturday, the next night. This fellow had saved, worked like a bugger for three or four years and had enough for a down payment. Then he had the truck and payments was due. Lord, payments due and no work. Well, there was work but even using the big scoop and working 16 hours a day there was no way he could haul enough grain to pay gas and payments, even if he did sleep in the cab. He'd worked himself into a state of frenzy, I guess you could say he was insane, that's what debt and frustration and bull work did to some men.

They found his truck, rolled over and smashed up where he'd either driven off the road or just aimed it off and said to hell with it all. Poor bugger. I think the police found him wandering around town later and they put him in the nut house at Brandon. Maybe he didn't belong there, but that's where the Depression put him.

Anybody could have told him you can't make payments on a new truck hauling barley and oats for debt-hounded farmers when they got wagon boxes and teams of their own and nothing to do in the winter."

———————————— • ————————————

My Son The Vegetable

"My son Raoul came out of school in 1932 when he was 18, a good looking lad, a bright lad, and that spring he sat on the verandah where we had a big swing and I'd hear the swing going creak-creak-creak until it used to drive me to my wit's end.

In summer he used to go down to the river, that was the place where all the fellows went and I don't think there was girls down there, but they would lie around and get brown, and that happened every summer.

In fall, sometimes it was swimming and down at the dock on the river but mostly it was the porch swing again, and in winter it was sitting beside this big wood stove we had in the kitchen, sitting in a rocker which was really my Dad's chair but he never got a chance to use it and that boy rocked back and forth, back and forth. And sometimes at three in the morning I'd hear him making a crackers and honey sandwich and he'd go back into the dining room and play some solitaire, and he did this every night. Once his sister stole three cards out of the deck and he couldn't win, you see, and it was about three days before he found out, before he had sense enough to count the cards and found only 49, and I thought he would go mad. He wanted to kill somebody. I don't think it would have mattered who.

Raoul did that for five years, from 18 until he was a man of 23, and all the time there was no work. Things were bad in Northern Ontario and in our town unless you could get into the mine. And if you had a job, then you would go to work sick, dying, dragging one foot after another and you'd do your quota, and everything depended on that job. There was no jobs, and a few times he went down to Toronto and he kept at it, I guess, for a week or so and he came back riding the caboose with a friend of his father's and he said, 'Mom, would you want me washing dishes in a cafeteria for $3 a week?' And I said no, that's not what I wanted for a boy like him who should have been well on the way to making his way in the world by that time. He was about 20, maybe 21, this particular time he came back.

He went up the stairs to this little room he had at the top there and I knew he was feeling so awful low I could just cry, and so I made some tea and took it up and I know I said the wrong thing, the worst thing I could have, but my very words were: 'Raoul, how come Jimmy Buchanan and his brother can go down to the Massey plant and get jobs? I've never thought they were a patch on you.'

Well, the boy jumped up and he grabbed that drafting thing, that big cel-luloid ruler and he broke it over his knee and he took his engineering books and he threw them all over and he smashed his hand, his fist, into this big mirror in his closet door. He broke that. He was yelling, screaming. You see, he was a quiet boy, he never did anything like this except the solitaire cards. This was not to his nature.

Then my boy started to cry and he yelled. 'Because I'm no good. You've got a no damn good son. Three dollars a week in a dirty kitchen working with a bunch of Chinks. That's what they thought I could do. Work with Chinks.'

A couple of years went by. He sat in the rocker and I'd have to ask him even to put in some coal. Our lawn was about the size of a blanket but he never got around to cutting it. He wouldn't stay home for Christmas dinner and said he just walked around. He swam a lot. I don't think he ever had a girl. I don't know what he did. He was handsome as Jean Beliveau and he did nothing. He didn't read and he didn't do crosswords or go for walks or even trim his fingernails. He was a vegetable. That's what his sister called him. It broke my heart.

In September, the ninth of September, 1939, he joined the army, the Canadian Army. He was killed at Dieppe, the summer of 1942. He was a wonderful soldier, very good soldier. You see, somebody wanted him. There was something for him to do.

His chaplain wrote and said he died bravely. I still have that letter. When I die, when I leave, I have told my daughter I want the letter in my hands. In the coffin, you understand."

————————————— • —————————————

We Were Hung Up On Food

"Looking back it seemed that we had a terrible preoccupation with food. We weren't hungry in our family, not in the way you read about families in oh, Biafra or Pakistan. Big bellies and huge dying eyes. Oh no, but month in, month out, a diet of porridge and bread and hamburger and wieners and cabbage and spaghetti and macaroni and the very cheapest cuts of meat and neck bones they chose to call spare ribs and bread pudding and chocolate pudding – no matter how good a cook a woman might be, it was still dull. Uninteresting. Dull, dull food. I forgot stewed prunes and pork and beans and the kid – and there were six kids in our family – the one who got that tiny, tiny piece of pork in the can was the winner that day. We never saw an orange except in the toe of our stocking on Christmas Day. A banana was something each child got, one, at the annual Sunday school picnic.

On Saturday mornings we'd head downtown, a few girl friends, and we'd just walk along St. Catherines and the side streets and look in the windows. The delicatessens. Or to Morgan's or the other big stores and we'd go through their meat departments, their food departments, and we'd drool. I mean, we would literally *drool*. Our mouths would begin to salivate, fill up, and if you ever saw four young girls spitting – and maybe it wasn't a pretty sight – then you'd know we'd spent five minutes in front of the window of a delicatessen.

Mind you, there was a lot of money around. It was just that about 25 percent of the population had a lot of it, 50 percent of the population had only a little and the rest had none. We were 50 percent. Our Dads all had jobs, but in those days $100 was something. My Dad made $20 to $25 as a jobber and if he had an exceptional week he'd make $30. Not often.

So people could afford those things. In Montreal, Westmount was English and I don't think there was much hardship there. We lived in N.D.G. in one of those funny apartments. Good God, two adults and six kids in three and a half rooms, and in some ways, we were doing good.

But the food bit. Years later a teacher in Outremont, which had a large Jewish population, told me that when she told her pupils to write an essay, a paper on anything, about half would write on food. How to buy food, grow it, cook it, eat it, how good food was for you. From A to Z, but food.

I have a friend, a quite respected businessman now, who in his Depression days did the artist-starving-in-the-garret bit and he used to draw still life, but not the wilting flower in the vase or the red apple and yellow banana and the highlighting of it all. No, he did still life of great plates of food. Filets. He sold some too. Bake at 400 degrees for 45 minutes and serve with garnish and a red wine. Hah!"

———————————— • ————————————

The Great Gideon Mystery

"This I have never told, and the truth is, I guess I forgot all about it about 25 years ago. But it is the God's truth. I was on the road selling groceries. Draw a line across Manitoba through Winnipeg and north of that was pretty well my territory. It was a good job for those days because people had to eat, and they could always find the cash somewhere.

You remember those $1 and 50 cent a night hotel rooms? Well, for $1 you got a bathroom and for four bits you went down the hall. I did an awful lot of walking down the hall in those days. I was in dozens of those hotels and in hundreds of rooms in them and one night I reached over and picked up the Gideon Bible and I couldn't care less about religion but I flipped through it and darned if there wasn't a ten dollar bill and a two dollar bill nice and flat in the centre. Finder's keepers, loser's weepers.

After that the first thing I'd do after taking off my shoes and lying on the bed in a new room I'd reach over for The Good Book. Now, without a word of a lie, I found more money in the pages! I guess in about five years, before I was moved into the front office, I must have found at least $300. Without a word of a lie. In the Gideon Bibles.

I couldn't figure it out. I still can't. But I have two theories. One is that some person went around putting money in the Bibles, figuring that if a person was religious enough to read a Gideon in a hotel room, then he should have a little reward. I think I reject that because the amounts would be three ones, or a five and a one, or a ten, or a two and a one, odd amounts. If this person was organized, he probably would put in two one dollar bills, or even a one, or maybe a five if he'd lost his mind. These were all different amounts, as high as 20.

Now, this is the way I figure it. These rooms had no toilets and they didn't have locks on the doors. I take that back – some did, but a lot didn't. So as times were so damned tight a man wouldn't want to leave his wallet in the room when he went to the can or for a bath, and he might not want to take all his money down to the beer parlour if he was going to do some drinking that night, so what would he do? What would be his reasoning? I figure that he'd figure the Bible would be a pretty safe place to hide it and so in it would go, some of his money. Who ever reads a Gideon Bible? Who ever looks through one?

If he came back tanked, he could very easily forget he'd stashed away part of his loot, and if he went to the can, he just might forget and go away next morning.

For what it is worth, that is my reasoning, and I'm not sure I accept either theory anyway. It is something that has always baffled me."

———————————— • ————————————

My Tobacco, Your Tea

"I guess I was 11 or 12, that very impressionable age, and there was this family across the street and their children would just walk into our house and we'd do the same. You know the kind of relationship. Everyone has one or two of them.

They had this gorgeous old house, an absolutely gorgeous house and while my parents were good friends with them, in those days there were a lot of things which were kept private. Personal things, you know.

We knew something was wrong, that this man's car business was going downhill because of the times. There was no money in our town, and especially not for buying new cars. I noticed they had stopped burning coal in the basement furnace and had set up a Quebec heater in the kitchen and it was there they got their heat. From wood. There was plenty of wood around.

This day I walked in, and in the kitchen I heard the most terrible fight. Screaming. Yelling. This is what it was. They were on the dole, money from the county and that was the most terrible and humiliating experience. My friend's father had done the shopping and he had bought a package of tobacco. Ten cents. That was the argument. How dare he buy tobacco! The money should have gone for something else. Yell, scream, curse. To young and quiet little me, this was horrifying. Two people I loved in such a terrible fight over 10 cents.

Finally the father yelled, 'Okay, I'll never buy tobacco again as long as I live, but I won't buy tea either! Not even a dime's worth.'

That ended the argument right there. You see, she was a woman who loved tea, to sit at the table in the living room and sip tea and read, or gossip with a friend or just to contemplate the day, or her life, or tomorrow. He was telling her she'd have to give that up.

Oh, it is a small story, I imagine, and not very interesting, but here were two lovely people at each other's throats. Their nerves must have been worn raw. They must have been near the breaking point, trying to live on the few cents a day they were given and to keep up a front, keep up a facade of being one of the town's important families.

If he couldn't have his beloved tobacco, then she couldn't have her beloved tea. How sad, and yet that's what the Depression must have been like for so many people."

———————•———————

Get That Guy Off The Street

"Everybody had their own way of beating the Depression. There was this Eaton's floor man, a big impressive fellow in a dignified uniform and he stood at the escalators leading up from the main floor and smiled and nodded at people, and helped little old ladies and women with big parcels, that kind of thing. He was kind of a symbol of Eaton's, and everybody in town knew him.

Anyway, he was fired. Canned. I don't think it was because of age, because he looked in pretty good shape to me. It could have been an economy thing, everybody was cutting staff right and left. This chap, and I'm sorry I can't remember his name, but when he got his pink slip he went over to the Winnipeg "Free Press" the same day and he bought an armful of papers and began peddling them right in front of the main entrance which opened directly on to his stand at the escalators.

The rest is talk, but everybody who went in spotted him, smiling and nodding as he used to, but peddling "Free Presses" at a nickel each. It never got into the newspapers and you probably won't find an Eaton's executive who would ever admit it, but the complaints began to roll in immediately and within an hour or two that man was off the street and back at his stand by the escalators, smiling and nodding. The whole town seemed to know of it, everybody was chuckling about it. Today, the company's hiring him again would be called Improving The Corporate Image. Then it was probably called Let's Get That Guy Off The Street Before We're The Laughing Stock Of This Town. Same difference, wouldn't you say?"

———————————— • ————————————

Gold Fever

"They said there was gold on the Fraser bars below Quesnel and because it was August the water had dropped and now was the time to go. You could make $5 or $6 a day just panning gold, just picking the nuggets out of the pan.

Well, that was rubbish but if you were living on 40 or 50 cents a day on the Skid Road in Vancouver and there was gold in them there hills, that's where you went. Hundreds went that year. Yes, '34 because the country was gold crazy. Miners in producing mines in Ontario were making more than bank vice-presidents. Well, almost. But not out on the Cariboo cricks.

Ever heard the term 'hungry ground?' Just what it means. You work a bar all day, shovelling tons of gravel, hundreds of buckets of water, up to your knees in cold water and a helluva cold wind coming down from the canyon above, and after dinner of beans and bacon you do your cleaning-up, picking up the gold with mercury and then vaporizing it off and what have you got left? You might have a nub of gold worth 60 or 75 cents or at most, a dollar. That is what hungry ground is. There was nothing romantic about it. It was just the roughest and hardest and wettest and coldest work a man could ever do.

But we did it, all through August, September, Christ, even into late October when even the bears were holing up and there was ice along the shore every morning and she was dark by 5:30. For what? A dollar button of gold that you cashed in at the Chinese grocery in Quesnel, and a week's work, seven straight days, didn't even buy a week's grub, even at those low prices. Twelve hours' work and you couldn't even keep ahead.

I think you could call it gold fever. You know, the Forty-niners. The Klondyke. We were no different. There was all the evidence in Christendom to prove there wasn't a bar worth more than a dollar a day but there were dozens of guys still working. Why? They had gold fever and you go a little crazy."

————————————— • —————————————

The Church Was My Wife's Life

"Much despair there was in this family. In those days the church was my wife's life, they would make all of it better. She'd light the stove and put in the bread at 5:30 in the morning to be ready for breakfast when she comes home again, and she'd tie her boots by the strings together and put them around her neck and walk four miles for early mass. Not when there is snow, she's not that crazy, you know, but every other time. Every day.

Just her. Sometimes, on bad days maybe, only she is at mass, but she makes that priest say mass. In Quebec, the men go twice a year, then, Christmas and Easter. Maybe St. Jean Baptiste time. Not that woman.

The priest charge her 50 cents a week to say mass. You know, that is his charge, like my grocery store charges 60 cents for a pack of smokes. To this guy mass is a business. To my wife it is going to end the bad days, that life we had, you know, of salt pork and beans. The kids, we had 10, would get cod liver oil again, you know.

One day Mrs. Cocteau I think her name was, she stops me in the village and she says why I should let my wife pay 50 cents for masses when nobody else does? Nobody else will. I say I don't know. I don't even know where she gets that 50 cents, you know. Maybe she has a secret treasure somewhere, you know.

This woman, and I forgot to say she is the priest's housekeeper, she asked did my wife know that on the Saturday, every Saturday my wife pays out the 50 cents for the masses, that priest has a nice big bottle of wine. She should know, I guess. She was his housekeeper, she serves him breakfast and supper, you know.

I say to her, I say, 'Mrs. Cocteau, you should tell my wife that. If I tell her that I might become dead.'

She says she won't, but do you know what she tells me? She says that when that fellow in his warm house and his big meal right there in front of him, you know, when he pours out the first glass of wine and sips it, he holds it out and waves it a little and says, 'Thank you, Mrs. LeBlanc.'

That's when I decided to tell my wife, you know. And she just said she heard the masses and if he wanted to spend the money on wine, well, that was fine, you know, the poor man worked so hard.

I am sorry. I forgot to say. The reason why my wife wore her boots around her neck, you know, she did not want to wear them out. At the church, she would sit on the steps and put them on. Like that."

———————————— • ————————————

He Never Let Me Forget It

"The man I married was a stock broker, and from 1925 to 1928 he made a great deal of money. Well, you know, anybody in that position could. Every sell order matches with a buyer and the volume was going up, up, up and up. In 1929 he interpreted the lull in the summer as the ordinary summer lull of trading, people on holidays and all that, and he was so confident that everything would keep going up and up that he went to the bank and borrowed on his personal stocks, and he had a great many, to buy more.

Then the Crash came, and the bank kept calling for more money to cover his margin on the new stocks. He lost heavily like everybody but he was a clever man and while he was very heavily in debt he had managed to keep a great deal in my name. We lived very, very well, I can assure you.

In 1932 things were just about as low as anyone thought possible and he started asking me whether he should sell everything and pay off our debts and be starting off even, or should he just hang on with what he had, or should he borrow on my good stocks he had left and buy some of the fantastic bargains around? How did I know? I was young and had two babies and I didn't know anything about these things. He was the expert. But that man pestered and pestered, he persisted and persisted, what did I think, what should he do, and on and on. Finally one day I yelled at him, 'Oh, pay off your debts.' I guess it was the Scots in me that said that.

He did, he sold everything and we were back where we had started from. And almost from that week in 1932 the market started going up, not much, a bit, then a fall back, then a bit more, and up and up, slowly, but it was getting up again. Of course, if he had hung on, we'd have been in very good financial shape and if he had borrowed more to buy those bargains, we'd have been much better off. So I had advised him wrong, what did I know about stocks, and until the day I divorced him he never let up on me, never let me forget it.

He blamed me for losing all that money, selling out just when the market was starting to rise again.

A perfectly irrational attitude, of course, but there were a lot of irrational people around in those days."

CHAPTER SEVENTEEN

Bartering Pork Chops For Babies

The Five Kids Barter Plan . . . Bedroom Deep Freeze . . . Love In A Taxi . . . Dad Just Couldn't Say No . . . The Exchange Mart . . . We'll Get Her A Piano . . . The Swap-Happy Society . . . Labour To Exchange . . . The Cow in the Showroom.

The barter system returned. It had never disappeared from the country, but now it moved back into the towns and cities.

An unemployed friend of our family did the monthly books for four small stores in our district, got $5 worth of groceries from each owner, and everyone was happy. A Nova Scotia dentist – fillings 50 cents, extractions a dollar – would do a family's teeth in exchange for them cutting down some huge trees, bucking them and splitting them into cordwood. An Okanagan farmer would take a truckload of apples and pears up to Kamloops and swap them for a beef.

And, of course, there was the oldest one of all, the tramp going to the back door and asking for a meal in exchange for weeding the garden. Only it was young men now, kids hopping the freights, looking for a hand-out; and often the woman would give him a sandwich and an apple and milk free, for no work, because the lad reminded her of her own son.

This whole system of barter, swap, bargain and make a deal undoubtedly put the fairly sophisticated marketing system back a bit, but it worked and it was necessary. The alternative was "to be in debt" and in the Thirties, that was the worst sin of all.

The Five Kids Barter Plan

"I call my kids vegetables and pork babies. My oldest boy, he was traded off for doctor service for a sack of onions, two jars of pickled eggs and enough pork to feed a good-sized family for a week.

Doreen, she was born in August so we swapped her for vegetables, right

214

out of the garden. I picked them myself before we drove in the wagon to the hospital.

So it went. Five kids, and that doctor all he got was vegetables, pork, eggs, firewood. That's the way things were done up there. No one had a dime. Just enough for shells, for a moose, and like as not you borrowed the neighbour's rifle. If you had a neighbour. Some of the ones that hung on in that country they made it. Rich. Land. Big cars. Trips to Mexico, London. Not us.

That last winter, 50, 60 below, was one winter too much. God didn't mean man to live like that. The Sisters of Providence, the priest in town, they said pray. Pray to the Lord. That wasn't enough. Nothing was enough. You have to have six gears' worth of guts and we only had three."

———————————— • ————————————

Bedroom Deep Freeze

"Dad was a doctor, north of Saskatoon and I had a big sleeping balcony in the front on the second floor of this big, old wonderful house we had. I'd sleep there from May to late September and then it would be kind of chilly so that's when Dad would take over. It became his deep freeze.

You see, people had no money. When I say no money I mean it. He practically worked for nothing despite what you hear about doctors refusing to go out on calls or operate unless they had cash on the line. Such nonsense. All through the summer Dad would be practising, visiting, night calls, babies, accidents, all the things that happen in a farm community, and the farmer's wife would say she just couldn't pay for Fred Kotowich's broken arm or whatever it was. Dad would say not to worry, but if they could, they might give him some produce or meat or a bit of venison, potatoes, anything, but bring it in October. They did too. Everyone, I think. Those Ukrainians were very honest people. Everyone was in those days.

Soon the sleeping balcony would begin to fill up, and by November it would be jammed. Vegetables, jars of strawberries, raspberries, canned corn, roasts of beef, even a side of beef or two, everything you could think of. We lived pretty high off the hog on that barter money and Dad even gave a lot of it away to patients who were in hard times. Some of the Ukrainians would bring jars of their home brew. White stuff, but if you mixed it right you could get a drink that didn't send fire out of your eyes and ears. Everyone was poor, the doctor was poor and the patients were poor but we all pulled together and got by.

To my way of thinking, the story of those years is one of the better parts of Canada's history as far as the people are concerned."

---•---

Love In A Taxi

"There was the tail. Waitresses, mostly. You'd get a call, say, to Child's, which was open late, and you knew damn well a waitress couldn't swing a cab fare out of her wages, tips were nothing. So if she said something about keeping the meter off, well, you'd just keep the flag up and away you'd go. Some lived in the North End but a lot out in the West End, past Furby and Maryland, that way. The fare wouldn't be more than 50 cents or maybe less but if she was going to sell herself for that, I didn't care. I'd just drive around into the lane and take her into the back seat and hump. A back seat ain't the best place for a piece of tail but I didn't mind, and these gals didn't mind either. I was young and tough in those days and you'd never see me turn it down so I got it two or three times a week, and show me the married man who got it that regular, week after week.

One little lady even asked me to be her pimp, she'd set up a room somewhere and I'd bring the guys. For that she got a backhand across the mouth. But she still came back and I still screwed her, often, many times."

---•---

Dad Just Couldn't Say No

"My father had this general store in a tiny village near Deloraine, the kind of a place where a stranger driving by would ask, 'How does he ever make a living?' We did well, Dad was a good businessman, but when the Thirties hit, things got tougher all over that country. The farmers would come in and they were broke. They literally didn't have a dime in their pockets, but their wives would have these lists for groceries and because Dad had been in the district so long they just naturally expected to get their groceries and hardware and things from Mr. Tubbs.

We had this big cement storeroom downstairs, it was dug into the ground, and it was cool in summer and many the time when it got to be a scorcher in summer in the early Thirties we'd eat down there. Well, Dad died suddenly and the lawyer told my mother to make an inventory of everything he had, everything, so us kids would go prowling around with a notebook making lists. In this big basement storeroom there was a section that Dad had boarded off, a place to store things in a cool place, and we finally got around to it.

Well, sir, you never saw anything like it. There were jars and jars and jars of butter, five gallon jars of farm butter, unsalted. There were crocks and crocks of eggs put down in preservatives, and jars and jars of pickles, and pre-served chickens and anything you could mention.

What had happened was this. These farm women would bring in a jar, five gallons of butter. To trade. And Dad, being the man he was, couldn't say no to those people. They had been his customers, and faithful too, for years. So he just kept taking in this produce over the counter as barter and handing out goods which he was buying on credit from Winnipeg, and I don't need to tell you, that is no way to run a business. There was no way he was going to be able to sell the butter, even fresh, when butter was about five cents a pound and every farm wife in Manitoba was making it. So it went rancid. The eggs were rotten too, and no market for them anyway. Same with the cucumber pickles. Same with everything. Dozens and dozens and dozens of crocks and jars and bottles of nothing.

It all showed up eventually on the books. Dad had actually been bank-rupt for some time but he just went on doing business in this crazy way. A lawyer came down from Winnipeg to talk to our lawyer and he said the big wholesale companies wanted Mother to keep the store going and work her way out of the mess. But how? She'd just have done what Dad had been doing, going deeper into the hole every week, helping people. They were quite a pair."

———————————— • ————————————

The Exchange Mart

"I ran an exchange mart. I suppose the idea is as old as civilization itself because it's the very essence of trade, but in the Thirties people thought it a pretty slick idea and I made a living, or I thought I was making a living.

I worked out of my house, a nice old home way up on Yonge Street, and to survive I had to do a lot of advertising. Say, if a dentist wanted some car-pentry work done and a carpenter needed some fillings done for his daugh-ter, then I would get them together. Maybe no money changed hands between them, but I charged 25 cents each. It worked fine. I've matched up people wanting to drive to the coast who had a couple of cases of eggs, and people who were driving out. You name it, I could match up. If you made four deals a day there's $2 right there, and a man and wife could live well on $50 or $60 a month. Maybe not well, but they could live.

Of course, I had to pay the phone. That came first. I put out a small newspaper, a give-away, listing what people had to offer and that made the thing go. The Work Exchange Market News, I called it. People from all over Toronto picked it up in grocery stores, theatres. Free, you understand. That's where I made my mistake. Printing was dirt cheap but the printer had to be paid, and even when I got more and more business and had two phones going, my wife and me on them, I never quite got even with the printer. Six years after the Depression ended I cleaned off the last dollar with that printer, so you can see I didn't actually make any dough. It was one of those things. You paid the rent, ate well, bought a crock on Saturday night. You thought you were doing fine but you weren't. It was fun, though, and I met a lot of nice people."

————————————— • —————————————

We'll Get Her A Piano

"This woman, Mrs. Cowan, she'd been a music teacher once and the kids had nothing to do so she decided to give them music lessons. Off sheet music. She had no piano but she taught the kids the music just from the notes, you see. Da dah dah da da dah dah. Like that. In their heads.

So a bunch of us farmers got together and said we should get this woman a piano and I said I know this little Jew in Regina in the second hand business, and I drop a note to him. Send us a good piano. I tell the fellows he's straight and if the piano is what he says it is, then that's what it is worth. Carrot River is about 220 miles north of Regina and he ships this piano, a good one, $150. That's an awful lot of money in those days.

I drop him a note and say we'll pay him when we can. Okay.

That winter I tell the fellows that some of the wood we cut goes to Regina for this Jew. The lady is doing more for the kids in the district than all the things money can buy. So we ship several loads down to this coal yard in Regina and I write the Jew and tell him there are so many cords in his name at this yard and he writes back and says, 'Very good.' That's the way we pay him off. With wood. It takes us three years but he never pushes us and it works out fine. He was a square shooter. If he said something was so, then it was so."

The Swap Happy Society

"We could catch the fish in the Fraser but a lot of the time we couldn't sell 'em, and if we did sell, prices were so low they meant nothing. White spring is good eating, a big, firm fish but you couldn't get 10 or 12 cents for a 25 pounder. Humpbacks, half a cent a pound. Coho, a cent or maybe two if you were lucky.

We swapped. Everybody swapped. We'd take a load of fish back into Surrey and stop at farms and swap salmon for eggs, fish for potatoes, turnips, chickens, meat. A five pound lard pail of fresh milk would go for a seven pounder. If you let it stand overnight, you got about five inches of the best cream on the top."

———————————— • ————————————

Labour To Exchange

"I believed then, and still do, that every labourer is worthy of his hire, and that is the way I operated during the Depression. It is true I had no money, but again, nobody else did either. There were days on end when I never had a solitary nickel, but I always had my labour to exchange. I would go to a house, always the back door, and I would ask the woman who came if she could give me some food, a sandwich, a meal, in exchange for chopping wood, shovelling snow, raking the lawn, taking out the ashes. Don't think I was just making a gesture, putting off her opposition. I was sincerely willing to exchange my labour for a commodity, and isn't that what the marketplace is all about? Of course it is. I never asked for money. Just goods in exchange. That was fair enough. When it was presented this way, in a quiet tone, with sincerity, with the obvious willingness to do the work in exchange for whatever, it was rare that you were turned down. You chopped the wood, or hauled the ashes, and you might eat in the kitchen, but hospitality goes only so far, and you usually ate on the back step if the weather was good, or in the barn or in the basement if it was winter or raining."

———————————— • ————————————

The Cow In The Showroom

"My grandfather had the Dodge dealership in our town and about 1933 or so he made a deal, and sold a car to this big family with this positively vast house. The down payment, or maybe it was most of the payment, was one cow, one calf, which was considered pretty well a dead loss, and three pianos. That house probably had four.

He had a showroom of sorts in those days – nothing like they have today, just no way – but he penned off a bit of showroom and stuck the cow and her calf in and hung up a sign and he wheeled the pianos in and put signs on them saying '10 percent down' and so much, you know, forever to pay, and by night he had sold cow, calf and pianos.

Granddad came home that night and said he'd sold a Dodge. That's the way he figured it. No money changed hands between him and the new car owner but he had sold a car. Barter, round the corner, up the hill, back around and down again. Any way to make a buck."

CHAPTER EIGHTEEN

You Made A Dollar Any Way You Could

A Beautiful Bird House . . . The Sure-fire And Deadly Potato Bug Killer . . . Street Car Tickets . . . Suckers And Fish And Chips . . . Who Needs A Sidewalk Anyway? . . . The Three-Gallon Oil Can . . . The Biter Bit . . . A Case Of Mistaken Identity . . . The Raffle-Your-Paycheque Plan . . . Living By Your Wits . . . Creating Their Own Jobs . . . Like Any Army Foraging.

———————————— • ————————————

If you could put one over on the next fellow, you were considered "a sly one" and so deserved the envy and respect of your relatives, friends, neighbours. Unless, of course the one you had done the dirty to was one of those relatives, friends or neighbours. Then there might be a bit of bad blood, but not for long.

Being sly was being crooked, sometimes, but always without malice. Sometimes it was just good fun. One up on the other fellow. Or better still, the government, like the chap in this chapter who stole one side of a wooden sidewalk one winter for firewood. The next winter he went back and stole the other side.

Now that was stealing, but not exactly. It was being crooked, but more than that, he was being a sly one. He was a man anybody could applaud.

It might be said that if all the ingenuity and brainwork and labour and cunning put into cutting red tape, slipping through loopholes, getting something for free or doing someone in, had been directed at straightforward enterprise, the Depression might have ended earlier.

But that would have discounted human nature.

———————————— • ————————————

A Beautiful Bird House

"There was a bird house competition in our school. The merchants had put up about five bucks in prizes and the first prize was $2.50.

My uncle was a carpenter and I went over to his house, to his basement shop, and he built me a beautiful bird house. He'd do 98 percent of the work and then he'd say, 'Here, give this screw one more twist,' or 'Take this brush and just touch up that corner.' So I really didn't build that bird house but I was there when it was built and I helped, and if anybody questioned me I was ready to lie like a trooper.

Of course I won. Mine looked like Joe Louis alongside a bunch of bums. Each entry had a number, not a name, so nobody could wonder how a scruffy little jerk like me could build such a masterpiece.

That $2.50 bought us our whole Christmas dinner – turkey, cranberry sauce, stuffing, potatoes, vegetables, jello and cream, cookies and tea. For five of us. Sure, it was cheating. You're damned right it was cheating."

●

The Sure-Fire And Deadly Potato Bug Killer

"The slickers were a mile a minute, and everyone had a crack at taking the poor farmer. Here was one. Maybe you couldn't grow much, but with a little care you could grow potatoes and they'd help you get through the winter. Nothing wrong with spuds. Didn't the Irish live on them once, and even make their whiskey from them? You could get a binful, but you had to watch out for the bugs. The potato bugs. They could ruin you.

There was this advertisement in a lot of the papers, the (Winnipeg Free Press) "Prairie Farmer," the (Saskatoon) "Western Producer," the farm papers and some of the others, and it advertised a sure-fire, quick-kill, instant, always ready potato bug killer. It never missed, and easy to use. Only $1.50, or $1.25. Even a child can use it, the ads said.

Well, there wasn't a farmer who couldn't scrape up a dollar and a half to save his crop, and until the papers got wise and stopped their advertising they must have sold thousands, more than thousands. When it came, it was two pieces of wood, about half an inch thick and about the size of a pack of cigarette papers. About five cents worth of wood, I'd say. The instructions were simple too. Just go out into the potato patch, pick up a potato bug, put it on one piece of wood and slam the other piece of wood down hard. Goodbye, spud bug. They were right, of course, because it was deadly and sure-fire and even a kid could handle one, but somehow that wasn't the point.

They sold an awful lot of them and it got to be a joke, even in the post office, where the postmaster, if a parcel was about the right size, would say, 'Okay, Joe, here's your sure-fire and deadly potato bug killer.'

Hell, in some ways it was worth a dollar and a half to get a laugh in those days."

———————————— • ————————————

Street Car Tickets

"Street car tickets for children were 12 for a quarter. We'd use a razor blade to start and then we'd peel each one in half. So then we'd have 24. We used to pray that when they dropped in the box they'd land right side up. Some kids had the idea that if you plastered the opened side with spit they'd fall right side up.

I was going downtown to high school and my Dad worked out East Hastings. So I'd get on the Commercial Drive streetcar two blocks from Hastings and get a transfer. My old man would be waiting down two blocks, at the transfer stop. There would always be somebody, usually quite a few, getting out. I had this tin case that eye glasses came in and when the door, the rear door opened, I'd toss out the case with the transfer in it. Dad would pick it up, cross the street and catch the East Hastings car. All done slick as a whistle. I don't think anybody ever caught on. Oh, we had our tricks."

———————————— • ————————————

Suckers And Fish And Chips

"Quite by chance, Billy Mackie and I discovered that the sewer just below the Legislative Buildings in Winnipeg, on the Assiniboine River, was boiling with fish. The warm sewer water made a hole in the ice about eight or ten feet across and the water was just swarming with fish, all suckers, about 15 inches long.

We were in metal shops in school and it was an easy thing to make fishing spears, the trident type, three prongs, and fit them into broom sticks. Every time you struck you got a fish. You see, it was impossible to miss. We'd go at night because we didn't want anyone to know what we were doing, we didn't want anybody else horning in our deal. It was just a few minutes' work to fill two coal sacks, and we'd load them on two sleds and take them home.

We made a deal with a Chinaman who had a big garden on free land below Clare Avenue on the prairie, and he'd give us a penny a fish, a cent each, and he'd put one in each of his potato hills. He only grew spuds. We took hundreds of fish out of that hole and there seemed to be as many as ever. They just kept coming and coming, and we sold about ten bucks' worth to this Chinaman.

Billy said once that his garden only had about two or three hundred hills but I said he must have another garden somewhere else. I mentioned this to my Dad, and he knew the guy and he said the Chinaman had a fish and chip shop over by Morley Avenue. A bell rang, yes, I knew the shop but had never been in it – and I never did go in it because to this day I believe he was using those suckers for his fish in the store. It just made sense. When I think of those suckers living on that raw sewage it makes me sick. It does now, I mean.

To us kids it didn't mean a thing. The next winter there we were back at the same old stand, spearing fish, but this time we asked for two cents a fish. We got it, too. That convinced me. Jeezus but that was a dirty river."

———————— • ————————

Who Needs A Sidewalk, Anyway?

"We lived near a housing area just outside of Winnipeg called Morse Place and there wasn't much you could say for it except that some time in the Twenties somebody had some big plans for it. In those days a lot of sidewalks in the suburbs were wooden, and there were some like that there and we had the last house on this mud street with board walks. There wasn't another house for two blocks. We were just sitting out on the prairie.

The old man was looking for work and he'd hike down to the trolley stop and the motorman knew him and he'd let him ride free. There was a lot of it in those days. No work, the old man would come home after lunch. He'd eat in the soup kitchen on Water Street and bring bread home in his pockets and sometimes spuds, and if there were a few apples lying around he'd manage a couple of those, too.

But anyway. There was one winter that was a bastard. Cold, 30, 40 below for weeks, it seemed. One afternoon the old man came in the back way and dumped two planks down in the basement and said, 'When they thaw out, Joe, saw them up into stove size.' I didn't have to ask where they came from. The good old sidewalk. All that winter, Dad would come home, plunk, plunk, down would fall two planks. There was nobody to complain, the sidewalk was really ours because we were the only customers, and by spring we'd burned up about a third of a mile.

Along about June a city official and a cop come to the house and they wanted to know where the sidewalk is and Dad said he didn't know, it was there one afternoon last winter and next morning it was gone. The city guy shrugged his shoulders and said it figured. Next winter, we burned up the sidewalk on the other side of the road.

That old man of mine was a character."

———————————— • ————————————

The Three Gallon Oil Can

"Jesus, boys, I'm here to tell you I think I still hold the world title for hitch-hiking across this land of ours. Vancouver to Halifax, seven and a half days. Even beat the railroad, I think. This was in 1936, no cars to speak of, no roads worth a dang except in Ontario and some on the prairies. No freeways. Travelling 15 hours a day, that's how I did it, boys, and with my own gimmick.

I was in Vancouver, stealing logs for a livelihood and a friend came into our houseboat down on the creek and he said I was in trouble. The log patrol were on to us, all three of us. I told the other two in Happy Home to give me my share of what was coming and they laughed. I woulda too, boys. I said okay, bugger you, and said I was heading back to my own true land and that, boys, is Halifax where they ain't no cedar to steal and no log patrol with beavers. A beaver is a sort of rubber paddle thing, and it slaps like a beaver's tail, but it doesn't leave a bruise. Slap, slap, slap and you're seein' stars, boys.

I had a brainwave. I got this three gallon oil can and took the shears and cut a hole in the side and I tacked the whole thing back together with leather hinges and there, you see, I had this suitcase which was really a three gallon can we once used to fill with oil for our boat. I washed her out, cleaned her out good and stuffed in my precious belongings. Then I walked out, right up to the tram depot a block away and bought me a ticket for New Westminister. Ten cents. That put me out on the highway and I'd stand there with my oil can and people thought it was a gas can and I was out of gas and needed a lift to go to my car down the road. You see how it worked, boys. Nothing wrong.

People just naturally stopped. Friendly. I wasn't a bum, a hobo, I was a fellow motorist in distress. They'd ask where you were going, how far and I'd say 'Halifax.' You see, the joke would be on them. They'd been taken in, but not mean taken in. Some would laugh, some would chuckle, everybody was friendly. It was shooting fish in a barrel. Rides, rides, and more rides. In big cars, old wrecks, pick-ups, big trucks, milk trucks.

Things were looking up then, and a lot of people who'd left the prairies and even further to go to British Columbia to eat apples and cherries right off the trees were going back home. Some relative would write and say to come home, things were better, they could get a job. I'd ride just a few miles with the lot, just down the road to their turn-off, their town, or a few hundred miles and I never turned down a ride. If they was going to travel all night, I'd spell them off and go right through with them. I just kept going as long as there was cars on the roads. Let me tell you, the roads was terrible. Mostly gravel. They didn't know too much about laying blacktop to last in them days and the frost and the winter would wreck it.

From Port Arthur, I rode a freight to Parry Sound and I thought it was pretty country so that's why I came back here. I'm not sure if there was a road through then. I doubt it. That's why I rode the rods, so to speak.

Right across the country. People used to invite me to dinner, knowing me only an hour. Stay the night with us, they'd say, and they didn't know me from Adam. If there was no room they'd fix me up with blankets in the car. Things like that. Some offered me money. I'd take it if I thought they could afford it. Other times, I'd just say thank you but no, I still have some.

In them days things was more free and easy. People trusted people more. Now they're more sceptical, always suspicious of the other fellow. Somethin's happened to us all. I don't like it."

———————————————— • ————————————————

The Biter Bit

"There weren't many laughs, but the whole countryside laughed until they cried over this one. I won't tell you his name because there are some of the family around. Around, hell. They've been around since about 1800. This fellow had 80 acres, and pretty sorry acres they were, and he had more kids than cows. Twelve. Six and six. Six boys, six girls, and that poor woman just burned herself out, carrying 12 kids in about 15 years, rearing them, milking cows, slopping pigs, keeping things together, and she just up and died. Just worn out.

He put on a big show of grief at the funeral, the lousy fourflusher. Then he went courting soon after. We'd see his Model T go chugging past our gate and Pat looking like Don Juan, all snazzied up. Nobody would have him. Widows knew what the score was and mothers asked around and found out what a poor sort he was and then they'd say sorry, but my daughter isn't home tonight when he came to call. It got to be a joke. Soon he was going further and further, chasing down every lead, so to speak, and out near Cornwall, somewhere along the river, he found a widow. I believe her name was Chappell. A fine woman, big, boisterous, happy, rosy-cheeked, could mix a cake batter with one hand and sew a patch on overalls with the other.

They went for each other like two freight trains on a single track and the flowers were hardly dead on the grave before they were married. He told my husband they were made for each other. The neighbours gave them a reception although there was quite a bit of coolness involved, but away they went to Peterborough for a weekend honeymoon. Must have been some honeymoon.

He only had 80 acres and a house that was overflowing. I've got to tell this right. She didn't know that he had 12 kids, because she had never visited his farm and he sure as hell hadn't gone out of his way to tell her. Anyway, when they were finished their honeymoon, maybe she got the inkling he was poor as a churchhouse rat but she wasn't letting on at that stage. When she got near town she told him to go on in instead of taking the concession road to the farm. They went in and stopped at the bus station and there was a real welcome. That woman was a widow, all right, but that doesn't mean she didn't have a brood. Not four, not six, not eight, but *ten*. *Ten kids.* Old Pat's eyes must have followed his heart to his boots. Instead of his own kids and a buxom widow to sleep with, he now had 22 kids, all under 16 or so, his kids and her kids, and he told me he had got the feeling during that honeymoon that she might mean business.

They all piled in the Model T leaving one kid to guard a pile of baggage ten feet high and away they went. That ended Pat's happy days. She took charge and worked his ass off. And there were no more babies either. None of this stuff about your kids and my kids are beating up on our kids. He worked his ass off. She got the kids organized, bought more cattle, put in about three acres of garden, a bloody big garden, and sold milk and cream and vegetables. They kept going, and by the time the war came along, those kids were moving out into the world and it was the best thing that ever happened. How she ever kept from Pat the fact she had ten kids, until the I Do's were said, I'll never know, but a woman who can do that can rule the world. I admired her guts, walking into a situation like that."

A Case Of Mistaken Identity

"Oh, those days. My, my. Those days. Folks sure used to do some funny things, things people would think crazy now. Absolutely daft. I mind there was this lad named Macdonald around Sydney and there was all Macdonalds around there and this boy was a hot head, you had to be careful every moment he was around. Fun and laughing one minute and raging angry, up and wild-eyed the next for no good reason a person could tell.

He was a hoist man, and over at one of the pits, there was an argument, some toughing about when he brought part of the shift up and it was words and then fists and the other fellow got a wrench on the forehead in the going-around and my boy, who saw it, said it put him down and he never moved. Things like this were happening, men were only working one or two days a week – and that was if they were lucky – and you know tempers, men, tempers. But this was different now, because the man died. Now this was big news in Cape Breton. Lots of knocking about and broken noses but a man dead from a blow, oh Lord, where were we all going, everyone said. It was like God was supposed to protect crazy Cape Bretoners, and here he wasn't doing the job.

The lad fled, his uncle driving him down to Boston, which was something of a journey in those days, and the next we heard he was in Toronto working in a coal yard. Why can't our lads stay away from them places? A coal yard isn't a pit but there must be something about eating the dust that they all need, like a dog chewing new grass in the spring. His folks all knew it, the street knew it but the police would come snooping around, then close mouth.

Then there was a notice, a write up in the paper that he was dead. Tuberculosis. They had found him in a place where the hoboes gather, dead of the dread T.B., and that was strange because he'd been such a healthy lad just six months before. But there it was, in black and white. Dead, and the police in Sydney told his mother that the police in Toronto wanted to know what to do with him. She said to bury him where he was. Now that's not like a mother and no Scots mother is going to act that way and I'll say it's not the way I'd act. Nor any mother in Cape Breton. The blood is strong. Folks sort of did not see her on the street after that.

Now perhaps you're wondering. A year later my daughter and I are going shopping and along comes this brawny lad and he says, 'Hello, Mrs. Macdonald, hello Jessie,' and I said, 'Good God, you're Ian and you're sup-posed to be dead.' He said he wasn't Ian, he was his cousin Alex from Toronto and I sort of blinked at that and my daughter said, 'Then how did you know my mother's name and how can you call me Jessie?' She had him there, and he just winked.

It was no mystery. His mother told me. It was Ian, all right. Of course it was. What happened was, he opened the coal yard one cold morning and here was this poor lad huddled up in the front of a truck but he was froze to death. That was where Ian had the brain wave. He got into the truck and drove it a few miles away, and here it was still before daylight in the winter so it was just another truck driving along, and he dumped the body off near a ravine and took some papers out of his wallet and put them in the man's shirt and put some pennies and a few nickels in the poor devil's pocket and somebody came along later that day and found poor Ian Macdonald of Cape Breton dead by the ravine. Dead of staying out in the cold and the dread lung condition.

That was all. Ian came back a year later and said he was Alex and he didn't stay long enough in Sydney to get into trouble and then it seems he went down to Truro or near there and the police never found out, or if they did, why would they care?

The thing is, you've got to be quick with your wits, and it's boys like Ian who are in those big buildings in Toronto and in this place, there are lads like Ian from Nova Scotia running the whole affair. Quick witted lads, like Ian."

———————————— • ————————————

The Raffle-Your-Paycheque Plan

"Nine dollars a week wasn't enough to live on, not with a wife and four kids, but that was all I got. Some got up to $12 a week, but I guess somebody didn't like me, so I sat down at the kitchen table one night and decided I'd figure out something, and I did. I came up with a scheme they're still doing. Hell, for all I know I might be the father of the Raffle-Your-Paycheque Plan. There were a couple of big beer parlours down on the Vancouver waterfront, and the Anchor was one of them and I forget the other. Maybe the Stanley. Anyhow, I'd go in and sell 50 raffle tickets on my cheque, a dollar a shot. Jesus, those guys were longshoremen and seamen and fishermen and they had a bit of jack in their pockets. They could sit there and drink beer all day, couldn't they, and a 50-1 shot for $36 was not bad.

I kept it pretty quiet but one day I found I had been selling tickets to a couple of detectives for months and they weren't doing anything about it. They just wanted to win. I had these poker chips, each with a number in crayon, and a guy would draw his and I'd write his name against the number and then I'd get the barman or the owner of the hotel to draw. I was getting in $50 for the $36 I was putting out and they could see I wasn't being greedy. Like no chip drawn was ever over 50. I wasn't being greedy, making $14, but let me tell you, those 14 iron men was often the difference between eating and going hungry."

———————————— • ————————————

Living By Your Wits

"Been this way since I was 14, in 1932. Forty years. I grew up in the lovely land of the Minas Basin, a little village with a white lighthouse and a red roof, called Barrsboro, and I helped my mother in the fields, potatoes mostly. My father was dead. I am not stupid, but schooling just didn't seem to be for me. I'd look out the window all day at the trees. I never got past the third reader but I've improved myself as I went along.

(He pulled a book out of his pocket and it was 'The Man Within,' by Graham Greene.)

I rode the rods, front end, between cars, inside box cars, and once I was locked in a car filled nearly to the top with green peanuts from Georgia going to Toronto and I ate them and had diarrhea so bad I thought I was going to die and they had to carry me out when they finally stuck the car alongside the factory. Somebody heard my last cries for help. I have been chased by railroad bulls and shared sandwiches and coffee with brakemen in cabooses and ridden in a parlour car with a handwritten pass from the manager, Prairie Region, C.P.R. but that is a story too complicated to go into. I have starved on the northern run through Sioux Lookout and Capreol and frozen to death in the Rockies in November and ridden railway barges to Newfoundland and Vancouver Island and I think I owe the Canadian Pacific and Canadian National Railways at least $100,000 in fares and meals.

At 14 I rode into Montreal. A fortress commanded by a few hundred Englishmen and Scotsmen to keep about two million French in line. I am half and half, English and Scots, but my sympathies were for Jean Baptiste. They still are. I'll give a quarter to a French Canadian and a penny to a Scot, and I don't care if he is playing the bagpipes and has 15 tiny battle flags fluttering from that vile instrument.

I arrived in Montreal, and I was poor. I had not yet learned the ropes. The ways of the road, how to sustain oneself in hard times, how to persevere and how to succeed. How to get the other guy, but in a nice way so he would shake your hand, later.

I thought, and I came up with a solution, a plan. Where is the Canadian Legion? I asked a man on the street, and I could tell he was English by the cut of his clothes and the sourness of his face. It was Friday night and I stood outside the door of the Legion and when a man came out, I told him I was a poor lad from the Minas Basin down in Nova Scotia and my father was a war veteran and my mother had written saying he was dying from his old wounds. Could he help me, just a little bit, sir, to get home to stroke that old white hair before he passed on. That would have elicited tears from Cathedral Mountain. I improvised my story, I elaborated on parts, I turned on the steam. In short, I was a great little liar.

And from that time on, I never was short of money. I often gave the appearance of having the shorts, but my Legion gimmick across the country always won out. It was not a true story, I'll tell you, but it had the appearance of being true. It was worth hundreds and hundreds of dollars, in nickels and dimes and quarters and crumpled dollar bills during the Depression, and when other men were sitting at home by the fire driving themselves and their wives mad, there I was out on the country. Just a lad. In a way, truly, I was sorry when it ended in 1939 when Hitler went to war and even Canada became a less than pleasant place to live in.

I never paid for a ride, even a five cent streetcar ride to get me out on the highway. I always had a little story, a tale of woe, and I had a voice that could sing to the angels.

I rarely paid for a meal, even in Chinese restaurants with sloping floors and stove grease caked on the ceiling and rats big as alley cats in the store-room. Fancy restaurants I sometimes was taken to by important gentlemen who had picked me up on the highway. Thank you, sir, thank you. It was against my principles to pay for a ride, a meal, and clothes, which the Salvation Army were more than pleased to offer to a homeless waif, or things like soap, stationery, chiclets, pencils, adhesive plaster, combs, flashlights, safety pins, shoe laces – which any manager of a stationery store would have been delighted to give me if he had known I wanted them. But I knew managers of such stores were extremely busy men seeing that their clerks did not steal them blind, and so I never bothered them.

I never worked. During the Depression a woman who I once befriended in her little home in Regina used to look at my hands and say they were the hands of a concert pianist. I was 18. She was a lovely woman, an excellent cook, and she was sorry to see me go. I used to send her a postcard now and then.

Another woman, on a houseboat in Coal Harbor in Vancouver, a boat filled with the fineries salvaged from her home, foreclosed by a banker, took my hand once and said I had the letter 'M' in my palm. That means 'mors' from the Latin and in palmistry, I believe, means an early and perhaps a violent death. Anyway, she said, a sticky end.

I had blond hair in those days, just a boy with big blue eyes, a face as shiny as the polished buttons on a Dutchman's vest, and a gift of the gab which would melt the heart of a woman or man of stone before they were 18 bars into the melody, 'Down With All The Rascals.'

I did very well then, but things were simpler then. I do well today too, for I could be living in a fine apartment. But here I am on the road. You don't throw off 40 years of wandering. I have good clothes stored with friends in Calgary, Vancouver, Winnipeg and Toronto. I can stay with them. Anytime. I never go east of Toronto any more. That is enemy country, Canada's South Viet Nam. I could live the easy life, but I prefer this life of the road. As I said, I bum and hobo and tramp, but I am not a bum, a hobo or a tramp. I am a man highly tuned to his senses and I mean the five senses, and if you will lift that off your tape recorder and use it, I shall be most appreciative."

———————————— • ————————————

Creating Their Own Jobs

"It never was much of a secret that some guys used to set fires, forest fires, so they'd get a job fighting them. I think the pay was a buck-fifty a day or close to it. I'm in that old hotel across from the C.P.R. station in Calgary and this guy comes up and wants to know where he could borrow a car. It was hot, in 1936, and the whole country was just drying up. You could hear her just sizzling away, and his plan was to get back into that country west of High River, up in the mountains, and set a big one off. That year it was funny, because it was about July, no, well into August, I think, and there were Chinooks. Even that big Chinook Arch in the sky, and by gee, it was blowing hard down those valleys. This fellow said one match would do it. My brother had this car, a Reo, and this fellow got the keys and away he went and sure as hell if he didn't set that big one. That was the Highwood Fire, they called it.

There was a lot of wonderful timber in there, little lakes, pretty country, as pretty as I ever saw before.

The long and the short is, we got a job. They were pulling them off the streets of Calgary and this bastard, name of Johnson, he knew just where to stand and I stood right beside him. Well, there were about five trucks of us and a sorry bunch, bums, winos, nobody with any real savvy about fighting fires and I think there was just two rangers with us. Well, you know how much good two rangers could do. They tried, mind you, but with about 100 or 120 men? All they could do was tell Calgary to keep sending the guys down and working with those who meant anything at all, putting them into small crews and sending them up into the hills. It was a joke from the start, but they had to do something. Mother Nature sure wasn't doing much helping.

It seemed the whole country was on fire, and you could see smoke for a hundred miles. Like the atomic blast. High, way up high and then a wind would come along and sort of skim off the top and it would blow out to the east. I can't remember who put out that fire, crews who were fighting it on the British Columbia side or guys from Calgary and High River and through there. I know a real sonofabitch of a rain, a real storm came just about the right time and we spent another week or so putting out stumps, stuff that was smoking.

Johnson wasn't around. He couldn't stand the gaff. In those days they conscripted you, like in the army – you, you, you and you! You're all volunteers. That sort of thing, but Johnson was so bloody useless that he wasn't any good even as bull cook, scraping out pots and pans. To my knowledge, he was sent back on the supply truck about four days after. He was from Port Arthur, said he was a lumberjack, and tough, but he sure couldn't hack that, and there he was the guy I suspect of starting that fire. Things like that went on during the Thirties I sometimes have trouble believing now."

———————————— • ————————————

Like Any Army Foraging

"People stole, but they didn't call it stealing. I can't really say what it was called. Perhaps it was like when an army forages, take everything you can. There was this Italian fruit vendor and every Friday, you could set your watch by him, he'd come down our street selling vegetables and fruit, but mostly fruit. Oranges and apples. Bananas, grapes, pears, peaches, and he had it set out in boxes, sort of slanted up so they would be on display. Anyway, you could see his products.

There were about six of us, oh, we'd be about 10 or 12, maybe older. We'd ambush this old Italian. The Dago, we called him. Or The Wop. He used to yell, 'Grapadafruit, muchada ripe!' He had oranges and peaches and pears, but he always yelled about grapefruit. Two kids would run at his wagon from the side, pretending to steal something and he'd jump down, pretty spry for an old guy but anybody over 40, I guess, was old to us. He'd have this long whip and he knew how to use the goddamned thing and while he was chasing the two kids the rest of us would be looting him, his wagon, from the other side. Oranges and bananas were the favourite. We'd probably get away with a dozen of each and some apples and maybe a few onions or beets.

We'd be off over fences and through yards and into the backlane and the other kids, the two, would meet us and we'd divvy up. This went on all one summer and I don't think the old man ever caught on, although it seems hard to believe, doesn't it? So we'd go home with maybe two oranges, two bananas and a few other things and give them to our mothers, or just lay them on the kitchen table and she'd never say a word. She knew damn well where they came from.

One other thing. You see, we had to rotate the jobs around and by that I mean, everybody had to take his share of being the diversion squad, the ones who got chased by the Italian. He was good with that whip and if you got in his range, pop, pop, pop, he could do a lot of damage to your back and arse in a short time. It wasn't all fun getting that fruit. He could really handle that thing, and I sometimes think he might have known the rest of us were grabbing his load just so he could get in his licks on the others."

With the onset of the Depression the Canadian farmers' markets fell apart. But falling prices were not the only enemies they had to fight. In the south of Manitoba, Saskatchewan and Alberta they had to contend with hail, hoppers, rust—and drought. Often, like this farmer near Moose Jaw, they had to travel many miles to fetch the water that would keep their farms going.

[AAFC-PFRA Photo/21802]

Even while "The Big Dry" got worse and the land dried around them, farmers doggedly kept working it.

[Agriculture Canada]

But "The Big Dry" continued and the wind blew the topsoil away in dust storms that became a common sight all across the Prairies.

[Glenbow Archives/NA-2496-1 (top), Saskatchewan Archives Board/R-A4665 (above), R-A3523 (left)]

Soon drifting soil, as fine as sand, had covered fenceposts.

[AAFC-PFRA Photo/6138-3]

Farm machinery stood useless, conquered by the sand.

[AAFC-PFRA Photo/22211]

With no crops and no cash, many Prairie farmers had to rely on relief trains from the east in order to stay alive. Long queues of horse-drawn wagons stood in the snow waiting for the relief train to arrive.

[AAFC-PFRA Photo/22150]

The relief trains often contained old clothes and unwelcome foodstuffs like turnips or dried codfish. But other supplies, like these, were more welcome.

[Saskatchewan Archives Board/R-A3341-1]

Prime Minister R.B. Bennett (left) found that his name had been adopted to describe the "Bennett buggies" that became popular as money for gas ran out.

Eventually hundreds of farmers could take no more, and simply quit the farms that had been the centre of their lives. The sand moved in, and soon only weeds grew around the deserted farmhouses.

[AAFC-PFRA Photo/372 (top), Agriculture Canada (bottom)]

To head west to British Columbia, or north to where there was land and water, was the aim of most burned-out farmers, and they were determined to get their families there somehow.

But most of the good land in the north had already been taken. Many families, like this destitute family from Saskatchewan, simply gave up in despair and headed for home again. This group was photographed in Edmonton in 1934.

Through all the horror and despair of real life, the Hollywood tinsel world twinkled brightly. All over Canada people of all ages scraped together enough money to enter the escapist world of the movies, where stars like Shirley Temple were huge box-office successes.

[*Toronto Star*]

CHAPTER NINETEEN

You'd Grab Any Job, Then Hang On

The Money Was Worth It . . . The Accordion . . . Mallory And Derek . . . Friendship Was For Sale . . . The Filthy Swine . . . The Port Arthur Soup Kitchen . . . We Ate Not Too Bad . . . Harvest Workers From The East . . . Working For Nothing . . . Blight College Years . . . A Line Around The Block . . . Memories Of An "Animal" . . . We Worked For A Salary . . . Be Safe, Be Careful.

———————————— • ————————————

In the Thirties any job would do. Had to do.

Men who had been pastry chefs in swank hotels or brakemen on the railroad took jobs as street car drivers or warehousemen because their brother-in-law had a friend who knew a guy who was looking for a man who would work cheaply, long hours and didn't mind night work.

But it was a job. It was rent money and hamburger and milk on the table and boots for John and Billy and, above all, it was security.

It was a thing to be treasured, a job, any job, for a man out of work soon found out that man was born to work. When he wasn't working, then everything was wrong.

———————————— • ————————————

The Money Was Worth It

"They were putting this road in from East Braintree, east of here, to Falcon Lake. It was never much more than a trail. Where we were working was about 30 miles from civilization, so if we wanted to get out for Sunday to see our people, get supplies, we walked from quitting time Saturday, spent about half a day or not much more with our folks and then walked in again.

Most of the time it was 10 to 20 below. We worked in snow, up to our knees, sometimes to our waist and it was axe work, clearing this right-of-way. We got $1.75 a day, a 10-hour day and we boarded ourselves. That meant we had to carry in our grub when we went in on Sunday night, but sometimes we had a horse. Not always.

We'd eat about three bowls of porridge with brown sugar and bacon and eggs we'd brought from home and for lunch we'd have a couple of sandwiches of head cheese, just about the cheapest thing you could buy, and an apple. For supper, we'd have a stew. Venison and vegetables. We'd start it before we left for work and by night it would be about right. We killed a deer a week and that fed us.

We got $1.75 a day, something like $10 a week. The work was hard, the weather was hard, everything was hard, but we figured the money was worth it."

———————————————— • ————————————————

The Accordion

"I was a farm hand and I considered that an honourable trade.

In the spring of 1937 I walked from Saskatoon to Regina looking for work and I got a job with a fellow west of Regina. He had a good set of buildings, and in those days it meant they were still standing, but this fellow even had paint on them and his line of equipment was in good shape. He was a decent fellow, called Tascot or Pasquette or something like that. He was frank with me. He did need a good hand but he didn't have any money, just enough to get him through until fall. I hired on with the deal I'd share a tenth of the crop, and that was an unusual deal, very unusual, and he could only have made it if he owned his own land and he did. He'd built up a big place but he was on his uppers in '37. We got the seed in, about 300 acres and it looked good in mid-June and if we got those first of July rains it would have been off to the races.

Then the sun boiled over and every day you could see that oats and barley and wheat just shrivelling. Then there were grasshoppers. Rust, yes, rust too. I think it did rain once, and it was hail. The long and the short of it was, there was no crop. Not enough to pay binder twine and axle grease.

I hung around until early October and then told these people I was going to the Coast. I wanted no more part of this country, it was finished. The farmer said, 'Well, Harry, we shook on a deal and it didn't work out for you or me but you've worked hard and you're a good man, so if you see anything you want around the place, something you might be able to sell, then I'll give you a bill of sale on it and the money might get you to the coast. I've been to that Fraser Valley and it sure is a nice place.'

What the hell, I could have sold a horse or a cow or a hay rake but those things was their livelihood, so I hemmed and I hawed and then my eye lit on their old accordion on a clothes chest in the kitchen and I said that would do. I probably couldn't sell it but I sure could play it and I told them I'd play my troubles away.

You should have seen the looks on their faces, the wife's, the kids, but old Tascoe, he said, 'Sure, Harry, take it.' I was in my room packing my few duds and I heard the little girl, about 10, she was crying downstairs and her mother told her to shush-shush and I remember that kid crying, and I remember her saying as well as I'm talking to you right now, she said, 'But what will we do, where will we get another one? What will Daddy play this winter when we have nothing to do, and we sing?'

Damn it all. That beaten up old accordion meant more to that family than any horse or cow or hay rake and I was too dumb to see it. I made a big clumping noise with my boots going downstairs and I walked into the kitchen and I said to the farmer, I said. 'What do I want with an accordion? Too big, too heavy. I'd lose it jumping the first freight.'

I stuck out my hand and then his missus, she gave me lunch. It was bread and cheese and two carrots. I shook hands with him, walked out the door and he followed me to the gate and shook my hand again and said, 'Thanks, Harry, there's not too many like you.'

I walked down that lane with my duffel bag and I hadn't one thing to show, not one thin dime, for five months of hard work."

————————————— • —————————————

Mallory And Derek

"The dole in Newfoundland was $1.80 a person each month, which was six cents a day and that used to be five cents a day.

I was on the wharf at Lunenburg one afternoon when this schooner comes in off the Grand Banks and she'd stopped at St. John's and a couple of these goofy Newfies had hopped aboard. Not stowaways. Pretty hard to hide out on a fishing schooner unless you're a mouse. The skipper let them work their way over.

One was a lad of about 14 and his brother was 16 or so and they'd come from one of those outports you read about and the whole family was starving on codfish. One big meal of cod and spuds and Indian tea a day.

They seemed like likely lads but knowing nothing of farming and I was a farmer, but I told the skipper that I'd see what I could do. It was the old story. Leaving home so there'd be more food for the younger ones. At six cents a day, that's hardly flour gravy for the cod and dried beans and apples, and if they ate more than rabbits you'd surprise me.

They had nothing, they carried nothing and I told them they could stay on my farm and help with the haying and I'd give them three good meals and maybe get their teeth fixed. Their teeth were in shocking state. Black. God!

Mallory and Derek, pretty fancy names for a couple of outporters, eh? Stayed with me for four or five years and they grew to be big strong men and never asked for a penny and were grateful for the few dollars I gave them. They wanted nothing. Brought up to hard work, all they wanted to do was escape that prison of Newfoundland. In the years they were with us, they never received a letter or card or anything from home. I guess a lot of lads just disappeared like that."

———————— • ————————

Friendship Was For Sale

"I worked in this little store on Bloor Street West. A little store but my boss had a good neighbourhood business, vegetables, canned goods. Well, it was just a little store like there were hundreds in Toronto. A family store.

I opened up at eight because somebody had to be there for the first deliveries, bread, vegetables, and I stayed to six at night and I got $7 a week which suited me all right and the owner would let me take home wilted vegetables and things he knew he couldn't sell that day. It wasn't much but my sister was with me and no job. We came from Timmins. So every bit helped and we got by. The room was $6 a month, the one we lived in.

This girl I went to school with in Timmins, Edith, she looked me up and used to come around to the store sometimes or up to the room to eat. She didn't have a job. Edith and I were girl friends in that I'd known her since I was a kid. You could say we were good friends.

One Saturday afternoon the owner, this Italian, he asks me if I would work for $5 a week and I said I was supporting my sister so how could I. It wasn't fair, I told him. Wasn't my work good? I didn't steal from him. So he said he was sorry but he'd have to let me go and there I was, one hour I've got a job and the next minute, and without actually saying I wouldn't take the $2 cut, like a 30 percent cut, I was out.

I went back Tuesday to get some things I'd left in the backroom, and guess who was clerking behind the counter? Sure. You don't have to guess too hard.

My friend, my wonderful friend Edith. She'd gone around behind my back and told Aiello, the store owner, she'd work for $5. That happened a lot in those days. When it was between friendship and a job, friendship just went out the window. It was four months before I got another job."

———————————— • ————————————

The Filthy Swine

"Them tourist people advertise, they say Nova Scotia is a pleasure land. Things like that. Maybe. You should have been around in '34.

I went underground, to the face, at 13. For Acadia Coal. They were the big cheese around here. That was in '30. In '34, and then I was 17, I could lick any man on my shift and that's why the foreman we had was such a big guy. He had to lick them all. I never tackled him although he would have been no match for me, but you see, he was a dictator. You worked if he said so. We were little white mice, happy to be in our little cage.

In '34 our pay was $2.80 a shift. That sounds a lot, I know, in what money could buy. I could buy beefsteak for six cents a pound and that was no fat on it. We had a new deal that the mine union had worked out and the Acadia men said no, we can't pay it, and instead of going up to I think $3.20 a day, the filthy swine wanted us to go *down* to I think $2.40. Bread out of the mouths of our kiddies.

There were about 2,500 men in the pits that company owned, you see, and we went out and the government, old Angus *(Premier MacDonald)* he said no, no help for you rotters. In those days the working man got it right where it hurt. Government wouldn't listen to him, but they'd listen to the companies.

So everything got real bad and I said to my mother, make me a lunch, I'm going up to Montreal and I'd be on the train for 24 hours. And so I went over to Halifax and took that train, the first I'd been on, and somewhere down the line the conductor came along and said everybody should shift their watches back one hour and right then and there, I said to myself that even if I should make a fortune I wasn't going to pleasure myself in a place where a man had to live a different time than the next fellow, and I stayed one night in Montreal and then I came home. I've been here ever since, working on the face until that pit prop split."

The Port Arthur Soup Kitchen

"Port Arthur had one of the best soup kitchens in the country and everyone knew it. In Vancouver or Regina or wherever, you always compared their soup kitchen stew with Port Arthur stew. If it was 'nearly as good as' then it was good stew.

After a couple of years of crossing the country I decided I'd settle down beside that stew pot, and I showed up for every line-up and every time the supervisor came along I'd ask him for a job. For board and 'baccy. That meant I would work for nothing, for a cot and blankets in the storeroom, three meals a day and enough money for rollings. You know, roll your own tobacco. After a while the staff started calling me 'Board And 'Baccy Dawson' and the name stuck.

I made myself handy and little by little I just moved in. I'd stay a night and then miss a night and then show up again and within a couple of months I had what I wanted. Nobody said anything, just glad of another hand, and I worked. Mostly behind the pots, because you could do yourself a lot of good by giving extra big helpings or forgetting that a guy had been through once before.

Two fellows I was favouring once cut me in on a warehouse they had lined up and we split more than $1,200 from the office drawer, $500 for each of them and $200 for me. Fair enough, I just was the lookout. I helped lots of fellows and they helped me and I made a lot of friends and once in a while, once in a year or so, one of them will show up here *(the Vancouver Skid Road)* and we'll go over to the Anchor and have a few beers. We're all old men now.

I spent about five years in that kitchen, as I recall, and kept one butcher downtown supplied with a quarter of beef every so often for which he made it worth my while. Nobody ever missed it and if it hadn't gone out the back door with me, those pieces of meat, and good grade meat too it was, would have found their way into some alderman's pantry or some city hall guy's kitchen. But believe this, I stole, but the boys on the line never went hungry."

————————————— • —————————————

We Ate Not Too Bad

"You ask me why I worked in a filling station for $5.50 a week, working 55 to 60 hours a week? Simple.

That was 10 cents an hour. With 10 cents my mother could buy more than a pound of hamburger. A quart of milk. About three pounds of dried beans or nearly two pounds of rice or two pounds of sugar or a bag of about eight rolls or a couple of small loaves of bread. A pound of peanut butter for 20 cents, good stuff with real peanuts in it.

I know these costs. They are burned into my brain.

That $5.50 kept my mother and my sister and me from starving. We didn't do too well in the other departments, medicine and movies and clothes, but we ate not too bad."

———————— • ————————

Harvest Workers From The East

"I often wonder what happened to men now like we had in those days? I'm just sort of thinking now, but I can remember men, some skinny little ginks, but men all the same, and they could work 12 to 14 hours in the field. Pitching bundles. There may have been parts of the West that didn't get a crop worth talking about, for three or four years, but there were places where it was heavy. You get a good crop of barley or rye, hell, anything, and you'll know what I'm talking about.

Men used to come out from the East on those harvest trains. I can't remember the years but take some college kid or factory worker down on his luck and you'd look at them and say to yourself you'll never get half a day's work out of them. First day you wouldn't. Second day either, but about the fourth day they stopped walking around like they had been pole-axed and the muscles started to toughen up and Jesus Christ, they were good workers.

Wages you wouldn't pay a Chinaman cutting rice, either. A dollar a day. Some years higher, but they never had any great hopes of more. A dollar a day, a dry bunkhouse, plenty of food and a ride into town Saturday night, that was the best they expected. It was what they got, too. Cheerful bunch, too. College kids, some of them, squeezed out of college because there was no money at home. No money anywhere.

They had fun, clowning around. They'd borrow the .22 and go after gophers and they usually got to know a few girls in the district. There were a few babies born in March and April, let me say, that didn't know their daddies. Oh, what the hell. My very own daughter had one. A boy. It was no great thing to cause alarm, as I remember. Life on a farm has its own way of straightening out things. The boy came back next August and married her. It was quite simple.

All in all, man for man, I'll stack the Canadian worker up against any worker in the world. Good fellows."

———————————— • ————————————

Working For Nothing

"I'm not at all sure I could do it again. No, I don't think any of us could do it all over. If I went out, my mother had to stay home in slippers because there was only one pair of decent shoes in the place.

I got out of commercial school with decent marks, short-hand, typing, you know, the rest of it, and this was in '32 and there were no jobs. I remember thinking I could get one over at the hospital and I very nearly did, yes, very nearly did, until some other girl got it. I found out she was the friend of a friend of the administrator's daughter. It was who you knew, not what you knew. That kind of thing. It still is today, I guess.

That winter I walked the length of Jasper Avenue *(in Edmonton)* about three times and I'd stop in every place and ask. No luck. Then something happened. You want to call it luck? My uncle had told me that law offices were good places to work because lawyers always got business, foreclosures and such, and I'd tried the Jasper Block more than other places because it had the most lawyers. Anyway, I went into the lobby one morning because it was maybe 30 below out and I was warming myself when a man from one of the law offices came down those marble stairs that wind around and he recognized me from the number of times I'd been at their counter and he asked me how I was doing. I said I wasn't, rotten, or something like that and then I had this brainwave and I asked him if I could work in their office free. I couldn't stay home and listen to mother whine, and at least I'd be in a warm place and would be able to practice my typing and shorthand.

When I said free, I meant I would work for nothing. I guess it didn't sound that much out of line because young lawyers out of law school work on the same basis. He said fine, come in tomorrow, and I did. In my mother's shoes and a cousin's blouse and my own skirt, and my hair done nicely. Oh, God, but it was a good feeling. Just 18 and a real job. The first week I worked like the devils were chasing me, and at the end of the second week they gave me a dollar. For carfare, they said, although I could walk to work. Nobody said I was on the payroll and I sure wasn't going to be the one to ask. Not any way, thank you.

A month later I was doing a lot of legal work, the forms, typing them, delivering to the court house, swearing to papers at the court registry, and about the fifth week I got a pay envelope. I can remember it yet. Yellow, and my name, Margaret Evans, written across it. In red ink. I still remember it. Three dollars. I went out at noon and bought a pair of shoes at Army and Navy for a dollar, gave Mom a dollar that night, and I had the other dollar. I was rich.

In another month I got a $2 raise and I stayed with those people for 20 years, until they sold the practice and retired, and they were the nicest people in the world. One went to the coast and retired and I still get a Christmas present from them. The other died. They were good men."

Bright College Years

"I was desperate. No job, a wife and three kids and a nice house in Norwood and the end was in sight. A friend named Lettner phoned and said there was a job in an insurance office, or he thought there was. I phoned the manager and we had a chat and then he said he'd like to see me for an interview, and remember this was only selling insurance which, unless you were very good, was a very poor way to make a living in 1933, but he said come on down and see him, and just before he rang off he said, 'Oh, I forgot, have you been through the university?' I said yes. He said good.

I got on the street car and went out to Fort Garry and I went through every building there was that the University of Manitoba had. Even the cow barns. Next day I had a good interview and filled in a form and when it came to the part which said university, I printed in University of Manitoba. Nobody checked up, and why would they? I got the job, and I turned out to be a very good salesman. I'll bet you could get away with the same thing today.

Have you been through university? Yes. Good, you're hired."

A Line Around The Block

"The five-and-dime, Woolworth's, I think, put this ad in the 'Edmonton Journal' saying they wanted some salesgirls, and next morning I got up at five and walked from Bonnie Doon, down over the low-level bridge, and got to the store by about six o'clock. There was a night watchman there and already there were some women, girls there, three across, 11 deep so I was the 35th or so in line and I figured, well, if they want quite a few girls, then I've got a chance because my own eyes could tell me that some of the ones in front of me couldn't be asked. Too shabby. Too scruffy. Half starved, you see. By about nine, when the doors were to open, there was a line going down the block and around it and they'd even brought in some police. Somebody wasn't using their head that morning. It was cold, too. Christmas.

About nine somebody at the back tries to break in ahead of us and soon everybody is going at it, just one mass of women pushing back and forward, up and down, shouting, yelling. The police could do nothing. They didn't even try. The crush got so bad I just had to get out of there, job or no job, and just as I made it to fresh air the big show window buckled and fell in. They'd pushed that big window in.

That's when the cops started at it, grabbing women and just throwing them out into the street. Oh, it was a mess. I went home.

Later I found out they wanted *three* girls. Why didn't they just go through their applications? They must have had a stack five feet high. Instead they caused all that trouble. Silly."

———————————— • ————————————

Memories Of An Animal

"They always got a crop in the Peace River Country. Maybe hailed out or rained out, but I don't think they were ever burned out. They grew a lot of oats and barley up there. I went up there in 1935, just when it was the worst down south, drought, rust, smut, grasshoppers, you just wouldn't believe so many things could hit at once.

Up north their season was behind, of course, and there was some snow on the ground but it was going. A farmer in Dawson Creek asked if I had field pitched. I said I had and he didn't think I looked big enough. Okay, he said, $2 a day. We were in the hotel lobby at the time and a big guy said, 'Dollar, seventy-five' and I said I'd work for one-fifty.

Now, you've got to realize, that is one-fifty a day, and you didn't have a team of your own but just went around that field helping everyone else. In other words, you didn't get a chance to rest, going to the thresher or waiting a turn or coming back, you were pitching sheaves all day. You had to be in the stable to help the other fellows, you helped feed and water and then break-fast and then harness, and you worked all day until noon and the same thing then, and then all afternoon until damn near dark. It was brute labour of the worst kind and you prayed for a breakdown, something going wrong with the tractor or the thresher, something that would give you a break. Of course the farmer was hoping nothing would go wrong. Luck always was on his side.

You ate well, there was a good lunch the women would bring out about 3.30 in the afternoon, but I've seen me so tired at night that I couldn't eat. Just take off for the bunkhouse and not know a thing until next morning. Sleep even in my overalls and boots. There was nothing considered wrong about that, either. The farmers would say, 'Well, if you don't like it, there's a dozen guys hanging around the elevators just itching for your job.' There were, too.

Hard days. We were treated like animals, and I guess that's pretty well what we became."

We Worked For A Salary

"I worked for a large store. Well, it was Ashdown's, what we called then a family store. Founded by old Phil and handed down through sons, through the family. They didn't pay well, but it was security, and before '29, the thing you worked hard for and could look forward to was a pay raise. It would be small, but if you worked hard you got it. I think I made $80 a month in '29 and we got by.

Then came the Crash and the Depression and from then on it wasn't a case of looking forward to a raise but whether a pay cut would be coming. You know, five percent this year or seven percent next year, just a whittling and scraping and pruning away. Still, sir, it wasn't all that bad.

There was no income tax on those kind of salaries, and we were proud to say we worked for a salary rather than a wage because a wage meant hourly rates, labour, bohunk work, factories, that kind of thing. I guess they were better off, but we had that prestige. It seems silly now when you think of it, wouldn't you say?

I worked very hard for Ashdown's and they were good to me. But the pay cuts. Yes. They had us there. There was nothing we could do about it and we had the sense to know that if we didn't work hard we could be let go. That was the term, a man was 'let go.' Fired. That increased efficiency. Companies probably got more out of their staffs those days than ever before or since. I'd take my pay packet, the money came in an envelope, and give it to my wife and she would count it and if there was no cut she'd smile and nod her head.

I think I got cut about three or four times, but you must remember that the cost of living, food, rent, clothes, were going down, too, so I guess it was a break-even business.

This went on for about seven years. We brought up four children this way. Three actually, because one died. He was hit by a car going to school. When the war came and I heard there was going to be work in the shipyards on the coast, at Vancouver, I bid Ashdown's farewell and that was that. My advice to young people is never work in a large store. Unless you marry the daughter of the boss, the sure formula for success."

———————————————— • ————————————————

Be Safe, Be Careful

"Well, I got out of high school in 1928 and I got a job in the Winnipeg Grain Exchange on Lombard Street as an office boy at oh, I think it was seven a week. Maybe $6. Times were fair but wages were never all that high unless you were selling. On a commission basis. People would buy anything those days. Anyway, I was just a clerk, doing clerk jobs, and then came the Crash in the U.S. Of course, Canada just got knocked over like a ten pin. We didn't have a chance, six million people utterly dependent upon foreign markets and especially the Americans.

I own my own company now and if I knew then, in 1929, what I know now, and could have got the message across, there would be statues of me in every city in Canada. It is far too late now. I worked for that company for two years and things got worse and worse. In fact, my salary was cut to $5 a week, but you just took it.

I wanted to be a pilot, to fly, and Winnipeg was a jump-off place for the north then. Quite a bit of mining activity going on. I knew this fellow who ran a small flying school and he said he'd give me lessons for my ticket if I'd work a year for room and board at a base up north, God's Lake or Cranberry Portage. Somewhere I just can't remember. I didn't smoke, I didn't drink, and I'd be around planes all the time and that was what I wanted. Shit, it was like going to sea with Sir Francis Drake. I said okay and we shook hands and I told my mother, and you've got to picture her.

She was about, well just short of six feet and big, a big woman, and a stern face and she always dressed in black and she was the kind that meant business. I told and she said no, and I said yes, and that's the first time I ever really stood up to her. The office was on the fifth floor of the Grain Exchange and that woman, for God's sakes, even today I've got to admire her for it although I hate her for it, my mother came down at noon, the lunch hour, and she walked me up and down that narrow hall, and I can see it yet, the walls were a brown-yellow and the hall was poorly lit and the elevator was always clanging its doors down the hall and people were passing back and forth and probably wondering what the devil was going on, and my mother just kept talking.

Airplanes are dangerous. Pilots are unreliable. They beat their wives, they chase women, they drink until they pass out, they only work part of the time, flying companies are going broke all the time, the competition is too tough, the weather is bad, the north is so cold you can't stand it. God, that woman did her homework, and all the time in a slow, monotonous voice, like this: 'Now, Kenny, you'll be dead within six months up there, a propeller will fly off and cut you in two just like it did to that poor fellow at Kenora last month,' and on and on.

Then she'd turn and blow the other way. This is a stable company. It is a good job, clean, nice people around, the money will get better, the plans for advancement are excellent – hah! – and on and on. For five days. Five noon hours and at home, breakfast and dinner. Finally I couldn't take it any longer and I said okay, I'd stay, for five bucks a week I wouldn't go. I wouldn't get a pilot's license and work in the north.

I phoned my friend, the chap I'd spent a lot of time getting to know, and told him and he just said, 'Okay, Ken, if that's the way you want it,' and hung up on me. I felt worse about that than giving in to my mother. It took me 16 years and a war to get out of that goddamn little grain company and I never did go flying. I got into this business and it has been good to me, but I've often thought of flying. Of course, I might be dead now but I never did give it a try.

Be safe. Be careful. Never take a chance. Always listen to mother."

CHAPTER TWENTY

Things Were Just Fine, If You Had Any Money

I Was Up And They Were Down . . . Living It Up On $145 . . . A Bum, But An Elegant One . . . Have Faith In $20,000 . . . The Great Days Of Cruising . . . Bridge Parties Kept Us Going . . . The Gambler's Grand Tour . . . Velvet Gowns For The Relief Train . . . The Big Boys . . . Aunt Mary Meets The World . . . Hard Times Are For The Poor.

———————————— • ————————————

Depressions are good for people who have money. Some Canadians I interviewed remember it as a wonderful time. One man in Winnipeg made $200 a month selling cars – to whom? – and had a hard time remembering anything about the Depression, except there had been some wonderful championship fights in that decade and he had attended them all. A friend remembered happy days at a tennis club and that he had a dozen pairs of white ducks. Why so many? I asked. He said he bought so many because "they were always so cheap and the Depression might end and then they'd go back up in price again." He was an intelligent man, but he still didn't see the fallacy in his reasoning.

People bought two-storey houses in Vancouver for $2,000. A new car was less than a thousand. One of the Canadian Pacific's fabulous dining car dinners was about a dollar. Or a hamburger, called a nip then, cost five cents and a milk shake, called a milk whip, cost another nickel.

You could be in a relatively low income bracket and live in clover, with no income tax. The tax began on incomes over $2,000 a year. That was about $180 a month, and that was big money.

If your income was $6,000 a year, by fair means or foul, then you could live like a millionaire. It was as simple as that.

———————————— • ————————————

I Was Up And They Were Down

"If you had money the Dirty Thirties were a good time to live in. I was senior apprentice to a master miller in a big flour mill and I got $100 a month and you bet ya, I was in clover. Yes, I can remember everything about those times.

As I said I got $100 a month and that was a good wage. For a single man that was $25 a week and there was no taxes, the income tax didn't start until you made $2,000 a year, and I had a fine little apartment and a garage for $17.50 a month, kitchen, living room, two bedrooms and bathroom and big storage space in the basement. Not bad, eh?

I belonged to the canoe club over on the Red River and I curled, and in summer two other fellows and myself had a cottage all summer at Winnipeg Beach and we went to all the junior hockey games, following the Winnipeg Monarchs in those days, and I had a big Victor Northern Electric radio. They weren't called radios in those days. They were called radio receivers, which makes sense, doesn't it? The set received radio signals. There was Moore's Restaurant, and Child's down at the corner of Portage and Main, and the Royal Alex had a fine restaurant and so did the Fort Garry but it was always too stuffy for me. Life was good, on $100 a month, and I saved money too. About $15 each month.

Oh, yes, I had a snazzy little 1929 Auburn roadster, painted sort of a silvery grey and as I remember I bought it cheap. I offered them $100 down and paid it off at $15 a month and they were glad to take it. I think it was Webb Motors. A lot of those firms went belly up later – just not enough $100 a month bachelors around. It was a great little car, travelled over mud roads like a skater on ice, and it was sure good to get the girls. Later I bought a big Nash from Leonard and McLaughlin Motors.

Food was cheap. Meat was shockingly cheap. You could buy a pound of fresh filetted pickerel straight from Lake Winnipeg that morning for something like 15 cents a pound. Lamb, 10 cents a pound. Stew lamb, why they practically gave it away. Sirloin, 20 cents, even less. Everything was rock bottom, and I heard the cost of living dropped more than 35 percent from 1927 to 1933.

No, we never thought of the poor people. The reliefers. We'd see them on these make-work jobs, cleaning up back lanes, digging dandelions, hauling coal. I never thought to pity them, or help them. Far as I knew, nobody did. They were just there. If I went up to the public library on William Avenue and I saw how the people lived around there, sometimes I'd wonder. But only how people could live in such poverty, such conditions. I can't remember ever asking myself what made such poverty, such conditions. I was up and they were down and I expected to see my name in the sport pages as part of the team that won such and such a race at the canoe club, and if those people, if their name showed up in the 'Free Press' as having been sent to jail for stealing from Eaton's or the Bay, then so be it. What I mean is, I equated poverty with the sort of low life that criminals led and, I guess, if you were a criminal or that way inclined, then you lived in poverty and poor conditions.

No, I can't really say that I had a social conscience. Of course, you must realize that such a phrase had not even been invented then. There were always people in Market Square in the evenings ranting about hard times and corruption and R. B. Bennett and why weren't more jobs being made. We would just say they were 'Commies' although I believe the usual word was 'Bolshevists.' The newspapers ignored them, usually.

I remember I was stopped for speeding by a motorcycle cop one afternoon, on West Portage, and it turned out to be a chap I'd gone to school with and we got to jabbering and he said he was making $19 a week and he was tickled pink with it. I said I was making $25 a week and he said, 'In that case, Ernie, you get a ticket. This way it sort of spreads things a bit more evenly.' I remembered that, not to blab about how much you were making. There were too many thems and not that many of us and it was best to just let sleeping dogs lie.

Good times. When I married my wife in 1939 I was making $120 and it looked like I was going to get a good shot at that miller's job. It didn't work out that way because I went into the army two years later and there was no job for a captain working as 2-i.c. in a 40-year-old flour mill for me after. I was a big shot and wanted a big shot job. I moved to Saskatchewan and started a feed store, bulk oil dealership and had a small mill on the side. Just to keep my hand in. I did well.

Does all that sound phoney?"

———————————— • ————————————

Living It Up On $145

"You never had to worry if you were in the army, but yet you'd hear people say, 'Oh, he can't make it in civilian life, that's why he's in uniform.' Stray cats and dogs, that's what people thought the army was about.

I'd like to tell them that my father was a sergeant major and we lived on permanent force bases. Kingston, mainly. He made $145 a month in those days and he used to laugh, 'Momma, even my broker doesn't make $145.' It was a big joke to him.

He got a good house for us, and his uniforms and we got dental and medical care and all the cod liver oil we could stand and my brothers took tennis lessons on the base and we had good holidays, and getting extra food was no problem. No problem whatsoever. You see, my father was in charge of messing. The non-commissioned officers' mess.

We dressed well, we ate well, we lived well and it was only when September, 1939, came along that we learned what the army was really all about. Then that was midnight. The ball was over. Everyone had to go to work."

────────────── • ──────────────

A Bum, But An Elegant One

"My father was a businessman, with about eight salesmen on the road. He'd take any line, provided it was made of cloth or leather or rubber. All through Ontario, down into Montreal. A buck was a buck to him.

I tried it, a territory which was pretty good, but on commission don't think I was making any fortune. Even in '29 you could see something was happening. The customers weren't buying so the stores weren't ordering and a couple of months, like August which should have been good for Christmas orders, I think I made $80 on commissions. I could edge that up to about $100 by sticking the old expense account but it wasn't my style so I quit and the old man, well, I shamed him into giving me an allowance. Fifteen a week. I slept at home. I often ate at home.

The Depression hit. My old man's jobbing business was just a pile of bills. Half the salesmen went, they doubled up on the territories and worked their asses off and were glad.

Then he said my allowance was being cut to $10. So who cares? Bennett is bringing in the dole and I've got friends, so I get $8 relief a week, so I'm okay. The guy at the relief office would say, 'Why don't you get a job?' And I'd say, 'Don't talk crap. Who would hire a bum like me?' I meant it. I was a bum, but an elegant one. At $18 a week and no expenses I was almost in the bankers' class. I never worked a day during the Depression and there was never a day I did not enjoy. Good times."

────────────── • ──────────────

Have Faith In $20,000

"Jesus Christ, I heard about one guy who got $20,000 when his mother died, this was about 1935 or thereabouts, and he kept his eye open and picked one house up here and another there and watched out for forced sales and bought up mortgages at next to nothing, all in the Kitsilano area and Fairview and around there. In a couple of years he wound up with about 60 houses, old ones, frame ones, but some good ones too, but mainly they were on good lots, some close to the water.

They'd be easily worth, and I'm being easy on it, at least one and a half million dollars now. A guy I know who knows this fellow said he didn't have faith in Vancouver, he just had faith in what $20,000 cash could do."

———————— • ————————

The Great Days Of Cruising

"I used to travel a lot. Once you sailed past Quebec or The Battery or out through the Golden Gate, then you could tell the whole world to go straight to hell. It was going there anyway. Beer was 10 cents a bottle and a double brandy 15 cents and if you watched yourself you could survive – and the food! Just thinking of that food today is still something beautiful.

They practically got down on their knees and begged you to travel. What they called winter cruises. They'd leave about the first week in October and you got back in late April. Around the world, around the old orange. If you left from New York, then you came back through the Panama or dropped off in San Francisco.

Plenty of women. First day out you ignored them. Be aloof. Second day, look interested at the one or two you wanted. Third day, smile gently, as if you were bored and wanted company. That night after dinner, move in. Be the big bad wolf. Blow their house down. It always worked, because, you see, that is what they were aboard for. Romance. To forget a lost love. Get over a divorce. They were very, very vulnerable. A pushover, as we used to say.

Say you left from S.F. Then to Hawaii, and to Japan and to places you've never heard of today. Korea was over the flat edge of the world then but the cruise ships stopped there. Everything done right. Manchukuo, the city of Mukden. The Japs moved in on that, starting the war with China. Half the population doesn't even know Japan had a big war with China for years before the last war. China. Hell, I saw the Great Wall three times. The last time, I was doing the guiding. Strictly amateur, but I knew as much as the guide. Shanghai! The International Settlement. What a town. Women by the score. White, black, red, brown and golden. The golden women! Anyway, Philippines, Siam, that's Thailand. Straits Settlements, that's Singapore and

Malaya now. Things change. Java, that's Indonesia now – *there* was a place for golden women, cute little things. Bali, Ceylon, and India when the Raj was still running the show. Egypt, Italy and then France and then Good Old Noo Yawk.

I forget. Two grand. Two thousand bucks. First class stateroom, on the upper deck. I mean strictly first class. There is nothing, absolutely nothing like it now and never will be again. That gave you all shore tours included and the very best.

About seven months. That works out to about $300 of living a month as good as any king got. Seven months away from North America. The thing would cost you at least ten grand now and you'd be made to feel like The Ugly American, The Ugly Canadian in half the places, more than half the places we visited. You know, there is something to be said for colonialism, keeping the bastards in their places. I'm all for it."

Bridge Parties Kept Us Going

"It was the bridge parties which kept us alive. Literally alive. I mean it.

My husband was on the Faculty at Saskatoon, the university, and contrary to what most people thought, academics in those days were graded pretty low, very low in the salary schedule. You talk about a janitor, pardon me, a structural custodian, these days making almost as much as a teacher in an elementary school, well let me tell you it wasn't all that much different in the Thirties. Tenure was a fine thing, you couldn't get fired, but don't you believe me, they knew how to cut in those days.

I had three children to bring up and I followed all the advice in the papers, like buying day-old bread because it was better and steaming it, and saving the water that greens had been boiled in and using it – but it still tasted awful – and using cheese and dried beans as a meat substitute.

There was one that was a dandy. Don't drink tea because it has no food value. Well, let me tell you this, I like my tea. It may not have food value but it has philosophical value and heart warming value.

But to bridge. October through to the end of April, and once a week, every Thursday, we started at 1:30, quite early, and played for about nearly two hours and then had a lovely lunch and talk and went home to another week of the Depression. One year it was two tables, eight ladies, but the rest, it was four ladies, just four good friends. We all lived near the campus and we did have nice homes but it was those days and nobody really did any entertaining. Couldn't afford to, that was the real reason. But we did have our lovely living rooms and our furniture and our best china, and we could still cook. So important. We were starved for talk. 'Socializing' as a farm woman might call it.

My turn came around every four weeks and the week before was the anticipation, the planning what to have. Let's see, Monday I'd do a bit of cooking and the floors, and Tuesday I'd scrub and polish the hall and bathroom and living room and kitchen, and Wednesday I'd prepare. God, how I'd prepare a luncheon. Scrumptious, I can tell you, just scrumptious. Somebody used to use that word, scrumptious, in one of the radio shows. We didn't compete to see who could put up the best lunch but we all did our best, and there was no jealousy. We were such good friends.

Poor bridge players, I might add. Contract bridge was really quite new in those days so we'd often play auction, which was simple.

It was the anticipation, that's what counted. Having them come to your house, your home, and going to their homes even though they just lived around the neighbourhood. When Mrs. Hensley died, it was like we had lost our best friend and it took a lot of deciding who would take her place. Oh, lots of ladies wanted to join. In that way it was a kind of exclusive club. Not snobby, but in a way, yes, you could say it was, if you understand.

Those were such hard times. As I remember there were times when you heard of somebody leaving, a fine letter of recommendation and all that, but the thing remained, he and his family wouldn't be around Saskatoon when the fall classes began. Saskatoon was such a nice town, such a pretty place with all its trees and the river, and it also was a place where everybody knew everybody else's business and there was an awful lot of talking at those bridge parties. Of course I should have said that it was very inexpensive, these little parties. You must remember that prices were quite low, you know, good brown bread for four cents a loaf and sugar at practically nothing a pound and a little money would go a long way and besides, the papers were full of economy recipes, oh they had fancy names for them, but they were still Depression recipes. I still remember those weekly tea parties so well. They were such good times."

———————————— • ————————————

The Gambler's Grand Tour

"Holy Jesus, do I sure remember those times. I knew them like my own face in the mirror. I came out of the 14-18 war, the navy, and got on with the railroad. That was then in the days of what I call the railroad families. My grandfather had helped build the railroad and my Dad, well, he was a conductor which was right up there, and Dad was able to slip the word to the guy in the hiring office, and so his son got on the board. I was braking, east and west out of Winnipeg. It was a good job and if I recall, I was making about $100 a month, which was enough. You could get by. But that's not what you want.

Right, and when '29 came along I was only 17th from the bottom of the list. People just weren't dying off like they should, and by '31, well, I got the notice that I was being put on stand-by, everybody above 50 on the list was standby, and you don't have to be a railroader to know you were down pretty low to get any part-time work. This was '31. Nothing to do. Shovelling snow for the city, or warehouse work a day or so a week. I set myself up as a painter, a house painter, and my capital just dwindled away because who was getting their houses painted? The municipalities weren't even painting the schools. Let 'em rot. So many people had nothing to do and when there is something happening like that, then there are other people who will always take advantage of that. There are people to whom people in distress are their natural prey. I refer to the gamblers. They set up games, and there must have been 20 or more operating around Winnipeg at any one time. They supplied the house and took the rake-off and did well.

Now, you may ask, where did the money come from? I will tell you this, my friend. You could set up a game at the South Pole and soon you'd have players, even if they were only penguins, and soon people would be coming in from New Zealand. This is the way Las Vegas flourishes. A gambler is a gambler and if not born a gambler he will soon become one. Gambling is like drug addiction. I know. A gambler will sell his wife's wedding ring and even his wife if he figured he could find a buyer.

So I became a gambler, and I was a good one. I knew the cards, the combination, the odds, and I had that one commodity you've got to have. You've got to have patience. And one other thing, my friend. I had luck. Not always, but more often than not.

To make a long story short, in about two years I had won about $10,000. That is a lot of money. That is a great deal of money. In today's terms I would be considered well off. I won in Winnipeg until I was told to move on, not by the police but by the game operators. They could have just barred me from the games but they wanted me out. Gone. Away. Their word was as good as the police.

Once I saw four or five envelopes sticking out of the pocket of one game owner and I said something like, 'What are you doing, answering the lovelorn columns?' and he laughed. He said, 'No, for my boys.' I didn't follow him, but about an hour later the door opened and a cop came in, in plainclothes, and he went back into the kitchen with the operator and when he came out he had the envelopes in his hand and was stuffing them into his pocket. Now, my friend, those envelopes did not contain pressed violets.

I left. To Toronto, and my luck and patience held and I won there and that was when I topped off my $10,000 with a weekend down in Montreal which added $2,000 or thereabouts. You see, there was lots of money around, and it was there to be taken. But I'd had enough, for then.

I went to a good tailor, a little Jew who must have been in the business for ever, and I said to the little fellow that I wanted two new suits, two sports outfits, the whole kit and kaboodle and I wanted to look like a fashion plate, but casual. You know, and he said yes. I gave him $250 in good faith money and you should have seen him blink. I was dressed like an English lord for about $500. Not bad for a brakey, eh?

Then I cashed the money into American funds and I took the train down to Detroit and went to the factory and bought a Lincoln Zephyr V-12. Now that was a car. V-12 motor. Lime green. It looked expensive but it wasn't. Only $1,200, something like that. It would be a $10,000 car today. I was registered at the Brooks-Cadillac and I got the head bell boy and I told him there was $50 for him if he could find a girl who wanted to travel around the States with me. The way I described her he must have thought I was ordering the girl next door. That kind of thing. But he got one. Jeannie. A wonderful girl, and we spent many months together, just touring in our big car. New York, there we stayed at the Ritz-Carlton at Madison and 46th for $7 a night and lived like a king and queen. Florida, the big hotels, $3 or $4 a night. The Greenbriar. Six days and nights on a cruise to the Caribbean, the very best, only $130 for both of us. God damn, but a man could live like a king on practically nothing. On that ocean trip I got in a game one night and took in more than a grand. I wound up playing only when I felt like it, maybe once a week, and wound up with more than I left.

Five months later, four of travelling and a month in the Ambassador in L.A., I gave Jeannie $1,000 and paid her fare home and said good luck. She didn't want to go, cried for two days, but that's the way I decided it would be.

I sold the car, took the train up to Vancouver and, well I guess I was tired of it all because I invested my money, made some on it, moved to Calgary and then back to Winnipeg but I couldn't pick up the strings any more and I just drifted around until the war started and I joined up. That's about all."

—————————— • ——————————

Velvet Gowns For The Relief Train

"Our town, Guelph, had manufacturing, you see, and that's the way it had been for generations and while some mills, some foundries, while they cut back, they never quite closed down so there was always work. Wages were cut, you know, but a man could work. Some of the immigrants who had come in in the past 20 years, Italians and so on, they would be laid off, but that would be in slack periods. No, our home never suffered all that much.

Yes, the relief trains. Well, I don't know if you'd call them trains but groups, like our church and others, we'd be asked to get together and try and get up enough goods, and I mean clothes, baby things, shoes and boots, mittens, ladies' things, and if we could, pots and pans and rugs and blankets and anything that we figured would be of some use to those poor starving people in Saskatchewan. Was it the prairies, or just Saskatchewan?

Our minister came up with the slogan: *From Green Ontario to Parched Saskatchewan.* Something like that. We had a meeting and I can't recall who asked us to call it. The Red Cross, maybe? Anyway, we were to set up a committee and we were assigned a box car to fill. None of us knew how big a box car was, but our minister said it was big and we named this committee and set a day for collection.

Well, you never saw anything like it before. Picture those old houses. Some big as fortresses, well, just as strong anyway, and for generations it seems, people hadn't thrown anything away and anything half way usable would go up into the attic. I know when the girls and I started in, we wondered why the house just hadn't fallen down of the weight. You never saw such stuff. There were trunks, clothes brought out from Scotland and never worn, bonnets and these big hats the like of you wouldn't believe, and dresses with three and four built-in petticoats. It was like a circus. My three girls just had the time of their lives, and finally I had to lay down the law and I told them to just keep passing the stuff to me and I'd decide whether it should be kept, thrown away or sent out to parched Saskatchewan. Things like high-button shoes went into the garbage and I wonder if I was right? After all, on a farm, I think such shoes would have had some use. Just slopping pigs if nothing else.

It was like a circus, all one day, this Saturday, and the girls were trying on clothes and coats and furs and hats. In the end we sent everything, almost, because it was of the best weave. A lot of Paisley, the best wool Scotland and the mills around Guelph could produce. I think we had 18 or 20 boxes of clothes, and on top of each we posted a little list saying what was in each box and let the people at the other end worry about who got what. Who would be strutting around in the dust in a velvet gown and an ostrich feathered hat? Things like that would send us off into laughing so hard.

Now, you must allow that this was going on in a hundred other homes in Guelph and in Galt and up in Toronto and Brantford and Hamilton and down at Woodstock and London, all over the place. All these attics. Is it any wonder it was announced that in that year, I think it was 250 car loads that were sent, and it must be remembered these were good clothes, warm clothes, and often they had never been worn or only once or twice and once you got the stink of moth balls out, why things would be pretty good out there in the west. To make a long story short, they were picked up and shipped out.

Now I have a strange observation to make. It happened years later, after I had moved to Winnipeg. I was talking to an old lady, my age, you understand, a neighbour of my daughter, and I mentioned this very thing, how we cleaned out the attics to send the relief trains out. I should mention that there also were food trains sent, many many box cars, but I had nothing to do with that.

This old lady stiffened and her face became hard and she said, 'Mrs. Monk, in all your days you will never know how the people of Saskatchewan resented those clothes. How they downright hated them. You people in the East got us into the Depression and then when the drought came and we could do nothing, you threw your old moth-ball clothes at us like a bunch of town ragamuffins throwing rocks at the local idiot. I must say this, because it's true and I believe in speaking the truth.' Those were almost her very words.

Needless to say, I was astonished. Astonished, for goodness sakes, and I said that they took the clothes and used them and weren't they good clothes and didn't they need them? She said, 'Mrs. Monk, it may interest you to know that for one winter I milked three skinny cows in a dress which could have been worn to a ball honouring the coronation of Queen Victoria. A lovely dress. A truly wonderful dress.'

We looked at each other, these two old ladies, and we couldn't help it, just the thought of it, and we both burst out laughing. Just picture it, and we hugged each other then, still laughing. We became good friends."

———————————— • ————————————

The Big Boys

"Canadians didn't own all that many bonds, stocks, securities, because a lot had been hurt by the Depression of 1919 when the boys came back from France and everything dropped. Remember, in 1929 our banks were sound. Our big companies were sound, or fairly sound. The government was in strong control. The big families of Ontario, of Westmount in Montreal, the strong French families, a few in the Maritimes, some in the cities of the prairies, and of course, the lumber and fishing and mining families in British Columbia, all these wealthy men, the financiers, they came through it okay.

Yes, they suffered losses but nothing which really dented their fortunes. You must remember a lot of these people were of Scots ancestry or Scots themselves. You've heard of Scots thriftiness. Well, it was so. Canniness. The bankers and financiers, the ones who did a lot of the buy and sell of the country and who advised others, their friends, they all came through in pretty fair fashion.

I know there was a terrible disenchantment among ordinary people with what has been called Big Business but I think this was an overflow from the United States. Remember, then as now, we were dominated by American newspaper news, especially financial news, and magazines and radio and the talkies, of course.

As I saw it, many of the wealthy just sat back to ride it out, and they knew their money was pretty safe. Their style of doing things didn't change much. Of course, a lot of little guys got wiped out, but in those days they shouldn't have been in the market anyway. It was for the big boys. The speculators were wiped out, just driven right off the map. It had to be that way. That's the way the system worked. The empire builders, and the friends of the empire builders, went on to double and triple their money in later years."

———————————— • ————————————

Aunt Mary Meets The World

"I had an aunt named Mary Hudson and she lived with us in Brandon, Manitoba. She was a funny little creature and nobody knew much about her

but she was my mother's aunt. She had her own room and toilet in our basement and she helped mother when she felt like it and she paid rent and for
food, and that helped, but really, we didn't know much about her. It would
be safe to say she was just somebody around the house.

She was from Toronto, and every day she got the Toronto "Globe" delivered, although it was days late. She'd spend all morning reading it. Why she
stayed with us I don't know, if she was still that much in love with Toronto,
which was a place which was very, very far away in those days.

One day at the supper table she announced she was leaving on a round-
the-world trip, leaving in two weeks. Just like that! This little biddy who
wouldn't even go downtown alone was going around the world. In the
Thirties, that was just unthinkable. A big trip then was to Riding Mountain
National Park about 70 miles away. In about a week, she had packed a big
trunk and got a train for Vancouver, and she was gone months and months
and we'd occasionally get a card. Off somewhere in the wilds, and nothing on
it but 'Love to you all.' Some inanity like that.

Just before Christmas, and this was months later, we got a telegram and
she was coming home the next day and Dad and I took the old car down to
the C.P.R. station and there she was. She had three trunks now, not just one,
but she didn't look or act any different. Same old Aunt Mary. The other two
trunks were filled with souvenirs and she passed them around, and now that
I think of it, just junk, but it was good then. I think most of it ended up in
our school museum.

Next afternoon when I came home from school there she was in the sun
room getting the last bit of warmth and the floor and the couch were piled
with about ten tons of Toronto "Globe" newspapers going back about six
months, and she was slowly going through the society pages of each one,
catching up on what had gone on.

But that's not the real point of the story. The real point is that she told my
mother that her trip had cost her no more than $600, and that was every kind
of fare, meals, hotels, those crazy souvenirs. Six hundred dollars. Six months.
That's what the Depression was all about. If you had money, it appreciated in
value. You could live like a king on peanuts. Nice old Aunt Mary certainly was
nobody's fool."

Hard Times Are For The Poor

"If you were on a salary, if you were in the civil service, whether the federal government or Alberta or Edmonton, if you did not take a paper or listen to the radio and just did your job and collected your money, you would never have really known about hard times.

In the cities, I feel, the Depression was for the people who are always in trouble. They have fancy names for them now, but they were the poor. Those that couldn't help themselves. The aged, old age pensioners. Cripples. Women whose husbands had run off, just up and left and not come back. Young men with no education, their brains all in their muscles. Men over 40 or 45 who had been in one job all their lives, say an insurance office or a warehouse, and knew nothing else and had no chance to learn anything else. Those with a shortage of grey matter, the semi-retarded. Girls with illegitimate babies, and young couples who had married and had too many kids all at once on really no salary at all. Think that list over, and you'll agree that it is just about the same as the categories we have today. The unemployed and the unemployable.

But if you had a job, you could do well. Hell, even a postie's job was good. Men fought to get them. Security, fresh air, a chance to kick dogs. The pay wasn't great, but when has it ever been in that sort of work? Civil servants always have been scared men. I know, I was there. There may have been pay cuts, like the 10 and 5 and 15 percent hacks the others got in the private sector, but again, raises weren't all that frequent either. Like never. Many a man got married on $80 a month. I was making $19 a week when May and I did the dirty deed. If you were making $125, then it was chicken every Sunday and a new Ford and down to Sylvan Lake or out to one of the beaches and maybe a good, long trip every third year. You could rent a house for $18 to $25 a month, a good house. You could buy a big one for $1,250, three bedrooms, living room, dining room, kitchen, bathroom, garage. No, I am not kidding you. And if you went at it the right way you could knock that down to $1,100 by bargaining. I know chaps who are wealthy today because they watched the tax sales and bought houses, good ones in good districts, for peanuts. Say, $500 or $600. That was nothing. Of course, you had to have cash or a very, very friendly garden. Everybody had a garden and a lot of people on the outskirts had chickens and some tried rabbits, although I never cared for the meat.

If you had $125, you were on Easy Street. Remember, no income tax. None. You had to be making more than $2,000 to pay income tax, and then it was damn little. How the country got along I don't know. Yes, I was making $1,500, and I was doing well. We had a house, and our payments were about $35 a month with interest. Of course, it took years and years to pay off, but nobody thought about that. When things got better, after '39, that $35 was a lot cheaper than rent and everybody who'd bought a house on time felt better and all those who pooh-poohed the whole buy-a-house thing felt lousy. I had a Ford, yes, a Model A and then later, about '37, I bought a 1933 Plymouth and that was a damn good little car. A little dandy. I drove her to 1948 and then sold her for more than I'd paid for it. She was in good shape and cars were hard to get. The big companies had just finished retooling after the war.

The wife and I could go down to the Piggly Wiggly *(a Depression supermarket)* and for $5 we could fill up the back of that car. On a Sunday in the fall we'd drive south of here, down to Trochu, a little town, and we knew a farm family down there, a second cousin, and we'd buy up on meat. Two sides of beef, and chickens, and as this was just about Thanksgiving, a couple of turkeys, one for Thanksgiving and one for Christmas. The cost was dirt cheap, a few cents a pound for the beef and maybe 50 cents for the big chickens and I forget what for the turkeys, but damn low. They were happy, they didn't have to go through a middleman, and we were happy.

I should say that farmers hated the middleman as much or more than they hated their local friendly Bank of Montreal banker. Can you blame them? Beef they sold at $12 or $13 a hundredweight wound up in the butchershops all over Edmonton a week later at five and six times that price.

Entertainment was cheap. You paid about 35 cents for the first-run movies on Jasper Avenue and they are $3 today. You'll remember most of them were crap, what we'd call escapism entertainment today. Get their mind off the Depression stuff. I heard that Roosevelt once asked Hollywood to only make happy movies in those days. He didn't have to ask that. People wanted happy movies, pretty girls and dancing and music and a loving kiss at the end, and that's what Hollywood gave them. I'm turning my mind back and I'm damned if I can remember one big grim movie about the Depression. Maybe "How Green Was My Valley," but that was in Wales, wasn't it? "The Grapes of Wrath" came out after. I bought the book about Christmas of '38 and so the movie must have come out later.

By 1937 we were getting back into business. The rains came again in '37 in some parts and '38 in others, and north of here it was always pretty good. What we needed was better price for wheat, and as I recall, it was around 55 cents in '39 and that wasn't too bad. Far from good, but the farmer and the Edmontonian ate out of each other's dishes and we got to be thankful for small mercies, as they say.

Clothes? I have bought good suits with a vest and an extra pair of pants for $20, the best cloth. Off the rack, of course, but good Scottish material. I have bought a good suit, not the best but good, for $13 which would wear like iron and I still have an old overcoat around that I bought in 1936 and it cost me $9.95 and I remember that price well, and when I die, that coat will go to the Good Will or the Salvation Army and some down-and-outer will wear it for another few years. Underwear, socks, shoes, shirts, hell, man, they were almost giving them away. Shoes, say $4, and good ones too. Shirts, 95 cents over at Eaton's. Anyway, I'm just throwing my mind back, but if you had a steady job, you could go a hell of a long way on $100 in the Thirties. Education was cheap. You could put a kid through to be an engineer or a teacher across the river *(at the University of Alberta)* for practically nothing provided he lived at home. Practically nothing.

But you mustn't get the idea that everything was rosy. What I meant was that if you shut your eyes to all the misery, then you could do fine. But if you were a man, a person who was concerned, then it worried you."

CHAPTER TWENTY-ONE

Home-Made Entertainment

Four Men At The Butcher Shop ... There Was Always The Baseball ... Love In Hidden Places ... What Happened To All The Pianos? ... Camping – 1935 Style ... Welcome To A Corn Roast ... Fun Cost Practically Nothing ... The Famous Winnipeg Rebels ... Everybody Played Hockey.

———————————— • ————————————

Forget the Roaring Twenties; that was an invention of Broadway gossip colum-nists. Remember that Canada was a country proud of being conservative, thrifty, and canny – in the Thirties Canada was still a go-to-Church-on-Sunday country. But it was not a solemn sober country where you never had any fun.

There were skating parties down the long stretches of river and hayrides along country lanes, big roasts of corn and pick-up hockey games on flooded corner lots and all-day Saturday baseball and stamp collecting and bridge clubs and Monopoly and come-as-you-are camping with sing-songs around the fire and hot chocolate and oatmeal cookies, and quilting bees when a lot of ladies got together and talked and talked and talked, and shooting gophers with sling shots, and putting messages in bottles and floating them out to sea and going down to the station for no other reason than to watch the 7.38 come in, and leave at 7.41.

All in all, the Depression was the biggest do-it-yourself fun-filled, action-packed show in the world. If you were able to forget ...

———————————— • ————————————

Four Men At The Butcher Shop

"It was August, 1934. I remember the date. Hell, I remember every date. I'll remember the day of my hanging. Anyway, I was in Vancouver and I was flush with about a hundred bucks in my kick and that was worth three months hard labour in a Hastings Mill camp up on the island, three months, spend-ing nothing, and the jack to show for it, but there was hundreds walking the streets. I figured I'd take her easy, a hotel down on Cordova, one of those places the Chinese used to run, and a couple of good meals a day and drinking around, beer, and talking to the boys.

I wasn't going to be too free and easy with handouts, last of the big time spenders. One hundred would go about two months. I reckoned. That didn't include a woman, you understand. Just room and grub and beer and smokes. No women. This was the Skid Road though, you see, and a woman wasn't all that much of a problem. They were so hungry you could just walk down the street and think, 'I want a woman' and there would be one, ready to spread out for a couple of beers and kind words.

Anyway, I was stakey and I wandered up from Cordova over to Granville Street. They didn't like loggers up that way. It cut down on the tone of the high-class business section. There was this butcher shop called Reid's on Granville and their window was a sight to see. Damn it all, man, just a sight to see. They had this electric apparatus, the first kind of barbecue I ever saw, and there were two chickens on the spit.

God, man, but they were plump and juicy and brown and there were three other guys standing there, the thing was quite an attention-getter, and we watched it and I said aloud, 'You know, if I had some place to eat that, I'd buy it,' and the guy next to me said, 'Well, I'd throw in for that pan of potato salad,' and the third guy said, 'I don't have a red cent, but my wife and I have an apartment down the street and over on Pender and if you want to, you're welcome to come with us,' and damn it all if the fourth guy didn't say he'd like to come, and he'd hustle over to the liquor store and buy some booze. So I bought those two big chickens, and I think they cost me a dollar each, and the other guy bought the pan of salad and a jar of pickles and the other guy picked up a 40-ouncer of Hudson's Bay rye and we went to the apartment.

Now, remember, we didn't know each other, hadn't even laid eyes on each other, and here we were having a good party. His wife was a lovely woman and we ate and drank that 40 and laughed and joked and had a wonderful evening and it was Frank and Doug and so on. We didn't bother with last names and we didn't impose on each other, didn't ask anything. The five of us were just friends and we didn't expect to see each other again so we were ourselves.

What I'm getting at is, things were done different then. Sure, some people were suspicious, naturally, being people, but people were friends, they helped each other out. I bought the chicken, Doug bought the juice, somebody did this and somebody did that and nobody expected anybody to sign on the dotted line. Nobody expected to be paid back. I know human nature doesn't change, I know that, damnit, but I've seen it change over the past 20 years, and I liked it more back in the days, like that day in August of 1934, when we were standing outside that butcher store on Granville Street. Sure, I may be wrong, but I don't think so. People were different then."

———————————•———————————

There Was Always The Baseball

"Baseball! God, if you came from the Prairies you had to remember baseball. There was nothing else to do. You'd work your land and put in the seed and watch the Russian thistle knock out the new wheat or barley and then the blistering heat would come and you could just see everything shrivelling. Then you'd get, maybe, the grasshoppers, and that was it for the year. No crop insurance, nothing, but there was always the baseball.

If you had a car you could get to a tournament every weekend. All through Manitoba, Saskatchewan, Alberta, and teams used to come out from the Okanagan Valley too. I remember one team that came from Penticton, I think, and they rode the freights to get to a tournament at Vulcan.

Each town would have a sports day, beginning early in June and running right through to Labour Day, sports all over the country. There would be men's fastball, just ordinary baseball, and then there was softball, and a men and women's senior team and usually a girls' and boys', or junior teams. Most towns, if they were big enough, and they had the surrounding farms and villages to draw on, they had four teams, and there were some damn good teams. I've seen senior teams from towns in Saskatchewan which could go up against anybody in the country today. It was just that they were stuck out there in the wilds and nobody ever heard of them, but some of that pitching was strictly big league. Mostly fastball, you understand. There wasn't much slider or curve. The boys got up there and for seven or so innings they just threw that ball as hard as they could and nobody can tell me there weren't a couple of potential Dizzy Deans or Lefty Groves out there in the Thirties. Hell, those fellows had nothing to do except practise, and they loved baseball. I've seen men of 40 playing just as hard as a guy of 20, and some of their women, whew! Those gals could play. Softball, of course, but you get a big, hefty Ukrainian girl throwing a big softball and it just comes screaming in.

Each town would have a tournament and they'd get the prize money, hook or by crook, from entries, small admission charge if they could, although not always, because a lot of it was cow pasture ballparks, and gifts from the merchants and the banker, and perhaps a rummage sale or two. Some of those pots got up to $500 and even – for a place like Swift Current or Weyburn or Brandon or Wetaskawin or Lethbridge – even higher. As much as $1,000, and that was enough to bring real good teams from all over hell's half acre and including up from the United States if their entry was allowed. I've seen 10 teams playing, in the men's senior, on three diamonds, from 10 in the morning and when the last fly was caught just as the sun was going down, several thousand people would have watched.

They were big events. Real big. An awful lot of fun. Some teams used to bring in ringers, a Yankee, or a guy from the East, if the pot was big enough. There was nothing wrong with it, I guess, but the ringer never got the royal type of welcome he probably thought he deserved. Not even from his team mates because if he was that good, then he'd have a deal to take a third of the pot, and a third could mean a lot of dollars from the other guys' pockets.

There was one guy that Stavely brought in and he was a pitcher, a fast-baller, but he had a nice curve too and a curve wasn't seen much at those tourneys, and he pitched a no-hitter the first game, a one hitter and a two hitter, and Stavely won the tournament. Naturally. If you don't believe me you can look it up. It was in Robert Ripley's *Believe It Or Not*. Three great games in one day. This big gink had played pro ball for Seattle or San Francisco and hadn't got the attention he probably thought he deserved, but he sure did on the Canadian prairies.

Sports days were fun days. Everybody came, and there was a dance and a lot of drinking, out in the cars and trucks parked around, and sometimes a fight or two. The cops usually stayed away, let the folks have their fun. Not like a Polish wedding where they stayed parked at the corner of the hall just waiting for the bomb to explode. They were good times, not prosperous times, but everybody did what they could to help the next fellow, and a lot of planning by the ladies and the committee went into them tournaments. Some of the rivalries between towns got pretty fierce, at the ball park level, for the big prize, but otherwise it was just people of Saskatchewan or Manitoba or Alberta trying to make the best of a tough situation.

Sitting in the little bleachers most towns had at the fairgrounds, you wouldn't know that if you dumped everybody's pockets, everybody in the stands and along the sidelines, you'd be lucky to come up with $50 in spending money. Nobody really cared that much. One thing I've always thought I'd like to have seen. Like to have seen some of those town kids and those big farm boys get a chance to try out for some big league team. Likely they wouldn't have made it anyway, but then again, you might have been real surprised. Some of those boys were real good."

———————————— • ————————————

Love In Hidden Places

"The times were hard on the young people. Courting, I mean, getting to know each other. It was called spooning, and about the best in the winter that a young couple could hope for was for the fellow to go over to her house and the old people to go visiting, and yet again that wasn't so hot either.

Some people just didn't get married. There are plenty of spinsters who never married in the Thirties, not because some young fellow didn't want them, but because he just could not, just could not afford to get married. On the farm it was different, mostly. The bridegroom could move in with his bride and her folks and he was expected to work his ass off, but in the city it was different.

If two young people had a severe case of the hots for each other, the best they could do was sit in the parlour or kitchen and listen to Jack Benny and Fred Allen on the radio on Sunday night or the dance in town Saturday night. No one had any money, although many's the cold winter night I've hitched up the cutter and driven over to a girl's place and taken her for a ride and away we'd go. Cold. You couldn't stay all that warm but you, if you were determined enough, you got what you wanted, and sometimes you even married the young lady. Too many single men, though. Ask any girl who was a school teacher in the country then. They came out of the woodwork.

In the spring, you see, that's when the fun began. In the country. In the city too. Parks were made for screwing and so were country lanes. Having a baby wasn't all that much of a thing, and no big lightning bolt was going to come flashing down and wipe you out, but still it was a problem. But that's not what I'm talking about.

There was just no money. My God, 40 bucks was a good wage, and a young fellow would give half that to his folks. There were no bars where you could take a girl and look dreamily into her eyes. You could go to the picture show and spark – that's another word for courting, sparking – but usually the last three or four rows of the show were filled up. Hell, you could just smell the lust, waves of it coming up and spreading all over.

I'm not saying there were not a lot of marriages during the Depression, because young people will always get together, no matter what. A lot of babies born, too. But I've heard a lot of guys say it just wasn't the same. What they meant was, it wasn't the way they had imagined it, and if that goes for the fellows then it will go in spades for the girls, being more romantic. But then again, they're pretty practical too.

What I'm saying is that things were tough for young people and it was something they didn't bring on themselves, something they couldn't be blamed for, and I guess some were bitter.

I know I was. I figure I missed about six or seven of the best years, the good ones when everybody should have been happy and gay and they just weren't happy and gay years for me. For others, maybe so, but not for me."

----------•----------

What Happened To All The Pianos?

"Did you ever wonder what happened to all the pianos? Think back. In those days everybody had a piano. Well, nearly everybody.

You could walk down any street in any town or city about 4.30 any afternoon, after school was out, and hear children practising on the piano. It was the thing to do. Girls just naturally took piano and a lot of boys too. I remember I took piano, for about four years, from a Mrs. Pearse and for the first two years she charged 15 cents a half hour and then 25 cents a half hour.

Lord, there must have been tens of thousands of pianos in those days. It seemed every house had one and most people could play. Maybe not play well, but play enough for Sunday evening sing-songs."

----------•----------

Camping – 1935 Style

"We used to go camping. Sometimes it was families, brothers and sisters and cousins and so on, or else it might just be two or three families which got along together. You could do it for nothing in those days, practically nothing. People didn't go in for camping all that much. There were a lot who had summer cottages and the railways used to run trains all summer out to the lakes and there were Boy Scout and fresh air camps around. Those kind of things. But there weren't too many private camp grounds, what we would call

commercial camps today, and they certainly weren't up to any standard. A
dam on a creek for swimming or a rickety pier, something like that. Toilets,
the hole in the ground type.

Things have gone a long way, but I'm not sure they have as much fun today
as we had. Everybody would load up a couple of cars and split the gas and
away we'd go, for a week or two weeks. I can't recall any working man or a
guy in an office getting more than two weeks of vacation. Of course, he could
have been out of work. A lot of them were. Each family would have a tent and
my, some of those tents had seen a lot. Some were the bell tent, you know,
white, that the soldiers used in the First World War and you could buy cheap,
all torn and mended. Others would be the umbrella kind with the stick in the
centre, the pole, and the kids would usually make some Indian teepee things
out of blankets and pieces of canvas or tar paper. You just set up like gypsies.

We'd carry our cooking gear in a gunny sack and our vegetables in another
and our staples and canned goods in another and we'd be in business. After
we'd stocked up, I doubt if we spent more than $5 a week. There wasn't much
drinking because nobody could afford it and as I remember, people just didn't
drink as much then as they do now. I think the war had a lot to do with that.

There would be a lot of fishing done, and there were quite a lot of fish
everywhere in those days, and baseball games. Always a baseball game in the
afternoon, and sometimes the girls against the boys, and the scores weren't
as lopsided as you might think. Some of those girls could play very well.
There was also volleyball. It was big. There always seemed to be a volleyball
game going.

At night, some of the young people would drive to a nearby town for a
dance or to watch a ball tournament, but there always was a fire and everybody would get together and sing. Everyone, even the little shavers, knew all
the old songs, just dozens of them now and it was always a good time. If it
was August, there would be big corn roasts. You could feed an awful slew of
people for just a few cents, and wieners and buns were practically nothing.
Everybody went to bed about midnight, or even earlier.

There always were romances, naturally. Summer sparking, it used to be
called. A few days, a few weeks and they found somebody new. But not always.
I know quite a few over the years who met their one-and-only during one of
those summers. Babies? Well, now, I can't say about that. Of course there
would be, because we weren't quite as prissy as this Now Generation thinks

we were. Not me, but the younger ones of that day. Yes, there was a fair amount of summer sparking. Human nature doesn't change, you know.

We had lots of fun, and I may be wrong but it seems that the sun always shone in those days. You could always count on two weeks of good weather, something you just can't now. In that way we were lucky. There wasn't any money around but we didn't think of ourselves as poor. Nobody had much money but we had fun, and all in all, I think we brought up a pretty good bunch of kids."

———————————— • ————————————

Welcome To A Corn Roast

"Somebody would get the idea for a corn roast. There were always plenty of kids around, from six or so right up to 16 and above. There were plenty of workers to go into the woods and get firewood. That would be done the morning or afternoon of the roast. But the night before, about five of us would pedal our bikes to the farmer's market. As I look back now, it was a hell of a place. You could buy just about anything there, even pottery and amateur paintings, but the main thing was food, fruit, vegetables, eggs, ducks, geese, chicken, sausage from every country in Europe. It's all gone now. A long time ago. There just doesn't seem to be much sense in these kind of decisions but I guess somebody wanted it for a parking lot, or a filling station. Sometimes when I drive by, I say 'God damn them all.' Oh well, that's progress.

So we'd wait until dusk, about nine or so, and then we'd buy the corn. It would have dropped in price. Those farmers didn't want to lug all their stuff back home. You could buy, as I remember, a dozen cobs for five cents, or six dozen for a quarter. Gold Bantam corn, five rows, as delicious as you can think of. What the hell is wrong with corn today? We'd buy about 10 or 12 dozen and load them up and take them home. I think we figured about six cobs a person. There would be about 20 or 25 people, adults and kids there.

The women would buy a couple of pounds of butter, and hell, it was just a few cents a pound, and wrap up chunks of it in cheese cloth. You used that to butter the corn and didn't waste a drop. Old Man Best would get out his tripod and copper cauldron and set it up the next night in the vacant lot beside his house and get a fire going and we'd shuck the corn and pop it in and wait around for it to boil. We'd wait, remember, for it to get dark because the sparks shooting up and the fire would give it a woodsy effect. Jesus Christ, I can see it now.

Each kid would bring a couple of potatoes from home and stick them into the ashes. Just as they were. Then we'd eat corn. We'd eat corn until it was coming out of our ears. Mrs. Best would make cocoa, and bring it out in that big enamel jug. I guess we brought our own cups too. I don't remember. We must have. We ate corn until we were cross-eyed, hot and buttery, lots of salt. Then somebody would get a stick and start flipping the potatoes out of the ashes. I can remember chipping off the hard crust, and the potato inside, the white part, was firm and steaming and white as chicken. I don't care if I hated baked spuds at home, I sure as Christ could eat at least two big ones at the corn roast. We'd be full of Golden Bantam corn and baked potato and cocoa, and then somebody would build up the fire and we'd sing.

Everybody, even the little shavers, Carter and Cliff Gill and those Raleigh kids, they knew all the old tunes. 'Long Long Trail A-winding,' 'Old Macdonald Had A Farm,' 'If You Were the Only Girl In the World,' all those. And the ones we sang at school, well our parents knew those.

Hell, I guess we didn't have much else to do. We'd do that corn roast about three times before the season was over. Have you heard of one since the war? I haven't, and I doubt if they have them. People have changed, and I know why. We were all in the same boat then. No money. I'll bet you a dime to a doughnut that a corn roast for about 20 or 25 people cost little more than a buck, a buck and 10 cents. Fifty cents for the corn. Fifty cents for the butter. Ten cents for the cocoa. The wood was free, just go out behind the bush and get all you want. That was about it. Christ, but I can still smell that smoke and hear the singing.

You're right, I can taste that corn too."

───────────── • ─────────────

Fun Cost Practically Nothing

"Grand Beach. It was really a hell of a place, about a mile of terrific sandy beach, lots of places for hiking, and some fishing for catfish, jackfish, perch and if you knew the score, there was good pickerel fishing. Everything was on the cheap. The cottages were dirt cheap, the food was cheap and everybody brought in their own by train.

There was a road in of sorts although you needed a good car and guts, as

I remember. If you did get there you couldn't drive it. Park it and walk. No roads, you see, because the railroad saw to that. They owned it.

The screwing was free too. Fantastic. I never got in on much of it because I was too young but we used to walk up in all these sand dunes at night and there would be couples lying all over the place. In hollows, on slopes, under those funny little twisted trees, all wind-blown that grew there. Here's one reason. Not too many couples could afford to get married, and the boy would live with his folks and the girl with hers. Well, where would they get a chance to make love? On the riverbank, sure, but that was like Grand Central Station. So they'd get on the Moonlight, and I forgot, that was the name of the train the C.N. ran every night up to Grand Beach. Two a night. They'd leave Winnipeg about 6 and 6.45 and it was an hour's run, a nice trip up along the lake, and when they got in, they'd forget the dance hall which the Moonlight really was all about. They would head out the board walk and down into the sand dunes and screw.

They had about four or three and a half hours before they had to get back to catch the Moonlight going back and you'd see dozens of these couples coming arm in arm back towards the station and they'd look pretty tired. Tired but happy, you know what I mean. How many babies were conceived on those sands I guess only they know. A lot, anyway. Some probably wanted it that way. Then they'd have to get married.

I said everything was on the cheap. The Moonlight ticket return was good for only that night, so if you were gonna stay a week or two you'd be left with a two bit return ticket, no good. Oh, yeah! You sold the other half, the stub, to somebody who already sold his weeks ago. For two bits. Everybody was happy, except the railroad. They weren't happy. Hell, even with that it must have been one of the few lines in the country that showed a profit from May 24 to Labour Day.

Tickets, cottage, recreation, carrying your own grub from Winnipeg, a few quarts of milk, five cents a quart, Jesus, a family of four could do it easily on $25. That's for two weeks.

Here is the thing. North of Toronto here, last April, I decide I'm gonna rent this cottage we got up there. I want the rent to cover the taxes and the special security patrol, about $500 all told for the year. I'm talking to my brother-in-law and he's been around. I say $500. He says I'm crazy. Ask $800. So I ask $800. What's to lose? It's a doctor, you see, and he doesn't bat an eyelash. Not an eyelash. Sure. So compare $800 for July, just for a month. Back in those other days, for a month, $50, and that's grub and tickets and fun too.

You figure it out. I can't."

———————— • ————————

The Famous Winnipeg Rebels

"What good was an education? We found that out soon enough, no jobs at all. But there was a lot of fun to be had. The city (of Winnipeg) had skating and hockey rinks around the city, green wooden shacks and boarding, and a caretaker to keep the fire going and all that. We'd hang around there, a bunch of us, oh, I'd say 18 to 25 years old, and we had nothing to do but play hockey. Scrimmage. We were pretty fair players and a few went up to semi-professional and that meant you played for a city or a town and they gave you a job.

About the second year, say 1934 or '35, a bunch of us were hanging around together, and Danny Lock, his father was a travelling salesman for Nabob, he asked his father to line up some games with towns on his route. That was easy done, of course. We were the Winnipeg Rebels, that's what we decided to call this team we were going to form, although we came from only a small part of the city. Lord Roberts district. So Mr. Lock got us about six games lined up, that was the easy part. All on Saturday night, and the town promised to show those Winnipeg Rebels a good evening. The game and food and moccasin dancing.

We only lasted one season but I remember we played a bunch of French Canadiens at Letellier and some Mennonites at Steinbach and over at Morden and at Emerson. Anyway, six games.

We didn't give a damn, of course. One of the guys had a brother who was interning at Winnipeg General and he would skim off a quart of that grain alcohol – it was head-busting stuff – and we'd each have an empty pint and fill it with part of the alcohol and dilute it with water or lemonade, or Kik, what we wanted. I think most of us used to drink it with Kik. Awful stuff, just awful. Awful cheap too.

We always took Mr. Lock's car and another guy's Dad's car and that was ten of us. One goalie, three defencemen and two forward lines and that was enough. We also had a pail, and that was important. We always arrived about half an hour before the game and we'd skate, loosen up, and meet the other team. They had pretty good rinks in those towns, sometimes open air but a good clubhouse, and a couple even had arenas.

Before we'd face off, we'd each drink about a third of our bottle and that would be about four ounces or so and we'd put them in this pail which we filled with snow. That kept the booze insulated and we wanted it cold, the way we drank in those days.

We'd get out on the ice for the face-off and we were pretty good. I'd say the score after the first period might be 4-1 for us, something like that. At the rest period we'd go out to the car that had the pail and we'd drink off about another four ounces, the goalie too and it would hit us warm in the belly and we'd play like madmen that second period. However we just weren't playing as good as we did before. We looked it, but the score might be 6-5 in favour of us, the Rebels, after that period.

People would begin to ask, 'What's wrong with those guys out there?' We were making a lot of mistakes, see, poor passing, bad checking, kind of like we were goofing. Another belt and goodbye, bottle, and we'd go out for the third period. We were having a whale of a time by this time. We should, we were stinko, and we'd make a lot more mistakes and do some clowning and everything seemed funny and the score usually ended up 9-7 or something like that. For them – not the mighty Winnipeg Rebels.

Everybody would feel good about this and we'd get dressed and go to the party and stoke up on food, hot dogs and chocolate and pie and the like, and then we'd start dancing and have one hell of a time. Everybody was happy for us, I mean for them, because their team had won, but nobody knew we were conked. After the game some village sports would usually have a jug and we'd nip at that. Sometimes one of us would manage to get one of the town girls into the back of the cars and have themselves a session. It was called petting in those days. Those towns closed down about midnight, so we'd pile into the cars and head for home and it was just one hell of a lot of fun."

———————————— • ————————————

Everybody Played Hockey

"Hockey was the thing in those days. The big thing. The Toronto Maple Leafs and Foster Hewitt on Saturday nights. Hell, he was better known than the prime minister. It was the touchstone to success, the way a kid could gain fame and a little fortune, playing for Toronto or the Montreal teams, Detroit, Chicago.

It was like the Negro before he was allowed into organized sports. The Negro could only enter the white man's world if he was a superb boxer, a champion. Remember Joe Louis?

So it was with hockey, and junior hockey those years was an exceedingly fast and good game. But everybody played. Hell, I've seen men of 40 going up and down the ice a full game in the intermediate leagues and every kid from the time he graduated from bob skates wanted to be a star. Corner lots were flooded and they became the rinks where the stars were produced, but this wasn't good enough. There were rarely boards, and almost never a club-house to change and keep warm. Then someone had an idea. I'd like to think it was my father and a few of his cronies who used to sit around the Legion on Saturday afternoons. Their one day out in the big-time. Ha! Fifty cents was a lot to spend on a beer bust those days. Or the idea might have started in a hundred places in Canada at once, like an idea whose time had come.

Look at the picture. There were hundreds of blocks of lots undeveloped and gone back to the city for non-payment of taxes in almost every city in the Thirties. So there was this land. The C.P.R. and the C.N.R. had thousands of boxcars lying on sidings across the west, unused from year to year, just rotting away, and those cars were of the finest construction, finest lumber, and built for the coldest weather a Canadian winter could throw at them.

There were fire hydrants everywhere, of course, and firemen sitting around doing very little. And finally, there were dozens of men idle, master carpenters, plumbers, electricians, you name it, who were willing to work for nothing, for a good cause, of course, just to feel they were doing something useful.

So put them all together and, yes, that's what you get. The neighbourhood would form a legal entity called a community club, the such-and-such Community Club Association, duly constituted, officers, treasury, minutes, and all that. The city would gladly deed over the necessary land to the association. I'm not sure how the box car deal worked but I think they were sold to the association for a nominal sum, say, $10 each, and the association had to get the cars off their trucks and to the site. Boards were always a problem, but there was always demolition work going on somewhere and somebody always had an old truck and there were always hands to load and unload, and soon you had boards.

The fire department would come two or three times, the first to soak and freeze the ground, and the other times to build up a good thick ice surface. At our club, we used to run a garden hose from a house across the street every time we wanted a new finish on the ice. Two box cars, fitted side by side, made a good clubhouse, and two Imperial Oil barrels welded together made a fine stove.

Of course there were problems, hellish big problems. An association never did get things all tickety-boo until about the third year, but from the first if they started about July or so they could function quite well. Money was number one, of course. Isn't it always? But the wives would hold rummage sales or tea parties or raffles, some merchant would donate a ham and another a $5 grocery order, and the paper boys would put the hard sell on their customers at 10 cents a ticket or three for a quarter. At any one time, in Winnipeg, there must have been 40,000 raffles of one kind or another going. It was a great raffle town, and I don't know anyone who ever won anything. Maybe the raffle was a great racket too. But these clubs survived, and grew, and they had full leagues, from 4:30 after school to 10 p.m. and skating on Saturday and Sunday and broom ball for the oldsters on Saturday night and then a dance.

They were the beginnings, the rugged, small and determined Depression beginnings, of these three and four million dollar community centres you see in every city and which they are still building, because they serve a very definite need, as much now as they did back in 1934. As I said, maybe it all was just an idea whose time had come, but I like to think it all began back with my Dad and his First World War pals sitting around the Legion on Saturday afternoon."

CHAPTER TWENTY-TWO

The Fantasy World

Two Worlds – Real And Fantasy . . . Chain Letters . . . They Always Found The Money For The Races . . . Miniature Golf – A Foolish Diversion . . . It Was A Grand Fair . . . Got WGN Last Night . . . A Little Dough Stashed Away . . . Kids' Day At The Movies . . . Good Old Joe Looee . . . Great To Be A Bush Pilot.

———————————•———————————

In any interview, whether on Vancouver Island or the Nova Scotia coast, it was only a matter of time until the radio was mentioned.

"It saved my life," said a woman in the Maritimes. "There I was, my husband cutting wood in the bush and me with three kiddies on that farm miles from nowhere. It was the world talking to me. I had never seen a hockey game but I think I became quite something of an expert listening to Foster Hewitt doing the Saturday night games. And the CBC news. That drama series, Baker's Dozen. I still remember. And Lux Radio Theatre, Pepper Young's Family, Ma Perkins, the soap operas."

The radio spoke to everyone and, I think, much more than television today, for it brought the world into the home for the first time.

And the movies, some great ones and many poor ones, all ground out by Hollywood's mills because the demand was so terrific. People wanted to escape into the fantasy world.

———————————•———————————

Two Worlds – Real And Fantasy

"I've often thought of this. Do you remember Jack Benny – his name always comes first because he really was good – and Fred Allen and Fibber McGee and Molly and Singing Sam and Amos and Andy and all those famous radio personalities we used to listen to as if our life depended on it? Do you recall any one of them, just once, ever mentioning the Depression, that times were tough, millions out of work, kids sleeping in ditches and barns? Can you ever recall one of them mentioning just once all these terrible things which were happening around them? Think about it. Kind of scary, isn't it? There were two worlds in those days, the real one and the fantasy world."

———————————— • ————————————

Chain Letters

"I was as bad as anybody about the things. Let me see, you got a letter and you scratched off the top name and sent a dollar to that name and added your own to the bottom and copied out six letters and sent them to your friends. There was supposed to be bad luck, the curse of the Irish, if you broke the chain. The chain letter craze seemed to come around about once a year.

I never got anything except once, seven tea towels, towels to wipe the dishes, all in different sizes and colours, and who would want that many? You were always hearing of some person who got $480 or $1,480 or something like that. Of course, that would be the person at the top of the chain, the one who started it all. Just a racket, but people believed. Goodness, but how they believed. If a friend sent you a letter and you threw it away and she found out, you could probably say goodbye to that friendship. The newspaper used to say that if a chain went through eight, I think it was eight, full completions it would include all the people in Manitoba. This was crazy, of course. It never got that far. They always broke down. There were crazy ones too, and I remember one which asked you to send nothing but good wishes, good luck to the people and I did that one. It made some sort of sense, wouldn't you say?

The only people who benefited were the starters of money chain letters, and they were little better than crooks, and the government who sold the stamps. Pity the poor postman who had to carry all them letters, maybe hundreds of thousands more during the chain-letter craziness."

———————————— • ————————————

They Always Found The Money For The Races

"In the summer I'd come down from Dauphin and work on the $2 window at Whittier Park and then move over to Polo Park, or maybe it was the other way around, but anyway, it was the races. I used to be surprised at the amount, there were a lot of bettors. Now the handle would be considered pitiful in relation to today's totals but again, if you want to consider this horse racing nonsense as the sport of kings and improving the breed and so forth, then the stock was pretty poor stuff. Most of the horses then couldn't win a race at Lethbridge today.

Exceptions there were, of course, but in the main I am correct. But the bettors kept coming. There wasn't much to do and these bettors, the newspapers called them punters – and where that name came from I don't know – they'd play the $2 windows. Where did they get the money? Well, I can only guess they scrimped and saved and by betting just six or seven races at my window, that was, say, $14, and if they got lucky they might win ten and if they were real cautious but lost, they might lose six.

So they were getting good entertainment, something they'd looked forward to all year and saved for, for five bucks lost, break even or a few bucks ahead. Hell, for the Depression that was pretty good. A sunny afternoon, among old friends, the kick out of wagering a couple of bucks, that was all they wanted. Nobody begrudged them their fun. It wasn't considered sinful."

Miniature Golf – A Foolish Diversion

"Don't ask me about the date, because I could be a couple of years out, but there was this craze for miniature golf. It was stupid, really, but it did have a few things going for it. You just needed a city lot, that size, and one man could put together 18 holes and they were only made of sand or hard packed crushed gravel or dirt. Not grass, it wouldn't stand up. You got pipes and tiles and cans and it was all like one of those Rube Goldberg inventions, hit the ball, and it goes along and plops into a hole and runs down a pipe and knocks aside a wooden arrow and then drops into a cup. Foolishness.

But a guy, or at least his wife and him, could build one and buy a couple of dozen old putters and some beaten up balls for a few bucks and you were in business. Yeah, miniature golf.

My Dad and his brother had one in Toronto and in one season they made a fortune. On Saturday and Sunday it would be going from 10 in the morning until, yeah, until it was too dark to see and then they had these Christmas tree lights, yeah, the blue and yellow and red ones, and people would keep going until midnight. Nothing to do, you see, and a dime to play, a couple could spend 20 cents and have some fun.

Then they could go down to the riverbank and screw if they wanted to, but at least, yeah, he could say he'd taken her out on a date.

I'm telling you, my old man would come home on a Saturday midnight with dollars, quarters and dimes weighing him down. Sixty, 70 a day, and all clear, was nothing. But how could it last? Next year there were dozens and my old man and his brother got smart and sold their layout, yeah, for $500 or so.

So that year every son of a bitch went broke. People were doing something else, bike races, contract bridge, fads were the things in them days. Chain letters. Hopes and dreams."

———————————— • ————————————

It Was A Grand Fair

"There were posters along the roads that the big fair was going to be at Outlook again on July 1 and the kids started pestering me and so I started putting pennies and nickels aside. I had just more than a dollar two days before the fair when the baby come down sick and we took him into Outlook and the doctor said, well, here's a medicine, get it at the drug store, and that druggist must have seen right into my purse because he said the medicine would come to a dollar.

On fair day, this was about '36 because we wasn't on the place next year, 1937, on fair day the kids was up early and we walked the three miles into the fair grounds about noon, the kids in overalls and no shoes but that was no matter, a lot of farm kids on the prairies didn't have shoes them days. It was a grand fair, popcorn, candy apples, little car rides that went round, a merry go-round, and the kids kept asking, 'Daddy, can I go on that,' and 'Daddy, buy us that,' and I just kept walking them along and I figured once around and I'd scoot them out and tell them their fun had gone to save the baby's life. The kids was big enough to understand.

Well, sir, we wasn't no more than 100 feet from the walk-out gate and there was dread in my heart, real sadness, and suddenly, flat up against the side of a hot dog stand, down low there was this blue thing and I knew in my heart soon as I spotted it. Snap, I grabbed it. That blue piece of paper was a five dollar bill and that was what it was. The wind had blown it there, maybe from last night when the fair opened and nobody had spotted it.

I know that my $5 gain's somebody else's grief but I wasn't thinking of such things. I just said to the kids, 'Well, you've been around this layout once. What do you want to do and see now?' And, sir, we was off. Rides, hot dogs, throw-the-penny, the whole works, and me nipping on a pint of bootleg I'd bought for a dollar behind one of the tents. Try as those kids would, they couldn't spend more than $2. Five cents this, five cents that, it don't mount up too fast.

Then we walked home and it was getting on for supper and there was still $2 left and when we got there my wife, well, she knew I was stony broke but she said I had to take the kids anyway and maybe we'd meet someone who would lend us a dollar. The wife looked kind of funny and I gave her the $2 and I said I'd explain later but here was $2 and I didn't want her to spend it on the baby or Susan or Edgar or Robert, or me or the house, I wanted her to spend it on herself. For a pretty, I told her, and I said God had given me the money, and that was the truth."

•

Got WGN Last Night

"I think it was 1935 when my old man bought his first radio, the Whistler and His Dog type. An RCA Victor. We used to read in Mechanics Illustrated how the English were working on television in those day, but even a radio was just about too much for us.

In the city, sure, there were lots of radios. In our area we could get Ottawa faintly and as I recall there was a big station at Cleveland. Cleveland? Yes, I think so, and if you pulled in New York on a cold and clear winter night then you'd be down at the store next day and telling everybody, 'Got WGN last night, New York. Clear as a bell.'

I remember one old chap, and we were sure he had gone screwy on us, but he went out and bought a deForest Crossley. Three hundred dollars. Where did he get the cash? I guess he and the Lord knew, but there it was in his tiny living room and it was like one of these opera singers. When it let go, turned up full blast just to show it off, the panes in the windows actually shook. Vibrated. They had these little shelves along the walls with chinaware on it and each piece would go into a little dance too. You wouldn't believe it. His name was Vance, and people would come all the way from Pembroke to listen to that big brown mahogany monster. It seems to me there was short wave, and that was something. Ships at sea. A ship approaching Strait of Belle Isle in fog, asking for a position, now that was something.

The rest of us had RCA Victor or small Stromberg-Carlsons and the kids had crystal sets. They weren't much but if you got one rigged out right you might pick up something, if the broadcasting station was in the hay field next to you. There was something better about radio in those days. There weren't all that many commercials, and in the next place, the commercials seemed to make sense. They'd say, 'Now, we've tested this soap and it is as good as we can make it, so why don't you try it? We think you'll agree with us.' And you did, and if you liked it, then you bought it. The same with jello or tooth paste or motor oil. Not all this razzmatazz like a kid running up and being a rude little brat and saying to her Dad that she's got 22.3 percent fewer cavities. There didn't seem to be much of that.

Radio drew people together, families together. There was good music. Jack Benny, Fibber McGee and Molly were funny, but the funniest of all was Fred Allen. *There* was a man who was just naturally funny. Everybody in any town could say, 'There's a fellow in our town who has a sense of humour like that.' One I never liked one iota was Bob Hope. Always thought he tried too hard.

This deForest Crossley that Vance had. Nobody had electricity, you see, except the old wind charger and that radio for some reason slurped up the juice like nobody's business so you were better off with a little one. This was in the mid-Thirties, mind you, and they were starting to broadcast the big fights so if you wanted to hear Joe Louis and them, then you went over to Vance's house. That, I reckon, was really the only advantage.

I ever tell you about the preacher in Flin Flon? He had this service at eight o'clock and, correct me if I'm wrong, but that was when Fred Allen came on and he wasn't getting too much of a congregation. So he switched it to quarter to seven to quarter to eight and that gave the congregation 15 minutes to high-tail it for home and hear Fred Allen, and he got in his licks at the devil too. Nobody seemed to mind. The fact is, it just sounded like a good bit of business on the part of the preacher.

Radio was king for quite a number of years but it couldn't compete with television. Or maybe you should put it this way, the parents couldn't compete with their kids who wanted to watch television."

———————————— • ————————————

A Little Dough Stashed Away

"I made $6 a month and my food and a place to sleep from May to September with Paddy Conklin (*Canada's famous carnival operator*) in Ontario and what we could steal gave us a living wage. I came to Vancouver after four years as a sailor and I was big and husky and I got on with a unit through British Columbia and I worked with that unit, on the flats, in the cookhouse, anywhere they wanted me, all through the Depression.

I always wondered where the money did come from. We'd be setting up and the police would come out to check us over and they'd tell the boss there wasn't a stray dime in the district and if there was, the Chinese candystore owner would have it by night. But we'd get the music going and the girls out and the little Jew would get that smell of hot dogs drifting over the grounds and by God, they'd come, and also by God, they'd have money. A dollar. Two dollars.

Where it came from I don't know, but after two days or five days we'd move on and it would have been okay, and this was in the mid-Thirties. Some of the guys on the games, crown, chuckaluck, would be telling about some guy who had lost 20 and another guy had dropped 35, and yet here was a town where they were supposed to fight you on the streets if you dropped a quarter. Always the same way, a little dough stashed away for a little fun. Carnie people sure as hell had hard times, but not as much. You get me?"

———————————— • ————————————

Kids' Day At The Movies

"You want the story of the Depression? Well, have a go at the movies, they'll tell a lot. The-Golden-Age-of-Going-To-The-Movies. Those were the days. I didn't know there was a Depression on. Nobody had any money to speak of, but if you were born in a cave 5,000 years ago and your old man painted donkeys and cattle and tigers on the walls, how the hell would you know that later there would be people like Rembrandt? Same with us.

Friday nights. That was for kids, say 15 and over. The lovey-doveys as we called them. Saturday night, for parents and teenagers. Monday, Tuesday and Wednesday nights for mothers getting chinaware and cutlery and gravy boats and crummy oil paintings and all sorts of crap along with their two bit ticket. The movies on Monday, Tuesday and Wednesday were incidental to the free chinaware, a saucer one week, a cup the next, a bread plate the next, and you had to go three times for a large serving plate, which probably cost a cent to make in some Japanese factory whose owner paid his workers 16 cents a day.

Thursday nights were for everybody because they usually had an amateur night, every screwball in town flocking to the theatre with his dumb little act. Tap dancing like Shirley Temple was very big, or elocution. I'm not sure I can spell the word now. A big word then. Some dame would get up and recite "The Highwayman" by John Masefield or some beefy, red-faced bloke would try "The Cremation of Sam Magee." Accordions. Every kid in town played one, and badly. First prize was usually two bucks, second one a buck.

Or there would be a sing-along, or the manager maybe would just pull a lucky number from a hat, based on a ticket sold the past week and you had to be there that week to collect, so he couldn't go wrong, and he could be pretty right if he pulled out a ticket number that didn't exist.

Saturday afternoons were for the children, say from five to 14. Then when you got into the big time, became a man, you went Friday nights and the cost jumped from 10 cents to 15 cents. But it's Saturday afternoons I'm talking about. That was like being on the barricades. No man's land. The war between the North and the South, cowboys and Indians, them and us. The doors opened at 12:30 at the Tivoli Theatre and there was a line-up then. Why, I don't know. If you got there at five minutes to one, you could always find a seat, but no, you had to be there before 12:30 and the line-up stretched half a block. At one o'clock, down would go the lights and that big MGM lion would go 'warrouf!' and that's the only film company I can remember. From then on, it was murder.

We all took our cap guns. Every kid had a cap gun and he'd hide it about his person because Mr. Beasley and his two high school girl ushers would give us the once-over like the police do at a big American murder trial. As far as I know they never confiscated a single gat. Yeah, a gat. A heater. The old equalizer. Cowboy movies – Tom Mix, Hoot Gibson, Ken Maynard, Hopalong Cassidy – and we shot right along with the hero. When he was boxed in behind some rocks and four of the rustler gang were firing at him and he had only about 20 shots left in his trusty six-shooter and the lead was zinging off the rocks and a bullet would suddenly take his hat off, every kid in the Tivoli Theatre was on his feet firing like mad at those bastard rustlers behind the rocks, and the girls were screaming, and I never saw a girl with a cap gun. I guess it was unladylike. The firing, well it took about five minutes of firing and the theatre would be so full of blue powder smoke that you could hardly see the screen. My God, but it was great. There's something in all this for a psychologist!

Cowboys and bad guys. Cowboys and Indians. That was the stuff. Show a sport movie or a romance and that afternoon was dead. A Shirley Temple movie would hold us, or some good solid adventure like "The Swiss Family Robinson," but anything heavy or with kissing or actually with anything to test our tiny mosquito brains and it was out. But when the firing was going on, that was what Saturday afternoon was all about.

Mr. Beasley would come striding down the aisle and all the kids would set up a chant, 'Here comes Mr. Beasley, Here comes Mr. Beasley,' and he'd get up on the stage and flick a light and the picture would stop and he'd go into his little set speech: 'If you don't behave, stop firing those guns, I'm going to send you all home. Now behave.' He'd done his duty, on would go the movie, he'd stride manfully up the aisle and the audience would begin firing again.

I can't say we were destructive, though. We never slashed seats or carved our initials or lit the carpet, setting a fire. We were just kids. The girls were our audience and the more outrageous the things we did, the more they squealed. A man's prowess was based upon whether he could sneak down the aisle, up on the stage, run across it making wild and jerky motions with his arms and legs, get down the other side and into his seat and not get caught. Now there was a man!

And remember, suppose there were 200 kids in that audience, and that was not unreasonable. Two hundred times a dime, $20. Would you do it for twenty bucks today what Mr. Beasley did? Open up, show a film, and shorts, give out those goddamned suckers, pay a projectionist, a ticket taker, two ushers who actually acted as lady cops, and then have your place filled up with powder smoke? Well, he did, because there was competition. Oh Lord, but there was competition. Every theatre manager in town, and there must have been 50, each one was hell for leather out for every kid's dime. And yet they made a living, and they got the kids into the theatre habit, which really zoomed during the war and in the late forties, and it wasn't until the late fifties that television began kicking the movies right and left."

———————•———————

Good Old Joe Looee

"Radio was the big thing and boxing was radio. It was entertainment, sometimes the only entertainment there was. Joe Louis was the big one in those years. The Brown Bomber. There must be millions of guys my age, guys who were kids in the Thirties who can remember Joe Louis better than they can remember any of the modern fighters, except Ali because he's something special.

There was Joe Louis and then everybody else about half a mile down the road, Braddock, Schmeling, Galento. Half the people called him Joe Looee. Couldn't pronounce his last name right but they sure knew him, and yet not one of us ever had a chance to see him fight. New York, now there was the fight town. Madison Square Garden, and all the whoop-de-doo that went with it. The sports pages were full of Joe Louis and what they called his

Bum-of-the-Month Club. He was fighting everybody and knocking them over, and I can still hear the announcer. Forget his name, but I should remember it. We know now that Joe never threw that many punches but the announcer threw a lot for him, to make the fight more exciting and sell more Gillette razor blades, Blue Blades. He would say, 'Louis has him in the corner, and it's a left, another left, a left, a right, one to the mid-section, a hard one to the head, a left, two lefts, a right . . . HE'S DOWN!!!!!!' and if the poor bastard got up, that was his problem. It's hard to think they were fighting a world champion for a couple of thousand.

Everybody knew, without one iota of proof, that the fight business was crooked. Not Joe Louis, but everybody else in it, the managers, trainers, matchmakers, even the guy counting for the knockdowns and if you want to go that far, even the ring doctors.

But Joe could go into white clubs, private clubs that even a Negro Nobel prize winner or the smartest Jewish scientist in the world couldn't go to, and he really was nothing but a big dumb kid out of the slums of Detroit.

Joe Barrow was his real name. Louis wasn't a thinker, you know. He'd been taught well, left hooks, jabs, combinations, and he knew how to go in for the kill, but old Tommy Farr baffled him. That Welshman. A big and tall man with a face like one of them Welsh mountains. In my opinion he couldn't hit worth a damn but he went 15 rounds with Louis and his face never looked the same, but he didn't go down. In fact, we went to the newsreels of the fight and the Welshman seemed to be stronger at the end.

Everybody was nuts about fighting, of course. More than baseball, and football was nothing. In fact, they used to leave the gates open at half time at football and you could just walk right in.

Fighting, that was it. I remember about 40 of us were in my living room in this big house we had near Bloor (in Toronto) and the kids would be acting out the fight, about 20 of us, moving around, throwing the punches the announcer said were thrown, you know.

Farr kept staying up, and the thing was, he wasn't winning, but he was still staying up and fighting. The streetcar stop was right outside my door, my folks' door, and after every round I'd run out and if there was a car coming I'd stop it and yell in: 'Farr still going strong after six rounds' or 'Tommy Farr fighting hard after nine rounds,' and everybody on the street car would cheer. He was a Welshman, you see, and Toronto was an English city then. None of these Italians and other tribes. So that's about all. Louis won, as we knew he

would, but Tommy the Welshman put up a big fight. In fact, they just about
made him a national hero at home."

———————————— • ————————————

Great To Be A Bush Pilot

"Stevenson Field, Winnipeg. Planes were pretty new affairs then and on
Saturday afternoons and all day Sunday there would be crowds lining the
fences just watching these crates take off and circle and land. It was a regular
circus, all these puddlejumpers, and the pilots were pretty big stuff, acting
casual, the Smilin' Jack bit, and taking pretty girls up for rides. God, but when
I think of the ass those guys must have got, it makes you wonder.

Three and four thousand people gawking on a nice Sunday summer afternoon was nothing. That's all there was to see, just planes taking off and
landing and occasionally one doing a few easy stunts. Nothing rough. What a
simple lot we were.

I remember once they did put on a bit of a show, with the double parachute drop. Now this may sound big but it wasn't. The guy has two parachutes
and he climbs out on the wing when they're up seven or eight thousand and
he jumps and opens the first. Fine, it opens. He floats down a few hundred
feet, pulls a strap and slips out of it, falls free for a thousand or more, maybe
two thousand, pulls the next rip cord and his second chute opens and he lands
okay and all he may have is a sore crotch.

But that was big stuff, and that Sunday they said more than 15,000 people
showed up. Fifteen thousand would have been about 10 percent of the population of Winnipeg, and that's not a bad turnout.

You've got to realize just how much flying had grabbed the public. Every
day, the "Free Press" would have stories of people flying all over the world,
trying to break old records or set new ones on distances never tried before. A
guy setting a new record, only because he was the first to try it, from
Wetaskiwin, Alberta, to Swan Lake, Manitoba, he'd get a story in the papers.
Anybody could. It was all a little nutty. The big flights, across oceans, to
Australia, over jungles, Christ Almighty, that was like the Second Coming.
Only bigger. Much bigger.

Flyers were heroes, and even if the bush pilot was a pretty grubby fellow
most of the time, covered with grease and stinking of gas, he was still a pretty
glamorous fellow. I knew a few, as a kid, and they had a certain style. Hell,

put anybody in a Norseman or a Stinson or a deHavilland in those days and he could have style too.

Anyway, you could get 5,000 people out any Sunday just to watch a few farm boys in leather helmets take these old crates up and dump them down again, people dished out five bucks for one or two circuits of the field as a passenger, and people may not have had any moolah for food and medicine and shoes for their kids but they could afford their first plane ride for five bucks for five minutes.

It was fun, it was new, flying was the big new horizon in a world which had gone pretty goddamned flat, so why knock it. I was a kid of 12 who would walk eight miles to the airport to see that double parachute jump. Kids today would laugh at you and say they'd seen a guy walking on the moon."

CHAPTER TWENTY-THREE

Kids

The Tale Of A Young Cree ... Flour Sack Fashions ... The Kid Who Robbed The Bank ... Garbage Can Bonanza! ... A Very Strange Lunch ... Does Shirley Temple Know? ... Sick Two Days Each Year ... Thank You, Boys ... My Friend, The Butcher ... 12 Miles At 20 Below ... One Of Those Slave Kids ... The Comics House ... Mother, The Mitt-Maker ... Mr. Marshall's Shoes ... Brain Work ... No Sense To It At All.

———————————— • ————————————

I think the kids survived the Depression best of all.

Remember, a child of 10 in 1936 is only 47 now. How many people that age bear Depression scars, the fear of going on relief, the fear of unannounced people dropping by for a chat creating the need for a late evening meal (a must in those days), when there was no food for them? The fear of the bill collector, the insurance man making his weekly rounds, the fear of just shaving, so close to the bone?

In winter, a neighbourhood lot was flooded or a pond scraped of snow and a thrice-mended stick, a pair of Good Will tube skates and any old object for a puck and 20 boys could play hockey all day. In summer, a pair of black pants, a sweat shirt and running shoes lasted through summer holidays. The total outlay was perhaps $2.

It was the same for girls. They could make a 50 cent set of doll's dishes last a lifetime, and baking oatmeal cookies for little parties cost nothing. In the Depression nothing was cheaper than oatmeal.

Below the age of 10 or above it, things were much the same. Everyone got by, always on their own resources. Conditions at home may have been dreadful, but how could you tell if all your chums lived in the same conditions? Fathers weren't jobless; they just didn't work.

Most Depression children didn't know that there was such a thing, and that they were living it, because they had no basis for comparison.

The Tale Of A Young Cree

"Dad had farmed around Shaunavon but the drought drove him out and we went north. It was there we lost Mom. She had a bad cough in the winter of 1936 and it got worse and we drove her to hospital in the wagon, it was full of hay, and we piled every blanket we had around her. But those 12 miles to hospital killed her. When Dad lifted her out to carry her into the hospital her mouth was open and her eyes were open and I said, 'Dad, it's too late.' It was pneumonia and it was 30 below and it took five hours to go 12 miles over those tracks they called roads in northern Saskatchewan. We buried her in town and then went back and told the kids.

There were five others and Dad took over our schooling, which mother had done. But he couldn't figure out algebra and he said about grammar that we should just put it down the way it sounded right, and we could all read, so he taught us history. Western Canadian history. He'd grown up with it. I can remember, he'd do the chores during the day, going with the team for marsh hay, and I was the mother and at nights after our meal of moose and turnips and coffee – which was just roasted barley with no sugar – he'd tell us of the old days. The Selkirk Settlers, the Nor'Westers and what a tough bunch they were, and the Riel Rebellion and the building of the Canadian Pacific Railroad, these things and more, and he'd act it all out. He'd establish about eight characters or more, or however many there were, and then he'd go through it as a play. Voices. Dialogue. Moving around, and there were the six of us staring open-mouthed, and if someone had looked through our window he probably could never have figured what the Sam Hill was going on.

A story might go on for a week or more, with Dad leaping and whooping and hollering and skulking around the shack, acting Indian, soldier, settler, cowboy, every part. It was crazy!

The best I remember was Almighty Voice. He was a Cree up around Batoche about 1895 and he killed a Mountie and it took half an army to run him to earth. Dad took about five days to tell this story, and naturally we were all in sympathy with Almighty Voice. Just a youngster, and fighting for what he felt was justice. Yes, he killed several men but it was white man's stupidity that caused it all. I don't know where he learned it, or whether he just made it up, but Dad sang us the Cree Death Song, the one Spotted Calf did for her son, and we went to bed crying that night.

That is the way history should be taught, by people who know it and love their country. Not these dry phrases out of a textbook written by some old man. We may have been hungry a lot of the time, but I can look back on those years as being pretty good years. Thanks to Dad."

•

Flour Sack Fashions

"You'd take an empty sack of flour from Maple Leaf Milling at Moose Jaw and give it a good wash and bleach out the lettering and then you'd turn it upside down and cut two holes for the arms and one at the top for the neck and tuck in here and do a little tightening and fixing there and put in hems and guess what you had? You had a dress for a nine-year-old girl.

I went to school in those dresses and so did my cousins. Nobody laughed. Then, as I recall, another company came along, I think it was a Mennonite mill, and they put out bags with coloured flowers printed on them and their name in small letters so you could bleach that out easily and mother did the same thing, and what did you have? You had a party dress, fit for a queen.

I've told this story to my own children and they just don't believe me."

•

The Kid Who Robbed The Bank

"When I was nine, a kid in Winnipeg, I found a rich man's dog in the bush. I took it home and fed it and washed it and my Dad saw the ad in the 'Tribune' and he and I walked over to Wellington Crescent and the man gave me a five dollar bill. The reward. That was something, believe me. My Dad cashed it and gave me $2 for myself. Next day I went to a store and bought 25 cents of candy, a whole big bagful, and the owner, a Mr. Wheeler, saw a policeman walking by and he called him in. Who was I? Where did I live? What did my Dad do? Where did I get a two dollar bill? Why? Why? Why? 'till I was blue in the goddamned face. This Wheeler bastard – none of his goddamned business anyway – finally phoned my Dad at work. He came back saying, 'Yeh, the kid's okay.' You see, in those days nobody had money and a nine-year-old with a two dollar bill, well it was pretty obvious that kid had just robbed the Bank of Montreal on the corner, wasn't it?"

•

Garbage Can Bonanza

"God bless Libby, McNeill and Libby. I don't know if they are still in business but they made life sort of worthwhile for a kid in those days.

This is how it worked. We had nothing, absolutely nothing. Enough to eat, and the relief would give us clothes to get to school, but that seemed to be about it. I was 10 or so when I first heard about what you could get by collecting the wrappings that went around the outside of Libby, McNeill and Libby cans. I didn't believe it, but somebody lent me a catalogue and there it all was, camping equipment, pup tents, better tents than that, knives, Boy Scout shirts and pants, socks, shoes, even CCM bikes, a vast array. All you had to do was send in the required number of wrappings. They wanted a lot, but I can't remember worrying about that.

We didn't use cans, food in cans, at home as the relief didn't allow for that. You got potatoes and dried beans and syrup, and usually through a voucher so you had to buy what the relief said you could have. But we lived on the edge of a good district, the best in Victoria, Oak Bay, and I tried one day after school.

I just started down one lane going through the garbage cans and Libbys seemed to be the big seller because it was Happy Days from the first can. I got 15 or 20 that first day in an hour. Even then I had some business sense because I could see that this thing could be made to work if it was done right, and two guys could cover a hell of a lot more ground much better than one, so I got Cliffie Newton into the act and we cleaned up. The Libby people must have wondered just who were these guys, Barstow and Newton. They must have thought we were buying the stuff wholesale just for the wrappers.

We worked as a team; I would go ahead and go through the garbage cans and throw the Libby cans out on the lane, and Cliffie would come behind with a sharp nail imbedded into a stick and he'd strip the cans and throw them back into the garbage cans. We always left everything neat. A couple of times the patrol car came around because somebody would see us out in the lane, but they saw we were keeping things clean and, hell, I guess they figured even a couple of kids had a right to make a living.

The garbage pickup in Oak Bay was Friday so we did one route Wednesday, which gave us five days of throwing away, and Thursday, which gave us six days. We worked two days, from about 3:30 to 6 o'clock.

We split the take right down the middle and got a mass of stuff. Some we'd keep, of course, and other stuff we'd sell or trade because trading was a big thing in those days. We were capitalists in a sense. I've still got a haversack and a set of nesting aluminum dishes which are as good as they were 35 years ago, and that says something for the workmanship they put into them. My sons and I still use them, fishing and so on.

You could tell the kind of income the families had, because no matter how big the houses in that district, that didn't necessarily mean they had money. I'd say fully half the labels we collected were pork and beans and spaghetti. There was damned little asparagus and things like that, let me tell you. Kids were pretty resourceful in those days but I never heard of any other kids setting up a regular route to go garbage hunting. But it sure worked for us."

A Very Strange Lunch

"Every day, winter or no, we'd walk four miles to school and I carried a bag with lunch. Lunch was this. It was a big loaf of rye bread Mom made herself and she'd cut off the heel, you see. Then she'd push back, pack the bread in so there was this long hole in the loaf. Then she'd stuff in baked beans she'd soaked and boiled and laced with molasses and chili. My God, can you think of such a combination ever again. I can't.

At lunch we all ate it, my sister Kay and brother Bob and me, we ate it like a big banana or ice cream cone or what have you. Nibbling from the top down. It took us about half an hour to finish it, believe me, and that bean sandwich cost her about 10 cents at the very most. Probably less.

A couple of cups of water and our little tummies were bloated up tight until supper. What a woman!"

Does Shirley Temple Know?

"Shirley Temple. That's what I remember about the Thirties. Shirley Temple dolls. One year they were the rage, everything, everybody was talking about Shirley Temple, going to see her movies, reading stories about her in the newspapers and in the fan magazines. Shirley Temple, Shirley Temple, Shirley Temple.

Eaton's used to turn a big part of their store into a toyland at Christmas and that year, the Shirley Temple year, they had these dolls along one end of the toyland. There must have been hundreds of these dolls, and they weren't cheap. Nine to about $16, I'd say, and $16 was a lot more than some families got in a month for relief. You could rent a cottage at Grand Beach for two weeks in July for that.

They moved girls from all over the store down to toyland for about six weeks before Christmas and I was one that year. We worked, well we had to be there at 8.30, door opened at nine, and sometimes we were on our feet for 14 hours a day except for half an hour lunch and if we had to go to the women's room. For $7 a week. They really didn't give us anything for nothing. I never knew a girl who wasn't glad to leave that place. Girls used to marry fellows they didn't even care for, to be free of Eaton's.

Oh yes, these dolls. I'd stand there and watch the faces of those little girls, from about four or five right up to about eleven. Some used to come at opening time and just stand there looking at those pink-cheeked, golden-haired lovely Shirley Temples. Little faces, they needed food. You could see a lot who needed a pint of milk a day a thousand times more than they needed a Shirley doll. They'd stare for hours. We tried to shush them away but it didn't do any good. They'd go once around toyland and be back. This, mind you, went on day after day, day after day, until some of the girls thought they would go crazy. One girl had a crying fit just over that, those hundreds of poor kids who would never own a Shirley Temple in a hundred years. They were lucky if they had breakfast that morning, or soup and bread that night.

The kids weren't the only ones, but the mothers too, and the hopeless look on their faces and trying to shush the little girls away, knowing they only had a dollar or two to buy gifts for the whole family. One day I had this crazy notion that I would give Shirley dolls away to the kids, here, little girl, this is for you, and here's one for you, and this big one is for you, darling. That sort of thing. I thought I'd do it until I was caught and then I'd plead insanity. I never did, of course.

Those six weeks with those goddam dolls were the worst I ever put in, easy at first but sheer torture at the end, all those big and yearning eyes staring at you. I wonder if Shirley Temple ever realized the misery those dolls must have caused children all over the world? I suppose she's never even thought of it."

———————— • ————————

Sick Two Days Each Year

"I was always sick two Fridays of every school year, that is when I was in grades 10 and 11 at Kelvin High School in Winnipeg. The first Friday was in early October and the second was late in June. I guess you can figure that one out.

Those two days were when the school had its big dances, the two of the year. Sure, I got asked. I'd get two or three invitations a couple of weeks ahead, and it is pretty hard to tell a fellow you like that you are going to have the flu two weeks ahead. But I managed it. I always had the flu, which translated means I didn't have any clothes. At school we wore a sort of black uniform, all the girls, so that's how I got by there, but at a dance, no way.

Kinda sad, isn't it? I might have met my one true love at one of those affairs."

———————————— • ————————————

"Thank You, Boys"

"Every kid in Calgary had a shovel, either one from the basement or one he made out of wood, the kind you push snow with. Harry Webster and I could hardly wait for four o'clock on days after a good snowfall. One that came overnight. We'd get up to the hill as fast as our legs could get us and pick out a house, a big one where the people obviously had money, and we'd get to work. We'd clear the front walk, the side walks and out to the lane and then – and remember, this took at least one hour – and then we'd go to the front door and when the door would open, we'd say, 'Lady, we cleaned your walks.' That usually meant a quarter, not a bad day's work for a couple of squirts.

But sometimes the lady would say, 'Thank you, boys,' and shut the door. There was no sense getting mad, we'd taken our chances. But it made you wonder about people, and you learned things about people in the Depression you never forgot. Of course, you also learned another thing, and that was you never went to that house again. No, sirree."

———————————— • ————————————

My Friend, The Butcher

"We lived in Windsor, my Dad, Mother and me and when they stopped production, when they cut back car production, my Dad was one of the first let out by Ford. There was just no work and for reasons I can't quite remember now, Dad couldn't get relief. He may have worked casual labour a couple days a month. I think it maybe was because he had an old car, paid for, and he couldn't sell that because no car, no job when one came up out of town. So the relief people read the rule and said you have a car, you won't sell it, so no relief. Something like that.

We were starving. I got gruel for breakfast, that's all, and went to school where other kids had had orange juice, porridge, an egg and bacon, toast, jam and milk. I looked it too. There are pictures at home, class pictures, and there I am, skinny and run-down.

Then I got lucky. Here's how. About grade 5 a butcher came to live next door to us, he moved in about 1935 as I recall. A big and fat jolly man. God, but that man loved to drink beer. He'd drink a case a night. He loved to eat too. He worked in a sort of supermarket near our house and he loved a hot meal at noon so he arranged with me that when I got out of school at noon I'd nip over to his house and pick up a lunch bucket from his wife, it had a hot meal in it, soup, some beef, vegetables, pie, all hot, you see. I'd take it to him and pick up the empty one from the day before because he didn't like to be seen carrying a workingman's lunch bucket. After all, for chrissakes, he was a butcher. He had figured out our situation at home and that I got no lunch for school so when I'd pick up the other bucket, it was never empty. There was always a slice of liverwurst or three or four wieners and always a pint of milk. This was stuff he could pick up where he worked without going into the front part of the store. So there I was, going into the store and past the check-out girl and as I went by I'd scoop up as big a handful of peanuts as my paw would allow, those salty Spanish peanuts that every supermarket had. Five cents bought a lot of peanuts and everybody knew they were loaded with nourishment. That went into my pocket, the nuts. Then down to the butcher's counter to exchange lunch buckets and back up another aisle and I'd snipe off a Parker House roll, they were loose in a basket, and as I went out past the fruit I'd pick up an apple.

Everybody knew I took the apple. In fact, the manager the first few days gave me one and then I just began taking one. A one cent gift. So there I was, sitting on a curb or a park bench in spring and fall, or in the lunch-room at school in winter, and I'd put the wieners on the bun and munch away and then I'd eat the big handful of peanuts while I drank the milk and then down would go the apple. In those days we ate the cores too. Everybody did.

That was a good lunch. It was a better lunch than I bet many of the teachers were making. They only made peanuts. Hah! I had it good and I never let anybody else on to it and it kept me going. You better believe it."

Twelve Miles At Twenty Below

"There was a small hotel in this town once. In the Thirties it was quite busy and one Saturday I made $1 by beating every rug in the hotel. I hauled them out and down the stairs and hung them up and beat them and then hauled them up again.

The dollar was Christmas money. Everybody saved Christmas money.

In December, that's all I still had. One dollar. I got a ride on the milk truck into Red Deer one Saturday morning and I shopped there because I figured the buys were better. They weren't, I guess, but it didn't do any harm.

For my Dad I bought a pair of wool socks, 20 cents. My mother got a vial of perfume, 10 cents, and a big package of bobby pins, 10 cents, and I got two popular songs of sheet music for my sister who played the piano and that was 25 cents. I bought two hot dogs and a milk whip which is like a milk shake now, that was 20 cents. Then I bought a bunch of silver tinsel and stuff for the tree for 20 cents and five cents for a box of crackerjack and I got out on the highway and hitched a ride down to our turn-off and then walked 12 miles home and it was 20 below.

I never thought a thing about it, buying all that for a dollar or the three hour walk in the dark. That was just the way things were done then. Nobody thought anything about it at all."

———————————— • ————————————

One of Those Slave Kids

"We moved to a little farm at St. Simeon, and that is east of Quebec City and real habitant country. None of this phoney tourist stuff then. Back then life wasn't too much different than 1800. The philosophy of life, you see.

The farm was poor and my father was a poor farmer. His father had been a good one, but if you can't feel the goodness in the soil, the green thumb you call it, all the pamphlets from the government in Quebec, telling you how to make a crop, no help to you at all. My father farmed by these pamphlets. Maybe he should have written a pamphlet saying how you couldn't farm by those damn pamphlets.

He had 16 kids. Just like steps in a ladder, up and up and up. A kid every year. Two girls, my oldest sisters went into a nunnery and two brothers too, so the Holy Father had his share of Beaubiens from St. Simeon.

We never had much anyway. Enough food but cash, what was that? Cash was something the other guy had. No cash and where was the clothes, the boots and the medicines and the other stuff?

One day a guy comes to my house. Dad and I are in the yard, we're bucking poles, you see, and this guy who lives down the road makes a joke and says, 'I see, Romeo, you have sons for sale.' My Dad says, 'I don't put up no notice on the board in the village.' They talk and I listen and what is happening is this. I will go to work for this guy for my food and clothes, and this means my Dad won't have to feed me and he gets $10 from that guy too. It is a good deal for him. It is good for the farmer from down the river. Of course, it is not so good for me.

I could do two things. I'm 14 and big and tough and maybe I can work in the shanties in the bush. Run away, you know. Or I can say no, I won't go, and then my old man will go into the village and the priest will come out with his buggy and black horse and he would say, 'Do what your father says.' Then I would have to go. So I got only one choice, eh? I run away. But that would make my mother unhappy – so I go to work for this guy.

It ain't so bad. He's not too bad and his wife is a good cook and I learn how it is right to farm. I mean, I learn how to farm so you can make a profit. I go to school a couple of months in the winter too. It is not too bad.

Next year, my father does it to Henri and André and Denis and out they go, and so does Annette and Marie and by God, there are Beaubien kids all over the district. Seven altogether.

About two years later I am 17, I guess, and I go to a card party at a house. We didn't have dances, the Cardinal says no. This card party, I meet a girl from another part of the parish and I like her to see her right off, you know, and I think she is the same and when I tell her my name because I want to see her again, she laughs and says, 'Oh, I know you. You're one of those slave kids.'

That is the first time I hear I am called a slave in that district and it bothered me but not much because, hell, what my Dad did made sense, you know. It worked out okay."

———————————•———————————

The Comics House

"We lived in Hamilton and my Dad got laid off from the steel company, and he went down to Nova Scotia to look for work in a mill there. So when he was gone my mother and me and my sister Annie moved up to stay with her younger brother who lived in a shack near a dump. I remember it was at the end of a street car line east of Toronto somewhere.

Well, we never heard a word from Dad anymore, he just disappeared. Dis-ap-peared. Gone. Then my uncle was arrested and sent to jail for breaking into a boxcar, and that left Mom and me and Annie in this little shack. This was around 1936 and it was fall and getting colder so we went into the dump and we got dozens of these Heinz beans and spaghetti and other cardboard boxes and Annie and I held and Mom nailed them all around the inside of the shack. It just had one big room and she figured that would help keep out the cold.

We got some food from the dump, the stuff restaurants and hospitals put out. It was mostly bread and cake and potatoes that if you cut enough you could cut out the rot, and there were jam pails and if you boiled water in them they'd come clean and you had a good sweetener. People around were doing this.

I found a big bundle of comics tied together and brought it home and mother said it would make good insulation too, so she got a pot of glue made of flour and water and we papered the walls with these comics, the Katzenjammer Kids and Little Orphan Annie and Tarzan of the Apes and Buck Rogers. The word got around that the Turnbulls had a house made of comics. They called it the Comics House. Kids used to come from all over the area and they'd just walk around, on the cots, kneeling on the table, standing up, and they'd read these pasted up comic strips. I noticed that the kids would make rude remarks about Little Orphan Annie so we pasted her over.

Really, that shack was getting like a social club. Grown-ups, the parents of the kids, used to come over at night and there would be talk, about politics, Mackenzie King, Mussolini, the Depression, although I don't think that's what it was called. Our shack was a social club. Men would bring wood for the stove and sometimes a woman would bring some cookies or something.

One little guy, he must have been 80, he came to the door one afternoon and he had a note and my mother read it and it said, would someone read the comics to him. He couldn't read but he sure could look. Every week, once a week he'd come and one of us, or one of the kids who were there, would read him a wall of comics and he'd laugh and go away happy. He must have read the same comics 15 times that winter but it never made any difference. He was an old, old man and he just wanted company.

One afternoon when he left he gave my mother two one dollar bills, all grimy and creased. Oh, by the way, he never spoke. She didn't want to take the money but he just kept pushing her hand back. Mother figured that was the only money he had to his name but we'd helped him pass a tough winter and he was just showing his gratitude."

———————————— • ————————————

Mother, The Mitt-Maker

"Winnipeg can be the coldest place in the world in winter, and this is where my mother came into it. I came home from school one day and told her that a little Italian girl in my class couldn't hold her pencil right because her hands, the knuckles, were split and bleeding because of the cold. No mitts. Little Connie had no mitts. My mother said, 'Give her your mitts.' What about me? 'Never mind,' she said. 'Give that child your mitts. Leave them in her desk if you have to,' and that started what I've always called The Great Mitt Knit.

Mother started making mitts, knitting them, unravelling old sweaters, anything woolen, and rewinding that wool and knitting mitts, big ones, small ones, and I gave them out. Some kids didn't want to take them but I always found a way. Mother, I can see her yet sitting by the radiator when I'd get home for school, and she'd be knitting away. I guess she did a pair a day and it got eventually that every poor kid had them, but Mother just kept on knitting. It became an obsession."

———————————— • ————————————

Mr. Marshall's Shoes

"There was this little, old man living next door to us named Marshall. He'd been a butcher for a Red and White store and got let go and he had no money put away, none. His wife was dead and he was lonely. He was about 50, I think, but to a kid of 12, well, that's pretty old. Mother used to take him in leftovers from our stews and sometimes half a pie or a loaf of bread and he and she knew it was straight charity, but if it is disguised under neighbourliness, then that makes it okay.

One night he came over to play cribbage with my old man and he was feeling low and when he left he said, 'Harry, I've been feeling poorly the past while. If you don't see smoke coming out my chimney, would you drop over? See how I'm doing,' and – he put his hand up to his heart as if to emphasize his point. My Dad said, 'Joe, I never knew you had a bum ticker,' and he said, 'I haven't. It's just busted right in two.'

About a month later my mother said she hadn't seen anything doing around the Marshall house for a couple of days and she sent me over. The front and back doors were locked, but there was a basement door and I got in that way. I didn't know where the light switch was and it was black as hell so I started feeling my way up the stairs when I felt two bumps on my chest, as if I'd run into two objects. I reached up and felt them and, you know, I guess my brain wasn't working because it took me a few seconds, in fact until I felt the ankles, and then I knew they were shoes. Feet. Old man Marshall was hanging there. He'd tied a rope around the beam, the noose over his head, and just jumped out into space.

Now that was a hell of a thing for a kid of 12 to find, something I always remembered about the Depression. Old man Marshall swinging there."

———————————— • ————————————

Brain Work

"Momma said we had to have an education, but here we were riding this old hay rick with the tent built on the top, going up and down the Fraser Valley and stopping to pick where anybody would let us. Picking was slim.

For two years we found a house in the fall and lived some way with Pop doing a bit of work in the district. Not much.

Momma tried to get us into the little schools, one in Silverdale by there, but we were from Saskatchewan – not wanted, you see. So she had this Eaton's catalogue and she gave us lessons from it. We'd learn composition by writing letters ordering dresses and underthings in our scribbler, and do our sums by multiplying 14 pairs of men's boots by the price in the catalogue. Things like that, you see. Subtraction and adding worked out that way too.

For what Momma called brain work she'd have us learn the names of the books of the Bible. I can still string them off, lickitty-split. She'd make us memorize long parts of the Bible, Psalms, Revelations, parts like that. That's the way we got our education on the road. It helped a lot later when we got settled in our own place."

No Sense To It At All

"Nothing seemed to make any sense. Not to me, or for me.

I grew up on a farm between Guelph and Galt and since I was knee high to a grasshopper I wanted to be a vet. A veterinarian. It wasn't the loftiest of ambitions, but that is what I wanted.

I had an aunt who knew this, a fine old lady of considerable years who lived in Toronto. When she died, at the reading of the will after the funeral there were 30 shares of Ford of Canada stock for me, the stipulation being that it be used to pay my tuition and expenses at the Ontario Agriculture College in Guelph. As they say, I was walking on clouds. This was, oh, she died late in 1928. December, I think. I was 15 so I'd be going to OAC in three years. Hah! You know what happened, what's coming.

The estate was tied up for three years. A lot of trouble about land titles, neighbours disputing old surveys, and a question of who owned what property here in Toronto. It wasn't until 1932 that all the i's were dotted.

When the will was read, Ford of Canada was up around $67 a share or so. In around there, and climbing. By 1932, it was down to $6. Those 30 shares at $67 would have put me in clover. At $6, only $180, I was as poor as the next farm boy. That in a nutshell is what the Depression did. It wiped out many a big businessman, it shoved the poor, the aged, the helpless and the kids who couldn't find work, it shoved them deeper into the hole and tamped in the dirt. And Robert King never did become a veterinarian."

CHAPTER TWENTY-FOUR

"You'll Be A Better Woman For It"

Every Last Cent ... Such A Sweet Girl ... Back To The Old Ways ... Eva Went To The City ... Children Have To Have Sugar ... The Oldest Profession ... Our Christmas Dinner ... Tougher On Women ... Queen Of The Canners ... Confessions Of A House Maid ... Not Even Mom's Chickens ... The Great Marriage Plot ... Whose Kids Are Those? ... When The Clothes Boxes Came ... I Talked To That Stove.

———————————— • ————————————

I met a woman years ago at Soda Creek in the British Columbia Cariboo who survived three Depression winters by killing a moose each fall, and getting two 98-pound sacks of flour from a store at Williams Lake by promising to do housework for a month. With a few other necessities, she fed herself and two children on that.

I asked about her husband and she said, "Oh, Jack used to go down to the coast and wander about until spring. He wouldn't have been able to live the life we lived those years."

This doesn't mean that all women were tough during the Depression, but many were. They stayed home and kept the home fires burning.

In the more destitute families, they learned to make $10 relief for food a month go almost all the way. They scrounged and scrimped and patched and glued and sewed and borrowed and copied and worked day in and day out with not much hope and took a second long look at every nickel they spent and kept their kids clean and visited neighbours who were sick, and I guess they did a lot of praying too. It is a terrible thing for a woman to help children decorate a Christmas tree under which there will be no presents.

They did other things, too. Trying to keep in touch with a wandering son, out riding the rods, consoling a desolate husband. Doing some spring cleaning – down on her knees scrubbing kitchens – for neighbours, feeding five people on five bucks a week, macaroni and spaghetti, spaghetti and macaroni, and always serving herself last.

304

Tens and tens of thousands of mothers lived this life, for years, and we should never forget them.

———————————— • ————————————

Every Last Cent

"I knew where every last cent of my money went, feeding a husband and three boys. My grocery bill for the month, if it was over $10 I was just sick. I can tell you what my grocery bill was, every month, since we've been married. I've got it down, and I know that in the Thirties if my grocery bill was over $10 I was sick. Didn't know how I was going to pay it.

If my grocery bill was more, then I'd go over my book, over and over again, and I'd find out what went wrong. Ten dollars, that was the top, and my husband, my kids, they never starved."

———————————— • ————————————

Such A Sweet Girl

"We had this girl, Loretta Livingstone. A wonderful girl, such a sweet girl. This was when we lived in Winnipeg. Loretta's people were Scots, the Clydebank, very large family as I remember, and very poor. She came before breakfast and cooked breakfast, did the dishes, most of the housework, although I had a woman from the North End for the really heavy work, scrubbing and beating rugs. Loretta was not all that strong.

The children ate lunch at school so Loretta and I would have a quiet lunch and we'd talk like a couple of old church wives. She might do the laundry in the afternoon, Monday was always laundry day in Winnipeg, and the ironing Tuesday, and generally keep her busy.

She loved our house, it was a lovely place. It had belonged to my husband's mother and she had a lot of lovely things. About four, Loretta would set the dining table and put the supper together, a roast maybe, or fish, perhaps a ham. We ate well, my husband always insisted on a good table, and I agreed. About 4.30 my sweet Loretta would go home, a few blocks away over on Macmillan Avenue. I paid her $10 a month, which was very good in those days and she'd often take home some of our children's clothes for her brothers and sisters, the ones getting big. They were a large family, as I told you.

One day Loretta broke down at lunch. I knew something had been going wrong, for a few days I sensed it, but I felt she'd tell me when she was ready.

We were such good friends. It came out then, in a great river of tears and gasps and sobs. Poor Loretta. What it meant was that she was sold in marriage. Perhaps 'sold' is not the proper word, not for those days, but give a dog another name, you know what I mean. It seems there had been a young man she'd gone to school with, at Kelvin, an Italian. I'd never heard of him, of course, but there was a pocket of them over, somewhere near the C.N.R. sheds. I believe they worked for the railway.

He had gone away, up to Flin Flon or Sherrit-Gordon, where there was a lot of mining activity, mines did well during the Depression, and now he was back on a holiday and had been around to see Loretta. That meant nothing to her, just a school friend who dropped by. But the upshot was, he asked her to marry him, this Italian, and she said no. She didn't love him, didn't even like him if it got down to that. I guess this is the way they do things in Italy because this Joe went to see Loretta's father and offered him money. Quite a lot of money, I understand. What would you do? I wonder. Here was a man, her father who had been on relief for five or six years, he had all those mouths to feed, and here was a good looking husky young fellow offering $400 or $500 for his daughter. Four or five hundred dollars was a great deal of money, more than that man had seen in his life, I should imagine. He ordered Loretta to marry him, and this was what the crying was all about.

I was so upset that I phoned my husband and he was at his desk and I told him to get home right away, this instant. I was quite firm, so he knew something was up and he was home in ten minutes. I went through it and Loretta just sat sobbing quietly. I remember my husband saying, 'They do this in Africa, but surely, not here.' The upshot of it all was that I went to see her father, an unpardonable thing to do, but I did, and he was as Scottish as they come and stubborn as a mule and he could see that $400, and that's all he could see. I offered to take Loretta into our home, she could live in a small suite we could build in the basement. I had no children, you see, and she could work for us, become sort of one of the family. George, my husband, agreed. He was a good, kindly man. But it was not to be. That terrible greedy old man just wouldn't hear of it. Of course it was unthinkable to buy her off, I mean pay $400 to him, for that would have solved absolutely nothing.

So Loretta married this Italian man and went to live up north, and about a year and a half later I got a snapshot of her and a baby. Just the snap and nothing else. Another year and I got a post card. They were visiting the Rockies, and then that was all I ever heard."

———————————— • ————————————

Back To The Old Ways

"One thing, we had to go back to doing things the way our mothers did. The old ways. The old methods. We'd had electricity but the windcharger, a Delco plant, it broke down and it broke down again and it broke down again and then there was no money to fix it, or for new batteries. Those big glass expensive things. Then coal oil lamps again.

I remember making butter. We had a big eight gallon dash churn which John found in our implement shed. I guess it had been there 20 years. He hauled it out and went to work on it and it was in good shape. His Dad always did buy good things. Scrubbed it up and it was raring to go. I had to get my mother over to show me how. It was like a barrel, you turned a handle, a crank. If there is anything more monotonous than working that churn, seems like hour after hour, moving that dasher up and down in that hole in the cover. That was the way you made butter. Then you'd hear the sound of the first globs of butter forming. Throw in some cold water. What that did, I never did find out. The butter then was starting to form. They called it 'gathering.' Yes, 'gathering.'

I was the one who ladled the butter into a big wooden bowl. Mother always said, 'You've got to have a wooden bowl.' I'd say, 'Why?' She'd say, 'Don't ask me why. You just have to.' Like in school. Why? Because. You washed that butter, and worked it with your hands, and that felt good. You'd created something. You had to salt it. City people were used to salted butter. A lot of farm people don't like salted butter, still don't. Oh, well. Never the twain shall meet – do you hear me, Mr. Trudeau? I used about a pound of salt for every 20 pounds, and that seemed about right. You worked the salt in, around, in and around. Next day you worked it again and got the last water out. Pack it in a crock, cover it with cheesecloth, or a thin cloth. These were about 10 or 12 pound sizes as I remember.

If we were selling in town we packed it in big round wooden tubs. Mostly we just churned in the summer and stored it cool for the winter. You appreciated that butter because a lot of work went into it. If you took it to town you usually traded, and it was worth about eight to 12 cents a pound.

When my mother was over one afternoon and we were churning, she said, 'This is what I used to do 30 years ago. What went wrong?' I said everything. I said since we had no electricity I separated cream by hand, and because we had no money I baked all my bread and John mended his own harness, right there at the kitchen table by lamplight, and if the cultivator shoes broke, he made new ones, and he'd learned to shoe the work horses and I was doing laundry by hand because we couldn't afford a gas-operated washer, and Lord God, that was hard work, and I was telling my mother this and she said, 'It will all work out in the end. You'll be a better woman for it.' God, I was never closer to killing a person in my life than right then."

———————————— • ————————————

Eva Went To The City

"My younger sister Eva was the pretty one in our family. Real pretty. Brown curly hair. She had big eyes, blue.

We had this nothing little farm near Selkirk. It was just big enough to keep us starving. I remember it was around about August or so, what year I can't say, but Eva went into Winnipeg and got a waitress job. She came back for Thanksgiving on that trolley they used to have, and at dinner my Dad – he was about three things, Polish, Ukrainian and Russian all mixed in together – he said that her clothes looked too good for her to buy as a waitress. That's what she said she was. Anyway he asked her a couple of more times how she could buy these clothes, and if she didn't stand up and say, 'Pop. I'm not a waitress, I'm peddling my ass.'

The old man got up and went out into the yard. He and the boys had gone out and brought in a load of poles for firewood and they were lying by the well house. Pop picked up an axe and began to chop those poles and he chopped and sawed and sawed and chopped for I guess it might have been five hours. When he came into the kitchen it was dark outside and he walked through into the back bedroom and he shut the door. I can always remember, he shut the door very softly. As far as I know he never spoke to Eva again. Not even at Mom's funeral."

———————————— • ————————————

Children Have To Have Sugar

"We had a little farm. Six acres and a little house and three kids and my husband's health wasn't so good. He'd gone underground, the coal mines at

Sydney when he was 14. He signed his death warrant right there. He was, well he couldn't breathe well and was stopped from getting decent work.

We managed in a way. There was food on the table. Nobody starved. We had a big garden and a cow and chickens and ducks and somebody would give us a runt which we'd feed with skim milk and garden tops and so we always had pork. We had no money. The only good thing about it was that we were young and things didn't worry us. If they happened now, well, I guess I could live because I know how I did live in those days.

Our big problem was to get the money that was needed to buy sugar. Yes, I know they say children don't need sugar and that it is an acquired taste, but you try bringing up children without sugar. Just try it. For baking, for one thing. For their porridge. For fudge on Sunday nights. For ice cream. You see, we had the cow and when she was fresh we'd have ice cream. All the time. You've got to have sugar. Children have to have something good. We never had a cent for store candy. Once in a while somebody would give them a stick of gum or something like that. But I made all kinds of different kinds of candy. At Christmas, my goodness! We grew our own popcorn too, so we had that.

There was never a time when I felt I couldn't go on, it's all too much. I can remember having only $5 at Christmas. That was all I was able to save in one year, by scrimping and saving and doing without, just $5 dollars. Most of that was from the sale of eggs and old hens. That had to buy everything for Christmas, everything, the four children's Christmas gifts, and once my oldest boy got a sweater that cost a dollar and a half, and that cut the rest down. A small tree, a big dinner, gifts, everything, on $5.

We wanted for a lot of things. People today, even people on welfare, would say they couldn't live the way we did, on what we did. We got along, you see, and the two boys went up to Canada *(Ontario)* and got themselves good jobs and the two girls are married around here. My husband died, the mine finally did its deadly work.

Really, there was nothing unusual about us. We had a little house, I milked a cow, I had a garden, I saved a few dollars a year from selling eggs and a few hens, and the family grew up and they always were neat and clean and we went to church regular and it all came out right in the end. We weren't unusual."

The Oldest Profession

"I wish she could tell you her story but I guess she's dead and blown to the four winds now. I met her only once, up in northeast Manitoba about 1935, '36, in around there.

Here was the set-up. The government was putting a road in east to a new mining area, east of Manigotagan, and they had let out the brushing of the right-of-way to a gang. Brushing is cutting down, clearing the right-of-way and burning the slash, and it's a dirty job. A good gang can move along at a fair clip and so you've got to keep moving camp. You move it about 10 miles ahead and then the gang works up to the camp and then moves about five miles ahead and then you move camp another 10 miles. Leap-frogging would be the way to describe it, and a good contractor who is organized can make a good pile of money. This contractor was a Bohunk and he had five Indians, lads from around Selkirk, they were doing the axe work and they burned on dull or wet days.

Now what this story is all about is this. I did some prospecting in those days, in the summer, and seeing as they were kind enough to clear a trail for me, well I'd use it. I had a pack horse and I came up on their camp about three one afternoon and figured I'd settle for the night close by. I was surprised to see smoke from the chimney angled out of the big tent and even more surprised to see a cute little gal come out. Maybe 20 or so. I think she was damned surprised to see me too. I forget her name but maybe I didn't know it. To get to the point, she was Irish and she'd come out to Canada the year before as a domestic. You could get them for almost nothing then, five a month and board. So this little Mick had been hired on by this contractor after the first couple of jobs as domestic soured on her, and you know what she was doing? She was cooking for that crew, six guys, one a Ski or a Chuck and five Swampy Cree. Imagine that circus!

She gave me a muffin and coffee and there was an obvious question to be asked and I did it as kindly as I could. Guess? How does a pretty little thing beat off the affections of six animals in the north woods? Something to that effect. She made no bones about it, just telling me as if she was saying how she washed the breakfast dishes every day. The contractor paid her five dollars a week and by God, you can't tell me she didn't earn every cent. Each guy had her one night a week and he paid her, each guy paid her, a dollar for the night. She had her own little tent. This little one with the blue eyes and black hair was running a whore house in the woods, and she looked like she wouldn't say boo to a goose. So here she was making about $20 a month doing the cooking and slopping, and maybe another $25 for taking on the crew and that was $45 a month, and with nothing to spend it on that little gal was doing well.

So there we sat, me eating her muffins and she pouring coffee, a regular Darby and Joan, and I could have used some of it, but it just wasn't the kind of thing I did as a regular habit. But she caught the flash in my eye and she stood up and gave me a wink and she said, and these were her words, 'I'm so deathly sick of serving those beasts that this is for fun, so c'mon now, and not a word of this when they come in.' We knocked off two in her little tent and when I got back to Lac Du Bonnet I thought I'd have a first rate beer parlour story. But then I got to thinking, and I didn't say a word because I didn't think anybody would believe it. I don't like being called a liar and that's what somebody with a skinfull would have called me. But it was all true."

———————————— • ————————————

Our Christmas Dinner

"I'm talking about Christmas dinner, about 1934 or so.

I sent Tommy, my oldest, down to the butcher shop near the Marquis Hotel and told him to buy a cow's heart. It seems to be in my mind now that one cost about 15 cents. Canadians wouldn't eat them, but being from the Old Country, well at least we did know what you could eat and what you couldn't.

I stuffed the heart with bread crumbs – we could buy second day bread for three cents a loaf, as I remember – and with pepper and salt and melted butter and a pinch of this and that, it was really quite a nice stuffing.

So we had this heart, and heart you know, no matter how you do it, there's just no way for it to taste other than a bit rubbery. But it was good. We had heart, and my own garden potatoes and beets and corn and I made a flour gravy and we had pudding and wheat coffee, we made it by roasting wheat in the oven, and rock candy, and that was our Christmas dinner and I think the cost would have been about, let's see, oh, 30 cents, oh, say 35 cents. And that fed five people very well, thank you."

———————————— • ————————————

Tougher On Women

"Vancouver was the place to come in the fall. No winter, you see. No work either, though. Carpenters, plumbers, pipefitters, furnace installers, stone masons, stevedores, well everybody, nobody ever got over $2 a day. Ten dollars a week. Ten. A sawbuck. Men would rob for half of that and risk seven years in the pen.

Imagine going home to wife and five kids Friday and laying down a ten dollar bill saying, 'Pay the rent, feed us, buy clothes, let the kids go to the Saturday matinee and give me half a dollar for beer,' and then step back and listen to the uproar.

Can't blame the poor women. There they are in old clothes from the Good Will or Salvation Army or relatives in Ontario. My wife used dried moss for Kotex. Yes, she did. Can you believe that? That's what women living in caves 4,000 years ago used to use. Or Indian women.

It was tough on men but tougher on women – but again, women are strong in times of toughness."

———————————— • ————————————

Queen Of The Canners

"Lord, what a time, but my husband used to say I held the all-time championship for canning. The Southern Alberta Championships. I had this big garden, large, and I put up vegetables galore and pickles and onions and things that people never thought of canning or packing. Then the kids would pick berries, everything that was edible, and there I would be late, oh very late at night, boiling – and melting wax and pouring and screwing on lids until I thought I would lose my mind.

Everybody around would say, 'If you have to give away those sealers, give them to Sarah Barnes, she wants them.' So I'd get jars and sealers from here, there and everywhere, and I had more than 500 and every year I filled every one, and every year my family emptied every last blessed one. These weren't cans like in Safeway, they were quart and two quart jars. We ate good in those days, I must say. Thanks to Momma."

———————————— • ————————————

Confessions Of A House Maid

"I came off the farm. That's where. Dear mother, but I was green. Fifteen miles from town. No running water. I'd hardly seen a picture show more than twice. No car. I helped Dad and my brothers picking rocks, tearing roots, cleaning out mustard. That was Mamie. Me. Strong as an ox.

There was Mr. Wilson, he used to hunt over Dad's land and eat with us, and Dad got me a job in Mr. Wilson's house. A big one, right down there in Ottawa. Dear mother, it was nice. My little room downstairs, little bathroom, little washbasin, toilet, little desk and bed. I worked seven in the morning until dishes done at night, every day but Thursday afternoon. To the movies then, Hollywood. Mrs. Wilson gave me old clothes and the daughter did too. A little bitch. Lots of things happen. Big parties and I pass drinks. Everybody drunk and some use my little room downstairs to make love. I don't like this but what do I do?

One night, it is summer, I am down ironing sheets and pillows and Mr. Wilson comes. Not drinking much, but drinking. He walks around, looking at old magazines I have there, and then Mr. Wilson takes my arm and says, 'Come, Mamie, we're off to bed.' Oh, sure what do I do? I'm a big kid but only 17. Mr. Wilson, he's a big man. To bed. Next time Mrs. Wilson goes out, to bed. I'm afraid for a baby and then I tell my girl friend and she says to get some money from Mr. Wilson. I tell him and he hits me on the ear. Like this. Not hard, but a hit. I'm crying. He says, 'Okay, I pay you, but you got to work for it. If Mrs. Wilson says, where do you get new clothes, you say I am paying you more money for more work. Not for this.' I say okay.

In summer, he has fruit trees. Apples, mostly. Crabapples too. I keep my window open, if I hear boys in garden, I run outside with thick stick, tin lid from garbage can and I bang bang bang and kids run away. Crazy, for five more dollars a week. In spring, I do same while no apples grow. Winter, I feed crumbs to little birds on snow, put ashes on walk. This I would do anyway. I make $5 more each week for silly things, banging tin drum, feeding sparrows, this kind of thing is pay for being screwed. I like Mr. Wilson, for him it could be free.

Ten years, I guess, and she never finds out. Not once in ten years. Never asks about banging tin, which I do even when no boys there.

Mrs. Wilson not so smart. Soon I get to think only Mamie smart. Twenty-five dollars each month, I am rich."

———————————•———————————

Not Even Mom's Chickens
"Dad said he can't remember who pushed him over the edge but it must have been some clerk in somebody's wholesale store in Winnipeg or Toronto who

looked over Accounts Receivable one day and saw that Major's store was months overdue, and he did it to us. That man probably filled out a form, filling in the figures and date and names quite impersonally and mailed it off and that was enough, that order to the sheriff's officer, to push all our hopes and dreams over the side.

My, but bankruptcy was an ugly word then. Still is, I guess. Then it was shameful. I never knew whether the debt was for $4.99 or $149. Little girls of 10 weren't supposed to worry their pretty little heads about these kind of things. All I knew is that mother told my brother and me that we were going to Grandpa's house at Swan River, on a farm and we could help with the animals. I guess it was best that I didn't understand what was going on, the ins-and-outs, the reasons for it all, but even at 10 I was a good enough observer to take it all in. I took it all in from the second floor window of the big empty house, and it was empty because there was no furniture left, but they hadn't taken down the filmy curtains and I peeked through them. It was a Saturday. I remember. No school. The auctioneer did his work up at the store a block over on Main Street, knocking off the stock and fixtures, the cash register, the accumulation of four years of Dad's hard, hard work and he later told me, 'It went for nothing on the dollar.' He laughed. He was a man who could always laugh, and that's probably why he was such a lousy businessman. Laugh and grow fat, maybe, but not rich.

There was a big crowd, Saturday, naturally every kid in our town was there and not many of our neighbours but the handbills had been up for 10 days so a lot of people we'd never seen before had come in. Our neighbours were kindly folk and they wouldn't embarrass us by coming. I don't know how it is these days, what the laws are, but they couldn't clean you out then. As I remember, we were allowed to keep a table and chairs, enough beds for the family, our clothes, pots and dishes and I think the stove. The chesterfield. I may be wrong but I don't think they took the old car. If they did, I don't remember how we got to Swan River so I think we kept the car. Everything else except dishes and cutlery went, and there it was, everything else we had all piled up on the front lawn. What a time it would have been if it had been raining, but rain wasn't something we saw much of in that part of Saskatchewan those days.

Every area, not each town, had an auctioneer. He might be the livery stable owner or the furniture store owner and he did auctions in his spare time. I was just little but I remember he started off by holding up a folded piece of carpet which looked okay and he asked for bids and somebody bid 10 cents and it went up to 20 cents and then he opened it up and it had a round hole cut in it and he stuck his head through it and everybody laughed and he said something like, 'No, I won't sell you this. This has got a hole showing through it. But stay around, folks, for the whole show. We'll be selling off a lot of bargains and you can see this is honest, this whole show.' I found out later from Dad that every auctioneer had a little funny trick like that to get the crowd in a good mood. That was his. Very funny.

Everything went, the pictures for five cents each, the sewing machine which was something Mother could sure have used later, and the rugs and the extra linen and tables and garden tools and two small barrels of apples and even the boxes filled with bottles of root beer which Mother had prepared. She'd taken away her preserves in jars but somehow she'd missed them and they went.

Years later I found the bailiff's list when I was going through Dad's stuff when he died, cleaning up his estate because he did get back on his feet during the war, and I remember the prices paid were pitiful. Just pitiful. A set of Royal Doulton with places for eight, and only a couple of pieces missing, and I think, it went for $4. Imagine, Royal Doulton!

There's a story there. The night before, the neighbour lady, mother's best friend, a Mrs. Collins, came over and they were talking and Mother said they had let her keep her kitchen china but the Doulton must go. The woman said she'd bid on it for Mother loved that china and I think it was the only elegant thing she ever possessed, outside of her rings. She kept those, by the way. So when the Doulton came up the neighbour bid and it got up to three-fifty and then she stopped and it was knocked down at $4. Just think, $4. It turned out that three-fifty was all the woman had, not a red cent more, and so it went to some woman we had never seen before. The harness for two horses and an elegant buggy went for five. That's what the list said. Our cow fetched six and it was worth at least 20, a wonderful Guernsey. God, its milk was thicker than the cream you buy today.

Anyway, it went on and on and the last thing to go was Mother's 20 chickens and a rooster. They were Rhode Island Reds and good layers and Mother apparently didn't know they were on the block. She was standing beside me upstairs there watching and she said, 'Oh, no!' in protest and she seemed to feel worse about the chickens than anything. They were in the chicken run at back, but the crowd didn't have to see them. Chickens were chickens and the rooster, he knew something was up, and he was making a lot of racket and everybody knows that a healthy and alert rooster means a good flock. So they went up to 40 cents each, a pretty good price I believe, and the town butcher got them. My mother said, 'Oh, no!' again but I thought nothing about it. It just meant our chickens had been sold and we would have nothing really good to take to Grandfather's farm. My mother, I'm sure, knew differently, because she walked down the upstairs hall to the back of the house where the window looked out over the cowshed and the chicken run.

I watched people gathering up things they'd bought and then I heard her running down the stairs. She was crying. I ran after her and out through the kitchen and into the yard and she was standing beside the chicken run and crying and yelling, 'God damn you, God damn you!' and the butcher was looking at her, kind of stunned. He was in the chicken run and he had two chickens by the neck and I guess without thinking he gave each of them a quick snap of the wrist, like you'd crack a whip, and they died of broken necks. He tossed them over the wire to his son who had four others laid out and he slit their throats to bleed them. The butcher was a big, red-faced German and he kept asking 'Yes, Mrs. Major?' and I'm sure he couldn't figure out what was wrong because he turned and swooped out his big hands and grabbed two more chickens where they had all backed into a corner.

Oh well, there's not much to say. My Dad came running back and he saw what was happening and he turned Mother away and he said, 'Hans, haven't you got one ounce of common sense in that thick skull of yours?' and he led Mother into Mrs. Collins' house and I went in and Mrs. Collins gave her some lemonade. It was a hot morning. All Mother could say was: 'They didn't even leave me anything to feed my family with. Even my little red chickens.'

Dad should have been outside tending his business – ha! what was left of it – but he sat beside her for an hour in the parlour and stroked her head and kept saying, 'There, there, Little Violet, everything will be all right. All right. All right.' I was only 10 but I remember it so well because I had never heard Dad call Mother 'Little Violet' before. I guess it was an endearment he used when they were courting, when they were married, and when I think of it now, it almost makes me want to cry."

The Great Marriage Plot

"We always had some sort of a Depression going for us in New Brunswick. Large or small. To me, the 1929 affair meant not enough money. To my mother it meant marriage. My three sisters.

Remember in "Pride and Prejudice," that sloppy-brained Mrs. Bennett was continually trying to marry off her five daughters. Marry them well, to young gentlemen with income. That was her goal in life.

Same with my dear mother. My stupid mother. God love her, but my dumb mother. She had the firmest of convictions that any girl could seduce, if that is the proper word, any man with food. So food it was. Mountains of the stuff. Everybody loved food. Love followed.

I was up at the university at Fredericton fooling around towards a degree. Now I know University of N.B. wasn't, and still isn't any great shakes for scholarship, but again, I was no great scholar. We deserved each other.

Every weekend my mother would tell me, no she'd *order* me, to bring back two or three of my pals. This when I was in the third year, and that much closer to the breadline. She'd even order up junior lecturers or assistant professors. Then she and the girls would begin preparing Monday for that three day orgy, from Friday night until Sunday night. Food. A food orgy. I'd just tell the guys to come on down to our farm, an hour's bus ride away, and they could eat their hearts out for three nights and two days. They didn't have to marry my sisters. All they had to do was keep my mother in a rosy glow of euphoria.

We lived near the shore, so close we could see the coal freighters throwing their bloody garbage over the side, but anyway, we had oysters and clams and mussels and lobsters and everything that swam, including salmon, which we poached year round. To hell with those Boston and New York and Virginia millionaires and their fishing rights.

There was every kind of meat, beef, veal, pork, quack quack and cluck cluck and every kind of vegetable from a garden bigger than a football field and pickles, about eight varieties, and buns and cookies and pies and beverages and booze galore. Our own home brew and hard cider. Old pop skull, the kind we made by freezing a milk pail of cider and when the pure and true dynamite alcohol had collected in the middle of the ice block, then we drained that off. Two drinks and you were under. We used to mix four ounces with a quart of Canada Dry and that was plenty.

You can see that this was a production. Move over, Cecil B. DeMille. His orgies were nothing, except ours were food.

The girls got a bang out of it – and I think I mean that figuratively – but you know what? It *worked*. Those dames got married. One guy held out for nine weekends. We were all set to present him with his own personally engraved napkin ring but on the tenth weekend, he caved in and Mary grabbed him off. The other two girls picked and chose and each got a good man, and mark it that this was in a time when guys were being very, very cagey about marriage. How to support them and all that.

I know that when the marriages came off, Mother didn't support them. It was business as usual then, porridge and salted herring in the morning, bread and a garden salad for lunch, and cod or mackerel, or a pork chop and greens for dinner. No orgies. No fancy tablecloth. No nothing. The battle had been won."

Whose Kids Are Those?

"I won't tell you my name but I'll tell you this. My husband walked out, just left like so many did in those days because they just couldn't take the shame of not being able to support their family. It was the women who were strong in those days.

I was left with two tiny children, one a baby, and the best I could get was a small room across from Vancouver General Hospital. My relief was less than $10 a month. Not $10 a week, a month. The hot water heater had rusted through and the landlord wouldn't replace it, so there was no hot water. So every morning I'd put on a white dress that could pass for a nurse helper's uniform and I'd take my two babies across to the hospital and go into the big room there and I'd wash them. Nobody ever asked me what or how or why, and after a while, because it was warm, I'd leave the babies in cribs and I'd wander in and do something useful. Take a mop and use it. Wash dishes. Feed the children, and my own. I made beds. Everybody thought I was on staff.

It was crazy. It was something you could laugh about for the rest of your days. But then some disease came along, I forget which, and I was with a group of employees and we were all herded into a ward and we had to get this needle. They checked you off as you got the injection, you see, and there I was. So the fat was in the fire, but I confessed and a few stood up for me to the boss and said I was a good worker, and he just kept shaking his head, but the upshot of it was that they did give me a job. There happened to be an opening and I got it, and from then on things were better.

But another thing. In the year I had been playing my little game and getting bolder all the time, mind you, not one person in that huge hospital ever wondered who those two little children were. Not one nurse asked why the hospital had two extra children. That's as strange as anything."

———————————— • ————————————

When The Clothes Boxes Came

"Recycling, that's the big thing now. Bottles are big. The kids think they invented it. Well, this is Regina and it used to be called Pile of Bones because they took all the buffalo skeletons off the prairie and lugged them here and shipped them east for some sugar chemical process. That was recycling on a massive scale. But what I'm talking about was the recycling during the Thirties. We lived here, right out at the end of Broad Street and we were poor as church mice. Really poor. Patches on patches, that kind of thing.

My mother's folks would send us boxes from Sarnia, and what excitement! There were four girls in the family and we'd go through these boxes of clothes, some really lovely clothes, hardly used, you know, and I'll take that, and Susie, here's a skirt for you. I'm sure you understand. When those boxes came, it was like Christmas, really like Christmas. And then we'd be passing our other clothes down the line, to neighbours, to kids.

I never saw anyone too proud to accept clothes this way. We never bothered giving to the Salvation Army. It was what the kids today would call a rip-off. Take free from the rich, sell to the poor. All during those years we exchanged clothes, patched, some of us became very good with a needle and thread.

Remember the comic strip Jane Arden? She was a newspaper reporter and they had little clip or cut out sections and they were for children to make, like paper dolls. We used Jane Arden's fashions and we could take anything and make it into high fashion. That was recycling and we had it down to a science. It was being done all across the country, and across the world for all I know.

I see the kids talking about recycling and I say, 'Go ahead with what you're doing, it's fine, but you really don't have the slightest inkling of what it's all about.' To them it's fun. To us it was a sort of survival."

I Talked To That Stove

"At night, you know, when my Walter and children had gone to bed I used to sit up and talk to my stove, and we had troubles, not two cents to rub together, beef getting you about a cent a pound and no doctor closer than Quesnel and the children having trouble at school not understanding their readers, and I'd talk to that stove like an old friend, and if she ever saw me weeping a bit, well, I can tell you this, she never blabbed.

My kitchen now is like out of a magazine, a stove, electric, and a washer and these things, and it isn't enough. You ask anybody who had a wood stove with a reservoir with 15 gallons of soft hot water all the time and apple pies cooking and ask them what they remember about that stove and they'll likely say they remember the sound of the crackling wood and the smell of the smoke and the warmness and niceness of it all, but for me that stove helped this lady get through the Depression. There are still a few of those stoves in this district and I think the people in them houses are happier people than a bunch of stove knob twisters. Don't you think so?"

CHAPTER TWENTY-FIVE

The Big World Outside

The King And That Woman ... Politics And Cinnamon Toast ... In The Spanish Civil War ... Nazis In Winnipeg ... Saturday Soldiers.

———————————————— • ————————————————

In all my months of interviewing, amazingly few people ever mentioned the events that were taking place in the big world outside in the Thirties. Hitler, yes, but only in connection with Canada's entry into the war or the loss of a brother or son. Mussolini never. Russia, but only in tandem with Communism in Canada. The ghastly Spanish Civil War, but only because hundreds of Canadians were smuggled out of Canada to fight.

The Abdication of King Edward the Eighth, the rise of Nazism in the large cities, yes, people mentioned them. But in the Thirties, the big world out there didn't seem to touch the average Canadian all that much.

———————————————— • ————————————————

The King And That Woman

"I never felt hard done by. You could say I was just a normal middle class girl living in Toronto. I went to school and I had my friends and I loved my parents, and because I was born in 1928 I really didn't know there was such a thing as the Depression. I know it now, but in such a superficial way you couldn't really count me in. I only remember one thing. The Prince of Wales. When he became king and Mrs. Simpson, who my father (who was a real United Empire Loyalist type and still is at 84) called 'That woman from Baltimore.' Do you think this is important?

Well, all right. The principal announced there would be a special assembly this particular morning in the auditorium, and it was the first I remember when all the classes were there, from the little ones up to the grade nines. I guess I was grade four. Or grade five? We all sat on the floor, these hundreds of kids and there was this radio up at the front on a table and the principal,

321

God, what was that man's name? He told us that the king was going to make an important announcement at 10 o'clock by short wave from England and he sort of put us into the picture, this talk of the king and this Mrs. Simpson, the American. I can remember the way he spoke, that this Mrs. Simpson had to be the worst bitch that ever drew breath. Didn't say it of course, but even the grade ones must have got the picture. Even in my own small way I remember thinking, 'The King of England going to marry *an American!*' Americans weren't very high on the scale in our family, in a lot of families in Toronto in those days. We loved the king, and I had pictures from magazines in my room of the young prince, you know, so handsome, riding a horse on his ranch in Alberta, inspecting a regiment, playing polo, and I guess you could say he was the darling of the world.

Now I just don't think he was very bright, I think that he let down his country and the Empire. Very badly. But enough, the man is dead now and I'm sorry.

His voice came over, quite clear. I mean we could hear the words clearly and the way he put it I don't think most of us realized just what he had said. I remember the part about the woman I love, or the woman I must have beside me to help bear the burdens. You know. Then the principal stood up again and a couple of women teachers were weeping, and that made quite an impression I must say, and the principal explained that we would soon have a new king, that he would be the old king's brother, the younger one. And then he asked us to stand and sing "God Save The King" and we did and I remember crying. Maybe it was because my own class teacher over by the wall, a lovely woman we all loved, she was crying, and then about three-quarters of the way through, the teacher who was playing the piano she put her head down on the keys and began to cry.

I think it was the most dramatic thing that I have ever seen. Looking back on it I think what a great movie those days would make, and what he ever saw in her I'll never know."

———————————— • ————————————

Politics And Cinnamon Toast

"Looking back on it all now we were quite a bunch of twits, but if we were, every university, every college, everywhere on this continent there were twits too. I mean young people who sat around and discussed Communism and Fascism and really had no idea of what it was all about.

Of course, the war in Spain was on and I'd say it was covered quite adequately in the newspapers, the magazines, the commentators on radio like old H.V. Kaltenborn. But to go to Spain, to join the Canadian battalion in the International Brigade, I don't think that was ever considered. I know of not one intellectual or, to put it more succinctly, not one pseudo-intellectual who ever went. By the way, we were all in the latter category.

We knew that Germany was building up a huge army and air force. Ethiopia, its destruction by the Italians, that truly showed the hand of Italy and Mussolini. What a comic he was, although we did not recognize him as such.

There was Russia, but they were the good guys. Any one of us would have said we had socialist leanings, if not outright Communist sympathies. You know the chap, can't remember his name, who came back from Russia in 1933 and said, 'I have seen Utopia, and it works.' That impressed us tremendously. Anyway, we talked more about Russia and Communism than we did about our new socialist party, the C.C.F.

In those days, Russia wasn't considered a menace. A little strange, perhaps, but it was obvious that Britain would have to fight Germany and the old alliances of 1914-1918 in Europe would re-form and Russia and Britain would be allies. So Russians were good guys.

We were young and elite, the chosen few who could go to university. Believe me, there were bloody few of us in those days. Far into the night, until the dawn we'd talk. Boys and girls. In some frat house bedroom. In somebody's living room. Tea and cinnamon toast. I can't remember any beer or whiskey. Just talk, talk, talk some more, taking the world apart and putting it together, a fresh jigsaw puzzle every night.

God! but we were sweet young people. So naive. So beautiful. Yes, we were beautiful in our simplicity, our faith. Even our stupidity was something very clean and appealing. We were the generation between 18 and 25, and there was no Depression in Canada, and no Indian problem, and no French problem because none of us had ever bothered to go into Quebec to see a very large and very sour French problem at first hand, and we would graduate with honours and go into the best universities in Canada or proceed with a regal grace and measured tread to Harvard – or Cambridge and then return. Always to return and take our rightful place in Canada.

I realize that only people around 45 or 50, say 50, and only of that class, the upper middle class we belonged to, will understand what I am saying.

Probably even that little group of 30 or 40 who were considered accept-
able by a sort of group awareness of who was right, correct, and one of us,
perhaps that little group in those late pre-war years at the University of
Toronto will not even recognize themselves now. Occasionally I see one. A
couple of women keep popping up on the society pages, on committees. A
few of the chaps are prominent in business. I only knew two or three who
went into the academic field. At least four I know were killed in the war, and
all in the air force, because that was the right service to enter in that war. Do
you see what I mean?"

———————————— • ————————————

In The Spanish Civil War
*A volunteer in the Canadian Mackenzie-Papineau Battalion which fought in
the Spanish Civil War.*

"Too much has been spoken and written about us and not enough, if you get
what I mean. We were just a bunch of guys who got caught in the middle. The
wrong war. No bands played for us.

People got up in Parliament and called us Communists. Bolsheviks. One
fellow said we had gone to Spain to fight for the Red Army and Canada was
best rid of us. Now, there *were* some Communists in with us, sure, nobody
will deny that, and there were a lot of guys who belonged to outfits which
would be affiliated with the Communist Party of Canada but they were not
Communists. I repeat they were not. There were a lot too who just joined up
for the hell of it. They were tired of bumming around the country without a
bean in their pockets and I guess some were tired of their wives. Doesn't that
happen in any war? But if you take the lot of us, if there ever were a bunch in
Canada at that time that had a social conscience, a unity of purpose, a sense
of what was right and what had to be done to defeat wrong, then we were it.

The Canadian people treated us like pariahs. No, not all. Not the majority. Well, the truth is, the majority of Canadians didn't know what the Spanish
Civil War is, was, or sweet boom-all. The ones who were in control, the government, the politicians and yes, even your precious newspapers, they knew
what was going on. Oh yes, they knew the score, and we were treated like rats.
But we died like men. What is the saying, if the cause be just, then does it
matter how you die?

Some of our men drowned. I mean in the ocean, but some others drowned and I mean drowned in the mud of the battle. Franco's *(the present General Franco)* boys executed some and Hitler's planes and Mussolini's guns got some more and those commissars *(the Russian commanders of the International Brigade)* just sent the companies into attacks where nobody could survive. Bugs, disease, lots died that way.

I think about 1,200 Canadians went over, and somebody I read later said that was the highest percentage from any nation in the world. I don't know.

But what's the point of talking? Ask anybody under 50 what the Spanish Civil War was and you'll never get an answer. Ask people over that and some will know, but you'll just hear it was the civil war in Spain where Russia and Italy and Germany tested out their modern guns and tanks and bombers on the Spanish armies. In a way, yes, that's right. It wasn't just a civil war. I'm not too sure most of us knew all the ins-and-outs of what was going on when we were there. Does a soldier know what is happening half a mile along the front? Does a lieutenant? Half the time the generals don't either.

It was the Retreats and the Battle of Brunette and Quinto and the Jarama River Valley. Those were all battles the Canadians fought in, and by the Lord Living God, we fought well. Bloody well. Boys of 18 or so, and I remember a few old timers at over 40.

No, there is no sense talking about it. Nobody remembers and I forget a lot. I remember a few names, the battles and I remember the Battle of the Ebro River, a tough one, and the few good times we had. Funny, but there were a lot of Finnish guys from Canada who joined up. A lot of English and Scotch guys too. There weren't many French Canadians. Maybe they had heard that the government might prosecute anybody who got back from Spain. They didn't, but we were treated like shit when we did get home.

Here was a bunch of guys in 1939 who were the only soldiers in Canada, the only battle-tested men under modern conditions. Don't tell me about the First World War guys. I'm not talking about them. Here we were in 1939, tough and we knew all the tricks, and they didn't want us in the army, the Canadian army. We were subversives. Like the guy said in Parliament, we fought in the Red Army. That is pure bull. Some joined up, I guess.

No point in talking, all the days are gone. Most guys want to forget. I joined up because I had studied history and the patterns of aggression and it was obvious what was going to happen and yet I can't say it was all that obvious, or else me and a few others happened to be the smartest men in the world. I also joined up because I really wanted some excitement. Yes, why not admit it. But I really enlisted because I thought I could help, stopping Hitler.

I don't remember much. I remember artillery at night and the Spanish kids in the bombed streets of Madrid. Piles of dead bodies everywhere during an offensive and damn little help for those guys wounded and the way whole companies were thrown in on an attack, up a long slope and so damn few ever got to the top of that hill or ever came down it alive. I remember the good guys in the Lincolns, the American brigade, and those big three-engine bombers the Germans had and the realization that we were going to lose the war and how we'd come out of the lines and sit in cafes and drink that really rotten cognac they had, really rotten stuff which would kill you as dead as a bullet if you drank enough of it. Those are some of the things I remember. I don't remember men's faces."

———————————— • ————————————

Nazis In Winnipeg

"You had to be blind not to realize that a lot of Winnipeg's Germans, were getting right in behind Hitler. It was probably happening all over the world, certainly in Toronto and in the United States and in South America, especially Argentina, but to see them in Winnipeg! It gave you a feeling. I remember thinking of their past history, Prussia and Bismarck and all that, and thinking, 'That's typical.'

They had this Canadian-German Bund set up. Bund means friendship society, or something along that line. They professed love for Canada and all that, but not for one moment did I think they were fooling anyone. They were for 'Der Faderland' and that was that. They started small, not rocking the boat, but talking to them, the leaders, you could see they were pretty proud of what Hitler was doing and they were getting their teeth in Nazism and biting deeper, just gathering strength. They didn't know what was coming but they were pretty rough on the North End Jews. Even about 1935 or so, they had their toughs, their bully boys since celebrated in story and song. There was a theatre on Notre Dame just off Portage that showed a lot of German films, Strength Through Joy stuff, and it would be packed with Germans, night after night. If I'm not mistaken, Marlene Dietrich made a couple of films for the Nazis on this glorification of the Aryan race.

Of course, the rest of us thought the Germans were fine people, and they are. Except when they've gotten their teeth into something like this. It's like saying, 'All dogs are good dogs until they get rabies.' Somebody would smash up a Jewish tailor's shop on Selkirk Avenue and the police blotter at the Rupert Street station would read, 'Suspect unknown.' The cops damn well knew who had done it. Not who, exactly, but by whom. There was one chap, a German, who was fighting the Nazis in Winnipeg, and he got his headquarters bashed up more than once.

You must remember, this was before the atrocities, Austria, all that. Canadians were the most sleepy, smug and insular creatures on earth at that time, they treated this new movement as just another thing, like the Icelandic societies or the St. Andrew's Caledonian Games. But the Canadian-German Bund was growing and it was getting big, not only in Winnipeg, but across the country. It was the Communists who were getting the kicking from the police and Mounties, headquarters raided, literature seized. The old harassment bit. The Bund just sat and grew fat like a German burgher.

The newspapers didn't say a peep. Not a word. Oh, they'd report their meetings and concerts, just like they were United Church Women's Auxiliary meetings or the Belgium Club over in St. Boniface. Except for old Dafoe *(John Dafoe, editor of the 'Free Press')* writing editorials which nobody read, the 'Free Press' was one of the slowest newspapers in the West and the 'Tribune' was in the same class. The reporters knew what was going on, but the top brass said stirring up the pot was bad for the stew. The profit stew.

The Jews in Winnipeg knew too because they were starting to get letters from home, a lot of Jews had their roots in Germany, about how uncles and aunts and old friends were being carted off to camps, and a few refugees were coming through too and they had stories to tell.

It was in 1937, I believe, and there was a Bund picnic scheduled for River Park, down at the end of the Osborne Street carline. I was living down on Jubilee at the time so I walked over to Osborne to catch the head of the parade. A lot of other people had done the same thing. After all, a parade was a parade. I believe it was on the Sunday after Dominion Day. It was a shocker. That parade took forever to pass and there must have been 10,000 marchers, all Germans, all smug and smiling men, women and children. Singing. It was damn well organized, in groups like platoons and companies with German flags, the Nazi emblems on their sleeves, lederhosen on a lot, but also a hell of a lot of brown shirts and swastikas on their arms. It didn't take half an eye to see this was well organized and they knew just what they were doing. Likely as not it had been rehearsed. It was damned impressive anyway.

In the park under the trees, down around the bearpits, there was tables and tables of food and kegs of beer everywhere, and this was on a Sunday in Winnipeg, in blue-stocking Christer Winnipeg. There were pictures of Hitler and Goering and the little guy, what's his name, the propaganda minister, Goebbels, tacked on trees and there were speeches from a platform, some in English but most in German and a lot of Nazi salutes going around. I had my father with me and we walked around and I was stopped by a couple of burly fellows so I pulled out my press card and they smiled, yes, by God, and they took me over to a tent and out came a little gink and he pinned 'Press' ribbons on Dad and me. We had a fine time. Everywhere we went jolly women were offering us sausages and bloody big plates of sauerkraut and pickles, mugs, steins of beer, and the old man and I filled up and got kind of drunk and listened to the German bands, and they were damn good, and watched the dancing and not a billy club or a gas chamber was in sight. After it was over, when we left, my Dad remarked that he had had a very good time and there was no doubting that. All those happy people at play.

In little over two years, some of those happy people were in concentration camps, the war, you see, the Bund was no more, kaput, and Germans in Winnipeg went back to making money and saying they didn't know anything about Adolf Hitler.

They bloody well remembered Hitler and those arm bands and the speeches, and a lot of the old timers still do today. I often wonder if the Mounties were at that picnic and were they taking pictures of the speakers and those who were there? I doubt it, because they were too busy running down the Communists, and at the paper we knew that the Mounties were getting a lot of their Commie tips from the Bund, the Nazis. It was a screwy world in those days."

—————————— • ——————————

Saturday Soldiers

"There wasn't much doing around our neighbourhood, so we joined the militia. The Saturday soldiers thing. Train Saturday afternoons and then drink the four bits or a dollar they paid us in five cent beer in the wet canteen Saturday night. This was Canada's pre-war effort, getting ready for Hitler. Jeezuzz!! What a sad-looking bunch and yet, there's one thing, there were goddamned few of those boys came out of the last war in one piece. First in, and they got it, that God-awful abortion of Hong Kong, Sicily, Italy, Normandy, so maybe I shouldn't laugh at them. I was one myself.

But there is sure a wide-open field for laughing about the Canadian government. That Mackenzie King. When they made him they threw away the mould.

I remember one thing, we'd go out to Shilo for two weeks manoeuvres. This was 1937, '38. We had uniforms and lived under canvas, tents. The wind blew that Shilo sand into everything, and here we were, in our World War One uniforms, some with Ross Rifles which, I'm told, caused a scandal in the First War because they always jammed, and a few old trucks. We'd practise Aircraft Action. That means offensive but also defensive action against enemy aircraft. We'd be in the hills and one or two of those old yellow Tiger Moths would come floating in, yep, just floating, you could just about hit them with a rock, and they'd bomb with little two pound bags, bombs, filled with flour. If they hit near you, near enough you were considered out of action. Sort of lie down and play dead. And there we were, crouched down with our rifles or even rifles made out of wood going 'Bang Bang,' just like we had done ten years before, playing cowboys and Indians.

Remember, just remember, this was in 1938 and Hitler's factories were turning out dozens of Stuka dive bombers and here we were, going 'Bang Bang' at yellow Tiger Moths. Makes you wonder, doesn't it?"

CHAPTER TWENTY-SIX

They Didn't Consider Indians As People

The Man With Two Names . . . Because They Could Live Off The Land . . . Somebody To Kick Around . . . Starvation Amid Riches . . . Just Take Off, Mister! . . . He Was 19, I Think . . . One Bear, One Man, One Shell . . . Indians From Across The River.

———————————————— • ————————————————

I remember talking to a man who owned a resort fishing camp on Lake of the Woods and he said he'd fired his Indian guide. He added quite casually that the Indian was a damn good man in the woods. Then why? I asked. Because of a Norwegian he knew, he'd hired him instead. But was he better than the Indian? No. Then why make the switch? Because, said the man, the guide was an Indian. No sense to it. He just did it.

Any Indian in Canada can probably tell you a dozen stories to match.

And an Indian, if he lived in a city, or near one, or on a reserve, was in far worse shape during the Depression. Under the thumb of the white man, the police, the magistrates, the relief people, the Indian Affairs bureaucrats, the residential school teachers, the store keepers and the whiskey peddlers, he and his family didn't stand a chance.

The only chance he had was to go back a hundred years, to pack up and go back into the hills, the bush, where there were still deer to kill, muskrat to trap, berries to pick and fish in every stream, every lake. Some Indians did, but most didn't.

———————————————— • ————————————————

The Man With Two Names

"You can use this, or you can choose not to use it. I really don't care. Would you take me for an Indian? A pure blood? *(I said I might, under different circumstances, and he smiled)* Yes, I am. I have my Indian name. And, of course, I have my white name. I represent several clients of some importance, and in Saskatchewan and here in Ottawa no one has ever suggested that he was a

330

pale face and I was a bloody redskin. Yes, I grew up in the Depression. Not on the reserve, but around Calgary, High River, west of there, Black Diamond, that country.

Of course an Indian kid didn't know what a Depression was. We had our own little Depression around us like a chief's blanket all the time. If I'd known then I'd have had a few laughs knowing that you people were getting it in the ass just like we had for 50 years. And more.

I worked on ranches and I was a good hand, a good cowboy. With eight years of study at the residential school I was able to earn two bits a day stacking hay. That gives you an idea of the value of a good education. I've broken wild horses, domestic horses gone wild, for $3.40 a day and I was doing the same work, and harder and more dangerous work, and you know what I got? Two dollars. I worked for one company and for one month's work they paid me off in stock. Fifty dollars' worth of stock and I didn't have to be a broker or a geologist to know that the stuff wasn't worth the price of printing it. It was a duster, and down there that area is still duster country. I went begging in Calgary once, just a kid of 19, skinny, and got hit right in the face, not a word, just hit in the face with a fist by a cop who saw me and I didn't see him coming. They had a soup kitchen down at the Exhibition Grounds, where they hold the Stampede, and I was turned away, pushed out of the line by the manager just as if I was a black in Alabama. West of Staveley a rancher took me in, picked me up on the highway where I was walking. An Indian didn't dare hitchhike. He gave me a job, and when after two months I asked for some pay, he told me my pay was my room and board. The next night he lost three stacks of good hay for that. Three kitchen matches, three stacks. The Mountie couldn't prove a thing on me but the rancher, and I think his name was Bates or Banks or Baines, something in there, he tied the can to my tail. I picked beets with women at Taber for almost nothing a day, but hell, they're still doing it down there.

I walked from Lethbridge to Fort MacLeod to Cowley and never got a single ride. How far? About 80 miles I should think. I'm not sure I ever met a man who was kind to me, one who was not of my race. Every hand was turned against the blood. From 1934 to 1939 I worked around Alberta. I'd been told if I crossed into British Columbia I'd be arrested. Pure crap, of course, but I didn't know it. I worked most for my board, and if you did get a couple of bucks it went on wine.

I've seen men die down on the river bank, the Bow in Calgary, on a warm sunny day, die of wine and malnutrition and maybe a few kicks by the yard bulls. Some of them knew how to kick a man in the kidneys so he would never be right again. It was murder, of course, but as they say, lo the poor savage. Men dying, Indians turned out of bread lines because they were Indians – go back to the reserve and starve, chief – and whites, you, fighting and kicking and back-stabbing and gouging in business like none of my people ever did. Actually, you know, the Indian is a gentle person. He'd rather be your friend than not, and a Blackfoot or Sarcee or Peigan will give you the shirt off his back, his pony for a long ride, if you need it.

The pictures in the *(Calgary)* Herald of the P.M. *(R.B. Bennett)* arriving at the C.P.R, smug, so fat-cat you wanted to wipe that look off his face with two barrels of heavy birdshot, and even then – and this was about '35 I guess – everyone knew he had screwed up the country and was on his way out but there were the businessmen and the politicians doing their little kiss-ass dances around him. It was disgusting. I took shit for six years, lots of it, and I don't think I made more than $15 a month and that was maybe once or twice.

Sure, I stole. Didn't white men steal? Funny how I can use that term, 'white men' but you've got me going. Once out on the Highwood River I was in a blizzard and I came across a bunch of cattle, tails to the wind, waiting out the storm in a gully, and I cut out six of them and drove them with the wind boring in my face and cutting fences all the way, crossing roads, and the snow filling in behind, and about two days later I pushed them into a rancher's yard and I knew I was risking 15 years in the Prince Albert pen, but I saw him, he was in his blacksmith shop, and I said I had six steers to sell. I said, 'No bill of sale, no nothing. Two bucks each.' He walked out and looked them over and took out a wallet and handed up a ten and two ones and slapped my pony's arse and said, 'Piss off.' And I did. I back tracked around a bit in case someone was following and next day I rode into Cochrane and got drunk and the $10 I had left I sent to my mother and I was back to nothing. A financier could steal half a million, but if an Indian drove off one steer you could hear the pen gates clanging shut for 10 years. It was a funny time.

In 1939 all I had was a horse with a bit of Morgan in it and a saddle and a pack and I had been working six years. And the war came along and, man, they were glad to sign up this poor Injun. Take the King's shilling. Weren't we supposed to be savages, good hunters, killers? There would be few Germans around when we got finished with them. I was a smart Indian by that time and I got smarter and I was made a lance jack and then a corporal and then a sergeant, and if a man didn't like taking orders from me I'd go into the orderly room and get two sets of boxing gloves and tell him to say it another way. It was perfectly legal. I beat hell out of every man who ever tried. Of course by this time I had one hell of a reputation and I was a captain when I got out. May, 45 and one bullet in the leg. Hardly enough for a wound stripe. I picked up my grade 11 in two months, went to university, "married white" as they say, a white girl, and here I am today. An important man, when you consider other men."

Because They Could Live Off The Land

"About 1931 when the federal government pushed through emergency assistance payments, the city family got $15 a month and the country family got $10 a month because they'd likely have a cow and a pig and a big garden – and the Indian family got $5 a month because they could live off the land.

Indians haven't lived off the land since the days of Custer, but you couldn't tell the bastards in Ottawa that. I honestly think they didn't consider Indians as people."

Somebody To Kick Around

"Me? A Métis, French Canadian grandfather, Cree woman. I'm half breed, my kids are, my grandchildren, all born shit, and are so long as they stay around here. Everybody north of here (*Prince Albert*) is Métis. Portuguese on the railway gangs, they're darker, but they don't take this bullshit.

Yah, the Dirty Thirties. We got a little house way up north of here, my two brothers, me and a cousin from Sandy Lake, and the Indians they hate us, the white guys they hate us. Everybody had to have some guys to hate, and we were it. We didn't hate nobody.

They're sending white guys up from the cities, Regina and that, to make them farmers, homesteaders but these city guys don't know a pitch fork from a wagon tongue. They're starving, I tell you. Those people starved, and us fellows, me and my brothers, we sometimes help them out. They got no money but what the hell. One guy gives me an old shotgun once when he quits. Lots of them quit. They know nothing and their kids starving, their kids freezing at nights. Too bad, a lot like that.

One day I meet the homestead inspector in town. He's not doing much, everybody's quitting the country on him and he says, 'Roy, there's a lot of good hay land over there,' and I knew where he meant, and he says, 'We should make a deal. Government'll buy the hay on it to ship south, so you give me $15 and I'll put you down for five tons for your own horses and you take off 60 tons and use what you want. I'll fix the permit to say you're okay, and you sell the rest to the government.'

It worked like this, see. A government permit was two bits a ton for hay. That's $1.25 I pay to government. But I give him $15, so he puts $13.75 in his pocket. Then he says, go ahead, take off 60 tons and sell it to the government for $1 a ton. So we've got nearly $60. That isn't what the hay is worth, worth much more but these are hard days and only the government is buying and the price is a buck a ton. Okay, some money is better than none. We're doing wrong, but the guy who started it is the inspector.

The boys and me put up about 60 tons. It's what we call midground hay, not marsh hay, tall and heavy you understand, and we put it up pretty damn fast. We got good horses and we know what we're doing.

The day we finish the Indian Affairs guy drives out to the meadow and he says the permit, where is it, and I show it and he says, 'You boys are down here for five tons. There's 50 or 60 in that stack.'

Well, we don't stand much chance. The permit says five and it's a hell of a big stack and the agent says he's going to seize the hay for the government – and keep our mouths shut or he'll sic the cops on us, so we shut up. But you know what? A friend of my sister works in the government office and she tells me that the Indian agent got no right to grab our hay. You're Métis, she says, not Indian. I'm tired of it all by this time and next time I see her she tells me that the agent sells that hay to the government for feed for $1 a ton and he splits it with that homestead inspector.

That's the way they screwed us guys. They ganged up, these government guys, and we were so dumb we didn't know nothing, or what to do. It happened all the time. I hope these Red Power guys beat the shit out of these government guys, the bunch of rotten bastards."

Starvation Amid Riches

"You never heard much about Indians in those days because I don't think Indians actually existed officially. By that I mean they weren't a problem, they were just allowed to starve and die quietly.

I remember once we were upcoast on an inspection and about half a day north of Campbell River our engine started acting up. Quitting. The skipper said we should put into a small village over in Theodosia Arm and we could get some help there, or at least we could tie up. Now here was this Indian bunch, about five families, a lot of kids, and they were living in a few shacks balanced on big cedar logs, and those logs were half waterlogged and so the last two shacks, their floors were a few inches underwater. This was July, I think, and the salmon were running out in the strait. Hell, half the salmon of the North Pacific were coming down that strait towards the Fraser River and those Indians were starving.

You see, they didn't have a boat. Well, hell, they had one but I wouldn't have given you five bucks for it, a 30-foot gillnetter and somewhere they had scrounged up a converted Star engine so she'd go, but their steering was bust and to get anywhere one guy would have to grab the chain down to the rudder on one side and another grab the other side and pull it around that way. Nobody could fish that way, and their net was all full of holes and not worth a dime. So with a million bucks' worth of salmon heading south every 24 hours and every fish good for cash those Indians were broke and starving.

They had a sack of corn meal, the cheapest stuff there is, and some lard and were living on a few rock cod they caught and somebody had shot a lynx back in the woods. That was all. They had no clothes to speak of, and the kids had sores on their bodies and, well, Jesus Christ, they were a sorry lot. We gave them what we could, which wasn't much, but we couldn't fix their steering apparatus and without that they couldn't go fishing. But they didn't seem to be caring about it. That's the thing, you see, those Siwashes didn't seem to care.

A week later we were back in Campbell River and Barney Fellows and Lionel Sanderson and I went up to the government office and told them about these people, especially for the children. The Indian officer seemed like a nice guy and he said, 'Where did you see these people?' and Barney went over to the wall map and pointed. The guy said, 'Oh, Takoosh. That's Takoosh. They still there, eh? We wondered what had happened to that bunch.' Just like somebody would say, 'We wondered what happened to the Phoenicians or the Carthaginians.'

He didn't thank us and he didn't say he would send a patrol boat over. That was the way it was in those days, the poor got the shitty end of the stick – and can you tell me anybody who was poorer than a bunch of Indians with just one beat-up gillnetter and half a sack of corn meal left?"

———————————— • ————————————

Just Take Off, Mister!

"My Dad hired Indians once to do the haying. There were plenty of whites around and they were better workers but he made one of those under-the-table deals with the superintendent of the Indian residential school and he got the kids, young fellows about 15 or 16, for about two bits a day. The superintendent got another dime per worker per day. If you had a bit of power you could pull a deal. By that I mean a crooked deal. A lot of people did.

First morning the Injuns worked along pretty good, but about 11 o'clock they jumped a big jackrabbit, the biggest I ever saw. It looked like a deer. These five kids took after it, and you ever seen Indians run down an animal? Something. They took out after it and sort of fanned out and figured out every way that fellow was going to turn and when they disappeared they were gaining on it. A big jack can only run so far so fast, you know. Dad and I lit out after them and about an hour later, more than a mile away, we spotted a bit of smoke. No, I smelled it. In a clump of trees we found them kids, lying around a fire and they had two, not one, jackrabbits spitted and roasting over the fire. It was a pretty sight, like the days of the Old West, I guess, but it was our time and money they were wasting and Dad told them so and to get moving or he'd know the reason why.

They all giggled and one of them said something to the others in Cree and then the big one just looked at Dad and said, 'Mr. Dickinson, if you don't get away from here pretty soon, you and your boy is going to get hurt.' That was all. We got. Dad went back to the house and got out the pickup and drove to town and hired a white crew. Safer that way, I guess."

He Was Nineteen, I Think

"They hanged an Indian kid out at Headlingly, and I can't remember the crime. Oh, murder, of course, but what kind. I believe he was the one who opened his brother-in-law up with an axe, from throat to crotch.

The condemned man gets his wish for his last meal, anything he wants, and if he wants a roasted 15-pound turkey and everything, just like Christmas, well, that's what he gets. An old English custom, I do believe.

Anyway this kid was off a reserve somewhere up between the lakes and everybody up there was poor in those days, but if you were an Indian you were the poorest of them all. They literally had nothing, and nothing was what they expected. So when his time comes, the deputy warden goes down to see him and asks him what he wants. The kid says he wants boiled whitefish. Christ, even in jail the grub was 10 times better than that. No, he wanted boiled whitefish. Anything else? Yes, boiled tea with lots of sugar. That all? Yes, just boiled whitefish and tea. They tell me he made a grand meal of it, but the poor bugger, all he'd known growing up, all those years, was fish and tea, and that tells something about how we've treated those people. Those people always had their own Depression. All their lives. Whitefish and tea. He was 19, I think."

---•---

One Bear, One Man, One Shell

"You know, one thing sticks in my mind. Just how poor the Indians were, and what wonderful people they were. About 1935 we took on the job of caretaking a summer resort for the winter. It was east of Kenora, a lovely place. We moved in from Toronto and got settled. I think that is the loveliest country in the world in the autumn, so quiet, those blue lakes and the trees a hundred shades of red and gold and orange. We had both been born on farms so we were resourceful and happy to have a place for the winter, and that sort of eased the pain of not getting jobs as school teachers.

We thought we might teach some of the Indian kids in the district, for nothing of course, but the Department of Indian Affairs soon scotched that idea. Those Indians were their property, to do with as they pleased.

Well, my husband had been born in the Rockies and had done some prospecting and one night he said that gold was the big thing then, everybody was looking for gold, there was good money in gold, so why didn't we take a few days off and go prospecting before the snow flew? I said fine and we got a small outfit together and we headed north and east, back packing, and followed old logging roads and survey lines, and it was getting pretty wild country. That's where we came across these Indians. They had been harvesting wild rice, you know, bending it over the canoe side and banging with a paddle, and they sold a bit to us. No, they gave it to us, and we gave them cigarettes. We camped nearby and during the night there was a terrible racket. A real showdown, men shouting, children screaming. I asked John where they could have gotten the whiskey and he said not to be so damned silly, that was not whiskey. By the time we got over there it was over. It had been a bear, and what a bear! He'd torn up nets, smashed a canoe, knocked down their drying racks, and one woman was lying on the ground with a broken arm. Bears don't act this way, but this one did, so it was sick or old or had gone mad. We all went back to bed and there was not a sound from the camp. Indian children don't cry much, you know.

Next morning we had a good chance to look around and they were just a pitiful lot, nothing to begin with and then that tornado last night. We joined them in kind of a council and when they thought we should know something, the chief would mush-mouth us in English. You know the way they have of talking. The girl's arm could be set by an old woman who had the gift, the power of healing. They'd mend the net and fix the canoe.

My husband John offered to go after the bear. He had to be around close. John showed them the fine rifle we'd brought from the resort. No, the Old Man would go. He knew bears, said the chief. He respected them, and he thought like them too. He said the Old Man had known a bear when he was a youth, whatever that meant.

Now let me get this right. This Old Man was about 70 or 80. He could have been a hundred. He had one eye, just the left. His left hand was off at the wrist. His clothes were in rags and he had a torn pair of rubbers over his moccasins. He went over to the flour sack and he took a dirty dish cloth and piled flour into it and pulled up the four corners and tied them together into a little sack and put that in a tiny pack he had. He put three big handfuls of tea in one of the pouches of the pack and filled the other pouch with sugar. He had an old fedora and he took it off and lifted the leather inside lining and dropped in a dozen fish hooks and some line and he put a pig sticker of a knife in his belt.

I heard my husband mutter that this was getting ridiculous. Well, you see, it was. Here was an old man all bent, stooped over, going after a bear, possibly a bear maddened by an old bullet wound, and he was just as casual as if he was going down to the store to buy matches. He came out of the wrecked tent and Johnny said, 'Jesus Christ.' The Old Man had this gun, a :22, and it was bound up with snare wire where the stock was split. It looked like a pop gun. I guess it was. My husband asked the chief how much ammunition he had and the old man opened his hand and there were four whiz-bangs, those little short-shorts and one long rifle. The chief said the shorts were for grouse if the Old Man got hungry, if he had to stay overnight, and the long rifle was for the bear. I'll say this for Johnny, he offered the fellow our rifle even though he knew that if anything happened to it, replacing it would cost us about three of our month's wages. But no, the old fellow shook his head. The chief said, 'That all we got left, but when we sell rice, okay again.'

If it wasn't so crazy you could laugh. Anyway, the Old Man went after the bear, its trail was easy, and we left and headed north where my husband thought some old claims might have expired.

Now, if I could only tell you the rest and not make it sound corny I'd be happy. Four days later, yes, four days, we were sitting under a big tree on the edge of a clearing where there was a spring, a marshy little place, and this was about 10 o'clock and my husband said he thought he heard something. We listened and I did too. Just an animal moving. Then we heard a crack, like breaking a quite thick dried branch. Crack! Just once. Anyway, we both knew it was a shot and we were miles from anywhere. We ran through the bush and there was a big bear on its side. I'll never forget it. It was huge, about 450 pounds I'd say, a brown or black one, and it had this big purple tongue sticking out of its mouth, and it was dying. It gave one shudder, sort of a convulsive leap and it was dead. We heard a voice and the Old Man was standing 20 feet away. You know, I started to cry. I was crying, but I didn't know why. Here was this huge beast and there was that crazy old man and his funny busted gun and it was four days since we'd seen him. This was going through my mind. This is the way it must have been in the old days. The Indian in the woods.

He'd trailed that bear and when he caught up and finally got a chance for a clean shot, he had killed him with one silly little :22 long rifle. I remember Johnny got down on his haunches and he must have looked at that bear for two or three minutes and then he just got up and shook the old man's shoulder, put his hand on that frail old shoulder and he pulled him to him, hugged him like a brother. Boy, was I ever bawling then.

We couldn't find anything wrong with the bear. Nothing wrong. No old wound, except for the tiny hole where the bullet had gone into the neck, and it must have cut the spinal cord in two. The really fatal shot. My husband said that night, he'd been doing a lot of thinking and he said, 'He didn't even try for a heart shot. He shot where he absolutely had to.'

We were tired of prospecting anyway, so John cut off the head and stuffed it into a sack and the Old Man skinned it out and tied it up and we gave him a good meal. When had he eaten last? We don't know. He couldn't speak English, but his flour was gone. It wasn't all that far back to the Indian camp, and we got in just at dark, about 20 miles maybe, and the old man threw the hide at a woman and she put it away and my husband rolled the head out of the sack and pointed to the Old Man and there was some talk in Cree, some translating for us, and the gist of it was that the Old Man had done well. The thing was, and listen to this, those people did not think this was exceptional. They expected the Old Man would track down and kill the bear, and they were glad he had. To us, the city slickers, it was the most amazing feat we'd ever seen. To those Indians, well, I guess you could say it was just part of their life."

———————————— • ————————————

Indians From Across The River

"The ground was good for turnips, potatoes and that, and it was pretty well free for the asking. I'm talking about the old road north of Williams Lake along the Fraser River. There was a good size ranch down on the flats, and the rancher said, 'Now, Mrs. Karpenchuk, if you folks fence off about half an acre of that pasture then you can consider that as being yours.' Well, we did.

You notice he called me Karpenchuk. Our name. I used to call it our Saskapoosh name, the name I was married under in Saskatoon in 1918. We call ourselves Carman now. Better. Mike was burnt out, hailed out, froze out, even flooded out, so we came west in this old truck. A policeman in Ashcroft, he's being friendly, he says why don't you go up north of Williams Lake. He said there was a pretty little road along the river and that there was cabins which only took just so much fixing and he was right. The road was pretty. Poplars and alder and aspens.

The cabin we found, it only took about eight dollars' worth of tar paper and nails and lathing and we replaced the stove crates, burned out, they were from an old stove in another house and the root house was in good shape.

What that policeman didn't say was you could get pretty sick of the Cariboo in one winter. We was too far from Williams Lake for the kids to go to school and I can't remember if Soda Creek had a school but I think they did not. We had no money and my oldest boy, Sandy, he trapped a bit for shells and flour, and we got by.

My man left, went to the mine at Wells that first winter and he come back fewer and fewer until he didn't come back at all. He was gone and he died in an accident up north somewhere. Mike didn't like home life anyway, splitting wood, hauling water for garden, calling kids to supper. Guess he figured that was part of his Saskatoon farming life, so he just went. I told the policeman, bury him where he is.

There was across the river some Indians and they came over on the ice, and looking around the cabin they see there is no food. Just potatoes and a sack of flour so they are talking in their language. Next morning two of these guys come across the river riding two horses, leading two others and what do you think they got? Moose meat on one horse, all the horse can carry, and dried salmon on the other. The same, all it can carry. We've got this shed out one side of the kitchen door and thump, thump, thump, thump, these big sacks go down. That got us through the winter. Kids used to complain, 'Moose meat, potatoes, flour gravy, agh!' and I'd say, 'Yah, moose meat, potatoes, gravy, agh! morning, noon and night,' and I prayed to the Virgin for those Indians.

Next fall, things got a bit better. We have lots of spuds, parsnips, corn, strawberries, wild plums, lots of them, but a bear gets the one calf we had, nearly grown, a broken neck, and when the ice is hard, who comes along? Yah, the Indians. Not the white guys from Alexandria or Williams Lake, but the Indians. They know. This time it is a moose, dressed out, on a sled and they hang him in the outhouse and God, such a big bugger. About 700 pounds. The boy, only 13, he gets two small deer with the rifle later and the rancher brings over a goose at Christmas. We live good. Kids might like milk but where in the bush do you get it?

The next summer me and kids go to the clinic in town. A doctor is there now. He says, 'Strong as a horse.' I said, 'Doctor, you get us a horse and then see how stronger we be.' No dice. A horse in that country you can buy for $15, but we don't have it.

Next day all over anyway. We get back next day and the cabin is burnt down and everything gone. Indians say some white guys come along river looking for gravel bars to hunt for gold and take over cabin the night. Just like that. Next morning they leave, and soon smoke comes from cabin and then fire and that's it. Everything gone, and they even turned their horses into my garden. Four of them.

Neighbour drives me to Williams Lake and the cop, he says, 'You didn't own that cabin, Mrs. Karpenchuk.' I said what about my sewing machine? What about my bed clothes? What about my children's clothes? The children's books, the Bible? My garden?

He said the river level is way down and the bars are showing and they get 50 men a day to work along the river for gold. Four men on horses? You get many of them? He said nobody could prove who. They gave me train fare for me and my kids to Vancouver, and there we knew what it was like to have an empty belly. Kids used to say then Cariboo was a pretty nice place, not like this stinking Vancouver. Bad as some places was, always there was some place worse. The Cariboo was a good place. Just the white guys ruined it."

CHAPTER TWENTY-SEVEN

It Gave Politicians More To Louse Up

Politicians And The Kids ... King's Five Cent Speech ... That Toad Of A Face ... Pompous, Smug, And Rich ... The Buggy R. B. Made Famous ... Gimme That Old Time Religion ... Bennett Was A Dead Duck ... Let Them Play Soccer ... Finally, A Dead Cat ... The Leadership We Deserved ... Plain And Simple.

———————————————— • ————————————————

A wise man once said that the best way to survive a Depression is to become a politician. He was wrong. The best way to survive was to become a successful politician. Few did.

On the federal scene, only the wily William Lyon Mackenzie King survived, and he has been called "one of the world's great compromisers." Otherwise, men rose and fell, reputations shattered forever. On the provincial stage, governments rose and fell, politicians came and went.

Everyone was trying to do the impossible – solve the insoluble problem of the Depression. Get the economy moving again. Get smoke billowing from factory chimneys again. Get the looms spinning and the farm equipment assembly lines rolling. Cut the railroads' soaring deficits, or eliminate them. Shrivel the bread lines to nothing outside the soup kitchens. Bring rain to the western farmer and stop the wind from tearing off the top soil and get the price of Number One Northern wheat up to $1.60 again. Stop the men from panhandling, the young-sters from riding the freights, and take that look out of the mother's eyes as she sends her two children off to school with nothing for lunch.

But the answer rested with the price of beef in Argentina, the men who ran Detroit's auto factories and Wall Street, the financiers who decided what the world's currencies would cost, a man named Hitler ordering his troops into the Sudeten borderlands of Czechoslovakia, Canada's extraordinary imbalance of trade with its American neighbours, and a hundred other factors – and all beyond Canada's power to solve.

The politicians tried, but they had to fail. There was no other way. All they had were temporary or half-measure solutions.

———————————— • ————————————

Politicians And The Kids

"In a way it was like a war. In 1915 when my battalion went into the trenches in France we were healthy and fit and alert young Canadians, and we were considered trained to fight. Of course we weren't, but that was something you picked up awful fast. But there was a deterioration and it wasn't too long, only a few months, before you were living in your own dirt, so to speak. Survival meant everything, each day was a little victory all its own. You didn't care how dirty you got, what the sanitary conditions were because you just went anywhere, and you ate the food, hot or cold, or sour or spoiled, and some days you didn't eat at all, and you vowed to survive any way you could. This business of King and Country and Motherhood went out the window pretty goddamned fast.

We go forward now to 1931, and these high school kids coming out, pretty fit because the Depression hadn't really got going and they were trained for nothing but trained to learn quickly, and so they went into the front line trenches too. Looking for work. No work. No sign of work. No hope of work. Just months and years ahead, although nobody dreamed it would be that bad then. Then came the breakdown, the don't-care spirit, the young people's minds turning into slums just the way those trenches became awful slums, rats, dirt, filth, stink, shit. I could see it happening and I used to cry out against it, write letters, attend meetings, and then suddenly one night it hit me like I had been hit by a bullet. The enemy of my generation had not been the German out in front of me in his own trench with his rifle and living in his own shit, the enemy was my own generals, and political pride, and governmental stupidity, and it was the same thing for that German lad I might kill tomorrow or who might kill me.

The Depression generation was the same thing, the R.B. Bennetts of Canada and that despicable little twerp Mackenzie King and big business and their continuous tactics of grab, grab, take all, steal and loot, the forests, the mines, the farms. Those kids of 1931 and after were as powerless before this kind of enemy as we were in '16 and '17 against the brass-bound stupidity of the generals. It was then that I began to fight them, and I didn't accomplish much but I was always ready to give a hand-up to some kid, a sandwich, a quarter if I had it and a few words of encouragement. It was all I could do."

———————————— • ————————————

King's Five Cent Speech

"The Depression. William Lyon Mackenzie King. Sure, I remember. They call him the Father of Modern Canada, William Lyon Mackenzie King. To me he was a rat. R-A-T. I never trusted a politician again and I'm 85.

It was 1930 and King was in power. He had been the protégé of Sir Wilfrid Laurier, his boot licker, and the Tories were hollering for some sort of relief to provinces for the unemployment that was building up. Here was King, a puny little man, in winter he always wore that fur hat we called a Dominion and a buffalo coat. He looked like a little mouse in some other animal's coat of fur. But he was shrewd. Cunning.

It wasn't really a speech but an exchange in the Commons. R. B. Bennett, the Tory, was hollering for some benefits, some money for the needy, the starving. King's battle plan was that the government should spend money to stimulate employment and not just put out money to feed and house those already unemployed. It was what you could call a confrontation of Depression philosophy. No direct financial assistance, that was King's point.

Well, it got down to name-calling in the House of Commons and King, the prime minister, lost his temper and said that he might consider giving some money to a couple of provinces which had good government, and he meant Liberal premiers, but he wouldn't give a nickel, not one five cent piece to a provincial government which was Tory. Conservative. Not a nickel, you understand, and he was putting it in dollars-and-cents terms, but what he was really saying was that if provincial governments wanted federal aid, then they had pretty damn well not be Tory governments. That was laying it on the line. Vote Liberal.

I think the little bastard thought he'd gain a lot of votes, but people started thinking the other way, that if that was all he felt about people starving and losing their homes, then he didn't think much of Canada and he wasn't much of a man.

A lot of us must have thought that, because we threw the rascal out in the next election. The Five Cent Speech. The Nickel Speech."

That Toad Of A Face

"Oh, yes, I remember many, many things. The politicians, I'll never forget them, the rotten, lying, no-good, people-kicking sons of bitches. My favourite was R.B. Bennett. If he went to hell, then I'm going to change my ways and get down there too, because I'm sure there is some way I can make him feel more miserable than he already is.

I'll never forget a picture of him, it was in the newspapers when he was prime minister. Here he is, on a luxury liner sailing to England and he is wearing this fine coat with the fur collar and one of those hats they used to call a bowler, but it is his face. A fat, sleek, contented toad of a face. Just the way he is standing, well, I know it infuriated a hell of a lot of Canadians, maybe thousands. Beside him is his sister, just as tall and smug and well-fed as R.B. Bennett was. He was a corporation lawyer, you know. A lawyer, God knows, is bad enough, but a corporation lawyer is pure dynamite. Steal the cents off a dead man's eyes and swear because they weren't quarters. Oh, yes, everything I remember bad about the Depression was right there in that picture."

———————————— • ————————————

Pompous, Smug, And Rich

"Mr. Bennett was pompous, smug, and rich. He had the most prestigious law firm in Calgary, and could pick and choose his clients. No, he was not a man of the people. I could never say that. I don't think he knew a thing about the Canadian people. No, even after four years in office, as prime minister, I don't think he knew anything about the people.

I'll tell you a story which might tell you something about him. He bought a new car, the jazziest in Calgary and while he was learning to drive it he ran it up a pole. He walked away from it, and as far as I know he never got behind the wheel of a car again.

Nobody could talk to him at any time and he had a secretary named Miss Miller and you needed eight master keys to get by her. He never married. Why? Well, I can't answer that, and I don't know of any kids he's got running around here either.

I do know that the biggest shock of his life was when he was defeated in '35. He couldn't believe it. Everybody else knew it was coming, but he was so arrogant, so far from the true state of affairs concerning the people that he just didn't believe it could happen. It came to him as a terrible shock. That's the kind of man he was."

–––––––––––––––––––– • ––––––––––––––––––––

The Buggy R.B. Made Famous

"You ask me what a Bennett Buggy was? There were hundreds of them, and I wonder if there is even one now in some museum, some farm exhibit somewhere. In the Twenties, farmers bought automobiles, Chevs, Fords, Overlands, Reos, the Hupmobile, oh, a hell of a lot that they don't even make any more. Then came the Crash and the drought and nobody had any money for gasoline, let alone repairs, and they'd thrown out all those fine old buggies every farm used to have, so what was left? A car that wouldn't run.

Somebody got the idea of lifting out the engine and taking out the windshield and sticking a tongue onto the chassis with double trees and that's where old Dobbin and Dolly got back to work again. Two horsepower. Five miles an hour, but those oat burners got you there. Then somebody got the idea, the country was full of wits, to call these contraptions Bennett Buggies. Poor old R.B. Bennett. All over Saskatchewan and Alberta there were these carved up cars, named after him, and a constant reminder that he'd been prime minister when the disaster struck.

Of course, it was wonderful advertising for the Liberals too. Bennett Buggies – there goes the guy who got us into this fix."

–––––––––––––––––––– • ––––––––––––––––––––

Gimme That Old Time Religion

"It wasn't all that mysterious. Not if you lived in Alberta then. When you look back it would have been goddamned surprising if Old Aberhart and his wild bunch of Social Creditors hadn't got in that year. In '35.

Why? The banks and mortgage houses were foreclosing left, right and centre. Winner take all. Everybody else was losers. The farmers didn't have two nickels to rub together, and there wasn't one who wasn't half owned by some loan outfit at eight percent.

You could smell it in the air. Those Tories in Ottawa and that bunch of half-witted farm politicians in Edmonton, both high up in the driver's seat and not knowing crap all what was happening. We couldn't get lower and we didn't intend to.

Along comes Bible Bill. Down with the bankers, down with high interest, down with everything the people were against. Everybody would get 25 bucks a month and that would stir up the economy. Do you know what $25 a month meant in 1935? All right, consider the fact that a family on relief might be getting $10 or $15, yes, $10 or $15 and you had to beg for that, and beg for coal, and beg for clothes for the kids and beg for boots to send the kids to school.

Then along came Bible Bill Aberhart and, sure, he was a phoney, but he was the phoney the people were looking for. They'd have voted for a guy selling snake oil if he could show them a way out. That's what Aberhart did. Old time religion, and down with those financial vultures in Montreal and Toronto, wringing the sweat out of the prairie farmer. Back to the Bible Hour. Every Sunday. Religion and politics. Follow me, boys, and I'll show you the way.

I was a travelling auditor for the C.N. in those days and I saw it happening. Aberhart, you know, he was smart. For all I know he might have been the first Canadian politician to really use the radio effectively. Maybe he took his lessons from Roosevelt. Remember Roosevelt's opening words, 'Good Evening, My Fellow Americans?' Well, when Aberhart was talking, quoting chapter and verse in the Bible, he was actually saying, 'Good Evening, you poor dumb Alberta farmers who are getting a shit kicking from those Eastern Canadian bankers and that bastard R.B. Bennett sitting in his big expensive house in Ottawa and eating T-bone steaks for breakfast, and those United Farmers of Alberta in Edmonton who are making a complete hash of everything you and your fathers worked for since you bust the sod with a hand plough and two horses.' Yeah, that's a long sentence, but that's what he was saying.

Now, it worked this way. Not all that many people had radios, I mean farmers, and people in the small towns that were dying. Oh, an awful lot had them, but how many were working? Couldn't pay for burned out tubes, or the batteries were dead, or it was just plain worn out. Anyway, somebody always had one in a district and people would gather at that person's house on Sunday afternoons. They'd make a picnic out of it, bringing what food they had and a little bit of homemade wine or bootleg whiskey. They became real parties, out on the lawn if it was sunny, or on the porch, or in the parlour or kitchen in bad weather. There might be 30 or 40 people gathered and all the guy with the radio had to do was provide the sound and the seating. The rest was brought. Those people would listen, and Aberhart bloody well knew they were listening and he poured it on, and when he finished they'd talk about what he said and discuss it until it was time to go home and do the chores. That's the way it happened, all over Alberta and there was some spill into Saskatchewan too. I know because I was there.

Aberhart gave them what they wanted to hear, that the main thing wrong was the money system which was controlled, in a tight fist, by the bankers in the East, and he mixed it up with religion, and he was in the right province for that because Alberta, as you know, has always been a bit kooky about religion anyway, Mormons, fundamentalists, holy rollers, all those kinds. This National Dividend he was going to pay, $25 a month to every adult, that was like a Christmas tree all lit up with lights and presents wrapped in golden ribbon. Aberhart had some formulas which I don't think even he understood and, of course, he must have known they wouldn't work, but the people didn't know what.

It was an interesting election, and I forgot how many Social Credit elected, but it was a landslide. It had to be. All those Sunday afternoon parties, all over the province for years. Why, those people would have elected Old Bill for no other reason than he provided them with a chance to get out of their own ruts for a while, if it was only a few hours on a Sunday, and they could sit around and drink coffee and eat cake and dream of that $25. Aberhart offered them hope, and spell that in capital letters, when nobody else offered them sweet bugger all but the old promises."

—————————— • ——————————

Bennett Was A Dead Duck

"There was nothing of an upset in the licking R.B. Bennett the Conservative Prime Minister and the Tories took in 1935 because the only betting must have been on how badly the Liberals would beat him. My Dad was a Liberal organizer in South Winnipeg in that election. I was just a kid and I don't know what politics was all about, but I do remember a meeting in our living room and I was lying in the hall listening. There was a lot of argument and the campaign manager was bitching about not enough emphasis being put on the fact the Liberal candidate was this and that, you know, and I can still remember my father shutting him up by shouting: 'For Christ's sakes, if that telephone pole out on the street had a name and address, we could nominate it and get it elected.' Needless to say, our man carried South Winnipeg easily."

Let Them Play Soccer

"I remember one prominent fellow in Vancouver, a major or a colonel in the First War. The Province newspaper gave him quite a write-up. You could just see him behind a big desk, he was a politician who was rewarded with a good job because he led the boys so badly in the First War, and he was the type who went into the Second War and led the boys badly again and came back a hero. I could name you a few. Anyway, you can picture this guy. Behind his desk, still in his head wearing all his ribbons.

His plan was to start soccer leagues right across Canada. Get us off the streets where we looked bad for business, get the young guys out of the jungles. You can almost hear him saying, 'A few hours of soccer each day will take the steam out of them. Then they won't go round talking revolution.' You had to read this article to believe it. He'd have teams playing at the Powell Street grounds and in South Vancouver and the West End, and travelling to Victoria and Calgary and all over.

Why, if you just went over to the soup kitchens and the sandwich lunch line-ups the nuns had over on Cordova, you'd know those guys couldn't have played ball five minutes. They were too weak, you see. There wasn't one that wasn't suffering from malnutrition, me included. But no, this ass says, 'Get the lads out playing soccer,' and that bloody paper gave him a good write-up. I don't know who was dumber, that colonel or the newspaper. It was jobs and food and money for tobacco we needed, not running our asses off in the rain playing a kid's game."

———————————— • ————————————

Finally, A Dead Cat

"There was this fella going around Ontario with this economic theory that if every family spent half a dollar a day more, then Canada would be able to spend its way out of the Depression. The idea made some sense, you know, except for one thing. That would have meant $15 a month more spending for every family, and about a quarter of people were on about $20 a month relief and about half were just getting by. They booed him in Toronto, and threw tomatoes at him in Hamilton, and somebody threw a dead cat at him in Windsor. They were sure waiting for him."

The Leadership We Deserved

"They say a people get the leadership they deserve, and in a way this is true. It was in the Depression. I had only Canada, our home and native land, and the United States to compare, one with another, but I would have preferred to live under the Stars and Stripes.

In the beginning, at Confederation, we had great leaders. They were radicals, I suppose, of their day. And then we sank back into that smarminess which has characterized every leader we have had since, and I include the present one. Trudeau no more knows what is good for Canada than does the man in the moon. *(He laughs.)*

But frankly, I am speaking of William Lyon Mackenzie King and R.B. Bennett, the Tory, and then his successor Mr. King again. The Depression was not King's fault, and Canada did not know, the world did not know, what lay ahead when Mr. King was ousted, quite severely, in the general election of 1930.

Without going into detail I can say that Mr. Bennett tried. Relief was not a solution to unemployment, but it eased the pain of poverty. His moves towards tariffs might have been good on paper, but they served to cut us off from some good and large markets and tie us tighter to Mother England. The relief camps for unemployed young men were a disgrace but he meant well. The point is, he meant well and he tried, but he was what he was, a rich and snobbish corporation lawyer. So though the solution might have been to smash in right and left and leave the debris behind, he hesitated about going into the private sector and demanding, saying, 'We are in an awful mess. You do this and you over there do that and we'll tough this out together.' Corporations could not be touched, tax structures were inviolate, laws were made, even laws of 1868, to protect free enterprise, because that is the rock we stand upon – and so the whole load of misery came down on the people.

Yet, you know, there was a solution. It was right there before our eyes, and from 1933 onward we could read about it every day in our newspapers. I refer, of course, to Franklin Delano Roosevelt. I refer to his New Deal. He came in in '33, and was the United States ever in a mess! Believe me, I saw it. Saskatchewan was worse than anywhere, but on the continent the United Sates took the cake. Get things going. Create jobs. This was his New Deal. What did it matter if the Supreme Court knocked down some of his actions as illegal? Not a bit. Start something and get it going and it becomes tough to undo, or you plant the idea strongly in the people's mind. So if the black crows on the Supreme Court bench knock it down, the next time around will be easier.

Franklin Delano Roosevelt wanted to get the factories turning again, have smoke coming out of those chimneys. He was bold. He was strong. He was tougher than I guess we will ever realize. He didn't expect to be liked, except by the people. Remember his fireside chats and he'd start out, 'My Fellow Americans.' We never had anything like that in Canada. Government was cold, reserved, all morning coat and trousers and that nonsense of the Knight of the Black Rod opening Parliament. Anyway, Roosevelt provided jobs, but more important, he provided hope. Not too much, but some.

Let us face it, many many thousands of those jobs were manufactured ones, make-work jobs, and they were financed by money which was borrowed and which had to be paid off in the future. But after all, he was the government and what was wrong with that? Isn't that what every government does now?

Roosevelt did not get the United States out of its mess. It was still in an economic mess when the Second World War came along, but it was not such a bad mess, and anything that affected the United States affected Canada. Good or bad. Bad or good. You know that, the village idiot knows that. So when they improved, so did we. Not as much, granted, but some. He created no Utopia but he helped spread out the money a little more, less for the rich and more for the poor. Isn't that socialism, in a form? *(He laughs heartily again.)* One of the financial wizards of those times wrote that F.D.R. had no answers that were good for 100 years but in a six-month crisis, he had six-month answers. That's what we needed in Canada, and I am afraid that is what we did not get.

No, Mr. King was no help because he refused to look at the problem back in 1929 and '30, and Mr. Bennett was little help because he really did not understand the problem in the five years of Depression in which he served. When King came back in again, a vindictive and scheming little creature, he thought the problem would go away by appointing royal commissions to solve it. The perfect refuge of the bureaucrat, the man beyond his depth."

Plain And Simple

"Anyway, they were good times and bad times and I think the Canadian nation came out of it with a tougher layer of skin. We aren't so naive. My God, but we were naive. Just plain and simple country folk, really, before all that. Fight the King's wars, trust our politicians, believe that big wheat crops were the economic cornerstone of the nation, and go to church every Sunday. The Thirties sure as hell changed all that."

CHAPTER TWENTY-EIGHT

So Many Problems And So Many Bureaucrats

That's The Way I Lost My Place . . . Mindless Make-Work . . . Government Generosity . . . Go Drown Yourself! . . . Codfish By The Carload . . . British Immigrants . . . They Were Just Trying To Help . . . The Day My Father Cried . . . Not Even A Dollar To Spare.

———————————— • ————————————

If you are dealing with people who are destitute, beaten down and have utter dependence upon you, then even a small amount of authority becomes a mighty weapon. This is a theme that ran through many interviews, and I can say that there is still a residue of hatred, distrust, and fear of the bureaucrats who were in authority in places like the relief office.

Inevitably, there comes a time when the small and run-of-the-mill bureaucrat believes that laws and regulations are there for his own convenience, and not to serve the people or the state.

Then the poor, the homeless, and the desperate in their necessary day-to-week-to-month dealings with these people come to hate them, and then they hate the laws and regulations the bureaucrats administer so autocratically, and finally they come to hate the state. This is the stuff of revolution.

And it can be said that the bureaucrat, even the lowliest, often came to hate the poor and the desperate because they intruded on the orderliness of things. They were often there to demand answers of the bureaucrats when, so often, there were no answers – and certainly no solutions.

———————————— • ————————————

That's The Way I Lost My Place
"I remember, it was 1934 and the tax slip came and the wife said I owed the municipality about $40. This was on the place my Dad had taken up when he brought the bunch of us kids up from Minnesota in 1910, and half the district was still Minnesota Norwegian. So we got no money. The kids are going

354

to school in shoes I make out of car tires and the wife stitches canvas off the old binder to make the shoe finished.

We hitch up the team and go in and see the reeve this day, the day he sat in his office and did business and I said I didn't have no $40 and he said, 'Tor, don't give me that. You got a tin can buried out by the chicken house. You all have. How much in that?' Well, he had me there, I did have $20 in one bill and that was for something awful special that didn't come along yet, but it would sometime.

I guess I was just too damn honest, so I said okay, I got 20 and this fellow Jefferson said to bring it in, to him next week, and he'd tell the clerk to strike off the debt. He'd take the tax off the books, you know. I did, I brought the $20 in and gave it to the reeve and dumb Swede that I am, I didn't ask for no receipt. In that country you trusted a man. Next year I get two tax slips, one says I owe something like $40 for that year and the other has a stamp on it, says 'Delinquent.' Well, I tell you, I don't like that, not when my oldest girl tells me what it's all about. I don't read or write all too well, understand.

So the girl and I go into town and see the clerk and he takes the two pieces of paper and looks at my name on them and says, 'Mr. Thorsteinson, you are the fourteenth man who has been in this office this week.' I don't have to go to school to understand that. We been hooked.

This reeve had pulled this stunt on a lot of fellows and then he'd been beaten in the election last fall and he couldn't farm worth a hoot and so he had lit out. Sold out and lit out. What he was, he was a politician. Yes, and he was also a crook.

That's the way I lost my place, the house my father built, the barn which was as good as any around, the buildings. After the third year when I still couldn't pay their $40 and they had the auction the way they did it then, well, the bill plus the lawyer's fees and the interest and all that, the paperwork you know, and it came to up over $200, and here was a good quarter section with good buildings and some machinery and when it was finished, I got about $90 after everybody had taken their lick at me. This didn't happen just to me, it happened to a lot of other fellows too. Lots of fellows. Two others right on my road.

They say it takes a Norwegian a long time to get mad – and the clerk said he had sent along some mail to this reeve, Jefferson, on Vancouver Island – and I thought we'd just head that way and if I found him, then there would be one less politician and crook walking around, but somehow it didn't work out that way. Oh, yeah, yeah, sure, we got there, but what with getting settled and all that, the beating up part just sort of left my mind.

I suppose if he walked in that door now, I'd just say forget it and ask if he wanted a beer. They was different times."

●

Mindless Make-Work

"I was born on a farm south of Regina in the Maxton area. I don't believe anyone who wasn't there in 1934 and '35 and '36 can believe how bad it was. The wind blew hurricane force and the soil went with it and it was colder each winter than the Yukon.

In 1936 I was 16 and there was no point hanging around. I was just another belly to feed and there were three kids younger. I left and worked my way east. Just a dumb farm kid, but there were an awful lot of dumb farm kids around those days. I got down into the Niagara Peninsula for the picking but there were no jobs and I decided to turn myself in as a vagrant. There wasn't much point starving to death. I wish I could remember the name of the town or little city down that way, but I can't for the very life of me. We hung around outside the jail and then they let us in and told us, 'Boys, there'll be a dandy breakfast for you in the morning. Sleep tight.'

Next morning, we were rousted out about six. About 20 of us. Then the sheriff or warden or jailer came out and told us to split into two equal groups. One bunch went to that end of the yard, and we stayed at the other end. 'Now, boys, each of you pick up two bricks from those piles and carry them down to the other end, then go back and get two more bricks and keep doing that until I tell you to stop.' We did, for an hour, and we got our breakfast. A good one as I recall.

The fellow next to me at breakfast told me he did it as often as they would let him, and there was a county regulation that vagrants had to work for meals. We weren't prisoners, of course, because we were set free after breakfast.

I often wondered, if they did want to get some work out of us, why they didn't make us wash the dishes and clean the jail. It was the most mindless sort of make-work I can imagine, back and forth, two bricks at a time. Why, even worse than digging a hole and filling it in. At least digging a hole you might strike oil. Needless to say, I never did that again. The bureaucratic mind will never, never, never cease to amaze me, or drive me absolutely batty."

———————————————— • ————————————————

Government Generosity

"We were worn right down to the nub in the south country *(of Alberta)* and the government agents came along and said we should go to the Peace River Country. A lot of rain there and good crops. A pack of lies, what they didn't tell us was mosquitoes, no grazing, forests you had to cut down to get even a garden, winters so cold you wouldn't believe it, and no schools and no towns and no nothing.

We decided to go, and sold out what we could and got a hay rack and reinforced it every way we could with strap iron and bolts and wires and new planks and she held up pretty good all the way, about 10 to 15 miles a day to the promised land. Now, this is my point. Those government agents said the government would buy my cattle. Fine, because you couldn't take a lot of skeleton stuff into that country in the first year, so when the time came to clear off the old place, the government buyer came round. All he did was run each animal up on a portable scale and that was it. No grading? He said no, we pay a flat dollar and five cents per hundred, live weight.

I said, 'Mister, would you repeat that.'

He did, and I'd heard right the first time. A cent a pound, and they thought they was doing me a favour. What could I do? Thirty cows I'd worked like hell to build up, a bit lean and mean but they'd come around mighty fast with some good feed, and I got a cent a pound. The cheque was less than $300, for all those years of work, and if that didn't make a guy go out and vote four or five times for Social Credit, I don't know what the hell would."

———————————————— • ————————————————

Go Drown Yourself!

"It got so I hated those people coming to our office for relief. Really hated them, and I guess now I know it was the system I hated and not them, because they were just the end result of the system. I didn't mean the young men, or even the middle aged fellows who were single or who had left their families. It was the chaps my age, in a way, the ones without jobs, of course, who might have had a house and certainly a wife and kids – in those days there were altogether too many kids born. Talk about the French-Canadians. Why, half the English too on the coast were like Papa Dionne. But beside the point, one could say.

It was the way these men had lost their spirit, almost their will to survive, and they'd come shuffling into that office and ask for something more and I'd sometimes scream at them, 'Get the hell out of here. Go down to False Creek and drown yourself. There's the way, right down the hill, and now, beat it.' They'd just stand there and take it and then say something like, 'My kids need shoes to go to school,' or 'My wife has pleurisy and I can't get no doctor to come and see her,' and you'd just have to grit your teeth and reach for a form.

I know what it was doing to these fellows, and I know that even without a Depression, most of them had been in a pretty lousy economic box even before. Talk about your Roaring Twenties! Roaring in New York, maybe, or roaring in the slick magazines, but in Canada it was just a lot of whimpering.

But back to me. I didn't like what was happening to me. In that office I could see the rottenness of the relief system, what it did to people, the graft, and oh yes, there was plenty of that, and the phoney contracts and the phoney people and especially the politicians. You know, there is something about politics that brings out the very worst in people. But to me. I couldn't do much, I was just the guy who was checking forms and okaying extra relief and initialing forms – and even I'd got my job the right way in those days. My uncle was a coal and wood and ice merchant and he did business with one of the aldermen who did business with, you know, somebody else.

So I'd blow up at these people who would come in, and after, I'd apologize, and they would usually just look at me with those goddamned eyes they had. They didn't hate me. Can't even give them that much credit. I found myself turning into a hateful person, spiteful, taking it out on some person when it really couldn't have been his fault. Yelling at my wife, cuffing my kids, snarling at my neighbours, and why? Why? Because I knew that I was part of a system which was wrong, and it was turning me wrong, and to protect my wife and kids I had to keep going wrong, and more wrong, just like you can't be a little pregnant.

This went on for years, three or four anyway, and it was a bad situation and I wasn't the only one up to my ears in it. Our office was full of them. You had to be a goddamned idiot not to see what was happening. Not enough money. Who in the name of dear sweet Jesus can live on $10 or $15 a month?

With kids. Yet some big husky guy, a single, would also qualify for $10. Not enough money. Too many people. A lot of that money going to the wrong people. Wrong people running the relief office. Forms so complicated you wouldn't believe, and you couldn't help the person fill them out – and to this day I'm convinced those forms were made so complicated that nobody could fill them out. I know I couldn't fill out three out of three correctly all the time. Getting deeper and deeper.

And yet, if I read the papers correctly, the welfare office situation today, right here in Vancouver, is probably just as loused up as it was back then, and all your forms and reports and surveys don't do you any good. You need people who understand people. In '39, when the bugles blew, I went right out in October and joined up and breathed the clean fresh air of war for a few years."

———————————————— • ————————————————

Codfish By The Carload

"We once had a freight car of dried codfish come in. Not relief, but for distribution. Various agencies, churches, groups in those days treated Saskatchewan like a disaster area, which it was, of course, no doubt about that, no doubt at all, south of Regina anyway, and they collected car loads of food and clothing in Ontario and such and shipped them west. As I recall, the railroads hauled these cars free. It wasn't much of a gesture when you consider that the C.N.R. debt, the interest payment on the debt, was bleeding the country white, but it helped. The United Church in Ontario collected hundreds of tons of stuff.

A car load of dried codfish came in. Ever seen the stuff? This was tied together with twine in stacks, like shingles. Some folks said it looked like shingles. There was a story around that Jack McCormick had actually tried to shingle his outhouse with this codfish, but the nails bent. Anyway, it was a good laugh.

Prairie people are suspicious, you know. Look at Alberta's conservatism. One example right there. Social Credit. Something like dried codfish was so alien to anything they had known that they turned their noses up at it. Same as they would at Japanese snails or Chinese bird's nest soup. Another thing, what did you do with it? Nobody knew, but there were some darn fine cooks in the district and they soaked it and made Finnan Haddie and they boiled it and smoked it, or something, but it wasn't too long until nobody could look a codfish in the eye. People actually turned down the stuff. Given in the best of interests, it was just wrong for the people. Canada is such a vast country with such diversity that even regional eating is vastly different.

People would accept codfish because they didn't dare not to, but then they'd dump it down their outhouse or soak it in a tub for a couple of days and feed it to the pig. If they had a pig. If they had a tub that didn't leak.

Same with turnips. People rejected turnips, hauled all the way across the country at the taxpayer's expense. Why? You can figure that one out. Turnips were cattle feed for mixed farmers. You grew turnips, maybe the finest in the world for all I know, but they were for cattle. I don't know the nutritional value of a turnip, but it was no deal in Saskatchewan."

———————————— • ————————————

British Immigrants

"There was a certain class of city dweller which was hit very hard by the Depression, and I refer to the British immigrants who came in their thousands to Canada, after the First World War, many, many of them soldiers and their families.

When the Depression hit, when times got very bad, starting about 1931, a great many of these people were thrown out of work and they were helpless. This became an alien thing and it broke them down. They just did not know how to cope. Some of us relief officials used to sit around and try to figure out ways of getting these people off their butts and to work. They were like the African native who so believes in superstition that if he knows someone has put a curse on him that he will die, then he will die. You could say these people had the same fear. Most were getting relief, you see, but they didn't know how to use it. A Canadian woman with gumption could make a 1932 dollar do the work of three 1928 dollars, and 15 of our 1971 dollars. But these people! They would buy firewood off the truck at the door and they were living in Kitsilano only three blocks from the beach and there was a cross-cut saw in the basement of their house. They just didn't think of going down to the beach and cutting their own firewood from the driftwood piled everywhere. That firewood they bought. Where do you think it came from? Cut by a Canadian on the beach.

They could walk two blocks to the Marpole tram line and pay five cents and ride half an hour out to Lulu Island and buy sacks of vegetables and quarts of cream and gallons of milk and 100 pounds of potatoes all for about $2. But no, they never thought of that. It was beyond their experience. When the smelt were running in English Bay they could have taken a bucket and brought back pails of good-eating fish, but no. They would go up to the fish market on Fourth Avenue and buy the same smelt at high prices.

Every backyard had a garden, or space for a garden. No, they didn't know how. They say the Englishman loves his garden, his roses, but that didn't apply to potatoes and corn and lettuce and spinach. Many backyards had apple trees, and yet I have seen, without a word of a lie, fine red apples, October apples, on those trees of these people and dropping off and becoming unfit to eat because they didn't think to pick them and store them for winter. In fact, if you want to believe this, I know Canadians who would go and ask these Englishmen, sitting at the table in the kitchen in their shirt sleeves sipping tea and eating biscuits, and bitching, asking if they could have the apples and they were told yes.

I've always maintained that nobody had to go hungry. There was no money but there was always food, or so it seemed. People always had something to fill their bellies with, unpalatable as it might have seemed to the people up in Shaughnessy *(a nearby wealthy district.)* There was always a dollar to be made somewhere, even if it was working by the day on a Hindu sawdust truck, distasteful as it may have been to many. The docks often needed an extra hand or a warehouse a sweeper. The people got sick, you know, and if your name was in at a number of places then it was always possible to pick up a dollar or two a week. This was over and above relief.

But they didn't, they couldn't break out of this circle they were in, and what it really amounted to was an emotional sickness. They came to Canada thinking it was a land of milk and honey, and when the milk soured and the honey hardened, they had nowhere to go."

———————————— • ————————————

They Were Just Trying To Help

"Music. Singing. I remember that. The Mormon Church was very big in southern Alberta and they had this system where their young men, these fellows would go into other districts and work for recruits for old Joe Smith. They never got any converts that I knew of around Wetaskawin as I remember, but they were good fellows. Didn't smoke, chew, drink or curse and they didn't sniff down their noses or purse up their mouths if people around them did. Good fellows. They were missionaries. Only thing was, they were in the wrong religion to get converts in that part of the country.

This was about 1935, around there, and things were pretty bad. Lot of people just packed it up and others couldn't even afford to do that. Aberhart, old Bible Bill, was about to win the election but it wasn't called yet. That year.

These two fellows, they came into the district and they had been trained since youngsters to go out and meet people, to smile and be friendly and work for the community, and they went to the school board and asked if they could use the school on a Friday night for a concert. Not Saturday night, that was the night everybody went to town to stand on the street corners and complain about everything. That was the only fun anybody had, seeing who was worse off that particular week than they was.

The school board chairman said there was something in the School Act about not having religion, or a special religion taught in the school, but these fellows said it was a concert. Just that. Nothing more. People could play whist or five hundred and the kids could play button, button and that paper, knife, rock, scissors game. You know the one. Forget the name, but all the kids played it.

People could bring lunches for a late feed and there would be sing-song. Our school had a piano. It might not have had much of any other thing but old Jock Thompson years ago had given it a piano when he went to the old folks home.

I thought that what this sorry broken-down district needed was a bit of games and music and so I said I would go along with these two Mormons and the chairman went along with me, and that was it. Each school kid took a note home and those that didn't have kids were told somehow, and two weeks later there was a big crowd. Everyone just sort of stood around, just waiting for things to go wrong, that show-me attitude. After all, these Brigham Youngers weren't all that popular, because the Mormon Church was kind of mysterious, even then.

It went off fine. A couple of the younger couples pitched in to help, and soon there were card games going, snap, hearts, whist and the older kids were fooling around outside and then the music got going and everybody soon was bellowing his head off. 'Where Did You Get That Hat?' Remember that old song? 'My Sweetheart's The Man In The Moon!' 'The Good Old Summertime.' I can still sing them. 'Annie Laurie.' 'The Band Played On,' the one about Casey and the strawberry blond. 'Clementine.' 'Nellie Gray.' 'A Long, Long Trail A Winding.' 'My Ain Folk.' 'Old Folks At Home.'

We sang dozens, and it all came back and the women would take the soprano and contralto and the men the bass and baritone, and people we wouldn't have dreamed of as having any talent turned out to be damned good singers, and we were doing songs some of us had learned in school 40 years ago, and everybody was feeling good. Not from liquor, but just from singing and being with people again. That's what that country needed, some love and kindness and human understanding, and we were giving it all to each other then.

Then we ate and there were jokes and laughing and when we drove or walked home that night, the moon was shining and things didn't look so bad. There wasn't going to be much of a crop but I remember putting my arm around my wife and saying things would be getting better soon, and that was the first time I'd done that in a long time. Most before, I'd just been too dispirited.

We had two more of them social evenings, two weeks apart each, and there was getting to be a real fine spirit. People from as far as 10 and 15 miles away, right out of our district, were coming, and there was talk of organizing a harvest supper and big dance, and that was something that had died out about 1931 when things started to get bad and folks just pulled back into their holes.

Then we got the word. The Letter. The school inspector said we were using the school for the wrong purpose. We told him to come down for a meeting and he did and we said what wrong purpose and he said, 'Those Mormons. Those fellows from Utah. They preach having more wives than one, don't they?' Of course they did, long ago, but that was because they was more women than men in the first colony and it worked out fine, a man having two or three wives. But there was no convincing that bastard. No more dances. No more Mormons sneaking their religion around behind our backs and into the heads and hearts of our young ones. I remember telling the inspector he was full of bullshit, and he said any more of that and any more music nights and the district would lose its grant.

So that was that. The two young missionaries went somewhere else, the church pulled them out and sent them to another place, and there were no more music nights and of course, no harvest dance and feed.

That was the last gasp of that community. After that, it just up and died until the war came along."

The Day My Father Cried

"My father was a bricklayer and a very good one, so people have told me, but by 1930 there wasn't a lick of construction work being done in our county and if he got two weeks work that summer fixing fireplaces in some of those big summer homes along the shore, then he was lucky.

It was the dole he finally had to accept. I can't remember what it was now but you got your rent paid and some wood and I think my mother told me that the real money and the voucher value, you were expected to feed a person on eight cents a day so that would make my family available for about $15 a month or so. My mother and father, my three sisters, and I was the only boy.

The county said there was work in the woods, that the men getting the dole were expected to work it off in the woods, at so much a day. Maybe a dollar a day. The county said this was expected of them, but they could not force them to.

My father was a proud man. The family had been in the county for four generations. He was Scots and Presbyterian and proud of his trade, thrifty and a good man. He even played the bagpipes. He was ferociously proud, and it must have torn his guts apart to have to take dole but he did, and he was one of the men who said they'd go into the woods to work it off. Cutting firewood for the court house, the registry, the schools and such.

What did he know about cutting wood? He was a tradesman, a mason. You have to be skilled in the woods and they went in and they did not know how to handle the axe and buck saw, and they didn't have the right footwear. The wrong clothes. Wrong everything. In the wet and the muck and freezing cold.

I remember one day he came home after dark and he was cold and wet, and supper was just a can of corned beef, and I believe a can cost 10 cents, and the rest of the meal was turnips and potatoes. A cousin on Prince Edward Island had sent us a couple of hundred pounds of each. Turnips were cattle food. My Dad just looked, and then he laid his arms out on the table and he put his head down and he started sobbing. You've got four kids around the table and they are, say six, eight, nine and 11 and there is your old man crying. What is he crying for? For himself? Us, his kids? My mother? The world? Or just that cow fodder on the plate? How the hell should I know?

Mother told us kids to take our plates and we ate in the living room and we didn't say one goddamned word to each other.

About a week later Dad slipped off the truck bed up in the woods and banged his hip and it hurt but he kept working. Then some bone disease developed and he was laid up, quite serious, and then he went to hospital and was there 18 months and it was there he died.

End of my Depression story.

No, it isn't. Dad and the others were the good guys, the honourable ones, the ones who cared hard enough to go into those woods and work. But do you know who the smart ones were? They were the ones who told the county agent, 'Bugger you,' and wouldn't work off their dole and spent the time sitting in the kitchen with their feet up by the warm fire. The smart ones. They were a rarity then, I guess, but they are everywhere today. Welfare. Just look around you. God damn them!"

———————————— • ————————————

Not Even A Dollar To Spare

"I remember a teacher in the home economics class in our school became concerned about the general appearance of many of the country children. Off the farms, from log homes in the bush, and she asked one class of these children what they had brought for lunch.

Some just didn't have any lunch. Nothing. Others had one piece of bread slathered with molasses. The bread was soggy, just gucky. That was all they had in their lunch pails and many of these children were walking miles to school. This teacher was from Halifax and some of the teachers thought she was a do-gooder, but they agreed these children were in no condition to absorb much that was being taught. I guess you could say they were fighting for survival.

So this teacher had an idea, and it was to get a project going so the home economics room would make soup, a thick and nourishing soup, and it probably would have made a world of difference to those kids. She went around to the stores and cafes and they were willing to give her left-overs, bread, bones, pieces of meat, and it could be made into a wonderful soup for these children at noon. Just the country kids, some who walked five miles each day. All that was needed was some organization and co-operation.

This teacher and a couple of others went to the school board and asked for a few dollars a month. Not much, but some things had to be bought. Not on your life, they said. Not even a dollar a day. She said could they spare

50 cents a day. They said no. Not even that small amount. Of course, we knew the money was there, but to this day I think they just didn't want to be feeding farm children in a town school. And I think a lot of people in the town agreed with them. Oh, those were desperate days."

Governments were embarrassed by the thousands of unemployed men under-
foot and were afraid of what might happen if they decided to revolt. So relief
camps were established—usually far from the nearest town—where the unemployed would get food, shelter, and a little money. There they would be out of
sight. This is a camp in the interior of British Columbia.

[Vancouver Public Library/8834]

A relief camp scene near Ottawa.

[National Archives of Canada/C 31058]

The relief camps were run on army lines, and the men were kept hard at work on "make-work" projects. It was hard, menial and often pointless work.

[National Archives of Canada/C 20013]

In time, the men in the camps rebelled. In this camp in Northern Ontario the men simply downed tools and went on strike.

[*Toronto Star*]

When the men in the relief camps walked out and mustered in Vancouver, the police reacted violently. The city was swept by a riot that caused $30,000 worth of damage, and many injuries.

[Vancouver Public Library/8811 (top), 1313 (middle, left), 1289 (middle, right), 1307 (bottom)]

All over the country unemployed men decided to march to Ottawa to present their demands for jobs. Here the march of Ontario men files through the countryside near Toronto.

Marchers and spectators listen to speeches in Queen's Park in Toronto.

The On To Ottawa trek involved so many men that housing and feeding them was a problem. But men used to a drifter's life did not expect luxury.

[*Toronto Star*]

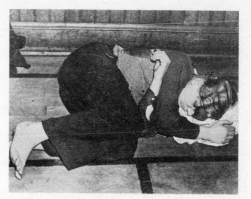

The march from British Columbia to Ottawa was the most spectacular. Here men clamber aboard an east-bound train at Kamloops.

[National Archives of Canada/C 29399]

By the time the marchers reached Alberta their numbers were swelled to many thousands.

[National Archives of Canada/C 29461]

In Regina the marchers were met by their leaders, returning from an unsuccessful meeting with the Prime Minister in Ottawa. Discontent flared when the police tried to prevent a public meeting, and in the riot that ensued a policeman was killed (on the ground, above) and many police and marchers were injured.

[Saskatchewan Archives Board/R-B171-2 (top), R-B171-3 (middle), R-B171-1 (bottom)]

Although the outbreak of the Second World War was what ended Canada's Depression in 1939, in the Thirties few Canadians were interested in political events abroad. Parades such as this one (in support of the International Brigade then fighting the Fascists in Spain) were uncommon.

[Vancouver Public Library/9446]

Snow was falling as this young man stood begging at the corner of King and Yonge one evening. He was arrested.

[Toronto Star]

CHAPTER TWENTY-NINE

Bankers And Business Walked Hand In Hand

The Interest Load On Our Backs . . . The Law Of The Jungle . . . The Wobbly Front Step . . . The Pride Of Possession . . . Two Dollars Short . . . Railroads Killed the Highway . . . The Way We Did Business . . . 48 Percent Interest . . . Bankers Had Problems, Too . . . How An Empire Fell.

⎯⎯⎯⎯⎯⎯⎯⎯⎯⎯ • ⎯⎯⎯⎯⎯⎯⎯⎯⎯⎯

Men of great business acumen of former days would roll over in their graves if they knew that today one could stroll down a main street and buy a suit, a set of golf clubs, a typewriter and have a $12 meal, just by handing over a small plastic card and signing a name. Even the $12 meal item would start them spinning.

In the old days of the Thirties, there was a little borrowing. For a house, a farm, machinery, a car, seed grain. Not much else.

It was fairly cut-and-dried. It made part of the world go round – mutual agreement on the amount, the interest rate, the payments, the time period, the collateral. Always the collateral. Good collateral. And when the cheque was handed over, a firm handshake. The banker considered the handshake good public relations.

But when the clerk in his neat red brick bungalow can't meet his $40 a month and eight percent interest, compounded quarterly, because he's lost his job at the store, what happens? Or the farmer, burned out for three years is told that his machinery is too broken down to cover the loan balance and that the problem will be handed over to the lawyer, what happens? Both men are out. One loses his house, the other his farm. It wasn't special greed or harshness; that was just the way things were done in those days.

"I remember hard," said one prairie farmer, remembering such a foreclosure which occurred 34 years ago. "Bankers and businessmen, nah!"

The Interest Load On Our Backs

"It was the interest that got us, that finally nailed us down. That interest to the mortgage companies and banks, we just couldn't beat that. I know, there was the dry years and grasshoppers and rust and smut and a whole combination of things, but farmers always have had those to put up with. The trouble is we got them all together but on top of it there was the interest load on our backs. It was our own fault.

In through that country, around Moosomin and east, we could always get a crop, sometimes not much, but something. Usually fair. We'd get good spring rains and then usually the July first soaking and things would look pretty good and off we'd go to the fair, our one holiday, and there would be Cockshutt and John Deere and McCormick and those beautiful tractors and binders and other equipment and we'd fall, suckers, every time. Machinery poor. The wife might not have a washing machine but the yard would be loaded up with all that equipment, and, of course, it had to be paid for and in no uncertain terms. The bank, it would lend you then. You see, the implement companies wanted a mighty good chunk of cash and they'd say, you've got a good year in sight so just take a loan now and pay off when the crop comes in. Trouble is, when the crop came in and essentials – taxes, water rights, bulk fuel bills, kids' clothes and the like – when they were paid there was not too much over. I mean we still had to keep something to tide us over the winter, Christmas, a couple of trips up to Regina, and then there was spring and we had to buy seed and more fuel, oil and distillate, and so the mortgage company or bank would say, 'Okay, we'll carry you this year' and the interest, at eight or nine percent on 3,000 or so dollars would be slapped on to the principal, and this would happen next year, until it was like the frog in the well, two jumps up and slide three back down.

Then we were deep into the Depression around '33 and the companies, they took out the bullwhip and said, 'Okay, you pay up now or we take over.' Thunder and lightning, a lot of good men left farming that way. Good men as farmers but not worth a doodle on the credit and debit side of it. You know what happened when they up and left? There was nobody to take over their land, the implement companies didn't want to take back their equipment, for who would buy it? Junk by then and everybody broke, anyway. The farms, the land went back to Russian thistle and the houses tumbled down and the wells filled up. Just plain stupidity.

If the government had come up with some sort of scheme at the start to keep those mortgage companies and the banks in the corral and given the farmer and rancher a chance to work things out, things would have been an awful lot better. As it was, it worked out to be a terrible disgrace, just a terrible disgrace.

What the hell is it, anyway, what happens to men's thinking when they smell what looks like easy money? It doesn't seem possible that it was all 40 years ago. It seems just like last year. I can remember every darn thing that happened clearly."

---·---

The Law Of The Jungle

"I never heard of any Canadian bankers or financiers jumping out of tall buildings into the streets of Toronto or Montreal. I never saw any businessmen in ragged and worn suits selling apples. I never heard anybody saying or singing 'Brother, Can You Spare A Dime?' except on comedy radio shows from the United States. I'm sure a lot of businesses went belly up but it wasn't the big businesses. Look at the big businesses in Canada today. Steel companies. Department stores. The food companies. The lumber companies. They survived and grew stronger during the Depression. Don't prove it by what I say, but I've lived too long not to know a thing or two.

The little guy went to the wall, thousands of them, but it often wasn't the economy that did it. In those days, the Law of the Jungle was at its height. Wasn't it Kipling who wrote a poem about the weak shall perish and the strong will always survive, and how it was a good thing. Well, I don't think it was. I'm not going to mention any names but let's take the case of a department store. Take any one. They're all the same.

Say I was a little manufacturer. Women's gloves, which I was. I employed 60 people, mostly women on the machines. In the Twenties, life was pretty sweet. We had a summer home in the Thousand Islands and spent some part of every winter in Florida or Mexico, which not too many Toronto people did then. Nobody ever accused me of running a sweatshop. Not a chance. I once heard a buyer say to another and he didn't know I was the other side of the partition and he said, "Isser is one Jew who acts like a white man.' He meant it as a compliment, but when I knew who was running the banks and big companies and stores in this country I wasn't sure that it was a compliment. It doesn't matter. I was small potatoes.

Comes Depression. Dirty Thirties. I had to let about 15 or 20 girls go in 1931 because there was no other way, and then this big company, this very respectable company, comes to little Isser and they say I put out such a good product and they are tired of being skinned and scraped by those Montreal garment houses so they'd like to deal with me. Just me. Exclusive. They'll take my whole production. Look, the man says, look at us. Stores across the country, every province. Look at the customers we have. Half the country. I fall right into the trap. That trap which even I, dumb, knew all about. Greed. That was it. I was greedy.

They took that year's production, spring and fall, and next year the same. I even hire back my girls. Next year at contract time they say times are getting worse and the whole country is sliding downhill so there's got to be a new contract.

My friend, there sure is. I can't live with it, but I gotta. Two years they get my full line, my production, and my old customers I haven't got a one. I don't have to tell you that I'm not going to get them back either. Their noses are in the air. Who needs Isser, that dirty little sell-out? My wife says, 'Don't give yourself a black eye, honey,' but I gotta. I walked right into the door knob. That year I just break even. We're about 1934 now, right? New contract time, and they cut me so low I gotta lay off girls and even then, I work the rest all that much harder. Now to stay alive I gotta cut wages and, God knows, they weren't all that good anyway. So now what have I got? I tell you. I got a sweatshop, and there is nothing I can do. I even got my wife doing books. I can't even afford an accountant.

Next year, I throw up my hands. What that big kind department store wants to do to me shouldn't happen to Hitler. But it does. Oh, yes it does. They've got me. All I can say, and this is what I do say, 'Okay, fellas, you've got me. You own me. I can't meet you any way, shape or form.'

They smile, and two days later they send a registered letter and they offer to buy me out, and for about half what I figure the business is worth and about a quarter of what it was worth four years before. They've worked me over real good and the only business I got is theirs, and if they don't want to buy from me, okay, so I don't sell to anybody.

My plant, my girls, my machines getting worn and old, my credit lousy at the suppliers. What do I do? Right! I sell. And they take over and I cash out and they do whatever they damn well want with my little plant we took the best years of our lives to build up.

This happened all over the country. The records show it. Big companies got bigger and little Issers went to the wall. So that is why I say to you I never heard of any Canadian bankers jumping out windows and no businessman ever sold apples and 'Brother Can You Spare A Dime' was strictly for comic shows, vaudeville, radio."

———————————— • ————————————

The Wobbly Front Step

"I married Jane in 1934. We just decided we'd do it. There was just no sense waiting. We got a little suite in Kitsilano, about $12 a month as I recall. It would go for $125 or more now. We wanted something better, something bigger when babies started coming, and my father-in-law told me about this house in West Point Grey. The owner had died and the widow couldn't carry the payments. There wasn't much else she could do in those days and she was going to sell it for the mortgage, then go to live with her son and daughter-in-law. I think she just hated to see that house go on foreclosure, the way the mortgage companies were grabbing up property. They knew the Depression couldn't last forever.

Anyway, hold on to your hat! The widow owed only about $400, something like $385. My father-in-law couldn't help me and I didn't know anybody who had that kind of cash, so I went to a finance company. Sure, they said, we'd be glad to look at it. They sent a man out and I and the wife met him and he walked up the walk, and mind you, this was a fine house. He started up the front steps and the first board he stepped on was wobbly. It was loose. Hell, the widow didn't know about fixing steps, but this guy stopped cold and turned around and he said, 'Poor maintenance. It's run down, you can see that. I'm sorry, but we can't help you on a place like this,' and he turned and walked back to his car.

Do you know who bought that house? That same finance company. That was just one of their tricks. No wonder people still distrust them. That house is still there today, lived in and still sound as a dollar, and it is surrounded by $40,000 to $60,000 homes, and it looks right at home."

———————————— • ————————————

The Pride Of Possession

"Canadians are a thrifty lot, they have a tremendous pride of possession. That's why a man would much sooner be paying on a mortgage on a house or farm than putting it into savings accounts or bonds. In the 1920s, this was the case. So although the average Canadian was a saving person, he considered his home or farm or business as his savings.

When the Crash came, with unemployment, heavy cuts in salaries and wages, low farm produce prices, businesses going belly-up, the average Canadian didn't have cash reserves to tide him over the tough times. You had to have a bank reserve, a savings account of considerable size, and I'd say not one Canadian in 10 had that. So an awful lot of people didn't last long. After all, they had to eat, too. So they couldn't make those house mortgage payments, those monthly payments to the banks. The Depression doomed them.

I won't say the banks and mortgage companies didn't do a lot of foreclosing, because we did, but if there had been some way out, some form of government assistance, some guaranteed moratorium, we wouldn't have. But we did, of course, especially on the prairies. I believe the directors of my bank, of all the banks, just could not understand that the Depression on the prairies was not the Depression in Ontario. If they had understood they were different an awful lot of farmers and ranchers wouldn't have been wiped out. Something would have been worked out."

———————————————— • ————————————————

Two Dollars Short

"Yes, let me tell you of one experience I'll always remember, because I think it shows what was wrong with the banking system then. The disregard for people. Our banking system was safe and not on flimsy legs like in the United States, but my husband used to say it was the closest thing to a Roman slave ship.

I was a junior teller in a bank in Kingston and my name was Dottie McLaren then. Banks were terrible places to work then. If you know a man today who was a manager or accountant in a bank in the Hungry Thirties, you take a good look at him because he will not be what he seems to be. Underneath whatever he appears to be, there will be a cruel man, a man dedicated to a cruel system.

It was hard for a girl or women to work for a bank, but they paid such low wages that they took women. I got $6 a week. I know fellows of 20, 22, or so, making only $8 a week. But the money was security. We know now you can starve easily on security but that pay envelope on the 29th of every month meant a lot, when everybody was standing around on street corners.

One day I totalled out $2 short. That's not much, but that also is not the point. It meant to the accountant and the manager that I was sloppy, stupid, dumb, not alert, not bright enough to walk through their front door and be part of that great and proud organization.

The thing is, I knew where I'd made that mistake. It was a woman on relief. A Mrs. Mackenzie, I'll never forget her name. I had cashed her relief cheque and given her $26. Two tens, a five, and a one. Silly how you remember the little things, isn't it? Now really, why should I remember that? Her cheque was for $24. I knew that, because it always was $24, so I had made the mistake. I was going to put in $2 of my own money but I forgot, and when the tally came I was short.

I'm not sure whether I was sorry for her because she needed the money and she was entitled to my mistake or whether I was covering up for myself. The manager called me in and gave me a talking-to and I blurted out that I knew where the deficiency was. That was a mistake. Wheeler was the accountant and the manager said Mr. Wheeler would accompany me to the house and get the $2 back. I was astonished. Ashamed, I guess, is better. Not the next day, but that night. We often worked until seven or eight at night so it didn't matter.

We walked down the streets to the Mackenzie house and I kept wondering if Mrs. Mackenzie had used the $2 to buy a cake or some candy or a new coat for one of her kids. Maybe they were having a celebration, and here we were, coming to take back the money. We found the house, a rattrap of an affair, probably rent free from the city. I knocked on the door and the accountant stood beside me. He was a tall man. Big. Tall. Mrs. Mackenzie opened the door and her eyes went from me to Mr. Wheeler and she said 'Just a minute' and she went inside and I heard her whispering and everything went quiet, no kids laughing or talking, and she came out and handed me two one dollar bills, but she was looking at Mr. Wheeler. I said thank you, and she shut the door and we left and walked back to the bank. Mr. Wheeler said, and this was the first word he had spoken since we had left the bank, he said, 'Whew, that was easy.' I walked on a bit and then I said, 'She thought you were a policeman.'

For two lousy bucks, $2, that's what we had to do in those days."

Railroads Killed The Highway

"You know, years after he was defeated, lost out as prime minister in 1935, R.B. Bennett told me that he could have ended much of the unemployment of the Depression. He wanted to build a Trans-Canada Highway, much as it is now, on the route it is now. But he couldn't. He was prevented from doing so by, well, guess who? The trans-continental railways. The Canadian Pacific and the Canadian National. They didn't want any all-weather road across the country, and they had too much political clout and Bennett said they were able to kill his plan. But if he had gone ahead with it, he could have created an awful lot of jobs and put a lot of money into circulation."

———————————— • ————————————

The Way We Did Business

"The greatest optimist in the world is the farmer, the Saskatchewan farmer. Jesus, once I sold a binder to a farmer's wife. She said, 'Mr. Cody, we can't possibly afford that binder,' and I said the one they had wouldn't go a week and maybe not another hour, it was a wreck, and I talked to her some more and she said her husband was in Moose Jaw and I said, 'Mrs. Cody, this is the last binder I have. I can sell it to your neighbour down the road,' and she said, 'Well, my husband will kill me, but I guess it'll have to be done,' and I made out the contract right there and she signed.

Now this was crazy. I didn't know if she had the right to sign. She said, 'How will we ever make the payments?' and I said, 'Well, Mrs. Cody, you've signed, so I'm going to make sure you make the payments.' I met her husband in his truck down the road and I figured I'd better face him then and there and maybe rip up the contract, and when I told him he laughed and said, 'Harold, you could sell a whale a week to a small town butcher,' but he signed too. The fact is, she couldn't have legally signed anyway, but his John Henry made it good.

That's the way we did business in those days. Anything to get a signature on paper. They never made a goddamn payment anyway, the grasshoppers had cleaned them out by late June and if they hadn't done it, the drought would have. It was crazy country."

48 Percent Interest

"There was this family, Italians, over by the tracks. The old man worked in the roundhouse on the steam hose, and a couple of the kids worked for the railroad. That was the C.N.R. They must have known somebody or else there was kickbacks to the foreman – and don't think that didn't happen, because it did.

One day a salesman got his foot in the door and he wound up selling them a Stromberg-Carlson radio, which you could say was the Buick of the radio world, a great big brown thing that sat in the corner of their tiny living room and when the old man turned it up high, it almost broke your ear drums. Damnedest thing in the world. It cost about $300, and that was a fortune in them days and there was no way that family was going to pay for it but they thought they were as good as Mussolini with it. The salesman had hooked them for about 48 percent a year interest. Just sign this contract, Mr. Josefa, right here, thank you, and we'll deliver it in the morning. Why, the poor dumb wopsies.

Anyway, the first payment, the down payment had cleaned out their bank account unless it was a sock tucked down Mama's bosom, which was ample, and they began to hurt after the second payment and it got worse. Of course they fell behind, and bang, bang, there was the credit collector at the door, and by the time he was through with them they had nothing. I think the law said they had to have beds and a table and chairs and a stove, but I think that collection agency for that well-regarded and upstanding furniture store down on Main Street took everything else, and maybe Mama's religious pictures and the figurines of Christ to boot. You had to be careful in those days, and a hell of a lot of people weren't. Some people got skinned clean. Democracy, hah!"

———————————•———————————

Bankers Had Problems, Too

"I often wondered if the hatred the farmers had for the bankers on the prairies would ever die down. But it did. Oh, some old men remember, but good times wash away a lot of the bitterness of bad times, and in a way it wasn't the banker's fault. It was the old story though. In good times, 'Borrow, fellows, and pay off when the crop comes in.' In bad times, 'Not a nickel for you guys and I've got orders to start proceedings against you for the land.' That was the way it went.

Who could ever tell that we'd get hit like we did right through the Thirties, a Depression and 40 or 45 cents a bushel for wheat and when grades were taken off that and freight rates, there just wasn't nothing left. Five cents a bushel, 10, 15 sometimes. That just ain't human. But the bankers was under the gun too. After all *they'd* made the blamed loans, and district office or the big boys in Montreal or Toronto didn't care. They just knew so many million dollars in loans was out and that was backed by land and if there was no money to pay back, then it was the bank's duty to go after the collateral.

It was the bank inspectors who were the hard-nosed ones. These fellows used to travel in pairs, like policemen through a tough district at night. They'd order the bank managers to grab that piece of property or that one, or this one, but who the hell wanted land? You couldn't *give* it away, but instead of letting the poor dirt farmer try and fight his way clear, they'd just close in, and they had the law on their side all the way. As I recollect, we never had the serious trouble up here that they did the other side of the line, but there was a lot of hatred towards the bank managers, or the banks, I guess.

Most of the bank managers themselves were pretty good guys, taking part in the town things, curling, duck hunting, smokers at the Legion, that sort of thing, but they still had the money and were taking away the land. When a farmer has lost his half section he worked his ass off for, and the bank is across the street and in an office at the back is the guy who signed the papers taking away that land, then it is pretty hard to explain to that farmer that it is some bank inspector travelling around the country or some fat man in an office in Montreal who did him in."

———————————— • ————————————

How An Empire Fell

"My father left me four houses in Toronto and it was no problem keeping them filled up and when I wanted to buy some more in the same district the bank gave me credit with both fists. They couldn't give it away fast enough, and the four rented houses, you see, they were collateral and the price of the money was 7 ½ percent but who cared? This was 1928 and things were going good. I say we thought things were going good. Looking back now, we should have seen something.

I bought four more houses, using half the $7,500 the bank gave me for the down payment and the rest to update them. Paint here, a bit of carpentering, a new bathroom set, fix the steps, plant a lawn. The little things.

I was on Easy Street. Rents from my own four houses, my Dad's, I put half of that plus the rents from the second four houses into paying off the loan. The rest of the rent, about $80 as I remember, went into a special fund and I was going to buy more property with that. I was going to be a millionaire by the time I hit 40. Ho! ho!

By late 1930, four of my eight houses are empty. Disaster. I cut rents way down to get in renters, but that is just putting off the evil day. The bank loan is still waiting. Month by month I'd lost tenants. Skippers. Gone in the night. I'd get more. So you've got eight houses and only four or five filled and you maybe are lucky to get $80 or $90 a month from them, and the bank loan is $120 a month with that wicked interest. You see, it's wicked interest by now. You've got taxes. Some maintenance has to be done otherwise you'll be in the slumlord business in a couple of years.

My little contingency fund of $80 a month, about $500, was gone soon. My job is my houses, the management of them, and I can't get a job. Who wants me? Never done a day's work in my life. I'm 26 and nothing behind me.

Then comes that day when the two converging lines meet. Pretty quickly. My own money is up the chimney and my rents don't come close to my bank loan and I go to the bank and I sit in an office with some accountant and out comes my file and there is some humming and hawing. Hmmm-mmm! Then the answer. It's like being waiting for the jury's verdict when you're on trial for murder and you know the death penalty is automatic. Crunch! That's my neck.

No, I can't have any more money. I don't blame them for that. Business. No, I can't have a reduction in interest. No, I can't have an extension.

So I'm out of business. The bank takes my father's houses. The trust company takes back the four houses I bought for half down payment. At 26, I'm finished.

Boy, was it easy to get credit when things were good! Boy, was it hard to even get a small smile out of a banker when things were bad! All their money was locked up and they weren't letting any of it out. Everybody was a bad risk. And I read later, a banker saying that this was what made Canada's banking system so strong in Depression time. I should think so. No lend, no risk."

CHAPTER THIRTY

Rough Justice

Judicious Use Of Tar ... The Big Fence Rip-off ... High Noon In The Relief Office ... A Very Ugly Story ... One Day On The Frontier ... Minus One Vanilla Milk Shake ... An Eye For An Eye! ... Dead Dog Down A Well

———————————— • ————————————

In this chapter there are several examples of rough justice, and probably every town east and west of Winnipeg remembers its own stories. It is probably true that many will never be told, for obvious reasons.

The story of the group of Maritimers who tarred and gravelled a village skinflint is probably true, because it has that bright ring of truth when tested on the heart and intellect. The story in an earlier chapter of the man who slaughtered his employer's bull, even though he liked it, is true, I'm certain, because when it was told to me, the man again became carried away by rage and frustration, and got up from his chair and advanced, arm out as though holding the knife, just as he had that night so long ago.

Often this sort of justice is meted out with an almost Biblical intensity. I think that it is usually spontaneous.

To people under real duress, suffering cruelly from economic pressure and political forces they do not understand, there will always be the populist philosophy that the big and powerful are stepping on the necks of the poor and that the big and the powerful are always favoured by the government, the laws and the courts.

In such situations there will be rough justice.

———————————— • ————————————

Judicious Use Of Tar

"Never heard of but one tar and feathering in Canada, real violence, and that was down home in '33, spring of, when a landlord got set to raise a widow lady's rent from $5 a month to $8. He might as well have put it up to $50 because he, this landlord, was just about taking the last bit of bread out of

378

that family's mouth. Widow and five wee kids. This lady went to the union boss and a few miners were standing around in the office and she said what was happening.

That night a bunch of the boys went around to this man's house on the edge of town, a big house, trees around it, and when he came to the door nobody said anything but they just grabbed him and dragged him down his driveway to where the tar was. Hot but not burning hot and they tore off his clothes and over him, from head to foot, went that tar. By the way, nobody was drunk. Not one. I said tar and feathering. I just used the thing that way. It was tar and gravelling, and one lad put a rope around this bastard's feet and another under his arms and they rolled him back and forth, pulled him up and down in the loose gravel and dust of his own lane. You never, never saw such a mess.

Then one lad he leaned down and he asked this bastard if he could hear him, and the guy went, nod, nod, yes. I got down on one knee and I said close to his face, 'Don't you raise that widow's rent one red cent. You got that?' He never did."

———————————— • ————————————

The Big Fence Rip-off

"I can't remember the year, but it doesn't matter. There was no work in the Okanagan and I walked through to Princeton from Keremeos and then took my chances over the old Dewdney Trail through the mountains and my grub was gone and by the time I got to the Twelve Mile Ranch I was pretty done in.

Now that ranch, let me tell you, it was a going concern in those days, big barns, championship cattle, fancy horses, quite a lay-out. The owner was a mining promoter, and while the place wasn't making money it didn't have to because he was promoting, and in those days that was like having your very own mint.

To make a short story long, I hired on with a haying gang there, mostly Indians and bums like me, and if you know haying, that bottom land hay, it is heavy and thick, and you sweat. I worked six days and got my pay on Saturday night and it was exactly, and I'm not fooling you about this, it was $1.20. That is 20 cents a day and board. Food was good because it came from the place, most of it, and lots of it. There was a Chinaman cooking.

I stewed all Sunday and next day the foreman, one of those bandy-legged little Englishmen, he told me he was putting me out with a team to pull stumps. For 20 a day? I asked. For 20 a day, says he. He said to get on out there as the owner was coming out from the city that morning and liked to see everyone working. The stableman got me a team. Big pair of draft horses and they were strong. That outfit sure kept their stock in good shape.

Well, being a dumb kid I figured I'd see the owner so I did my pulling along the trail out to Hope and pretty soon, about 11 or so, along he comes riding a big shiny horse and on a saddle that would keep a family in grub for a year. I whoaed my team and walked over and respectfully told him who I was and that 20 cents for a full day, especially haying and pulling stumps, just wasn't right. I told him they were slave wages and I wasn't any man's slave, and he turned to one of his friends who were in a smart little wagon and he said that if this thing kept on another year or two – and he meant the hard times – people like this, meaning me, would be glad to work for him all day for nothing, just grub and a blanket.

That was my answer. Jesus, but I was mad. I pulled another stump and then I said to hell with it. I had nothing back at the bunkhouse but a shirt and shaving stuff and a study book and I was about half a mile out of sight, so I sort of angled, not too deliberately, but kinda steered that team towards a corner of the fence where a gate was set in. The chain sort of caught in the logs and when the team felt that on the chain they dug in and pulled, and that goddamned barbed wire was strong and those cedar posts were tough, but they was set in soft ground, a lot of peat, and about 200 yards of fence just peeled out like you was peeling a banana. It was kind of a pretty thing to see, them coming out that way. I got those horses moving hard down the trail – more of a road because of the ranch traffic – and they dragged and hauled that banana peel of fence, wire and posts, oh they must have hauled it another 200 yards until it started getting all balled up and caught in trees and the like.

I unhooked those fellows and put on their feed bags, tied the reins to a tree and just walked on down that road, right into Hope, and I hopped a freight into Vancouver and I never heard another word about it.

If that owner hadn't ripped me right down the middle with his snotty remark and had acted like a Christian, he'd have had the best damned farm-hand around.

That's what it was like for some big shots in those days. If you had it, keep it and get more, and screw the little guy."

High Noon In The Relief Office

"You'd walk into this office which was in the basement of a firehall downtown and that's where they passed out the cheques, the vouchers. You know, the relief. One guy on each line, but one guy, a rat, was the boss.

One line for married men and women. Another for single guys. Don't ask me why. Don't ask me about anything in those days.

I was in the single line and there was several women in the family line and at noon the boss, this little jerk, slapped his hand down and said to come back at 1.30. Some of these women had been standing in line for three hours. Their kids were crying.

I said where was his assistant, the guy who handled the other line. My line. This boss was trying to do both jobs and he was a real creep. He wouldn't answer but I stepped in front of him, and then he said he'd fired him the day before because there wasn't enough work for two, and was it any of my goddamn business anyway?

I reached over, and he was a little jasper, and I grabbed him by the tie and I said it was my goddamn business and there was enough work for two guys or even four, so he was going to stay in line and look after these women until they was finished, and if he missed his lunch and supper too, then he could just go piss up a rope. And every time I wanted to make my point I jerked up on his tie and bounced my fist off his chin and he looked like he was strangling. I asked if he understood. You're goddamn right he understood. I told him if he tried to call the police then he should call an ambulance too because I was going to stand there and see he looked after those poor miners' wives and their little kiddies and by God, he got that work done and everybody else in that place got finished with too.

He said he was going to report me, that I'd be off the dole. I said if he did that then I'd beat the daylights out of him and drop him down the old Number Three colliery. I meant it.

He said he knew who I was, he had my file and I'd be cut off. I told him, I said, 'I know these women. I know their husbands, too, and when I tell them what is happening down here, they are going to come up with me this time next week and when we walk in that door you are going to have my voucher, my cheque ready and you'll be serving these poor starving women, and if you call in every cop in Cape Breton, it still won't matter a bit to you because you will look like an alley cat that has been hit by a main line locomotive.' And I told him to get that assistant back.

That was the last of that little fandango. There wasn't enough of it in those days, not enough of the poor and kicked around goddamned Nova Scotia miner sticking up for his rights. Those were very hard times."

———————————————— • ————————————————

A Very Ugly Story

"It was always very interesting to me, even then, to see how money worked upon a man's personality, how it coloured, almost dictated his every action. Here's an example. In about 1933, I worked with the Hastings Mill people north of Campbell River. The pay was about $35 a month. We worked six days, Christmas off, and if they wanted you to work the Lord's Day, then you worked. There were plenty who wanted those jobs.

My best friend, we'd have died for each other, was a Calgary boy, and I'd grown up with Frank, we went to school together and rode the rods to the coast together.

We worked in this woods gang, about 15 or 20 of us, and Frank worked the donkey, stoking it, oiling it and keeping an eye on the pressure gauges. The job didn't pay any more than us on the ground but when our straw boss, sort of an assistant foreman, was killed by a falling snag the superintendent gave Frank that job. Apparently watching those gauges did mean something. I think my pay was a buck-thirty a day and the straw boss got one-forty a day and a lot of paper work to do. No union there. It was fine if you wanted to be a superintendent one day when you were getting on towards 50 years old.

The day Frank took over he showed up on the job with new clothes, khaki hat, khaki shirt, khaki pants. All dressed up and no place to go. That's what we thought. Under that round and happy face there was a dictator. First, he fired an old guy who wasn't much use but did a lot of other things, bringing water, patching us up if we got nicked, cutting laces out of deer skin for our boots, that kind of stuff. Generally useless, but useful too. Every camp has one. Frank sent him packing his ass off down the track and that was that.

Then he started in on me. His best friend. Told me to smarten up, said I'd been dogging it for months, yah yah yah. I gave it back to him and he pointed his finger at me and said, 'One more crack out of you and you follow Old Billy down the track.' It went on like this all that morning until he made everybody pretty aware that he was boss.

Some wit came up with the nickname for him, 'Old Ten-cent Cigar' which was now the difference between his daily wage and ours. One thin dime. He made life miserable, and to this day it has made an astonishing difference in the way I've treated men since. I saw the utter contempt that men, all his equals and some better, had for a man like him. It was like taking a cover off a roast of beef and finding it swarming with maggots. He never understood, either. Just drive, drive, drive, and the more he did the more we dug in, but he always had an excuse for the superintendent or the foreman on why we weren't getting the logs out.

He was clumping along the board walk from the cookhouse back to the tents one night when somebody stepped up behind him and damn near killed him. He lay in the mud until he came to, and nobody made a move to even roll him over to see if he was alive. And yet, that man never caught on.

He's a fairly important man in Vancouver now, his name is in the papers sometimes, and I wonder about this often. Was he always a rat and I just never saw it, or did he become one overnight because he wanted that extra ten cents a day, or did he want to keep that job because of ambition and didn't know of any other way to do it? Power. He wanted that. I know one thing. He didn't have to work hard at being such a shit. It just came natural, overnight."

———————————— • ————————————

One Day On The Frontier

"Once, it was up in Edmonton, I'd just got out of Prince Albert *(the penitentiary)* for breaking into a box car at Estevan. Three years that time. Why I did it at Estevan I'll never know, for there ain't no place around there, just farmers, where you can sell the stuff. Never even had a chance to see what was in the car. Boom, the bulls were on me soon as I bust that seal. The town on my release ticket said Edmonton, so that was my hometown. I didn't ask for Edmonton, but in them days it was as good a place as any. Had a good soup kitchen until I hear the boys wrecked it.

I got out with a guy named Charlie and when we got to Edmonton we were checked twice between the C.N. station and Jasper Avenue, east Jasper down around 97th where the boys hung out. The boys in blue seemed to know we was in town.

Fellow came into the cafe, asked anyone if they wanted a job. Seems he was hiring two men for a packing house. I said I'd take it, and I told my mate to come along. I wanted company, but nobody else said yes so we went out and got in the guy's truck, and before we got in I said what's the rate, what were we going to get paid, and he said the rate was 35 cents an hour. Now,

mister, that wasn't bad. But you should have seen the work. Backbreaking.
Just plain backbreaking. More than that. Ever seen a side of beef off a big
steer. Dressed. Would you say about 150 pounds? Well, Charlie and I hauled
them things all day. Even the Hunkies wouldn't do that kind of work. Just
the white men they could get. Lift one of those hind quarters off the hook,
heft it onto the old shoulder, walk about 25 steps into what they called a
freeze room – Goddamned cold let me tell you – and hook it up again. Six
hours we did that.

Quitting time we staggered, and I mean staggered to the office for our pay
and the clerk said, 'Oh, you're part time.' Mr. Somethingorother, forget his
name, would pay us. 'He's down on East Jasper' and he gave us an address
down on East Jasper.

Well, Charlie and me hiked in, it wasn't far, and Charlie said there was
somethin' fishy here and I could but agree with him and we knew when we
got there and saw the door sign. It said the guy was a hiring agent, you know,
employment firm. Well we went in and a big guy came to the counter and I
said 'Harmon and Mitchell.'

The fellow said six hours and then said a buck-twenty each and I said bullshit! Charlie said quietly, 'Mister, six hours at 35 cents works out to $2 and 10
cents. Now fork it over.' We knew the packing house was paying this outfit for
getting us on, that's the way the decent ones worked it, and here was this little
jerk-off outfit trying to gouge us on 15 cents. The big guy said, 'It is $2 and 10
cents, and our agency fee is 15 cents an hour, and it is $1 and 20 cents for you.'

I guess he saw Charlie tensing up because he turned and yelled, 'Paw, will
you come out here and explain to these two punks what it's all about.'

I said, 'I know what it's all about, mister,' and then the little guy came out
and I told him off. He said he didn't work for the packing house, but just hired
for them. Charlie said he made out in the cafe like he worked for the packing
house and never told us he didn't. It went back and forth, and then the big
guy, this bastard of a son, said, 'Shit, quitting time. Here's your money and
get out before I call the cops,' and we did. What else could we do? One day
out of P.A. and in trouble again. Whew!

So we left and went down a side street towards a cafe and it was getting
dark but I spotted the old man's truck. Charlie did too. He said let's go, and
we waited and hid down on the far side. Nobody could see us, we were in a
lane. Soon a door closed and we heard those guys coming and I went around
one side and Charlie the other. He took the big guy, the son, and Charlie was

as hard as a sack of packed concrete and he took the guy with one fat punch right behind the jaw. Jesus, it whomped like you was throwing a baseball for all you were worth against a barn door. I never even gave the old man a chance to yell. Just bang, bang, bang, bang, and that was the end of him. We stood around kicking them for a while, just for the fun of it, and I'll bet you to this day that big guy still rubs his bones in wet weather. I went a little easy on the old man, but I guess I bust his jaw with a kick. Felt something give. And I stamped on his hand, breaking the fingers. Made sure it was his right hand, his writing hand where he put down all those nice figures. We went through their pockets and got their wallets. There was about $400 in the old man's and the big kid had about $120 as I remember. We walked away from there fast, and grabbed a cab about four blocks over and got out of that about a mile away and got another and then walked over to a hotel after picking up our suitcases at the station. Next day the papers had a story about two guys badly beaten and robbed in an alley, but they was okay. Didn't say why. Just robbery. If the police looked at the last two names on that work sheet, and saw the names Gerald Harmon and Charlie Mitchell, they weren't going to find them in that dumb town. They wasn't our real names.

We left for the coast on the train two days after."

Minus One Vanilla Milk Shake

"I wasn't a bad kid. In fact, I guess you could say I was a model boy, and that had no connotation of being a sissy either. Football, which is soccer today. Hockey, which I played well and could have gone much further. Excellent marks in school. But they were hard times, very hard times. I needed a job desperately, everybody needed a job desperately in Regina and I got one with a neighbourhood druggist.

Not a bad fellow, actually. He paid 10 cents an hour, and you made deliveries, swept the floor, carried the empties out to the back room. I think I could have run that store quite well if I had stayed a couple of years. Magazines, milk shakes and cigarettes. The prescription end of his operation was almost nil so it was a straight sales operation. I made 10 cents an hour, and that was summer, spring and autumn which was fine, and winter which was sheer hell. Pushing a bike with a loaded carrier around those streets, ice, slippery, and a Regina street was all ruts. I even worked all Christmas Day, and New Year's Eve, and Sundays, and for about 25 hours' hard work. And remember I was going to high school at the time, I would get $2.50, and maybe, if it was a special season or occasion, maybe 50 cents in tips. Let me tell you, it was not a very lucrative job, but $2.50 was almost enough to put us over the top and give the family just enough extra food to live on. For that we were grateful to Mr. Abercrombie.

But Mr. Abercrombie was not the most lovable of men. In fact, Scrooge would have been Santa Claus if they had lived on the same street. He'd skin a louse for its hide and tallow, as we used to say. So we get to the great disillusionment. It was one summer night and about midnight and I'd cranked down the awning and swept the store and got things shipshape and Mr. Crombie – that was it, Crombie, not Abercrombie – asked if I would like a milkshake. He said I'd worked hard that day, and I said thank you and I'd like vanilla and he made me one, a big foaming one. Drug stores had soda fountains in those days, milk whips, milk shakes, sodas, banana splits, that type of thing. Then when we were locking up he handed me my pay. He always paid at the end of each shift. I put it in my pocket and when I got home, well I counted it and it was 10 cents short. It should have been 60 cents and it was 50 cents. I couldn't figure why, and Mr. Crombie certainly had never made a mistake before.

Next night I asked him, and this is what he said: 'Why, Dick, that's right. Six hours, 60 cents, minus one vanilla milk shake, 10 cents. Total, 50 cents.' I think I could have killed him, or set fire to his store. But I didn't, I just kept quiet and went about my business, cleaning around, deliveries. And you must remember, it was my first experience with a small businessman in the realm of money. But I honestly felt he had offered me that shake as a bonus for a good day's work on one of those dreadfully hot days of August.

I told Harry Roya, a kid who delivered for a grocer, and he said I should just get it back. And I did. Believe me, I did. For months. I stole Kodak films, and I'd sneak behind the counter when he was downstairs in the toilet and I'd steal a few packs of French safes from the secret drawer, and I stole iodine and cigarettes and cigars and magazines, and I'd sometimes push the coke lever down when he wasn't around and let the syrup run into the sink and, My God, when I think of it, I took things I would never use in a thousand years. I guess I could have stocked my own drugstore. Most of the stuff I just pushed down a sewer but I sold the cigarettes, and gave the cigars to my Dad and he appreciated them, and I used the film. I've never figured out how much I stole, but it must have run into the hundreds of dollars over several months.

Crombie never suspected, as far as I know. Then I got an offer from another store at 15 cents an hour and decent hours and I left and Mr. Crombie said he was sorry to see me go because I was a good lad, a hard worker. And I'll tell you this, when I went over to that other drug store I never stole a cent's worth of goods. Not one cent.

All for a 10 cent vanilla milk shake. Incredible when you think of it, isn't it? For 10 cents. And remember, I was a model boy. As Mr. Crombie said, a fine lad, a hard worker."

--------------------------------●--------------------------------

An Eye For An Eye

"Yes, looking back I guess we were a stupid and passive lot, just a bunch of statistics that were brought up in Parliament every year. So many unemployed, percentage for Ontario up or down, with season fruit picking help thrown in to make the picture look better than it really was. It was bad. I was 16 and I hiked, I didn't hitchhike, I hiked down to Simcoe because they had a good peach and apple crop that year and, of course, knowing nothing about the fruit business I got there at least a month too early.

I wasn't in any way going back to Toronto, to that house with a drunken father, a harassed mother and five other kids, so I went into the newspaper office and I asked the girl if she knew anybody who was hiring. Right off, she pointed to an ad in the paper which was going out that day and she said if I'd scoot off to this farm, well maybe. Then she said I could use her phone and I got the farmer and built myself up and he said to come out. I guess he regretted that. Hell, the man has to be in his grave these past 10 or 20 years, but I'll bet his daughter remembers. Anyway, that comes later.

I went out and he had a fine farm, cattle and forage crops and fruit, acres and acres. Yes, he'd hire me. Two dollars a week, food, and I could sleep in the back room of the equipment shed. What's $2 now? Nothing. In 1934 it was okay. Not great, but okay. I worked a month, hard work. God, have you ever made hay in July in Southern Ontario in the afternoon and no water jug in the field? Rough.

Then the pickers started to come in and I thought my deal with the farmer was that when picking started I would go on picker's rates. That's what I thought. He saw me working with the gang and I had my tally book along with the rest and I was making good money, up to $3 a day and also helping milk his herd, Holsteins, and they take a lot of milking, but I felt I owed it to him. I felt that because I had hired on to milk, and I was being decent. A point here too. He knew that I was picking fruit and being tallied by the checkers. He *knew* that.

Okay, it was about a five week harvest all told, and when the big pay-up time came I was in line with the rest. He asked me what I was doing there. I told him. He said, 'Oh, no, buster, you're a farm hand. You're no picker. You know what you were hired for.' He handed me my tally book, and I put it back on the table. It was set up on the lawn. He took it and just like that, he tore it in half. Up until this time I had thought he was a good guy, and now he was trying to beat me out of more than a hundred dollars. I remember saying, 'God damn you, Sylvester,' and he reached out over the table and whacked this little guy, which was me, a brutal one right across the mouth and I went down.

The other guys were, well, what the hell could they do. Half hadn't been paid off yet and he could have called the provincials *(the police)* and said he had a farm workers' mutiny on his hands. Then it really would have been good-bye to their wages. This farmer said, 'I'm paying you off when these men are through, and at your own rate. Then get off the place. Go down that road and don't come back.'

After the pay-off, I got my 12 bucks and he said, and I remember him clearly, 'Your week isn't up until midnight tonight. Put on a clean shirt and pants and help park the cars behind the barn and keep a watch on them and when they're gone, well, you just clear out.' I remember those words. What he meant was this. His eldest daughter was getting married the next weekend and he was having all his friends in for a big garden party and dance on the lawn. We spent the next two hours laying down a rented dance floor, a small one, and putting and rubbing on talcum and stringing up those foolish Japanese lanterns and setting up tables for food and drink. The guests started coming about seven. They could park themselves because we'd put out lines of whitewash on the grass so they knew where to go, and I went back to my bunk and wrapped my few worldly goods in my windbreaker. Then I got out my big jacknife and I went over to the forge and I sharpened that knife like it had never been done before. Then I got a roll of electrician's tape.

I guess you know what I was going to do. I hid the windbreaker in the big hedge down the lane and when it was dark I started keeping watch on those cars. There were big cars from Brantford and London and Toronto and

Oakville, from Woodstock, all over. When the party was going good I took that electrician's tape and I taped the open knife to the bottom of my shoe. Put it on hard and tight, no budging about, and then I began to walk up and down the lines of cars and of course, anybody could see I was doing a good job of guarding. Yes sir. But at every car I'd kick each tire a couple of times with my right toe. Sssst! Ssssst! Ssssst! It didn't take me more than 20 minutes, I guess, and then I unwound the tape, walked over to some bushes and threw it away, put the knife in my pocket and went to the big caragana hedge and picked up my windbreaker. Then I walked down the road and I was whistling.

On the highway I got a ride right away, into St. Thomas, and then I stayed there in a park and went down to Port Stanley and stayed there a couple of days and even there I heard about the vandal who had punctured about 500 tires at a farm party over by Simcoe. Of course, they were wrong. It was only 192 tires. I know, I counted them. God, but there must have been guts to clean that night.

The only time I've ever been really mean in my life. It was fun."

———————————— • ————————————

Dead Dog Down A Well

"Some very bad men lived in Maine in those days. Those hard times. They were French like us, those farmers with their big fields but different kind of French. Call themselves Franco-Americans with the nose, the nose high in the air. Five, six generations they were our families once here in Quebec, this province, but now they are something special. When we would go down there to pick their potatoes, those guys would call us 'those Canucks' like a person was saying 'those Ne-groes.' You understand?

We used to go down in the wagons, families, old people and baby children. You understand? An old woman could mind the babies, keep the eye on them. Even a little boy could carry potato pails to the bin. All worked. We took our food, pickled and boiled fish in jars this big, smoked too, and deer, vegetables.

You could say these were our relatives, they should be our friends, don't you think, but they would cheat. We'd work two weeks, they'd pay us for the first week, one week in the fields, their potatoes, that is very hard work, bent over all the time and say, 'Get in your wagons and go. There is no pay for you.

I'll call the Immigration and if those guys come, you are headed for jail.' What could we do, I ask you? We went. This happened lots of times.

Their noses in the air, eh? They say we will go to jail for going into the United States wrong, and they don't have to pay us. They got the law. Then they wonder why their barn burns down or somebody kills a dog or a porcupine and drops it in their well at night. They didn't have to wonder far. I can tell you the easy answer!"

CHAPTER THIRTY-ONE

The Rosy Pictures Of The Timid Press

Who Were They Fooling? . . . Good Days in Moncton . . . The People Got Lost in The Numbers . . . Everything But The Bad News . . . It Was A Gay, Exciting World.

———————————— • ————————————

If there are ten men in a bread line in January and four more in February and eight more in March and so on, six and three and 11 and 14, at what point in time does the local newspaper, studying City Hall's figures, declare that the city faces an unemployment emergency?

Never.

These men in the growing line-up, the increase at the Salvation Army old clothes depot, the emergence of a hobo jungle in the east end of town, the five percent cut in wages at the flour mill, the discharge of ten clerks at the department store, these all were meaningless in themselves. In the big picture, they meant a great deal. Hard times ahead, or already here. But they actually were only statistics, in monthly reports or year-end statements. And the papers never took on the job of tying it all together. The role of the Canadian press in the Depression was a strange one.

———————————— • ————————————

Who Were They Fooling?

"Wherever you went, newspapers in Canada worried about the survival of the country. That is to say, if the country went down, so would they, and the country – and especially the Prairies and Quebec and the Maritimes – was in the worst shape.

So they tended to put the best gloss on things they could and I guess you couldn't blame them. So, in 1933 and '34 when things were very bad, when the prairie farm economy was reeling and in a deficit position and cities were going bankrupt and the stock market wasn't worth looking at, with stocks which were $40 and $60 down to $3 and $4, at that time, the newspapers painted a rosy picture.

Stories which would really only be worth three or four paragraphs buried on the financial page would get an eight column, 48 point bold headline, and the stories were about a sale of maybe 25,000 bushels of apples to be shipped to Hawaii or a three percent increase of lumber exports through Vancouver, or the fact that such and such a liner would make a special call at Halifax or that dried cod shipments to Jamaica were up by $5,000 for the quarter, or news about construction of a $100,000 addition to a shoe factory or a Canada Packers plant. Such piddling things. Really piddling things.

You've got to wonder who they thought they were fooling, especially when the actual indicators, the New York board and the Canadian Exchange and the price of wheat on the Winnipeg Grain Exchange and the relief figures, and talk about riots or semi-riots, and your neighbours moving down into the poor end of town because the factory had failed, all these indicators were showing that things were bad. But they weren't reported with the same prominence as these piddling little things, like a small order of Okanagan apples to Honolulu.

So who were these editors actually fooling?

Not the public. Of that I am sure. They could look around and see the old ways didn't work. Not any more. With pretty well every farmer on the ropes, and about a quarter of the working men on relief and another 50 percent just hanging on, taking wage cuts and short weeks and so forth and only about 25 percent making out okay, the country knew something was very wrong."

———————————— • ————————————

Good Days In Moncton

"I began to work in, I think it was 1934. This was on the Moncton paper. I used to work six days a week. Start off at two in the afternoon, work to five, cover city hall, the police station to see who they had in jail, the courts, the hotels in town and sometimes some sports. Then I'd go back to the office, write my stuff, go home to supper and be back at eight o'clock at night and work until six o'clock in the morning for $5 a week. Editing. Head-writing. Layout. Reading proof. Everything but running the press, almost.

That used to get me through the whole week and I saved more money proportionately than I do now. And I gave my mother $2 for my board. So I had $3.

I can't say we covered the Depression. You grew with it. It just came, and every year it just got worse. You just didn't think it could get worse. The railroad – and Moncton was a big rail centre – laid off more and more men. The lumber industry was very bad. Everybody would say next year it would get better. But it never did. It just kept on and on.

I was doing okay. Five dollars a week. Paying my mother board. A big 50 cents meal at Alcorn's Cafe on Saturday night. My own clothes. I was doing fine."

———————————— • ————————————

The People Got Lost In The Numbers

"In the Depression, on the prairies in particular, the newspapers were faced with the problem and worry about survival. No matter what happened they tended to put the best gloss they could on it. I've used the phrase 'the descent of an ice age,' to describe the relief thing, it came so slowly and then it was there, and it was there, and it was there for ever, and there was nothing to do about it. It just got gradually worse. And the newspapers just didn't cover it.

The city hall reporter once a week went down to the relief committee meeting where the finance report was read and there was a report on the numbers who were on relief. And aside from that, there was no reporting job done. It would get into the legislature and it would get into the numbers game and the picture would get lost. The people would get lost in the numbers. The poverty, the despair, the desolation. I lived through the damn thing as a reporter on the prairies and I know this is the way things got ignored.

After the war, years after, people would say, 'Well, you were in it, on relief, what was it like?' and I'd tell stories about what it was like to go down to the place to get relief. I was kind of an amusement centre, Jimmy Gray will now tell you what it was like to be on relief. No one knew except the people who had suffered.

God knows, so many suffered, but it was a different Depression on the farms, the prairies, a different kind of economy, and different in Ontario, the industrialized part of Canada, and far different in Quebec and, of course, the Maritimes was a different story altogether. In 1945 I was told that somebody should do the story of the Depression and by the time I got the manuscript to the publisher, top people had changed and the reaction now was, 'Who the hell wants to read about that?' "

(The manuscript in question was finally published in 1966. Under the title of "The Winter Years," James Gray's book soon established itself as a Canadian classic.)

———————————— • ————————————

Everything But The Bad News

"We never really covered the news. Here it was, this Depression busting about all around us, and Canadian newspapers didn't cover it. They didn't ignore it, but they didn't send reporters out to hustle, and I think there was a couple of reasons for this. First, the Depression, especially in the Maritimes and in the West, was part and parcel of everyday life, woven right into the fabric. What was the point in sending a reporter out to cover an eviction or a bread line dispute? Remember, even in the hardest-hit places, say Saskatchewan, life went on and on and on. There was still police court to cover, and city hall, the courts, the hotels-and-rails beat because people still travelled, and newspapers had a lot more sacred cows than they have now and they were reported, and the papers were filled up with much more social news, and sports was big, very big, the World Series, the Stanley Cup, the big Joe Louis fights, Jimmy McLarnin from Vancouver, and then it was a crazy time. There were fads, and six-day bike races, and dirigibles crossing the Atlantic, and expeditions up the Amazon, the newspapers then were just jammed with all that stuff.

Mind you, the big things of the Depression got handled, premiers' conferences, Bennett's pronouncements saying the poor were just too goddamn lazy to get out and get jobs, the Rowell-Sirois hearings into Canada's economic depression, some mayor saying he was going to kick all the bums off the relief roles, the weather which affected the wheat and the fall-off of wheat prices, and news like that.

But the day-to-day nuts and bolts of it all was just something everybody got used to. Life went on, and I guess I could say it went on just about the way it had, but everybody had a lot less to spend if they had taken pay slashes or had been laid off.

We never covered the rooster towns, the shack towns, the places with living quarters made of cardboard and wooden boxes. We never covered, not on any paper I was on, the hobo jungles, or only did if there was a murder or the cops cleaned one out. The trains hauling in box cars of clothing and fruit and vegetables from Ontario, they didn't get any play. I think nobody wanted to admit the West was on a charity basis with the East. No reporter that I know of was ever sent to live on the slop handed out at soup kitchens. Hell, I could go on and on, but you get the picture.

Newspaper editors just weren't aware, but if they were, they kept that awareness to themselves because they could tread on a lot of big toes in civic and provincial government, and that meant nothing but trouble for them. Another thing is, of course, that the reporters themselves never thought that the nitty-gritty, the real story of the Depression, was worth covering. They all had this, 'Screw you, Jack, I'm in the lifeboat,' attitude.

We didn't cover the Depression because it was not in the best interests of our publishers and the stockholders to do so, but I will admit that papers in Western Canada did a better job than those in the East. But they had to, because the Depression and the drought and the foreclosures and the misery was around them in such profusion that to deny it or ignore it would have been to deny that the sun came up in the morning.

We didn't cover the Depression the way a first class newspaper would now, but in defence of all of us, people were just so goddamned sick of the whole business that I don't think they wanted to read any more about it. In this sense, the newspapers were doing their job, reflecting the wishes of the reader. Crazy, isn't it?"

———————————— • ————————————

It Was A Gay, Exciting World

"Looking back, I can still marvel at the way life went on, as though there was no Depression, that life was as it always had been. It was as it had been before, of course, but with a difference.

Men and women and children were dying of starvation in Vancouver. I've seen them dead. Cause Of Death? Malnutrition, starvation, no food, weakness, the inability to withstand the winter's cold, and that was because they had no lodgings. Perhaps only a fire of packing cases burning under the Georgia Viaduct or on the False Creek Flats.

Newspapers didn't report this news, on page one or elsewhere. The inside pages were filled with sports and society. Sports was a terrific source of interest. Vancouver, Canadian, American, international. If you didn't have a team in every sport and were ready to fight to the death defending that team, Aston

Villa in the English League or Chicago White Sox or Montreal Maroons, why you just weren't a red-blooded Canadian boy. A very great interest in sport. It was all vicarious, of course. A newspaper cost only five cents.

There was great interest in the comings and goings of society. Far more than now. Column after column and pictures by the score, the Junior League promoting a dog show or a spring dance. Always something. Do they still have a Junior League now? Hadassah was big. So were the many women's institutes. Special days at the races. Skating parties at the arenas. Dances and balls when every woman was listed, along with a detailed description of what she wore. The women would send in the information days before the event. Military balls. Gymkhanas. Cricket matches. The Royal Vancouver Yacht Club, a function every weekend, it seemed, and plenty of ink.

Every newspaper across Canada and in the United States always played up the silver lining. Except it was a gold lining. There were no such things as starvation, hunger marches, store front windows being kicked in. Yes, they were reported, but always these were called incidents and incited by 'highly-paid professional agitators.' Communists. I knew some of these agitators and many were like you and me. Far from being professional agitators, and, for Christ Sakes, not highly-paid. Anything on unions, it got back on page 37 under the late classified ads.

One editor once told me newspapers were as concerned as any other business with making a dollar, showing more black ink than red ink, and they had to play up the town, the economy, the future, and by Jesus, play it up they did.

And the reason? Big business. The clique of businessmen who ran every town. If the newspaper played it down the line, their line, then they would get those full page advertising lay-outs from the big stores, all those quarter and half pages. But if the word on page one was gloom and sadness, then the 'Vancouver Sun' would get that advertising and the 'Province' would be in trouble. It was big business playing two gutless wonders off against each other.

They were always running editorials, puffing Vancouver up with hot air, with sentences which would read something like this – "The decision of the dash-dash-dash company to invest $80,000 in a new annex can be considered a monument to the forward looking attitude and that high optimism which has made Canada so progressive in a highly competitive world." Dah dah dah dah dah dah, et cetera.

No word of Depression. Tens of thousands out of work. Relief a lousy $10 a month for a family of four. We're raring to go. Just watch our speed. Gung ho.

And, of course, for the 75 or 80 percent of wage earners who were still hanging in there, it was no see-no want to see. They didn't want to hear of the other 25 percent and of bread lines and hunger marches and socialists, just as long as they were getting a monthly wage and scraping through each year with only a 10 or 15 percent pay cut. They were the ones who bought the newspaper. So the publisher had his powerful business and political friends applauding him and the 75 percent employed, often at starvation wages, were silent as the grave. He couldn't lose. It was a pretty dingaling publisher who went broke those years.

Nobody cared, it seemed. Oh, some newspapermen cared, the working ones who were able, day after day, to see the news ignored. There was nothing dramatic about people starving slowly, or children fading away from malnutrition, or the long lines at the soup kitchens day after day after week after month after year. But they had their consciences and that is why the good ones embraced the socialist movement, the organized Commonwealth Co-operative Federation, when it came along. That is why so many newspaper types are socialist-bent today. Not Communists. Too much sense for that. Not pinko either. Just intelligent people with a sense of social justice and a yearning, deep inside, to try and put things right.

Of course, their fight was a lost one from the start.

There was one columnist, Bob Bouchette, a fine writer. He drowned, and whether he drowned himself or he just drowned, we'll never know. He was one of the ones I am talking about. But it was, 'Oh, Bob's up on his soapbox again.' When he was being sarcastic, those idiots who okayed their firm's advertising budgets thought he was funny. Clever. Isn't it something for a newspaperman to be able to write so good. Ha ha! When he took off on them, they always thought he was writing about some other guys. When he slammed into the government, it was okay if he was slamming the party the big shots were against. When he wrote about the little guy in the rain, sleeping under cardboard in an alley, that was called human interest. Interesting, but it couldn't happen in Vancouver. He made most of it up, didn't he?

So maybe Bouchette did walk into English Bay that night and swim west until he could swim no more and then he drowned."

CHAPTER THIRTY-TWO

Law And Order

The Man With The Brick ... Crime On The Prairies ... Crucified On A Boxcar ... Brian On The Hillside ... The Railroad Bull ... All Good Guys ... Avoiding Relief Camps ... A Kind And Gentle Man.

———————————— • ————————————

Retired policemen have told me that the men who rode the rods, the down-and-outs drifting from city to city, gave them the least trouble of all. "Just nice kids, like my own, travelling," one said.

I would have thought that men without a dime in their pockets or a decent coat on their backs, pushed from town to town by the law, would hit a point of desperation where they would borrow or steal a gun and rob the nearest bank, Chinese restaurant, or corner grocery store. This rarely happened. James Gray, writer and historian living in Calgary, says that after extensive research he found that crime actually dropped during the Depression years. Had people lost the will to commit armed robberies, murders, thefts from homes, stores, people?

Canada didn't have its John Dillingers, no Bonnie and Clyde duos. There were no gangs such as sprang up in the States. No extended rampages where bank after bank was knocked over, and lawmen killed.

There was rum running, of course. Millions of dollars, tens of millions escaped Canadian customs duty as the traffic to bone-dry America flourished from Atlantic to Pacific, but only the small fry were nabbed.

One type of crime soared, though, according to those who travelled the freight cars. It was a crime to ride free and to trespass on railroad property, and many men I interviewed who remembered those days believed that a railway bull, a cop, earned his pay in direct relationship to the number of skulls he could bounce his club on.

These men I interviewed felt that the railroad bull was a crime.

The Man With The Brick

"My father, a policeman, told me this one. The main police station in Winnipeg was on Rupert, a big red brick building which could only be a police station. One night in October there is this hell of a crash and a couple of cops rush out and there is this little guy standing outside with a brick in his hand. He's right outside a big plate glass window that has been smashed all to hell. Next day he pleads guilty and gets six months. Six months in Headingly Jail.

Another year goes by and the first hard frost of a night in October, bang! Sure enough, there is the little old man again, second brick ready if the first doesn't do the job. Up before the magistrate next morning, guilty, your honour, six or eight months in the can.

Next year, the first real cold night in October, the sergeant at the desk tells one of the beat men to stand just inside the door and if a little old man comes along with a brick, then grab the little bastard. Sure enough, about 10 o'clock, along he comes and the cop hauls him in, brick and all. The sergeant says, 'Okay, you're not going to Headingly this winter for a nice warm bunk and three meals,' and he tells the cop to lock him up and they'll put him on a bus for Regina or Kenora next morning, run him out of town. The little guy just laughs, grabs the brick off the sergeant's desk and hurls it just over his head, smash, right through the big window in the office. What are you going to do about a guy like that? So he gets another jolt in Headingly, and then the next year my Dad said he did the same thing in Regina. One way of surviving."

————————— • —————————

Crime On The Prairies

"There was crime. Sure. Always will be. Cocaine was the drug then. Every drug store would be knocked over two or three times a year by the boys. It was never any problem, or not as we recognized it as such.

There were the usual killings. Man murders wife. Neighbour kills neighbour. Domestic stuff and old feuds.

Some gangs, and they usually formed up in jail or the pen, they'd go on the merry-go-round and hit small towns, five or six break-ins in a night when the town cop was asleep or passed out, usually in the livery stable. We'd always get them. They left tracks like elephants in a dried-up river bed. Always the same types.

I don't know why but there seemed always to be good safecrackers on the prairies. Peel a can as slick as a banana. We knew who they were and sometimes if they got too busy we'd set them up. That's called entrapment now. Then, though, the chief pinned a medal on you for sucking them in.

A lot of violations under the Railway Act. Clipping the boys on the road, riding the trains. I'd tell the kids I'd meet that if a railroad bull told you to move, then you would move by running. The railways didn't hire nice old professors to do the job. Those guys were tough."

Crucified On A Boxcar

"I wasn't there, but I heard about it plenty. There was this railroad cop missing at Regina and they got some of the crews out searching the empty cars in the yards. They found him, nailed up just like Christ was, and his own billy club had been rammed up his ass. We often wondered if they did that to him when he was still alive or had he died. The whole thing was hushed up.

I'll tell you, there were railroad cops and railroad cops, but some of them guys who worked for the C.P.R. were the meanest bastards on the face of the earth."

Brian On The Hillside

"Our first baby died, little Brian, and we never did know from what. We'd gone north of Prince George to homestead and we hardly had a bean and the baby died within three days. Just turned blue and stayed that way until he died. I couldn't get out to a doctor because the wife was sick, too, so I tried the doctoring myself.

I made a little coffin and we put little Brian in it and as there were no cemeteries around anywhere, my wife and I decided to walk to a bluff looking out over the river where you could see a long way and it was peaceful. I carried the coffin on my shoulder and my wife carried the shovel and when we got there I dug the little grave and pounded in, no, I planted four small saplings, at each corner, and then we both said the Lord's Prayer, and I guess you could say that was that.

In a few days the road dried up enough you could get over it and as the wife seemed to be worsening I hitched up the team and drove her into town. The doctor was a decent sort and he gave her some medicine, didn't charge us for a big bottle. Just before we left he asked where the baby was and I said he had died and we'd buried him. The doctor said that was too bad, how sorry he was, and we went back home.

About a week later a policeman came to the shack and this man was a son of a bitch. He was all set to throw me in jail, not reporting a death, unlawfully disposing of a dead body, a lot of nonsense. I said to him that little Brian was peaceful out on that hillside, and my wife was crying by this time, and I said that if he didn't get off my property there was going to be one less policeman in this country. He left. In fact, he got out real quick and I expected to hear something more about that, threatening a policeman or something, but I never did. Not a word.

Those saplings must be real tall trees now. That was a long time ago."

———————————— • ————————————

The Railroad Bull

"Yes, I was one of those railroad bulls they still talk about. C.N.

You got to remember, there were two types of men out of work in those days, and I'm not counting your professional hobo. The two types were the married men, and they got relief, a pittance, hardly enough to buy lunch and two beers today, and they pretty well stayed home, and there were the single ones, the hoboes. I've seen them as young as 12 years old, but your run-of-the-mill chap was 19, 20, around there, up to 40 or so. Then the life got too hard. It was a hard life.

Sure, I used to talk to them. All the time. There was a great degree of hopelessness among them. They seemed to be numbed, you know, by what was happening. They were all decent fellows. I talked to lots of them. I'd talk to a fellow, say, who had ridden the rods all the way from Toronto and I'd say, 'What the hell do you expect out here? Winter comes, they'll find you frozen stiff in an alley.' Remember, this was in Edmonton at the time. Down to 40 below! Oh, they didn't know where to go. Mixed-up. Confused. No doubt about it.

There was some bitterness, but I put that down to the professional agitators. The Communists. The guys with the red card. They were having a real go of it at that time.

Did I ever detect a feeling of revolt? Impending revolt? No. Everybody was in the same boat. Fellows that had had good jobs were on the tramp, fellows who had worked in the construction trades, in steel mills, running

402 TEN LOST YEARS

machinery. Everybody was in the same boat. When you lined up at the soup kitchen it didn't matter who you were. A bowl of soup and a hunk of bread. They were just one identity. Just one identity. If you did have a revolution and it did work, who would you shoot and take his money? Nobody had any money. Nothing to make it worth your while.

People did some talking about reforming or changing the system in those days but they were the trained agitators. The ordinary guy only thought about money. Where he could get a job and get some money. There wasn't too much deep thinking in those days, and an awful lot of shallow thinking too, if you ask me. I mean at the government level."

— • —

All Good Guys

"When I graduated from Regina *(RCMP training school)* I was assigned to a small detachment on the main line of the C.P.R. Most of our work was with transients, men and boys and the odd girl riding the rods going from place to place. It could have been dangerous work because we were enforcing the Canadian Railway Act against riders and it was our job to get them off the trains. Not necessarily because we felt it was right, but because we had orders.

Often it was at night and I'd be alone, walking along a freight with only a flashlight. I'd pull open a boxcar and say, 'Okay, fellows, come on out, end of the line.' Something like that. Sometimes it would be raining or snowing. Usually it was dark. Somebody could just have reached out of the car and smashed me on the head with a stick or come up behind me with a stone, but it never happened. Not even the threat of it.

They were all good guys, just guys down on their luck, without jobs, travelling back and forth. They'd get out, grumbling a bit, but they were used to it, and they knew I was just doing my job. Maybe I didn't like this kind of police work but it was my job.

Those fellows were essentially good and decent. Life had just given them a dirty crack. That was all. When their chance came they took it and became good citizens, good Canadians."

— • —

Avoiding Relief Camps

"I remember this very well. I was a member of the B.C. Provincial Police, before the Mounties took over, and one of my jobs was, well, I was posted to a squad which kept an eye on single men. Unemployed single men. We used to check them a lot and they would have an unemployment card and on many of the cards there were letters 'C-L' on the top right hand corner and I was unaware what those letters designated.

I asked a stenographer and I wouldn't dare say what she told *(this was given on an open line radio show in Vancouver)* but it meant to say they were attending a clinic. Do you follow me? So this can be said without exaggeration, rather than be forced to go into the federal government's work camps and work all day for food and a roof and 20 cents a day in these camps, a lot of these men, and this is absolutely true, would get themselves a venereal disease so they could stay in Vancouver, remain in Vancouver, and attend a clinic. They were doing it the very hard way. Nobody wanted to go into those camps.

If they stayed in the city they wouldn't get paid, but anything was better than being sent into those camps. That's how bad it was."

A Kind And Gentle Man

"It is funny how things stick in your mind. After all those years, just some things stay.

I remember going to the Moncton Station one night to meet Daddy as he was coming back from somewhere, and there was a freight train coming in, from Montreal, I guess, and this was in the Depression and these young boys, young men were jumping off the box cars and running. There was this friend of ours, a neighbour, a very good friend of ours and I always thought the world of him, and there he was chasing these kids, you know, with a great big club and he was a great big brute of a man but as I said, I had only seen the gentle side, and I saw him chasing these kids and really hitting them with this stick and I just couldn't believe my eyes. I just could not believe my eyes. You see, he worked for the railway. This was his job.

You know, I've seen those boys, mostly from Western Canada, I'd say, I've seen those boys come in and sleep around our kitchen stove. Bunked for the night, you know. Maybe eight or so sometimes. We never turned a person away. If they knocked at our door they were welcome. Always welcome. My mother said she would never turn a boy away because it could be my brother next in some town somewhere far away. Whatever we had, they had part of it, and they were good boys. Not bad boys. Good boys.

I can still see this man I'd always looked up to, thought so much of, striking out with that club of his. Like that *(making a smashing movement)* and that, and that. Horrible.

Such a kind and gentle man, with his family, with the neighbourhood, the kids. I could never understand it. Never."

CHAPTER THIRTY-THREE

Was A Revolution Possible?

Agrarian Trade Unionists . . . There Was No Leader . . . The Regina Riot: One View . . . The Regina Riot: Second View . . . On The Road To Regina . . . A Minor Revolution . . . 100 Cuban Rifles . . . Nothing To Hope For . . . The Shape Of Their Heads.

———————————— • ————————————

Was a revolution in Canada possible? Some of the people I talked with believe that one would have broken out in Canada if the war had not come along. Others discount the idea on the grounds that there was no leader who could have organized and inspired such a revolution. Canada had no such leader. She had no man who even came within a country mile, although there were many men who might have been. A name crops up here, and another there, but they all faded away like the morning star.

Canada wasn't ready to accept Communism. There was still great faith that things would work out. What were a few bad years? The good years would come again. Maybe next year. And then the feeling was: "Who wants some Toronto Jews and some Russians, those Communists, to be telling us what to do?"

Communism never was any threat – although for theatrical and political reasons the government sometimes treated it so.

One newspaperman offered this theory. In British Columbia, which had considerable unrest, there was a standing militia. They made $2 a month on parades and summer camp. If they had been turned loose on a bunch of revolutionary marchers, the revolution would have been over in an hour. And why? Because by quashing the revolution they were making sure they were keeping their jobs in the militia – and their two bucks a month.

———————————— • ————————————

Agrarian Trade Unionist

"In districts where there was crops, everybody flocked there. I remember jungling up with a bunch of guys in a quarry waiting for the harvest gun to

fire off. This was by Portage La Prairie, in 1934. We were asking ourselves what
the day rate would be, talking it over.

In 1928, '27, before that, wages was up to $3 a day just for a common field
pitcher or stocker. Wheat was real high. We knew wages would drop because
of the times we was going through. Wheat was lower than whale shit. Didn't
call it the Depression then, I don't know where that word came from. Portage
La Prairie had good crops, and you know, that is some of the finest wheat land
in North America. Deep loam. With one part of that land and four parts of
pulverized granite and enough rain, you could grow a good crop. We knew
times was tough. Damn tough. So about 60 or 80 of us figured a dollar a day
and board and room would be enough. We wanted to be fair. Except them
farmers didn't want to be fair – they offered 50 cents a day. From sunup to
sunset. Damn right.

Nobody's gonna work for that, we said. Or *I* said. I was spokesman, 'We
want a dollar a day and everything found, that's what the boys in my union
want,' and I waved to the boys. They'd elected me spokesman. One man who
wasn't a farmer but owned farms said, 'Oh, you got a union now, have you?
Well, we've got the police,' and I said, 'Bring 'em on.' We weren't official. No
authorization. No affiliation, nothing. But by God, at that moment, we were
just as tight and organized as any union and remember, unions were a shit-
word in them days. So, yes, we got a dollar a day, and every man insisted on
collecting it each night.

One farm guy held off and the next day, with Sunday in between, luckily,
so we could pass the word, nobody went into his fields. A strike, you might
call it. Anyway, a wildcat. Well, there is nothing a farmer hates more than to
see a crew standing by while the sun is shining and the ground is firm, and
how is he to know the next day might bring rain, or even snow. So that was
the end of that nonsense.

I believe that might have been the first farm union of harvest hands in
Canada. I don't mean a political party in the light of being a union like in
Alberta and other places. That was made up of the farmers themselves. I'm
talking about us, the hands, the guys what they wanted to work for four bits
a day, and we weren't having any of their shit. It worked that year but I don't
know if it ever worked again. Of course, far as I know, they never offered men
50 cents a day again when the wheat was standing belly high and it would go
30 bushels. I don't think they ever stooped that low again, but it sure showed

a lot of guys they had to stick together if they wanted anything. Those farmers had us by the scruff of the neck until I decided to shake them out."

———————————— • ————————————

There Was No Leader

"I often wondered why there never was a revolution, or even a try at one. I've never considered the Regina Riots and the boxcar march anything more than a skirmish, a poor thing led by the Communists, and when all was said and done in those days, nobody really had much use for the Commies. I think the people who deluded themselves more than anyone in the Thirties were the Communists. They thought they had everything going for them, and really, they had nothing.

No, we didn't have a revolution, because what did you fight for? Canada? It was in rough shape even before the Depression. The U.S. was bad off, so no help from that quarter. They never even had much more than a ripple. Europe, nothing there either. It was as though we were all bogged down to our waists in swampy goo and had given up trying, but I think there would have been something if we had had a real leader, I mean a real dyed-in-the-wool Canadian leader with fire in his guts, lots of fire.

The C.C.F. were pussy cats, little intellectuals, a few farmers, no hope there. It didn't take Canadians too long to figure that one out, and even though I admire much of what the C.C.F. did, it was a far cry from what was needed. This country needed a leader and we got Prime Minister Bennett and then Mackenzie King, and if they weren't a couple of non-leaders, then I've never seen one. But there just wasn't that one man around, or if he was, he just didn't seem to be there at the time when we needed him most. We had no Roosevelt, to put it another way, if things were to be done in a legal and peaceful fashion, or a man with a musket and a dagger in his teeth if it was to be done by force. It was a sad situation, and it still exists today.

There really is no hope for Canada, you know."

———————————— • ————————————

The Regina Riot: One View

"I wouldn't say it was a riot, not at first. We were behaving peaceably enough there in Regina, and then the police on one side and the Mounties on the other started to pull the guys, our speakers, off the platform. There was whistles blowing and horses charging and you could say it was the police doing the rioting, clubbing and charging. We took it for a few minutes and then we let go, against them.

There might have been about 1,500 of us, all pretty pissed off, and those newspaper reports that there was about 4,000 of us was crazy. There never was more than 2,000 trek boys at any time. What the others were, they were Regina people down to Market Square to hear the speakers. Then when trouble started they were gone, just like that. Citizens of Regina, and not wanting any trouble.

It began for me after I'd been in a relief camp at Deroche which was about 50 miles up the Fraser Valley from Vancouver. We got bed and blankets, meals, tobacco and 20 cents a day. Not even two bits. Twenty cents a day to buy luxuries. The camp was lousy and the food was lousy. Oh, it was good enough food, I guess, but it was cooked so bad, in the same pots, not cleaned, day after day. There was fights over the smallest things, like a game of checkers and whose move it was, and the Reds, the Communists were everywhere. Whenever there was trouble beginning, they had been there before to start it or had their hats off fanning the flames. They were easy to spot, in fact, as I recall, they never made much of a try at saying they weren't. Most of them came from the Old Country.

I just can't remember why I walked out of the camp and headed for Vancouver but it had something to do with chickenshit regulations. Most of the administrators were First World War veterans, friends of politicians. The whole relief camp business, you must understand, was a political thing. They wanted all the young guys off the streets and stuck hellandgone up in the woods where they wouldn't start no revolution. That was a laugh. We did a lot of bitching but not much about revolution. That was just talk. I think the main thing was that we felt we were just dumped into the bush to rot, and the food was awful. That ass, Mayor Taylor of Vancouver, said the food we got was better than the food on his own table. If that is so, then his wife must have been married for her looks and sure as hell not her cooking.

About 100 of us got to Vancouver, hitching, in boxcars but a lot just plain walked. As I recall, we bunked down at the Ukrainian Hall and then a labour temple. People brought food, and I think the city helped out, and we had enough to eat.

I just can't remember too many of the details and I never believed anything I read in the newspapers. There was a few newspaper reporters along and they gave us a few laughs. They tried to be unemployed, trekkers, but they didn't dress right and they didn't act right and they sure as hell didn't know the lingo. How could they? We let them come along, though. The Communists were behind the whole thing, you know, from the beginning and I guess to the end, although a lot of them would fade out at the final curtain. They didn't believe in going to jail.

There was Arthur Evans, Art Evans, and he was a real hard nut but his trouble was he couldn't get along with anybody. Even with this, Evans could organize, but we all thought he was more of a front man. I was 19 at the time, or 20, and even I could see it took a lot more than one man to get a thing like this going. But he was doing something, and that was more than anybody else was doing. His idea, his speeches said that the only way to get things was to go down to Ottawa and see R.B. Bennett – now there was a man who was easy to hate – and get something going for us. Decent relief, or jobs. Evans insisted that we behave ourselves. No violence, none at all. No stealing, and that was going to crimp an awful lot of guys' style. Be polite. Thank people when they gave us food or allowed us to sleep beneath their apple orchards. Evans was right, of course, and while I think very few of the boys were Communists, they could see he made sense. It was a case, more than anything, of follow-the-leader.

Vancouver had a mayor then, Gerry McGeer, and Gerry was a smart boy. He was a Liberal politician and if he could stick it up the ass of the Conservatives and R.B., those initials to us meant Rotten Bastard, then he could get some votes, and also he'd like to see a lot of us single fellows to hell and gone out of town. Let us be Ottawa's headache, if we got there. So Old Gerry tapped a lot of his rich friends and he set up a tag day in downtown Vancouver and they came through with about $5,000, which was an awful lot of do-re-mi in those days, an awful lot. In a way, it was bribe money for us to get out of town, and there we were, led by Arthur Evans, jumping a C.P. freight and heading to Ottawa.

I read that about 1,000 left Vancouver, and to a lot of Vancouver people it must have been good-riddance-to-bad-garbage. Along the way about another 1,000 or so joined us and we worked our way across to Calgary. We bunked down in Kamloops one day and got a soup kitchen set up by the town and tobacco passed out, and it went okay. It seems we spent another day in Golden, a divisional point, and the people were nice and Calgary was okay too, as I recall.

In fact things were just going along like free beer out of a spigot until the C.P.R. said they weren't going to let us ride their freights any more. That was a laugh. A million guys were riding freights in Canada, and suddenly no more riding. Evans and his boys told us it was a dirty plot to stop us, but we all knew that. What we didn't know was whether the C.P.R. or the Bennett government was behind it. It didn't really matter. The railways and the government were so close in cahoots together you couldn't tell them apart, anyway. I read something later that the interest paid by the government every year on the Canadian National debt was more during the Depression than was ever paid to men, women and children in Canada during those years to keep from starving, to be able to go out with decent clothes and to keep a decent roof over their heads, and, god damn it all, to keep from going mad. So we weren't going to be allowed to ride the freights, and Regina was the last stop.

Okay, so Evans and some of his boys went down to Ottawa to see old Rotten Bastard Bennett and that didn't work out too well. In fact, it didn't work out at all. Evans was hot-headed and couldn't work with people who didn't do just what he said, and you've heard of R.B. Bennett. I remember Evans calling the prime minister a liar, and if I know Evans, he probably swore when he did it. So you see how it would go. It was after this that Bennett must have decided that that was it.

As I recall we were going to have a mass meeting in the Market Square in Regina. We'd been sleeping on the ground and getting handouts and hanging around town for more than 10 days, two weeks and some of the boys had gotten into a little trouble, some stealing, theft by night, that sort of thing, and the locals weren't all that kindly disposed towards us.

Bennett ordered that Evans and his boys were to be arrested at the meeting. That was on Dominion Day. It was a stupid thing, but just about everything you care to name which the government did in those days was stupid. Well, as soon as the meeting got going they jumped us. I don't think our boys had any guns but the police sure as hell did, and they were using them. Shooting at legs. We didn't even have rocks, nothing but our bare hands, but if we could pull a cop off his horse, then we had boots and he got it. One cop was dead and some people were wounded, shot. A lot of guys were arrested, and I can't remember what happened to them. Probably three months, taking part in a riot.

I can't remember even what happened to Arthur Evans. He'd get jail, of course. He'd never be able to talk his way out of that one. But it wasn't all that much of a riot. The papers played it big but it wasn't all that much. A lot of guys just thought it was a lark, a chance to yell at cops and snap a lighted cigarette in their faces and then run like hell.

The C.P.R. assembled a train and got us sorted out and we got on it and went back to the coast, although there were guys dropping off along the way. It was a free ride for some, both ways. A lot of fun, a chance to break the monotony for others. I let off a little steam and so did a lot of others and we were fed pretty well.

That's about all I remember of it, except Old Gerry McGeer did a pretty good job of sticking it to the Tories. They got a lot of bad publicity. If my dates are a little off and I'm out on some things, well, it was a long time ago and I haven't thought of it for years."

———————————— • ————————————

The Regina Riot: Second View

"I always thought the Regina Riot was what you would today call a snow job. A police riot, and against us, the trekkers, and believe you me when I say an awful lot of those smashed windows and stolen goods were the work of good Regina citizens. I know. I saw them. Men in good clothes who weren't with our bunch who came out from Vancouver and so I can say, those guys that did the looting were a lot of Regina people. Well, mostly.

Look, look at it this way. We were disciplined. Art Evans told us it had to be this way, that being polite and organized and neat even in our old duds was the way to gain public support, and we'd got it all along the line. Suppose a trekker was found with a pen and pencil set or a wrist watch or something in his pocket. Well, they would have thrown the key away. Five, eight, ten years. Looting was the worst crime against property and you know what property was in those days. Like the Trinity, God, the Son and the Holy Ghost.

There were a lot of store windows bashed in. I read that the square looked like a battleground. Holy Hell, those reporters then never saw a battleground, and I have. For three years, '15 to '18. There was a lot of damage but two days later, after Dominion Day, you couldn't tell the difference.

I'm sorry the policeman was killed and some of our boys got arrested and it made a lot of noise across the country but as I said, it was a snow job. Old R.B. Bennett wanted a showdown and he got it, piling all those cops into vans and banging them into the square. Guns were firing. Guess who had the guns? He wanted to discredit the trek and he did. Oh, yes, he succeeded. We were, in the eyes of a lot of people, just a bunch of Reds. Carrying the card. It wasn't like that at all. We were just a bunch of ordinary guys, but Bennett stuck the label on us and it stuck. He did a lot of harm that day, that guy."

———————————— • ————————————

On The Road To Regina

"The boys were getting a bit restless. Nothing was happening, and they would wander around town and back to the grounds for meals and back and forth. Of course, the Communist agitators were working on them and there was one good slugging match with police and RCMP in a vacant lot across from the city hall and a shouting match another time, but nothing really happened.

Of course we knew the Communists, and while they hung around the soup lines, I don't think I ever saw one of them in the line. They ate up at a cafe and ate pretty well, I'd say. Then the gang came in from Vancouver, mostly boys out of the relief camps and this was the start of the March On Ottawa. You know, it only got as far as Regina, where they had the riot.

To this day, I don't think that riot had to happen, and Miller (*the policeman who was killed*) didn't have to die. They just didn't handle it right. I mean, the boys down at Victoria Park, they weren't ready to start any revolution but Art Evans was determined to push it through. You know, I never thought Evans was really a bad actor, and who is to say 35 years later that he was all that wrong. Anyway, about 250 of the boys at Victoria Park got sick and tired of sitting around so we joined the march, pretty much all together, and away we went for Ottawa. We were on a freight and if the C.P.R. arranged it this way, I don't know, but only the last six cars were empty and everybody piled in these and away we went.

It was late at night when we got into Medicine Hat and there was a lot of shunting and pushing around and nobody thought much of anything of it. There always was that kind of activity in the yards, but in an hour or so, the cops came along and said we all had to get off. What had happened was this. They had just unhooked the last six cars and pushed them on to a siding. The boys were all herded into a warehouse and told they would be charged with violating the Railway Act, trespassing on C.P.R. property.

The boys took it as a joke, saying they'd go on the next march, things like that. I had to stay with them, of course, and nothing happened. No charges were laid and they were put on other trains going back west or told to hit the road and as far as I know, none of that bunch got to Regina.

If someone had used his head they could have done the same thing at every divisional point between Vancouver and Regina, quietly, no fuss or muss, and nothing would have happened. You would have had a lot of screaming agitators but nothing else. As it was, there was a lot of trouble, and Evans and his merry little band, about 10 in all, I think, did cause a lot more trouble than they should have. They made it a lot tougher on the unemployed man, believe you me."

—————————— • ——————————

A Minor Revolution

"My Dad, the old man, he and some other guys would sit around our back-yard, there were trees all around it and drink beer they made and just talk. All afternoon. Talk. Politics. Fishing. Maybe some talk about women in the town, you know how guys are. That kind of thing.

I'd sit with them sometimes but I got no beer. I'd ask but my old man would say, 'What if the priest comes by, Jesus, then I'm in the soup.'

He's sitting there and he starts scratching his leg a bit and then he pulls up his pant and he tells me to go get a safety pin and then he picks away, he scrapes and ticks away and in a moment he's got a little hole in the skin and he uses a thumb nail and soon a little bit of iron, metal you see, this comes out and she's about the size of a shotgun pellet and he lets it roll on the table, and the other guys, they're looking at it, and the old man he says, 'Souvenir, German souvenir. The war, you know,' and the other guys they shake their heads. They know the old man got a good one in the war but Jesus, this is 15 years later. What's he gonna do?

The old man laughs and says he's got a pickle jar half full of this stuff, it comes out all the time, first a little itch and then a bump and he takes it out and it don't hurt none. He don't mind. Lots of guys got it worse, he says, and shrapnel isn't so bad. These are just the little pieces left, he says.

One guy there, he's called Jean, he says it's a goddamn crime a veteran he goes and fights for his country and comes back and works in the furniture factory and they close it down and he's got 11 kids and no relief, no money coming in except what the old lady can make doing laundry at the seminary. A goddamn shame, he says, and he's real mad. This guy is pounding his fist into each other and he's sure mad and let's do something about it, a guy who fights for his country and is kicked around like a piece of dog shit in the street. They'd all been drinking wine and beer, you see. They got going harder and there are all these real bad words in French and they start talking about going down to Quebec to see the premier, he was a crook in those days. Hah, aren't they all? The voices get higher and the kids are coming home from studies, the school, and women are yelling to the men to shut up, shut up, shut up you dumb guys, and one guy who is drunk by now, he gets up and tears a board off our fence and you know what he does? He splits it with the axe into about five pieces and then he sharpens each end real sharp and then he says, 'Come, you guys, we're going to war again. Money for Henri and his woman and 11 kids.' Well, it was crazy. Everybody's nuts.

My old man just sits there, he knows the score.

Somebody's kid runs for the police and four of them come up in a car and everybody is yelling, some for my old man and some telling the police to go away and leave poor people alone and the top guy of the police, he asks what is wrong and the guy who is drunk says they are going to Quebec. Oh, what for? asks the cop. The guy says they are going to get a pension or the relief or a job or something for this guy Henri here, our friend, and then they are going to stick the government guys through the belly with the swords. Then he says, 'We're gonna start with you, bastard,' and he makes like he is going to do this thing, although I don't think he is, he's mostly fooling around. The police have these clubs, you know, and I think they were made of rubber, and out come these clubs and whack, each guy picks one of my old man's friends and it just takes one whack. Those were some whacks. Jesus!

The women are screaming, kids are yelling. You ever heard 40 women and kids screaming in French? Some fun, I'll tell you.

They drag these guys with the swords off to the provincial *(police)* barracks and my old man he waits about an hour or so, has another glass of carrot wine, and then he goes down and he talks to the head guy. Sure, they mean no trouble and they make no trouble, they get all upset, you know, they got no jobs, kids hungry, they don't know what's going on.

The policeman tells the old man something has got to be done, some sort of report has to be filled out and the old man, he's no slow thinker and he says, 'Okay, say they tore a board off my fence and charge them with destruction of private property. Say 10 days' suspended sentence.'

The chief says nobody is going to believe that, four men stealing one board, and my old man says nobody cares about who does what so long as a report is made out, so the head cop says okay, and that's the way they do it.

That's the story of the great revolt against the government in my home town."

———————————— • ————————————

100 *Cuban Rifles*

"We had a lot of fun with these Mounties. We were honoured by their presence. That was comic interest, let me tell you.

They were infiltrating our ranks to find out when we were going to blow up the bridges and knock out the power stations. All they ever heard was talk about jobs we'd had, jobs we missed, jobs we'd get. Oh, there was some talk, quite a bit, about Roosevelt because he was doing his best to get his country moving, the United States. The way they went, we'd go too, so there was a lot of interest in his New Deal. There wasn't much talk about what Canada was doing, because from where we stood, it was just a lot of talk, moving back and forth around a fixed point of inactivity and doing nothing.

We used to kid these Regina Cowboys. We could spot them as soon as they joined any group. They walked like cops, and you could see where their hair had grown in over their regulation haircuts and when they talked it was like they were questioning a suspect. They didn't have the jargon, the road talk.

We used to kid them. Things like there were 100 Cuban rifles hidden under the Georgia Viaduct, all oiled and wrapped in heavy cloth and ready for the boys. Once we made a map of the Fraser Canyon and marked (x) by two big rail bridges in the canyon and wrote on the side, '60 pounds of forcite.' Enough to blow up the road. We left it where one of these Yellowstripes would find it. Kid stuff, but what the hell. We were just fooling."

———————————— • ————————————

Nothing To Hope For

"Revolution! Now that's an awful question. Doubtless there were some people who would have liked a revolution but what would they gain from it? After all, after the Winnipeg General Strike of 1919 when it was put down so effectively and after all the trials, just 10 years before, there wasn't much you could do. And then we had a lot of British immigration after the war, and they just weren't the kind of people who would revolt. Remember, they were joining hundreds of thousands of others, of British stock, to whom the

416 TEN LOST YEARS

word 'revolution' was just out of the question. And besides, the only place you could promote a revolution was in the cities, and we were not urbanized then to the extent that a half-assed revolution in the city was going to do anything. The people on the farms, why, they wouldn't stand for it.

Anyway, during the Depression there was nothing to hope for from a revolution. You didn't have people that waxed fat and saucy, and nobody is demanding revolution when they are scratching for tomorrow's dinner. That takes all their energy.

Anyway, there was nobody here who would know how to make a revolution anyway. Not in Canada. Or in the United States. Yes, there were riots. You can start a riot any time you want, on a breadline, in a camp, but that's not a revolution. There simply wasn't the potential for a revolution. No leaders, and people had too much sense anyway. Even the Commies weren't really preaching revolution. As a matter of fact, it was so peaceful that American millionaires were buying up B.C. islands, even then, so when comes the revolution in the United States, they had a place to hide."

———————————— • ————————————

The Shape Of Their Heads

"I think it is quite simple why the Communists never made much of an impact. They didn't make the splash they could have, you know, although they were busy in the relief camps, some in the jungles, in Vancouver and places in the east where there was a lot of industrial unemployment. Places where there was desperation.

You see, Canada was mainly Anglo-Saxon, the Maritimes, Ontario, the West Coast – and Quebec, of course, was Quebec. Most of the Reds were Ukrainians and Jews. They could change their names all they wanted, and an awful lot did, but they couldn't change their accents or the shape of their heads. They were still Jews, kikes, yids, hunkies, bohunks, hoonyaks, ukranskies, call them anything you like. They could be spotted a mile away, even if Rabonovitch became Robinson and so on. The names didn't change the man.

So all these Anglo-Saxons, English, Scotch, Irish and the Scandihoovians and Germans who were considered Anglo-Saxon, they would say, 'No damn bohunk is going to tell me to salute the red flag and sing the Internationale,' or they would say, 'No Montreal Jew is going to push me around and say I have to spit on the Union Jack.' Things like that. There was a great distrust among the unemployed for these organizers, and when they came in to the camps, undercover so to speak, they were spotted almost immediately.

They caused some damage, the Regina Riot for one, a few minor riots and soup kitchen battles, but no matter what they say, the Commies just weren't anything to be afraid of.

Like they said of the girl singer, she had all the words but didn't know the tune."

CHAPTER THIRTY-FOUR

1939 . . . Lining Up To Die

As an old soldier would say, "It's a helluva way to start a war."

First, general mobilization was ordered September 1, 1939. Then Parliament was called and spent three days talking before formally declaring war on Germany. Date: September 10.

Canada's lack of preparedness was ludicrous. There were plenty of rifles, First World War vintage, for the 4,000 permanent force army officers and ranks, but the inventory of modern weapons as of September 1 was 29 Bren machine guns, 23 anti-tank rifles and five three-inch mortars. It was laughable.

The navy with 1,800 men had not a ship worth sailing and the R.C.A.F., with 4,500 men, used most of its old crates for training and forest fire spotting.

Who was to blame? Everybody and nobody. A nation small in population, chopped to the canvas repeatedly by economic forces beyond her control, ravaged by one of the worst droughts in history and wracked by internal tensions, a nation in truly desperate trouble could not be expected to fashion a major war machine. It had trouble enough just breathing in and breathing out.

But to tens of thousands of men on the roads, hanging around street corners, standing at closed factory gates, without hope, the war seemed a godsend, the end of their troubles. The rush to navy, air force and army recruiting offices was heavy. By September 30 the army had recruited 45,000 volunteers and simply did not have enough instructors and equipment to train them. But still, the First Canadian Division of 20,000 men reached England in late December.

Boarded-up factories were opened up and converted to making munitions and the thousands of items needed for war. New factories were built, and government orders flowed out in every mail. Within 18 months, there was no excuse for anyone, male or female, young or old, who did not have a job. The work, at decent pay rates, was there. Unemployment had vanished.

And, as if at some mystic signal, the incessant winds stopped blowing across the prairies, the rains came again, the crops were heavy and prices rose.

The Depression was over.

1939: **Lining Up To Die**

"I came out of high school in 1936 and never even got a chance to look over the fence into the promised land. Just walked out of that school with my diploma, went right to the bottom like everybody else and scraped around there for several years. No, I won't tell you about it. Nothing to be proud of, but nothing to be sorry about, either, because the whole thing happened somewhere over in Europe and in Washington and Chicago and Ottawa, and the little people just didn't know which side was up.

Anybody can tell better of it than I can, but the war came along. Anybody saying the war wasn't the end of the Depression just doesn't know what he is talking about, because it was. Somebody once said war is good because every few years it reduces the surplus population. Maybe true, but it sure took a lot of us off the streets and the rods. I was in Winnipeg in 1939 in a jungle where the two rivers meet, when war was declared, and when Canada got into it a bunch of us went down to sign up. It was the MacGregor Armories. Heard it burned down a few years back.

Anyway, about a dozen of us from the jungle hiked over there and goddamn it if we didn't see hundreds of guys around, all lined up, and corporals and sergeants running around shouting orders. They just didn't know what to do. I'm not sure if they had many recruits before the war, but they had more than they could handle now, and they just didn't know what to do. Anyway, about 10 o'clock there was some sort of order and I remember a sergeant yelling, 'Don't rush, boys, there's room for all of you.' God damn, how right he was.

You keep buying the beer and I'll keep going.

First they were going to line us around in circles out in the yard, but that meant standing, and maybe some of us didn't look in too good standing shape. There was every type. There was us, out of the jungles. Lice on us, every one. Clothes from the Sally Ann, curse that organization, and most pairs of boots or shoes you could wriggle the toes at the sunlight. There were men in business suits and college kids, I guess, and kids that looked like they should have been in school behind their books. There was old guys just itching to get in, guys from the last war and they was the ones who made sense. They knew how to carry out orders, how to form lines and that, and already they had a new look to them, straighter back, you might say. I shouldn't have called them old guys. Hell and blazes, most wouldn't be over 45 and some younger, because time fades the memory, but the '14 War was only gone about 20 years before.

I wasn't patriotic. None of my buddies were. I just wanted some good clothes and hot showers and three decent meals a day and a few dollars for tobacco and beer in my pocket, and that's about all I wanted. You found out later that the others wanted other things. Like some of the older guys just wanted to get away from a complaining wife or a lousy job or a shit of a boss, that kind of a thing. One college kid wanted to impress his girl, and he was the biggest fool of all. The high school kids wanted adventure, and when all is said and done and the last dog is hung, that is probably what we was all looking for. Not adventure, maybe, but a new life. Same thing.

So anyway, you know, they decided to line us along the curbs, so we could sit down, and that morning there must have been 500 men if there was a thousand lining about three blocks of curbs away from the armories and housewives looking out the windows, and deliverymen coming, and newspaper photographers shooting us, and we just sat in the sun, it was September, and talked.

Every quarter hour or so, there would be a shout down the line and we'd all get off our asses and move about 20 seats or so down the curb. That's what they were doing, taking us in bunches of 20 or so. By the end of the day we had a sort of gang going, of the eight or 10 guys on each side of you, and we got to know each other.

Then they told us to go home and come back next day. Going to war and you couldn't even sign up. I got through the gates the afternoon of the third day and by that night I was in the Canadian Army. The school kids didn't get in, naturally, but they missed three days of classes and books and had an excuse. Poor little bastards, they must have come in about three years later when it was worse, much worse. Chickenshit right up to your eyeballs. My uniform fitted and I slept on a bunk that night and things were pretty good. I forget what the pay was, but it got better. A few bucks a month. I had no wife.

I often remember that line. We didn't do much talking about the war, and if we had known what it was gonna be like I guess we'd have taken off down that street like a cut cat. We talked about things we'd always talked about, and how we were going to get a meal that night, just as if we were back jungling, and how some of the other guys, the city guys – funny but I can't remember any farm boys, harvesting I guess – and these city guys just couldn't believe we could live like we did, on the road, in the jungles.

Everything was disorganized as hell but somehow they got things straightened out. The army always does, they never do it the right way but somehow it always gets done.

Everybody got a ticket with a number on it so nobody would muscle in on the line, you know, get it first and get the best seat, that sort of thing. If they'd only known they could have waited a couple of years. Some would have missed that Hong Kong business, for sure, and Dieppe too. You know, that was a massacre and the Germans knew we were coming. An officer told me so. And I remember the little girls in their frilly dresses and the little boys, the first graders, going down the sidewalk by us guys on the curb and to their first classes at the school down the way, and one guy said, 'They're starting out a new life and so are we.' Always remember that.

A lot got discharged early when they started sorting out the cards, and some were in the Hong Kong thing and we all got messed around a little. A lot of that bunch, if you had any brains at all, became officers. I'd see them around. I never made but corporal. A lot got wounded, and me too. I picked up this half leg. Shot clean off at Caen. I saw the German who shot me. He stood up with a machine gun and let go and it sawed 'er off below the knee. Just this leg. I saw him and I couldn't do anything, but it was all like it was in slow motion. Somebody else got him. A lot of our boys went for a shit and a lot came back without a scratch.

It was funny, lining up for days to get into a war, to get yourself killed."

CHAPTER THIRTY-FIVE

Lasting Effects

A Dime In Your Pocket . . . Save And Never Spend . . . How Many Busted
Dreams? . . . Mom, I Need These! . . . Any Loose Change? . . . How To Sell A House
. . . Forget Those Hard Times . . . Three Percent Interest People . . . I Had
Depression Trauma . . . Mom, This Isn't Real . . . What's Finnan Haddie? . . .
Saucers Of Left-overs . . . They Just Don't Understand . . . Enough Food To Serve
An Army . . . But We Survived.

———————————— • ————————————

*I said in my Preface to this book that the Depression still deeply affects everyday
life in Canada today. I believe this to be true – and I believe that the stories in
this chapter on the Depression's lasting effects prove it. But many people are quite
unaware of this.*

*For example, as I travelled across Canada asking my questions, people
would ask, "But why would anyone want to know about those days?" I would
say, "Just tell me what you did," and out would pop a story, so quickly, and told
with such feeling that it could have been hiding within them for years just
waiting to be freed.*

*There might be just one story, about some event, some moment so deeply felt,
so traumatic, so shameful, so crazy that to them that alone symbolized the whole
Depression. And others would talk for a 90-minute tape – say 15,000 words –
and be sorry that I had to leave because they could have remembered the whole
morning away.*

*There was a thread through these conversations, often expressed forcefully
but more often implied. It could be called the Depression Syndrome. The Fear
Syndrome. It is the Depression's most impressive and saddest legacy.*

*It could be illustrated by the man who said he never went out now unless he
had $100, $200 in his pocket. He would never be broke again. And yet, while he
was secure in the knowledge of having the money, he was forever slapping his
wallet pocket – just to make sure!*

*It shows in the case of the mother in New Brunswick who was always urging
thrift on her daughter and telling her of the tough days – and being shut up by
the girl saying, "Mom, this isn't real."*

These and many more.

*It shows, too, in the frustration at the younger generation, their own chil-
dren, in anger at the hippies, and in the occasional remark: "What some people
today need is a Depression. That would smarten them up." Perhaps the only
Generation Gap that counts is the one between those who remember the
Depression and those who don't.*

*I wish I could give you one quotation from this book which would wrap it all
up neatly. I'm sorry, but I can't. Those Ten Lost Years meant so much in so many
different ways to millions of Canadians.*

*I hope you will take this whole book as the complete statement of those years,
those years that we hope will never come again.*

—————————— • ——————————

A Dime In Your Pocket

"A hundred times a day, I guess, I suddenly put my right hand into my pocket
and feel for money. Yep, there it is. Things are okay. That's a throwback to the
Depression, and I'll bet there are tens of thousands of men my age, 55, 60,
who do it.

You just didn't have money. If you had money before 1930, then you had
to get used to not having it after that. If you didn't, then you didn't actually
know what money was. More than half the people in my block in Ottawa were
on relief, didn't have jobs, and there was a lot of laughter and people worked
together on things and I'm not sure I heard of anybody starving, but there
just wasn't any money. That's what I can't get across to the kids today. My
youngest girl is in grade nine and I asked to see her Canadian history book
and there was three paragraphs on the Depression, saying what a tough time
it had been, but there were chapters on Champlain and the founding of
Quebec and Lord Durham's Report, all useless as far as I can see, but just three
paragraphs or so on 10 years of absolute misery for Canadians. Nothing about
no money. You figure it out.

A few years ago my son and I are in a sporting goods store and he wants a
new fielder's glove, $9 or so, and I say I haven't any money and he says, 'Okay,
dad, just charge it on your credit card!' And when I was his age, 11 or 12, I

didn't know what a quarter looked like. I doubt if I'd ever had more than a dime in my life.

When I was older you'd get sweet on a girl at school and ask her out, and it would be one of those warm evenings in May, the kind when you just wanted to take a girl's hand and hold it forever, and you'd pick her up and walk around, through the park, downtown, past drug stores, and you didn't have a dime in your pocket. How the hell can you take a girl out if you can't buy her a banana split, or even an ice cream cone?

That's why I'm always diving into my pocket, just to make sure I've got change. I'll be doing that until I die because of the number of times I've taken a nice girl out for a date and had no money to buy her even an ice cream cone. Five cents."

———————————— • ————————————

Save And Never Spend

"It stuns me! I never really get over the last one and then another pops up. Teachers. Ninety percent teachers. I get a lead on one who is retiring, at 65, maybe History or English or something, and I drive down to Galt or that way and yes, there she is in her own house. I mean she owns the house and I start talking to her. How much money has she got? You know, smoothing them down and telling them how well they managed their money but now at 65 it is time to put it to work under highly skilled management so they can enjoy their lives. Their retirement.

It is fantastic! They're like children. She'll own her house and usually a good one. She'll have $40,000 in Canada Savings Bonds. She'll have $60,000 in insurance. What spinster needs that in insurance? She'll have $20,000 in something like Massey-Ferguson and $15,000 in the teachers' fund, and when you've got it all totalled up, that little old gal sitting in her cluttered living room has about $100,000 or so to play around with. Now it's my job to jerk that money out of where it is into my mutual fund, and I do, but that's not the point here. Oh, yes, she may have $15,000 in the bank. In the bank, for Christ sakes! At three percent or something.

The point is, and the woods are full of them, is that dear old Miss Whoopsadaisey, she got her first job teaching in the Depression. She worked for peanuts. She learned early that what can be given can also be taken away. So she saves, saves in the most careful way she knows. Probably on the advice of her bank manager. So she saves and saves and spends nothing, no trips to

Europe or Mexico, and she saves and saves and when she retires at 65 from Dingaling Secondary, she's got about a hundred biggies. A hundred big ones. Like a $100,000.

That's the Depression. In her bone, blood and mind. Save and never spend. Don't enjoy yourself. Save for your old age. Remember, there can be another Depression. Remember. Save. Be frugal. Save for your old age."

———————————•———————————

How Many Busted Dreams?

"I've learned something from standing here a lot of years looking, talking to the back of a guy's head or his face in that mirror. The Depression changed most men's lives much more than they realized. They haven't thought much of it, some of them, and some won't admit it.

I've been a barber about 38 years and you get regulars and they stay with you until they die or move away, and if they're sick I'll still go around at night. Today that's called super-service. In the Thirties it was just part of your trade. Part of the job.

You get to know your customers and I've got a good memory, a card file index and you may say something today and I could connect it up with something you said, something casual, two or five years ago and something you said seven years ago, and it's like fitting a crossword puzzle together, the puzzle that is you.

Here's my point. I have met few men sitting in this chair who are really happy in their work, men of 50 or 55 and over. He may be successful, have lots of money, park a Chrysler Imperial in front of my shop right out there, may be a president of his own company but that man may have wanted to be a sea captain. Or a guy I know is a super-salesman, he might want to be a maker of documentary films, or a bass fiddle player may have wanted to own an intimate restaurant downtown. Those are just three cases. Real cases I know. I could tell you 20 more, ones I know of. Hell, 40 more.

The Depression screwed everyone. You lost your job, got laid off, the plant shut down, and there you were, on the street with 5,000 other guys and all these bright kids coming out of college and high school and you took the first job you could get. You jumped at it. In the stockyards across the river, shovelling shit. If it was a job, you took it. And you stuck with it. Oh boy, did you stick with it. Like a tiger defending her young.

Well, everyone was scared. Everyone. Men and women. Boys and girls. You looked for a job, for months. It should be a good job and I mean a respectable one, but it had to be a job. Man was made to work. That was drummed into you since childhood. If it was $5 a week, four, six, then things would get better. You stuck it out. Just existing, one day after another.

The war came along, and after it there wasn't all that much changing of jobs. If you were not in it, maybe you were frozen into your job. If you were in service, you came back and grabbed the old job because you figured the Depression would just carry right on and by God, you had a job. Things just didn't seem to change. Then there was a wedding, say, and then one kid and the upstairs half of a house, rented, and another kid and the wife wanted a home and you wanted some kind of car and hell, you just kept going on in the old rut. Don't change. Things might get rough again.

Christ, I've heard it all so much. All the little things they say that I can add up. These are guys, most of them, who are leading lives of quiet desperation, as Shakespeare said. He said it all.

What about me? I'll tell you. My mother thought I would make a good lawyer. So did my Dad. But after school, I went out on the bum and when I got back in about '37 my folks had moved to Calgary and my mother knew a guy who ran a hairdressing school, and he could slip me in free. Two nights a week and I did odd jobs to pay. What's another kid with a barber's diploma? It was something and I didn't have a thing and that's why I'm a barber. I should have been a lawyer. You think about it and you'll see I'm right. I'm a good barber and I'm a good listener and I'm a bit of a psychologist and a philosopher, but a barber is still a barber."

'Mom, I Need These.'

"My son, he's 14, and I were in this sporting goods store downtown buying a new pair of ski gloves for his sister. They like to buy their own things but it wasn't convenient this time. My son came up with a pair of German hiking boots, about $25, and said, 'Mom, I need these.' I said I didn't have enough money and he said, just as happy as ever, 'Well, write a cheque then.'

I don't know, something inside me snapped and I yelled at him, 'Damn it all, what you need is to go through a Depression,' and the man next to me, an old man, Jewish I'd say, said, 'No lady, no, please don't ever say that.'

I told Robby to put the boots back and he wandered away, and the old man and I got to comparing and I said that when I lived in Fort William we had a tiny store and by working from eight in the morning to eight or nine at night, my Mom and Dad, too proud to take relief, made about $25 a month. That is, if they were lucky. Many months less, and there were times when we thought we were lucky. Anyway, here is this old man and myself talking about these things and he had been a tailor. He looked 60, but he must have been 80, but you know how some of these old men are. He said if he was lucky he would work one day a week and get $3 or so and somehow he lived on that and then he said, 'But my people were used to adversity,' and then I knew he was Jewish.

We must have talked for five minutes more, things just spilling out of us, old friends in just a few minutes, and finally the young man – 18 or 20 I guess, no more, and very blond and tanned and just right to be behind that counter selling expensive sports equipment – this youngster said, 'Pardon me, but what is this you are talking about? Is that the Depression you're talking about? I've heard my mother speak of it.'

The old man looked at the clerk and he said, 'Son, the difference between your life now and the Depression is this lady's son coming up saying he has to have those $25 boots right now, and her mother and father working all month in a little corner grocery for $25 to support their family. That's the difference, son.'

He turned to me, he really was such a sweet old man, and he said, 'Madame, if you have a little time to spare, could an old man offer to buy you a chocolate eclair and a cup of coffee at a little cafe around the corner?' I said yes, immediately. He said, 'Perhaps your son would like a banana split?' and there was a twinkle in his eye. I said no, I thought he would prefer to take the GO train home, as old people's reminiscences had no part in his life. The old man agreed, and we spent a lovely hour laughing and talking about the old days.

I'm glad we can laugh with each other about them now."

———————————— • ————————————

Any Loose Change?

"The hippie kids today say, 'Got any loose change, mister?' as though we were to empty our friggin' pockets to them. Not me. I might give one a quarter if he doesn't look too bloody smart-ass and to me, that's more than the equivalent of a dime, which is what I got in the Thirties. Then, if you panhandled, you were hungry or wanted a cot in some upstairs Chinese flophouse on the

428   TEN LOST YEARS

Skid Row. You didn't want it for dope or to buy another pair of flare pants. You goddamned well panhandled because you were hungry. Your belly thought your throat was cut. Usually I don't give out anything, and if they are standing in front of me, why I just walk right through them. That's the way I feel. Sorry."

———————————— • ————————————

How To Sell A House

"I'll tell you something, and if an agent has been in this *(real estate)* business any length of time and hasn't learned it, then he shouldn't be in it at all. He should be in a hardware store selling lawn mowers.

There are two kinds of people. There are what I call the Depression Babies, see, and the War Babies. I've heard them called the Bomb Babies. Now, there isn't that much difference in age if you take a kid born in 1935, so he's 37, 38 and his wife will be around 34 or 35 on the average, and a War Baby, who came along about 1942 or '43, so he is around 30 or so. When they come to me, the house, the kind I sell, that's going to be their last big investment. Their class house, in a nice neighbourhood, trees, nice neighbours. You get it. They'll retire in that house and they'll probably die in it. Right? So when I get a prospect in that age grouping I can usually tell whether they are Depression or War. If I'm not sure I ask a few questions, ones they never suspect. Fine, so then I know.

This couple, call them couple A, are Depression. At their age they probably knew boom-all about it but in those later years when they were growing up, they heard plenty from their folks, how tough it was. Sure it was tough. But people always exaggerate. Hamburger at seven cents a pound and only once a week. Potatoes like they were going out of style. No decent clothes. Wealthier relatives looking down their noses at them. But most of all, no money. The parents might not have exactly told them all this, but by their actions, the way they saved every penny, vacations done on the cheap, putting all those stupid little bits and scraps of food in the fridge for a rainy day, that got through.

So, and here is the secret, I talk cost to these people. I don't mess around with the $150 chandelier in the dining room. I tell them the house was built in 1938 and is solid as a rock and it will outlive them and that there is not a builder in the country putting up houses like this. It is listed at $40,000 but the owner will take 35 and I let them cut me down. Say 37. Cost, cost, value,

value, a good neighbourhood, reliable. A place to bring your friends, have barbecues on the big patio in the back. And it works. This sells them, because cost and quality mean everything. A special kind of wood especially imported from Turkey for the can means nothing.

Now the others. The War Kids. They never had it rough and when they came along their parents were in the chips, the war on, plants going full blast, quite a bit of money around. They don't care about the Depression and cost doesn't mean a hell of a lot. Why, what's $4,000 down and $160 a month for ever and ever. They just consider it as rent. They don't think of the interest. Why should they? So I sell them on the view, or tell the woman how nice a dinner party would look in this dining room. And I say dining by candlelight. Or this big cupboard can be easily converted into another bathroom. Look how high this ceiling is, that's perfect for a rec room in the basement. Look at those drapes, worth $400. They were made special. These Dutch front doors, why Mrs. Jones, they are the only ones on this street.

The little touches, putting them in the right setting. How pretty she will look, and how the house will add glamour to their lives, and how gracious a house it is to entertain the company executive from the East. If that doesn't show I consider the buyer a man on his way up, nothing will. It gets them every time. Well, almost. Anyway, I sell a lot of houses and good old psychology does it almost every time."

———————————— • ————————————

Forget Those Hard Times

"Oh God, don't tell me about those days. They were some days, eh! There were 17 in my family, and while today that is a very big family it was not so big in those times. My mother's sister, Marie, she had 21 and they were all alive. Yes, all alive. That may be a rarity but it was not a miracle.

Relief, my father did not believe in it. There was no baby bonus for big families. There was no help. How could there be help when everybody in that district had nothing? The priest, what help was that guy? Nobody worked at being in the church anyway. What a laugh. Those guys! You ever seen a skinny priest? So there were all these babies anyway. Long cold nights and no television, that's what I say. (*She laughs.*)

When I was 13 my mother says no more foolishness. I can read and write okay, can't I? Okay, you go to work. School is fine as far as you are concerned, ma petite, and in a French Canadian house you might think the husband is boss but he is not, it is the woman, and it is my mother who says what is for me. I have four older sisters and four older brothers and they are all working making garments, in the textile plants run by these Jews and I get it. Yes, I sure get it. I get ten hours a day and six days a week and I get $4 when I am 13, and if you don't smile nice at those damned foremen they can make you out of work right there. My sisters know my salary so I give my $4 to my mother and she gives me 50 cents a week for my car fare which is six tickets for 25 cents and the ride is one hour each way, and she gives me 30 cents to buy a soft drink to go with my lunch. That is 30 cents a week, as it comes to five cents a day. If I want a silk stocking, and it was only silk because there was no nylon then, that was 19 cents, because my sisters would not loan their silk stockings if I had a date and I had no silk stockings. When I had these precious stockings I would not loan them either. It was war over stockings in our house on Saturday night.

Girls would just marry to get out of the house their parents lived in. We had five rooms, and that was good, but there were as many as 20 people living there sometimes. That was not too bad. We had no cousins from Trois Rivières or Chicoutimi or one of those places. It was like an army barracks, good times and some bad times, but we ate. We should have. There was money coming, my sisters worked and my brothers and we ate okay. Not all so fancy, but French Canadian cooking is not like French cooking. There was no wines and cognacs. There was pea soup and hamburger casserole and beer my old man made downstairs, and we got by.

Times never did get no better. We just started to make a little more, some bonus money, a better job, things like that. But not better. There was more money coming in but prices were going higher too. Nothing is good for poor people.

Nowadays I go back to that district to see my mother and she says, 'Colette, you drive in a taxi now, heh? Pretty big stuff,' and Mrs. Sylvain, who is her best friend, comes over and says, 'Colette, I see you are getting out of a taxi, heh? Times must be pretty good. There is a rich boy friend, maybe a big shot downtown, eh?' and that Mrs. Morel comes over, poking her big black bosom, as big as way out here, she pokes around the door and says, 'Your mother takes the Metro, I see her when she goes to the hospital to take her shot,' and you see, we're all talking in French and they are meaning that I am a bitch for living the way I do, that apartment and the taxi, oh my sweet Jesus, that funny little $2.50 taxi ride and finally I tell those two old black gossips to take off, just take off, go away, and I don't say it nicely like that, either.

What I am saying, nobody down there, they are the slum now, can forget the hard times. Everybody should still wear shoes with auto tire rubber inside. I like $40 shoes and I wear them. Should Trudeau wear patches on his pants? Should a woman like me not get $900 a month, every month of the year, just because somebody in the Depression said woman, her place was in the home. I don't want 18 babies. Or eight. I don't want one-eighth of one.

What I am saying is this. These are good times here, good money, good food, good everything, and they are good for us but there are tens and tens of thousands of people in this province, Quebec, this country, Canada, this goddamned, excuse me, this goddamned Canada who still think of those hard times, and they think that because somebody went through them, then they should still go through them. It is as if they wanted to throw all the good money, ten dollar bills, into the river there. Why are people like this?

I remember those ten years. From girl to woman. I grew up in those ten years and why should Mrs. Sylvain or that Mrs. Morel or a Mrs. Jesus Christ herself come around and say, 'Colette, you suffered and you've got to suffer some more.'

Ah, what's the use. I can get mad sometimes. Excuse me."

———————————————— • ————————————————

Three Percent Interest People

"I can pick a Depression Westerner out on any street, anywhere, and I'd rather have their company than of any other kind. Mind you, they are cautious folk. They keep the bird in the hand until they squeeze it to death. Give them three percent interest on their money and they'll love you to death. Offer them a nice piece of land that reeks of profit and they'll say, 'No thanks. I knew a time when they couldn't give whole sections of that stuff away.' They plod onward and upward towards that pension, giving the boss his due, and they get downright dewy-eyed when the day comes that they get their gold watch. They marry and sire and sigh and die and friends gather in the parlour and drink the widow's tea. And that's the end of it, except they made an honest mark.

The trouble is, of course, that children of the Depression rarely realize their true potential because the experience of it glued them to the safe way. Breadth of thought must have budded in thousands of brains back in the Thirties, only to shrivel in the face of too many dust storms. Myself, I would quit my job right now and take a whack at something I like better but I dasn't because, deep down, I figure we're overdue for another grasshopper plague. See, that's Depression thinking."

———————————●———————————

I Had Depression Trauma

"The reason I'm not a millionaire today is because I was born in the Depression, just a kid when it ended. My old man drilled it into me, save your money, sock it away, government bonds, the Bank of Montreal, don't spend it, never get sucked into anything where you can get trapped like he did.

Land, what is land? Everybody's got land to sell, nobody wants it. This was about 15 to 20 years ago, and my wife and I were saving for a house. Had to have a house. A goddamned house.

A friend said to stop socking it away and stop messing around. He said I should be buying land around Calgary, any land. Small down payment, low monthly payments, long term, low interest. You could pick up big chunks then, oh, for $200 down, $500 down, $1,000.

You know what that land is now? Sub-divisions, $40,000 homes, $50,000 homes, shopping centres.

Jesus Christ, my own common sense told me to go into land, but there was always the voice of my father, the warning, hard times come in cycles, we're due for another, you'll get caught, be wiped out. That's why we saved, socked every penny away when today I could be a millionaire 10 times over. I didn't have the guts. Instead I had Depression Trauma, a disease."

———————————●———————————

"Mom, This Isn't Real"

"I never dreamed, it was beyond my wildest dreams, that I'd ever be living in a $50,000 house. That we'd have two cars. There is no way you can consider that you don't need two cars, now. As soon as you have a thing you begin to think that that is a necessity. The Depression, people today will hardly believe it happened.

My children looked at that wonderful film, 'The Drylanders,' on television, and they wouldn't look at it, they got bored, and my daughter said, 'Mom, this isn't real.'

I don't see how my four children can relate to those days. They don't teach them about it in school, you never see it in movies. It is a non-subject. I don't see how you can tell them what it was like. It is like war. How can you make a person understand what war is unless they've been there. The children, when I talk about those days, usually when they want something expensive which they won't ever use, they'll say, 'Oh, yea, Mom, oh, yea, Mom,' but that's all.

They just don't understand that people didn't have cars in those days. That's just one small example, but I think they believe that people from the beginning of time have always had cars. So I don't talk about it any more."

———— • ————

What's Finnan Haddie?

"I don't, I don't think I have anything to say. Really not, thank you.

Well, just a few weeks ago a friend took me down to a restaurant at Pictou, just down the road here a ways and the specialty was lobster. It was a place where there was an American trade in the summer. That's fine. Lovely people.

But I couldn't help thinking. Being offered a lobster dinner for $8.50 – and that is what they were asking for one lobster dinner – when in my younger days you didn't even bother with bay lobsters up around Pugwash, they just weren't considered, really. A few fishermen would go out for them, but they weren't considered anything.

So here I am, in this restaurant with all the trappings and being asked if I wanted an $8.50 lobster dinner, and I said to my companion: 'Do you realize that when I came out of Normal *(a type of teacher's college)* my first school paid me $8.50 a month. Not a week, no, not by a long shot, by the *month!*' He was amazed. I got by, living with a nice family, a daughter and a son I liked. I got along that first year because they gave me board.

So I asked my escort if he minded if I would have finnan haddie. He laughed. What is it, he asked? I said finnan haddie is smoked haddock and it is not very good but it kept more people alive during the Depression than anything I can think of. So I had it. It wasn't good, but I think I enjoyed it much more than I would have that month of teaching at the little school. I mean the $8.50."

———— • ————

Saucers Of Left-overs

"If you want to know how your mother, if she was old enough, got through the Depression, just look in the refrigerator. If it is full of junk, saucers with a few left-over sliced carrots or tomatoes, little jars with pickles that have been there a month, slices of fatty roast beef that not even a hungry dog would eat, then she was through the Depression and her family wasn't well off. Probably poor.

You never threw anything away. Keep it. Save it for a stew next Saturday night, or a casserole of junk covered with a tomato sauce, a bread pudding with a lot of stuff in it. Keep. Save. Don't throw away. You never know when you'll need it. Make every cent count. Eat your crusts, they make your hair curly. Finish your porridge, don't you know there are starving children in China who would love to eat what you've got there. That kind of stuff.

Sometimes they pinch a nickel until the beaver on it screams, and you want to scream, too. It's not their fault. The times were so hard, and food was so scarce for some that most people just got into the saving routine. The habit. Of course, what happened, actually, was that they saved and saved and saved and soon they couldn't get milk or butter or meat in the fridge, all these little jars and bottles and saucers and cartons, full of junk.

Somebody has to come along and clean out. Into the garbage, sock, sock, sock. I do this about once every two weeks and my mother, dear person, will say, always she'll say that she was saving something for something. A casserole. A meat loaf. A stew. My parents have good money now and it is ages since we've had a casserole, a meat loaf. Lord, a stew! My Dad would never eat it. It's funny, but kind of funny ha ha. Like a friend of mine was over and I was going to make him a sandwich and he looked in the fridge and he said, 'Ah ha, Depression habits,' and I said 'Right' and we both laughed. Nothing to laugh about, I guess.

Mother, I know, went through hell in those days and the funny thing is, she wasn't the one who actually did the saving, the putting away, the hoarding of little bits of food. It was her mother. My grandmother. She just picked it up from her as a girl. Well, here's where the chain stops. With me. Here."

—————————————— • ——————————————

They Just Don't Understand

"When I try to tell my children what it was like out there in the Ontario bush without more than a couple of dollars from one month's end to another, and my folks and us kids living worse than any Negroes in the South, my kids pretend they each have a violin and they play all together, the Hearts and Flowers bit, and it's just Mom going into her Depression act again.

I mean, I used to try to tell them, because I felt they should know, that everyone should know, *everyone*, but it was no use.

I told them about my little brother, their Uncle Donald, going to school his first year and the teacher enrolling him as Donalda, as a girl, and thinking he was a girl for months because the only clothes he had to wear were the hand-me-downs from my sisters and me. When I told them that, they laughed so hard they rolled on the floor, so I said, 'Never again.' There is just no way to make them understand."

———————————— • ————————————

Enough Food To Serve An Army

"I have a big fridge in my kitchen and another one downstairs in the basement and there is a big deep freeze on my back porch, and I never feel right unless they're all bulging.

That's the Depression for you. My hang-up from it is food. The kids are gone, in college, to Toronto, but I've still got enough food to serve an army. I can't help it. I never throw away a bone. I've got half a dozen large coffee cans filled with frozen soup. Wonderful soup. Thank God my husband is a soup-freak. I never throw away vegetable scraps without thinking, 'I wonder if there is something I can use these for?' That's the Depression thing.

You were hungry for so many years, not starving but hungry, and it's like some men I know, some men who have to have $300 or so in their wallet, just something to fall back on. Because for so many years when they were kids, you understand, or young men, they had nothing. Not a bean.

We go down to Kent County and load up on fall apples, bushels of them, and there is just my husband and me here. We buy four sacks of island spuds because we get them a little cheaper and anything cheap is a bargain, or it used to be. I can't help it. We're relatively wealthy. Money hasn't been the slightest problem for many years. It's just my hang-ups, I guess. Sure, my husband is just as bad as I am."

———————————— • ————————————

But We Survived

"Can I put it this way, my way?

I was 14 on the home farm near Swift Current in those days and I didn't know things were that bad, but years later I read that between 1929 and 1933 the value of farm produce in Saskatchewan dropped 94 percent. That's not out of a hat. That is a statistic.

My own common sense told me to pull up stakes and leave, and I heard I could get a job in the Baldwin shops in Montreal. Who was buying locomotives in '33? And in the same report, years later, I found that 34 percent of all employable men in Montreal that year were on relief.

I tell that to my grandchildren and they listen respectfully, but you see they think the old geezer's a bit of a nut.

I hear the boy, he's 16, ask his mother to give him $5 . He wants to take his girl to a show, or for a ride. His Dad's car. I tell his mother that $5 in those days was half the relief, it was $10, to feed a family of five in Saskatchewan, summer or winter, and she says, 'Oh, Pa, I know. Sure, I understand but the kids don't.' You see, she's telling me to shut up. Well, it's her house, I guess. I'm just part of the furniture.

I'm proud of what I did in the Depression. I didn't have to eat grass, as the saying went. I always worked and I made nothing in wages, but I kept going and it made me tougher. It made us all tougher. It affected every man-jack of us. You can see it on my face and I'm not being dramatic. I couldn't, even if I wanted to be.

It is important to me that people know that I was in that time, that I did my share. It's like a badge to me, you know, a ribbon saying I was there. Like in a war. There were bad times, very bad times, and there were good times and we survived. Yes, by the Lord Harry, it was a war and we survived it. Our battle flags still flying."

HITLER VERSUS ME: The Return of Bartholomew Bandy *by* Donald Jack
Bandy ("a national treasure" according to a Saskatoon reviewer) is back in the
RCAF, fighting Nazis and superior officers, and trying to keep his age and his toupee
as secret as the plans for D-Day.

Fiction/Humour, 6 × 9 , 360 pages, hardcover

PADDLE TO THE ARCTIC *by* Don Starkell
The author of *Paddle to the Amazon* "has produced another remarkable book" *Quill
& Quire*. His 5,000 kilometre trek across the Arctic by kayak or dragging a sled is a
"fabulous adventure story." *Halifax Daily News*

Adventure, 6 × 9, 320 pages, maps, photos, mass market

CONFESSIONS OF AN IGLOO DWELLER *by* James Houston
The famous novelist and superb storyteller who brought Inuit art to the outside
world recounts his Arctic adventures between 1948 and 1962. "Sheer entertainment,
as fascinating as it is charming." *Kirkus Reviews*

Autobiography, 6 × 9, 320 pages, maps, drawings, trade paperback

THE MACKEN CHARM: A novel *by* Jack Hodgins
When the rowdy Mackens gather for a family funeral on Vancouver Island in the
1950s, the result is "fine, funny, sad and readable, a great yarn, the kind only an
expert storyteller can produce." *Ottawa Citizen*

Fiction, 6 × 9, 320 pages, trade paperback

AT THE COTTAGE: A Fearless Look at Canada's Summer Obsession *by* Charles
Gordon *illustrated by* Graham Pilsworth
This perennial best-selling book of gentle humour is "a delightful reminder of why
none of us addicted to cottage life will ever give it up." *Hamilton
Spectator*   *Humour, 6 × 9, 224 pages, illustrations, trade paperback*

HOW TO BE NOT TOO BAD: A Canadian Guide to Superior Behaviour *by* Charles
Gordon *illustrated by* Graham Pilsworth
This "very fine and funny book" *Ottawa Citizen* "updates the etiquette menu, making
mincemeat of Miss Manners." *Toronto Star*

Humour, 6 × 9, 248 pages, illustrations, trade paperback

ACROSS THE BRIDGE: Stories *by* Mavis Gallant
These eleven stories, set mostly in Montreal or in Paris, were described as "Vintage
Gallant – urbane, witty, absorbing." *Winnipeg Free Press* "We come away from it both
thoughtful and enriched." *Globe and Mail*

Fiction, 6 × 9, 208 pages, trade paperback

THE PRIVATE VOICE: A Journal of Reflections *by* Peter Gzowski
"A fascinating book that is cheerfully anecdotal, painfully honest, agonizingly self-doubting and compulsively readable." *Toronto Sun*

Autobiography, 5½ × 8½, 320 pages, photos, trade paperback

A PASSION FOR NARRATIVE: A Guide for Writing Fiction *by* Jack Hodgins
"One excellent path from original to marketable manuscript. . . . It would take a beginning writer years to work her way through all the goodies Hodgins offers." *Globe and Mail*

Non-fiction / Writing guide, 5¼ × 8½, 216 pages, trade paperback

OVER FORTY IN BROKEN HILL: Unusual Encounters in the Australian Outback *by* Jack Hodgins
"Australia described with wit, wonder and affection by a bemused visitor with Canadian sensibilities." *Canadian Press* "Damned fine writing." *Books in Canada*

Travel, 5½ × 8½, 216 pages, trade paperback

DANCING ON THE SHORE: A Celebration of Life at Annapolis Basin *by* Harold Horwood, *Foreword by* Farley Mowat
"A Canadian *Walden*" *Windsor Star* that "will reward, provoke, challenge and enchant its readers." *Books in Canada*

Nature/Ecology, 5⅛ × 8¼, 224 pages, 16 wood engravings, trade paperback

HUGH MACLENNAN'S BEST: An anthology *selected by* Douglas Gibson
This selection from all of the works of the witty essayist and famous novelist is "wonderful . . . It's refreshing to discover again MacLennan's formative influence on our national character." *Edmonton Journal*

Anthology, 6 × 9, 352 pages, trade paperback

UNDERCOVER AGENT: How One Honest Man Took On the Drug Mob . . . And Then the Mounties *by* Leonard Mitchell and Peter Rehak
"It's the stuff of spy novels – only for real . . . how a family man in a tiny fishing community helped make what at the time was North America's biggest drug bust." Saint John *Telegraph-Journal*

Non-fiction / Criminology, 4¼ × 7, 176 pages, paperback

ACCORDING TO JAKE AND THE KID: A Collection of New Stories *by* W.O. Mitchell
"This one's classic Mitchell. Humorous, gentle, wistful, it's 16 new short stories about life through the eyes of Jake, a farmhand, and the kid, whose mom owns the farm." *Saskatoon Star-Phoenix*

Fiction, 5 × 7¾, 280 pages, trade paperback

THE BLACK BONSPIEL OF WILLIE MACCRIMMON *by* W.O. Mitchell *illustrated by* Wesley W. Bates
A devil of a good tale about curling – W.O.Mitchell's most successful comic play now appears as a story, fully illustrated, for the first time, and it is "a true Canadian classic." *Western Report*

Fiction, 4⅝ × 7½, 144 pages with 10 wood engravings, hardcover

FOR ART'S SAKE: A new novel *by* W.O. Mitchell
"*For Art's Sake* shows the familiar Mitchell brand of subtle humour in this tale of an aging artist who takes matters into his own hands in bringing pictures to the people." *Calgary Sun*

Fiction, 6 × 9, 240 pages, hardcover

LADYBUG, LADYBUG . . . by W.O. Mitchell
"Mitchell slowly and subtly threads together the elements of this richly detailed and wonderful tale . . . the outcome is spectacular . . . *Ladybug, Ladybug* is certainly among the great ones!" *Windsor Star*

Fiction, 4¼ × 7, 288 pages, paperback

ROSES ARE DIFFICULT HERE *by* W.O.Mitchell
"Mitchell's newest novel is a classic, capturing the richness of the small town, and delving into moments that really count in the lives of its people . . ." *Windsor Star*   *Fiction, 6 × 9, 328 pages, hardcover*

WHO HAS SEEN THE WIND *by* W.O. Mitchell *illustrated by* William Kurelek
For the first time since 1947, this well-loved Canadian classic of childhood on the prairies is presented in its full, unexpurgated edition, and is "gorgeously illustrated." *Calgary Herald*

Fiction, 8½ × 10, 320 pages, numerous colour and black-and-white illustrations, hardcover

FRIEND OF MY YOUTH *by* Alice Munro
"I want to list every story in this collection as my favourite . . . Ms. Munro is a writer of extraordinary richness and texture." Bharati Mukherjee, *The New York Times*   *Fiction, 6 × 9, 288 pages, hardcover*

THE PROGRESS OF LOVE *by* Alice Munro
"Probably the best collection of stories – the most confident and, at the same time, the most adventurous – ever written by a Canadian." *Saturday Night*

Fiction, 6 × 9, 320 pages, hardcover

THE ASTOUNDING LONG-LOST LETTERS OF DICKENS OF THE MOUNTED *edited by* Eric Nicol
The "letters" from Charles Dickens's son, a Mountie from 1874 to 1886, are "a glorious hoax . . . so cleverly crafted, so subtly hilarious." *Vancouver Sun*

Fiction, 4¼ × 7, 296 pages, paperback

BACK TALK: A Book for Bad Back Sufferers and Those Who Put Up With Them *by* Eric Nicol *illustrated by* Graham Pilsworth
This "little gem" (*Quill and Quire*) caused one reader – Mrs. E. Nicol – to write: "Laughing at this book cured my bad back. It's a miracle!"

Humour, 5½ × 8½, 136 pages, illustrations, trade paperback

PADDLE TO THE AMAZON: The Ultimate 12,000-Mile Canoe Adventure *by* Don Starkell *edited by* Charles Wilkins
From Winnipeg to the mouth of the Amazon by canoe! "This real-life adventure book . . . must be ranked among the classics of the literature of survival." *Montreal Gazette* "Fantastic" *Bill Mason*

Adventure, 6 × 9, 320 pages, maps, photos, trade paperback

THE HONORARY PATRON: A novel *by* Jack Hodgins
The Governor General's Award-winner's thoughtful and satisfying third novel of a celebrity's return home to Vancouver Island mixes comedy and wisdom "and it's magic." *Ottawa Citizen*

Fiction, 4¼ × 7, 336 pages, paperback

INNOCENT CITIES: A novel *by* Jack Hodgins
Victorian in time and place, this delightful new novel by the author of *The Invention of the World* proves once again that "as a writer, Hodgins is unique among his Canadian contemporaries." *Globe and Mail*

Fiction, 4¼ × 7, 416 pages, paperback

THE CUNNING MAN: A novel *by* Robertson Davies
This "sparkling history of the erudite and amusing Dr. Hullah who knows the souls of his patients as well as he knows their bodies" *London Free Press* is "wise, humane and constantly entertaining." *The New York Times*

Fiction, 6 × 9, 480 pages, hardcover

OPEN SECRETS: Stories *by* Alice Munro
Eight marvellous stories, ranging in time from 1850 to the present and from Albania to "Alice Munro Country". "There may not be a better collection of stories until her next one." *Chicago Tribune*

Fiction, 6 × 9, 304 pages, hardcover

MURTHER & WALKING SPIRITS: A novel *by* Robertson Davies
"Brilliant" was the *Ottawa Citizen*'s description of the sweeping tale of a Canadian family through the generations. "It will recruit huge numbers of new readers to the Davies fan club." *Observer* (London)

Fiction, 6¼ × 9½, 368 pages, hardcover

THE RADIANT WAY *by* Margaret Drabble
"*The Radiant Way* does for Thatcher's England what *Middlemarch* did for Victorian England . . . Essential reading!" *Margaret Atwood*

Fiction, 6 × 9, 400 pages, hardcover